This Is Detroit, 1701–2001

This Is Detroit
1701–2001

ARTHUR M. WOODFORD

WAYNE STATE UNIVERSITY PRESS
Detroit

Great Lakes Books

A complete listing of the books
in this series can be found
at the back of this volume.

Manufactured in the United States of America.
05 04 03 02 01 5 4 3 2 1

Library of Congress Cataloging-in-Publication Data

Woodford, Arthur M., 1940–
This is Detroit, 1701–2001 / Arthur M. Woodford.
p. cm. — (Great Lakes books)
Includes bibliographical references (p.) and index.
ISBN 0-8143-2914-4 (alk. paper)
1. Detroit (Mich.) —History. I. Title. II. Series.
F574.D457 W66 2001
977.4'34—dc21

2001000689

Jacket design by Mike Savitski, Ann Arbor, Michigan
Book design by Sanford Barris, Business Graphic
Services, Inc., Bloomfield Hills, Michigan

Detroit300

Grateful acknowledgment is made to

COMMUNITY
FOUNDATION
For SOUTHEASTERN MICHIGAN

To Frank B. Woodford
1903–1967

newspaperman, author, historian, father,
and
city of Detroit historiographer
1966–1967

Table of Contents

Preface

On July 24, 1951, the city of Detroit celebrated its 250th birthday. In honor of the occasion, a number of special events were held. One of the most impressive was a grand parade down Woodward Avenue. Along with my father and mother, I had the privilege of watching the parade, not from the sidewalk along Woodward, but from high atop the balcony on the north side of the old city hall, where we were guests of longtime family friend and city treasurer Charles N. Williams. As I remember, it was a beautiful sunny day.

What impressed me the most that day, when I was a boy of almost eleven, had little to do with the actual history of Detroit. It was not the beautifully decorated parade floats, the gaily costumed parade participants, or even the high-stepping marching bands. It was the troop of red-coated Royal Canadian Mounted Police astride their handsomely groomed horses.

And so it was that I was introduced to the history of our city. Over the years I developed an interest in Detroit and its past, an interest nurtured in large part by my father and his circle of friends who studied and wrote about the history of Detroit and the Detroit River region. One important member of that circle was Dr. Milo M. Quaife, the longtime secretary of the Burton Historical Collection at the Detroit Public Library. This same Dr. Quaife edited a pictorial history of Detroit, published by Wayne University Press (as it was then known) for the city's 250th birthday. The title of his book was *This Is Detroit: 1701–1951.*

When plans were made to celebrate Detroit's 300th birthday, Wayne State University Press decided to publish a new history of Detroit. It, too, would be an illustrated history for the general reader, and as the manuscript neared completion, we decided that this new book would also have as its title *This Is Detroit.*

With any book of history, the author is indebted to many people—historians, authors, librarians, and archivists—for their help. This book is certainly no exception.

First and foremost I must express a very special thank-you to librarian and archivist Cynthia S. Bieniek, whose principal responsibility was photo research. Her knowledge of special collections and sources of historic photographs proved indispensable. Cindy also typed this manuscript, and on more than one occasion she caught an error or an omission, suggested a way to clarify a phrase, corrected an awkward paragraph, or found and added an obscure fact or date.

Once the photographs were selected, they needed to be copied. For this task Cindy and I turned to Thomas Sherry. An accomplished photographer in his own right, Tom has considerable knowledge of reproducing various types of historical photos and documents. To him we owe a most sincere thank-you.

Those of us who study and write about the history of this great city are fortunate to have close by several outstanding libraries and historical collections. Principal among these is, of course, the Burton Historical Collection at the Detroit Public Library. Special acknowledgment is due Burton Collection manager Janet Whitson, assistant manager David Poremba, and photo archivist Cheir Y. Gay. Working under the most difficult circumstances, these professionals proved themselves a credit to the field of librarianship.

Also at the Detroit Public Library I would like to thank Mark A. Patrick, manager of the National Automotive History Collection; Barbara Martin, manager of the E. Azalea Hackley Collection; and Jon E. Cawthorne, assistant director of the Main Library.

Across Cass Avenue from the Public Library is the Walter P. Reuther Library at Wayne State University. Here we were fortunate to have the assistance of archivists Thomas Featherstone and Mary J. Wallace. At the Detroit Historical Museum we called upon Patience Nauta, James Conway, and John Polacsek, curator of the Dossin Great Lakes Museum on Belle Isle. At the Henry Ford Museum and Greenfield Village Research Center we were assisted in the selection of photographs by Melissa J. Haddock.

I would like to acknowledge John C. Dann, director of the William L. Clements Library at the University of Michigan, and Brian Dunnigan, the library's map curator. These two fine historians assisted us with the selection of photographs, and Brian reviewed passages of the manuscript and made several important suggestions.

The Manning Brothers Collection, now maintained at the offices of Forbes Management in downtown Detroit, proved another important source of historic photographs. Here I would like to thank Alyn Thomas for her many courtesies and for her assistance in selecting photos from the collection and in obtaining photos and information about the restoration and move of the Gem and Century Theaters.

For their assistance with the selection of photographs, I would like to acknowledge Sylvia Inwood, Detroit Institute of Arts; Patrina Chatman, Museum of African American History; Camilo Vergara, who shared his images and offered encouragement and commentary on urban photographic history; Bill Imberto, director of Indian Urban Affairs; S. Kay Young and longtime friend Charlie Meyers, who assisted with the selection of Native American images; Jackie Napoleon Wilson, for sharing items from his African American collection; Matthew C. Switlik, director, and Ralph J. Naveaux, assistant director, Monroe County Historical Museum; Robert Garcia, Fort Malden National Historic Site; Margaret Roets, Flemish American Genealogical Society; Katie Lewis, Detroit Lions; Kathleen Kennedy, Olympia Entertainment-Fox Theater; Marissa Mackowiak, Fox Theater; Cecelia Aska, Detroit News; Marci Schramm, Michigan Opera Theater; Jill Woodward, Detroit Symphony Orchestra; W. C. Burdick, National Baseball Hall of Fame and Museum; and Thomas P. Ford, Houghton Library, Harvard University. A special thank-you as well to Jim Clary, Bill Moss, Joe Maniscalco, and John Stobart for sharing their artwork.

In addition to acknowledging those who helped with the photographs, I would like to thank those individuals who assisted me with my research. I would like to acknowledge the assistance of Dr. Charles K. Hyde. Charlie was always prompt in answering my many hurried telephone calls, and he read portions of the manuscript dealing with the automobile and automobile industry. I would also like to thank Sam Logan, *Michigan Chronicle;* Jane Danjin, librarian, UAW Library; George Charbonneau, International Institute; Eileen White, Youtheater; Pat Zacharias, librarian, *Detroit News;* Laura Berman, columnist, Detroit News; Joe Grimm and Bill McGraw, *Detroit Free Press;* Genevieve Sylvia, Pewabic Pottery; Carolyn Deis, director, and Anne Tokarz, librarian, Macomb County Library; Marilynn Crince, UAW-Ford National Programs Center; David Littmann, vice president and senior economist, Comerica Bank; Mary Kramer, associate publisher and editor, *Crain's Detroit Business;* Larry Kulisek, University of Windsor, and longtime friend Alan Douglas, also of

Windsor; Mike Smith, Walter P. Reuther Library; Michael Harvey, Charles H. Wright Museum of African American History; Roger L. Rosentreter, *Michigan History Magazine;* Dr. DeWitt Dykes, Oakland University, who recommended titles to include in the list of suggested reading; and Dr. Norman McRae, Detroit's leading authority on the city's African American history, who was kind enough to share his research.

I would also like to thank William M. Anderson, Laura R. Ashlee, Richard Bak, John Bluth, Judge William A. Crouchman, Kenneth M. Davies, Paul Ganson, Fred Hessler, Deborah Kingery, Glen Calvin Moon, Bruce Mugerian, William C. Rands III, Stuart Rankin, Bob Shugart, Robert L. Stewart, Charles Wolf, and of course Peter J. Seares and Mark M. Woodford.

I would be remiss if I did not mention the staff at the Wayne State University Press—its director, Arthur Evans; its associate director, Alice Nigoghosian, who was supportive and encouraging; and editors Kristin Harpster and Jonathan Lawrence. A very personal thank-you goes to my friend and colleague Dr. Philip P. Mason, editor of the press's Great Lakes Books Series, for his wise counsel always given when it was most sorely needed.

Finally, a special thanks to the members of the St. Clair Shores Public Library Board of Trustees for their support; to St. Clair Shores city manager Mark Wollenweber for his encouragement during my leave of absence; and to the staff of the St. Clair Shores Public Library, whether for typing this preface, researching a reference question, interloaning a book, or answering the phone and taking a message—thanks to each of you.

Lastly, to all of you who took the time to stop and ask, "How's the book coming?"—thank you.

ONE

The River

THIS IS THE STORY OF A RIVER, and of the great metropolitan city that grew along its north bank. Today the river and the city both share the same name—Detroit.

One of Detroit's most unusual geographical features is that it is the only major city in the continental United States that is north of Canada. This is due to the sharp turn to the west that the Detroit River takes soon after it leaves Lake St. Clair on its way to Lake Erie. This bend continues west past the downtown center of the city. After a short distance the river twists back to its proper direction, which is south, but for a mile or so anyone standing on the Detroit shore looking at Canada looks almost due south.

At Hart Plaza in downtown Detroit the river is at its narrowest, little more than half a mile wide, and flows past with a current of about two and one-half miles per hour. Forming the connecting link between Lake St. Clair and Lake Erie, the river has a total length of about thirty-two miles, and over this distance its water surface drops nearly three feet. The average depth of the river (due to channel dredging) is now thirty-five feet, and its course is studded with about fifteen islands, some of them on the Canadian side of the international boundary line. Among the larger islands are Belle Isle, which has been a public park since 1879, and Grosse Ile, which is large enough to sustain a city-size population. Both are United States possessions.

The history of the city is inseparable from the ages-old story of the river. This story began a billion years ago when a fracture in the earth from what is now Oklahoma to Lake Superior generated volcanic activity that almost split North America. Over a period of twenty million years, lava flowed intermittently from the fracture. This geomorphic age created mountains covering the regions now known as northern Wisconsin and Minnesota, as well as the Laurentian Mountains of eastern Canada. Over time these mountains eroded, while occasional volcanic activity continued. Below the highlands to the north, molten magma spewed out to the fracture, causing the highland to sink and form a mammoth rock basin that would one day hold Lake Superior. Eventually, the fracture stabilized and the rock tilted down from north to south.

Then for millions of years much of the region's surface, including the present Detroit area, was covered by salt seas. When these receded they left behind layers of sandstone and limestone which the early settlers quarried to build their walls and chimneys, and which their successors found necessary for the manufacture of steel. They also left behind thick layers of salt. Until recently that salt was mined from huge caverns under the city, caverns whose chambers were loftier than those of the grandest cathedrals.

The process of making the land did not end when the seas subsided. There followed ages in which glaciers covered the surface of most of this region. These glaciers moved slowly back and forth, ebbing and flowing like an icy tide. The last one is believed to have receded from the Detroit area about twelve thousand years ago. The weight of those mighty ice fields gouged great scars in the land which their melting waters filled to form the Great Lakes. They were also responsible for the soil composition, the lakes and marshes, and the many small streams found in this part of Michigan. Like a giant bulldozer, the last glacier left a wide plain, fairly level and split down the middle by the Detroit River, whose course has not appreciably changed for thousands of years.

This plain is almost flat. One has to go back almost fifteen miles from the river to find anything left by the glaciers that has even the appearance of a real hill. The elevation of the city is about 581 feet above sea level, and from the river the rise is so gradual as to be almost imperceptible. This flatland was drained by numerous small streams or creeks. The most important of these is the River Rouge on the southwestern border of the city. Draining a large, closed-in area, the Rouge has been made navigable and is today an important channel of commerce, serving primarily the fleet of giant freighters carrying cargoes of coal, iron ore, and limestone directly to the furnaces of the industrial complex of the Ford Motor Company. There were many lesser streams nearer the present center of the city, but these have mostly vanished, having long ago been converted into drainage ditches and then into enclosed sewers.

One of these smaller streams was the "Ruissau des Hurons," today better known by its later name of Savoyard Creek. This creek was originally named for the Huron Indians, whose fortified town stood on the west bank of the stream's junction with the Detroit River. The stream had its origin in some marshy land behind the present Wayne County Building at Brush and Congress Streets. It flowed westward through a meadow, cutting across what is now the center of the city's business district, following closely the line of Congress Street. If one stands today at the corner of Fort Street and Griswold and looks south, a fairly sharp dip in the street can be observed. That depression marks the course of the Savoyard. Once wide and deep enough for scows, the stream meandered on a few blocks, then turned south just west of where Joe Louis Arena stands today, and there emptied into the Detroit River. In the early nineteenth century some of the city's building material, stone and lumber, was floated up the Savoyard. Today it is an underground sewer that passes beneath the Buhl Building.

Other important streams were Conner's Creek, May's or Cabicier's Creek, and Parent's Creek, all named for early French families who settled near their mouths. In the early years of the city these creeks served useful purposes, furnishing access to the country back from the river and occasionally providing waterpower for a mill. Today these streams

This map of "The River Detroit from Lake Erie to Lake St. Clair" was prepared by British army captain W. F. W. Owen and published in 1815. The map clearly shows the town and fort at Detroit, the town of Amherstburg, Peche Island, Hog Island, and Grosse Isle. Many prominent buildings and landmarks are also indicated. Author's collection.

have virtually disappeared, suffering the ignominious fate of being turned into parts of the metropolitan sewer system. Only a pond in the center of Elmwood Cemetery, near Mt. Elliott on the city's east side, remains as the last visible mark of Parent's Creek, which we will hear of later under the more intriguing name of Bloody Run.

Long before the river's banks became populated, its shoreline varied only slightly from today's contours. Originally its edges were scalloped in a series of shallow bays, but these have long since been filled in and the shoreline straightened. Before this was done, however, a bluff about twenty feet high bordered the shore. At the bluff's foot, a narrow shingle barely wide enough to accommodate a cart track provided a place where small craft could be pulled out of the water. Today one can see where this bluff stood. Let the viewer stand on Jefferson Avenue before Hart Plaza. From there at Jefferson, which once marked the approximate edge of the bluff, the ground slopes sharply down toward the river. Grading and landfill below Jefferson have provided two to three hundred additional feet of man-made land between what was once the bluff and the river's edge and where the waterline is now. Standing at the spot suggested, one can look across the river to the Canadian shore and see the reddish-brown bank of earth stretching along the water's edge, its appearance almost the same as that of the American shore as it was until the 1820s.

Although the river's shoreline has indeed changed, the river itself has not. It accounts for the city's existence, and it has determined nearly every phase of the city's destiny. Today the river carries 1,000-foot ore boats, just as it did the fur-laden canoes of Native Americans. From time immemorial the river has flowed swiftly and smoothly past the site of the city, as predictable as tomorrow in its movement toward the lower Great Lakes and on to the Atlantic Ocean.

Two

The First People

WE DO NOT KNOW THE NAME of the first people who inhabited the Detroit River region, but we do know that Native Americans were living here long before the first European explorers arrived. The best estimate is that the first Native Americans may have been here as early as 6000 B.C., possibly coming from the central plains of the United States or even from Canada. These first people found this a strange land. It is said they hunted the bison, the mastodon, the giant beaver, and other huge beasts. Venison is believed to have been one of their food sources, since the white-tailed deer, still plentiful in Michigan, is the only mammal known to have survived from those times.

Later visitors to the area are a little better known. They were the Copper People, so named because they worked the copper deposits of Isle Royale in Lake Superior. Archaeological studies indicate that they may have been here as early as 4000 B.C. and that they continued to live and work in the Lake Superior region for nearly three thousand years. Who they were, what they looked like, and where they came from remain mysteries. They attained a relatively high culture, as evidenced by the copper weapons and utensils they made, as well as by the tools they devised to work the copper. Some historians claim these copper products were widely traded and have been found in many distant parts of the United States. There is no evidence that the Copper People ever lived in or around Detroit, but it can be assumed that in carrying on a commerce with distant tribes they may have passed along the Detroit River and knew this region at least as visitors.

The Copper People were followed by the Mound Builders, another group whose place of origin and antecedents remain unknown. The Mound Builders occupied a large part of the present American Midwest. Compared to the Native Americans first known to Europeans, these people were fairly sophisticated, as proven by their pottery, jewelry, and tools. Some of their mounds were huge and elaborately designed, exhibiting considerable engineering skill. It is not entirely certain whether

These Native Americans, the Copper People, so named because they worked the copper deposits of Isle Royale, lived in Michigan's Lake Superior region as early as 4000 B.C. From Henry R. Schoolcraft, *History of the Indian Tribes of the United States.*

the mounds were burial sites only or whether they were also used for religious ceremonies. The most spectacular mounds are in Ohio and Indiana, but some smaller ones were built within what are now Detroit's city limits. One was near the River Rouge not far from the present Ford industrial complex; another was within the Fort Wayne military reservation; and a third was in the city's northeast section, giving name to the present Mound Road. Perhaps there were others that have long since been lost to recorded history. The Mound Builders, whoever they were, occupied the region from about 1000 B.C. to roughly A.D. 700, when they vanished or, as is more likely the case, were absorbed by the Indians who may have been their descendants and are known to have been in the Detroit area as early as A.D. 800.

It was not until the early 1600s, however, that the innumerable and glaring gaps in the archaeological knowledge and evidence of the region's first people began to be filled in from the written records of the European observers who entered this area and reported on what they found and what they saw. In all of Michigan, the Europeans found relatively few Indians. In the entire upper Great Lakes region, the Native American population in the early 1600s is estimated to have numbered approximately 100,000. This figure is small when compared to later population standards for this same area, but on a larger scale these Indians made up one-tenth of the total Indian population for all of North America north of Mexico at the time Europeans first began to have extensive contact with this continent.

The French were the first Europeans to explore the upper Great Lakes, and they would eventually identify seven tribes that would play a role in the development of the Detroit River region. These were the Huron (or Wyandot); the Ottawa; the Chippewa (or Ojibwa); the Fox; the Sac (or Sauk); the Miami; and the Potawatomi. Although the French at first had difficulty distinguishing between these tribes and the bands or clans into which the tribes were divided, the names that now identify these different groups were actually used at the time and are not terms arbitrarily assigned by later archaeologists, as is the case with such prehistoric groups as the Copper People and the Mound Builders.

The Native Americans the French encountered in the Great Lakes region, depending on where they lived and their background, were hunters and fishermen. Many were agriculturists; remnants of their gardens can still be found. They moved about from locality to locality, depending for transportation on canoes or pirogues. Some of their hunting and traveling paths became Michigan's main highways and important Detroit streets.

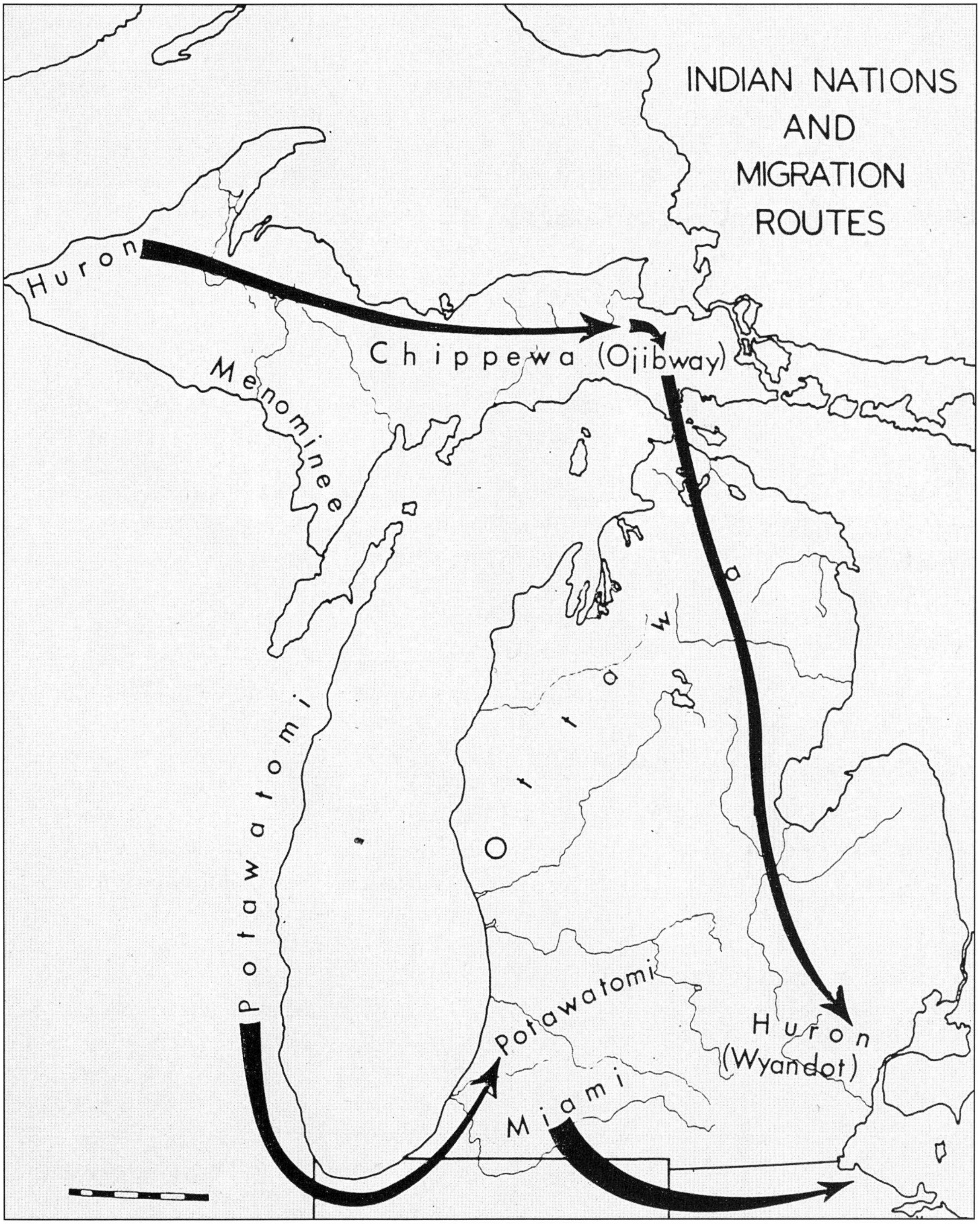

When the French began to explore the upper Great Lakes, they identified seven tribes that would play a role in the development of the Detroit River region: the Huron (or Wyandot), Ottawa, Chippewa (or Ojibwa), Fox, Sac (or Sauk), Miami, and Potawatomi. From Willis F. Dunbar, *Michigan, A History of the Wolverine State.*

These sketches were drawn by British Lieutenant Governor Henry Hamilton during the period he was commandant at Fort Detroit. This unnamed "Jibboway Indian" *(above)* is believed to have been an occasional visitor to Detroit from the north. Tzentoritzi *(right)* was a civil leader of the Wyandot tribe of the Detroit River region and was present at a conference with Hamilton in June 1777. By permission of the Houghton Library, Harvard University.

This portrait of Keesheewaa, a noted Fox warrior and medicine man, first appeared in Thomas McKenney's *Sketches of a Tour to the Lakes.* McKenney describes him as a man "of good character" and as a "firm, onward, fearless chief." From James D. Horan, *North American Indian Portraits.*

This painting first appeared in Thomas McKenney's *Sketches of a Tour to the Lakes,* 1827. McKenney described the Chippewa women as "strong and resourceful." From James D. Horan, *North American Indian Portraits.*

Streets such as Woodward, Grand River, Gratiot, and Michigan were all originally Indian trails. These Indians knew how to make maple sugar, one of their staple foods. They built huts of saplings, the ends of which were set into the ground and the tops bent inward to form a conical house covered with bark or skins. The early European explorers commented on other aspects of the lifestyles of these Indians, such as their hospitality toward strangers, their courage and stamina, and the love shown by parents toward their children.

The Indians who lived around the borders of the Great lakes were of two language groups: the Algonquin, who generally lived north of the St. Lawrence River and along the rims of Lakes Huron and Superior; and the Iroquois, who were for the most part centered along the south shore of Lake Ontario and the north shore of Lake Erie. The Algonquin tribes included the Ottawa, Chippewa, Potawatomi, Sac and Fox, and Miami. The more prominent Iroquois tribes were those of the Five Nations of central and western New York, the Hurons around Georgian Bay, and the Neutrals. The Neutrals were closely allied to the Hurons, but they were caught between that tribe and the Five Nations. They were less warlike and received their name because they acted as a buffer and traded with both sides. In the tribal wars that developed between the Hurons and the Iroquois, the Neutrals were nearly obliterated. So fierce were these battles that when the first French explorers arrived in the Detroit River region

The Indians of this area were skilled at making maple sugar, one of their food staples. From Henry R. Schoolcraft, *History of the Indian Tribes of the United States.*

they found a land that had been deserted since the 1640s when the last occupants of the area fled westward in the face of these Iroquois raids.

The Indians had several names for the region on the river which became Detroit. Some called it "Yondotega," meaning "the great village." Others called it "Wa-we-a-tun-ong," which refers to the bend in the river and has been translated as "the crooked way." Another name was "Karontaen," or "coast of the straits," while the Iroquois referred to it in their own tongue as "Teuchsa Grondie."

We do not know for certain who was the first European to see the Detroit River region. Possibly the first visitor was from one of the two groups of men indispensable in carrying out the French fur trade. The first, called "coureurs de bois," went out into the forests, hunted and trapped, lived with the Indians, and bargained with them for furs. Sturdy, rough, and independent, they often lived among the Indians for years and took Indian wives. The other group was made up of the "voyageurs," or boatmen. Seemingly tireless at the paddles of a canoe, they could drive their frail craft upstream for hours on end, keeping time with their strokes to the lilt of a lively song. Thus a coureur de bois or a voyageur may very well have camped on the shores of the Detroit River, but because they were illiterate and because to them one day's journey was much like another, they left no record of where they went and what they saw.

A better choice for first visitor would be Étienne Brulé, a protégé of Samuel de Champlain, the father of New France. Brulé was one of the group of young men sent from Quebec by Champlain to travel among the Indians for extended periods to learn their languages and customs. Brulé first reached the Great Lakes as early as 1610 and is believed to have reached Duluth on the shores of western Lake Superior in 1618.

Sainte Claire of Assisi, for whom Lake St. Clair is named, a voyageur, and a coureur de bois, as depicted in this mural by Gari Melchers. Courtesy Burton Historical Collection, Detroit Public Library.

There is a report that he crossed the Ontario peninsula from Georgian Bay to Lake Erie in 1625 or 1626, and some historians conclude that he must have passed by Detroit. The supposition is reasonable because the explorer returning from Lake Erie to the upper lakes and the Ottawa River back to Quebec would very logically have gone north through the Detroit River on his way to Lake Huron. But it still remains supposition, just as it is that some English or Dutch explorer accompanying a raiding party of Iroquois might have been the first to visit Detroit.

The first Europeans, however, to make any written record of the straits between Lakes Erie and Huron were the Jesuit priests Jean de Brébeuf and Pierre-Joseph-Marie Chaumont. They spent part of the winter of 1641 in a village occupied by a people previously unknown to them. The place was called Khioeta, and the Jesuits renamed it St. Michel. Its unfamiliar residents might have been Miamis, Algonquin people who were later reputed to have been the original inhabitants of the Detroit region. Evidence suggests that the village the Jesuits renamed St.

Michel was located on the Canadian shore of the Detroit River just up from Lake Erie. Unfortunately, these original inhabitants of the Detroit River region were driven out by Iroquois war parties.

The next European to see Detroit was a young French explorer named Adrien Jolliet. In the spring of 1669, French officials in Quebec sent Jolliet along the shores of Lake Superior in search of a copper mine of which the Indians had spoken. He failed to find the mine, and on his way back he stopped at Sault Ste. Marie. There he learned that the Iroquois were temporarily at peace and that it was safe for a Frenchman to cross Lake Erie. At the Sault he rescued an Iroquois prisoner who in gratitude offered to guide Jolliet home by an easier route than that which the French had followed for many years. So Jolliet and his guide set off paddling across Lake Huron, the St. Clair River, Lake St. Clair, the Detroit River, past the site of present-day Detroit, and on along the north shore of Lake Erie. Here they abandoned their canoe and set out cross-country. This was in September 1669. They had not gone far across the Niagara peninsula, reaching the vicinity of present-day Hamilton, Ontario, when they met a group of French and Indians on their way west.

The leader of this party was Robert Cavelier de La Salle, who was on his way to the Ohio country in search of a river that might prove to be the long-sought waterway to the Indies. Accompanying La Salle were two Sulpician priests, François Dollier de Casson, who had given up a distinguished military career for the priesthood, and René de Bréhant de Galinée. Dollier was described as "a man of great courage, of a tall, commanding person and of uncommon bodily strength." He came out to New France in 1666 as chaplain of a regiment sent overseas to fight the Iroquois. Galinée was more of a theologian, full of missionary zeal.

Jolliet sketched out a map of his travels down the lakes for La Salle and the two priests. He also told them of a large tribe living near Sault Ste. Marie, the Potawatomi, among whom no missionary had yet gone. The two priests immediately became determined to seek out this tribe. Dollier and Galinée separated from La Salle, who went off to the Ohio River. The priests wintered at present-day Port Dover, Ontario, and in March 1670 they entered the Detroit River. What was most notable about their trip is that they were the first to make a written report about their journey, although their narrative did not contain a detailed description of the Detroit region itself.

Actually, when they discussed the strait through which they passed, Dollier and Galinée included all the waters between Lakes Erie and Huron. Somewhere along the way—the best guess has put the spot near the mouth of the River Rouge—they came upon a strange object, a peculiar stone formation resembling a human figure. The Indians had made it an idol, painting and decorating it and placing before it thank offerings for safe passage across the oftentimes treacherous waters of Lake Erie. The sight of such a "heathen abomination" greatly offended the priests, and their zeal demanded that they do something about it. They proceeded to demolish it with a consecrated ax, and then carried the pieces of stone out into deep water in their canoe and dumped them overboard. Legend says that unrepentant Indians fished the pieces out of the river and set them up on the lower end of Belle Isle. Having accomplished their labors for the Lord, Dollier and Galinée continued on to Sault Ste. Marie, and then to Montreal and Quebec. They never visited Detroit again.

La Salle returned to the Great Lakes in 1678 and set up a shipyard near present-day Buffalo, New York. There, despite hostile Indians and mutinous workmen, his men built a ship during the winter and launched it early in the summer of 1679. They named the ship *La Griffon.*

On August 7, 1679, aboard the *Griffon,* La Salle and his party set sail across Lake Erie, and on August 11 they entered the Detroit River. The *Griffon* thus became the first sailing ship ever to traverse these waters. The next day they sailed onto the lake, which they named Ste. Claire in honor of Sainte Claire of Assisi, whose feast day fell at that time. The *Griffon* sailed on to Green Bay, and after loading the ship with furs collected there for him, La Salle ordered the ship back to the Niagara region while he continued on to explore Lake Michigan. On September 18 the *Griffon* sailed out into Lake Michigan and was never heard from again. It was almost a hundred years, according to one historian, before the next sailing ship of any size was to pass Detroit.

Accompanying La Salle aboard the *Griffon* was Recollect priest Father Louis Hennepin, chaplain of the expedition. It is from Hennepin that we receive the first descriptive account of what the Detroit region looked like. He wrote:

> *This strait is finer than that of Niagara, being thirty leagues long, and everywhere one league broad, except in the middle which is wider, forming the lake we have named Ste. Claire. The navigation is easy on both sides, the coast being low and even. It runs directly from north to south. The country between these two lakes is very well situated and the soil is very fertile. The banks of the strait are vast meadows, and the prospect is terminated with some hills covered with vineyards, trees bearing good fruit, groves and forests so well disposed that one would think Nature alone could not have made,*

On August 7, 1679, French explorer La Salle set sail across Lake Erie aboard this ship, the *Griffon.* On August 11 he entered the Detroit River, and the *Griffon* became the first sailing ship to traverse these waters. From a painting by James Clary. Courtesy St. Clair Shores Public Library.

without the help of Art, so charming a prospect. The country is stocked with stags, wild goats, and bears which are good for food, and not fierce as in other countries.

Those who shall be so happy as to inhabit that noble country cannot but remember with gratitude those who have discovered the way by venturing to sail upon an unknown lake for above 100 leagues.

Traffic increased considerably in the years immediately following the expedition of La Salle and Hennepin, and as long as the Iroquois were peaceful the lower lakes route to Montreal and Quebec was far easier than that by way of the Ottawa River. French travelers came to know the region well, and they gave it a name. They called it simply "the Strait," or in their own tongue, "*le Detroit.*"

This map of the Great Lakes, dedicated to King William II of Great Britain, appeared in the 1697 edition of Father Hennepin's *A New Discovery of a Vast Country in America,* which also contains the first description of the Detroit River region. Courtesy St. Clair Shores Public Library.

Three

The French Village

On the morning of July 24, 1701, the French explorer Antoine Laumet de Lamothe Cadillac and a party of fifty soldiers, fifty traders, farmers and artisans, and two priests paddled their twenty-five canoes up the Detroit River. At a point where the river narrowed, Cadillac and his men turned their canoes from midstream and headed for the river's north bank. They pulled their canoes onto the narrow strip of sandy beach, climbed the twenty-foot bluff, and surveyed the terrain. Deciding the location was a good one, Cadillac set his men to constructing a small fort. He would name it "Fort Pontchartrain du Detroit," and thus the city of Detroit was born.

Cadillac's wilderness outpost was founded for two purposes: to control the rich fur trade in what is now Michigan and the Northwest Territory (the region between the Ohio and Mississippi Rivers and around the Great Lakes), and to prevent the British from encroaching upon the region. While the world trade in peltry is no small business today, it in no way exerts the powerful influence it did in the seventeenth

Antoine Laumet de Lamothe Cadillac, whose plan for a French outpost laid the ground for what would become the city of Detroit, was memorialized in this statue by Julius Melchers. Courtesy Burton Historical Collection, Detroit Public Library.

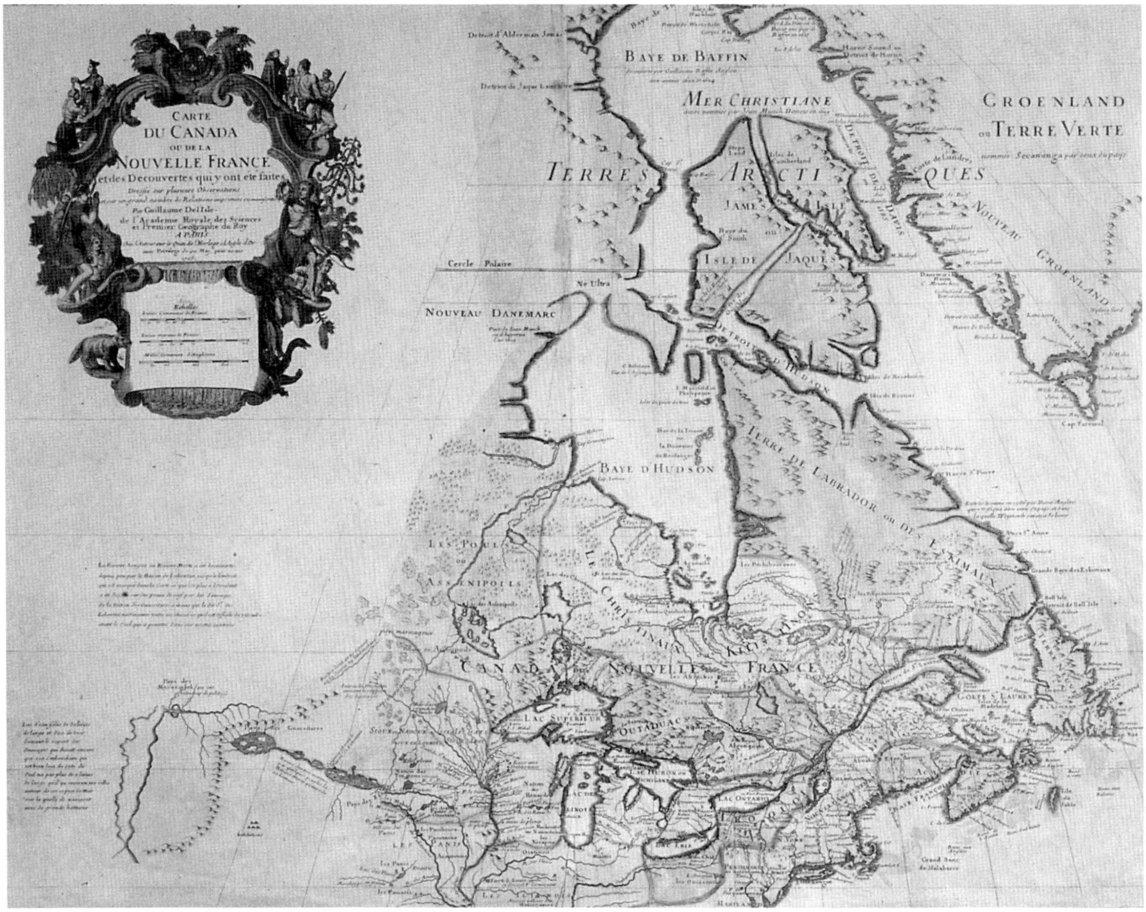

This is the earliest known map of the Great Lakes region showing the location of Detroit. The map was first published in 1703. Courtesy Burton Historical Collection, Detroit Public Library.

and eighteenth centuries. Furs were worn by French aristocrats and by the more affluent members of the middle class. Because France had become the fashion center of Europe under Louis XIV, the wearing of furs had spread to other European countries. Also of special importance in creating a demand was the vogue for the broad-brimmed beaver hat in the seventeenth century. For some time Europe had been able to meet the demand for furs, but eventually the harvest for peltries ran short. And when Poland, which had been a chief source of beaver for the French market, became trapped out, France turned to the New World and Canada. However, the stage for the founding of Detroit in 1701 was set more than 165 years earlier.

France's claim to Canada dated back to 1535, when Jacques Cartier discovered the St. Lawrence River and sailed up it to the site of what was to become Montreal. Samuel de Champlain arrived at Quebec as governor in 1608, and at about that time the period of settlement began. Many of those first immigrants found the fur trade an easier, more profitable existence than the drudgery of farming. To control the trade, a string of outposts was established, some where missionaries had already settled. In fact, years before Detroit was founded, several of these forts or trading

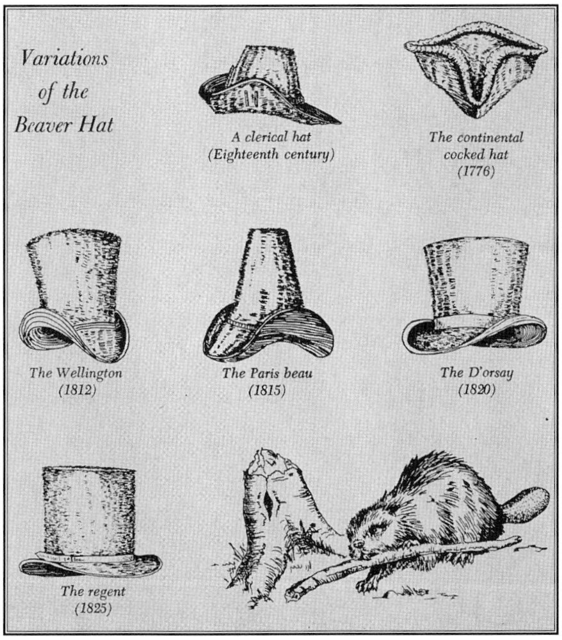

Cadillac's wilderness outpost was founded by the French to control the rich fur trade in what is now Michigan and the Old Northwest. A variety of skins were brought to Detroit for shipment to Montreal and Quebec, but the most important was the beaver pelt, from which the famous beaver hat was made. From North American Fur Trade Conference, *Aspects of the Fur Trade.*

posts were flourishing in Michigan: Sault Ste. Marie as early as 1668; Fort de Baude at St. Ignace in 1686; Fort St. Joseph, where Port Huron is now located, in 1686; and others at or near the present-day cities of St. Joseph in 1679 and Niles in 1691.

Within a few years, this system to control the fur trade through government outposts began to break down as independent traders dealt more and more outside government control. As a result, a flood of furs went downstream to Montreal. The price of beaver dropped so far that the warehouses were full of skins that simply lay in storage and rotted because it did not pay to send them to France. In addition, the Jesuit missionaries were pressuring the government to close the outposts because, in many cases, the Indians were being cheated out of their furs. The traders at the outposts were shamelessly and without restraint using brandy as their chief item of exchange.

As a result, in 1696 the government decreed that all furs had to be delivered to Montreal by the Indians, and the forts strung around the Great Lakes were ordered closed and abandoned. Only the Jesuits were permitted to maintain mission settlements in Indian country. Unfortunately for the French, this plan was equally unsuccessful, because the Indians, feeling no particular loyalty, turned to trade with the English. There was one man, though, who was developing a different plan. He was the former commandant at Fort de Baude at St. Ignace—Antoine Laumet de Lamothe Cadillac. Cadillac felt so strongly that he returned to France to present his plan to Louis XIV.

Cadillac's plan was to stop treating the West as a mere outpost and to plant a genuine colony there. He wanted to bring in farmers

These fur canoes, made of birchbark, were more than thirty feet long and could carry four-ton loads. When a rocky reach of water blocked their way, the voyageurs would unload the canoe, swing a ninety-pound pack of furs or goods onto their backs, and trot along the portage path to a place where the canoe could be launched again. Courtesy Burton Historical Collection, Detroit Public Library.

and artisans, develop towns, and urge the Indians to establish their villages nearby. The farmers would make the town self-sustaining, while traders and Indians would bring in their furs and make the towns financially stable. Cadillac realized that Michilimackinac was not the place to start because the northern region was too cold and too barren. A better place, he insisted, could be found lower down the lakes, at a place like "le Detroit." Cadillac recommended that a fortified town be built there. If this model settlement should work out satisfactorily, others would be constructed. Cadillac specifically had in mind a place at the mouth of the Mississippi, and another partway up that river. He was never able to build them, but his plan was used by others, resulting in present-day New Orleans and St. Louis. The king and his chief counselor, Count Pontchartrain, whose jurisdiction extended over the colonies, were enthusiastic about the plan, and in early 1701 Cadillac returned to Canada with the king's approval.

Cadillac receives orders from Louis XIV to establish an outpost on the banks of *le Detroit,* to control the rich fur trade of the Great lakes region. Courtesy Burton Historical Collection, Detroit Public Library.

Cadillac immediately set about obtaining provisions and supplies for his expedition, and in early July the flotilla of canoes pushed off from Montreal. Because of the peace treaty that was being negotiated with the Iroquois, Cadillac thought it best not to travel the easy route up the St. Lawrence and through Lakes Ontario and Erie. Instead, he chose the old wilderness road of the voyageurs up the Ottawa River, through Lake Nipissing, and down the French River to Georgian Bay. Although this entailed some backbreaking portages, it was a far safer route. Once in Georgian Bay and out into Lake Huron, the expedition followed the eastern shore south to the entrance of the Detroit River. They passed the present site of Detroit and, on the night of July 23, camped on Grosse Ile, which was seriously considered for a location of the settlement. But, because of the width of the river there close to the head of Lake Erie, Cadillac had second thoughts.

The following day the expedition headed back up the river and reached the location of the new town. The site Cadillac had chosen for his settlement was on the north bank at a point where the river was at its narrowest and where the high banks made it the most defensible. As far as can be determined, the landing point was at the foot of present-day Shelby Street a few feet below Jefferson Avenue. Today the Veterans' Memorial Building stands upon that spot. Cadillac had selected for his new town the river's north bank—rather than the south bank—for one very important reason. Because of the bend in the river at that point, it was possible to see farther both up- and downriver from the north shore than from the bank opposite, and thereby to derive longer warning of approaching sailing vessels or canoes. From the site of Fort Pontchartrain one could watch, in one direction, the main channel south of Belle Isle all the way to Lake St. Clair, and in the other, skimming past Montreal Point on the south shore (today, just beyond the Canadian end of the Ambassador Bridge), at least as far as the mouth of the River Rouge. A point on the south shore opposite Fort Pontchartrain would have afforded virtually the same sight line upriver, but the view downriver would have been so limited as to be nearly nonexistent.

Cadillac at once paced off the limits of his planned village between the Detroit River and the small twenty-five-foot-wide Savoyard Creek to the rear, marked the corners of his stockade, and within two hours sent his ax men into the nearby woods to fell timber for construction. The next few weeks were spent clearing the land and building the fort. The stockade consisted of a wall of twenty-foot logs, of which four feet were embedded in the earth. A bastion was set at each corner and a moat dug outside. At least two gates provided access, one on the river side wide enough to permit large loads to be brought in, another in the east wall. There was really only one street—Ste. Anne's—that paralleled the river along the top of the bluff. A shorter street above Ste. Anne's and two north-south streets, more properly alleys or lanes, were the only other roads in the village.

The first building erected was a church. It has been said that it was completed in two days and that the first mass was sung on the feast of Ste. Anne, in whose honor it was dedicated and for whom it was named. The present-day Ste. Anne's Church is located on the corner of Howard and Ste. Anne's Streets on Detroit's near west side, not far from the Ambassador Bridge. Ste. Anne's is the second-oldest continuously operating parish in the United States, the oldest being a parish in St. Augustine, Florida. After the church was completed, lots were marked out and houses built. The original house lots were no larger than twenty-five feet square. The houses were made of small oak logs or posts set perpendicularly into the ground, chinked with grass and mud, like the stockade, and roofed with bark slabs. Shortly after this a large warehouse was built for storage of public property and furs and for use as a trade store. The whole village—stockade, streets, and buildings—occupied an area that today consists of about one

Detroit's first major street was Ste. Anne's, which ran parallel to the river along the top of the bluff. Courtesy Burton Historical Collection, Detroit Public Library.

city block, bounded roughly by Griswold, Jefferson, Shelby, and Larned.

In September 1701, Madame Cadillac and Madame Tonty, the latter the wife of Cadillac's second in command, arrived at Detroit. There had been no women in the original expedition, and Cadillac wanted to convince the Indians that Detroit was intended to be a permanent settlement. In October 1701 ground was broken adjacent to the fort and about fifteen acres of winter wheat were sown. There was a crop the following July, although it was said to have been rather poor. Nevertheless, it demonstrated that the land could be cultivated and that the village could be made reasonably self-sufficient.

Madame Cadillac and Madame Tonty, the latter the wife of Cadillac's second in command, arrived at Fort Pontchartrain in September 1701. They were the first women to join the garrison at Detroit. Courtesy Detroit Public Library.

From the standpoint of trade, matters went well from the beginning. A band of Hurons set up a village where the Savoyard Creek emptied into the Detroit River; the Ottawas settled along the river near the foot of Belle Isle (in 1706–8 they moved across the river to the Canadian shore); and the Potawatomis and Miamis set up their villages a short distance downriver. Before long Cadillac reported two thousand Indians in the area, and in the spring distant tribes from as far away as Lake Superior and the Illinois country came to trade their furs. The pelts that were shipped from "Fort Pontchartrain du Detroit" included bear, elk, deer, marten, raccoon, mink, lynx, muskrat, opossum, wolf, fox, and beaver. Thus within a very short time Detroit was established as the center of the Great Lakes fur trade.

Pleased with his new settlement, Cadillac wrote to his superiors in Quebec:

The banks of the river are so many vast meadows where the freshness of those beautiful streams keeps the grass always green. These same meadows are fringed

Indians came to Detroit from as far away as Lake Superior and the Illinois country to trade their furs. It was not long before Detroit was established as the center of the Great Lakes fur trade. Courtesy Burton Historical Collection, Detroit Public Library.

with long and broad avenues of fruit trees which have never felt the careful hand of the watchful gardener; and fruit trees, young and old, droop under the weight and multitude of their fruit, and bend their branches toward the fertile soil which has produced them. . . . On both sides of this strait lie fine, open plains where the deer roam in graceful herds, where bears, by no means fierce and exceedingly good to eat, are to be found, as are also the savory wild duck and other varieties of game. The islands are covered with trees; chestnuts, walnuts, apples and plums abound; and in season the wild vines are heavy with grapes of which the forest rangers say they have made a wine that, considering its newness, was not at all bad.

In 1706, Cadillac made one of his periodic trips to Montreal and Quebec. When he returned he brought with him several families of settlers, and for the next few years the settlement prospered. In 1710 he was appointed governor of Louisiana Territory,

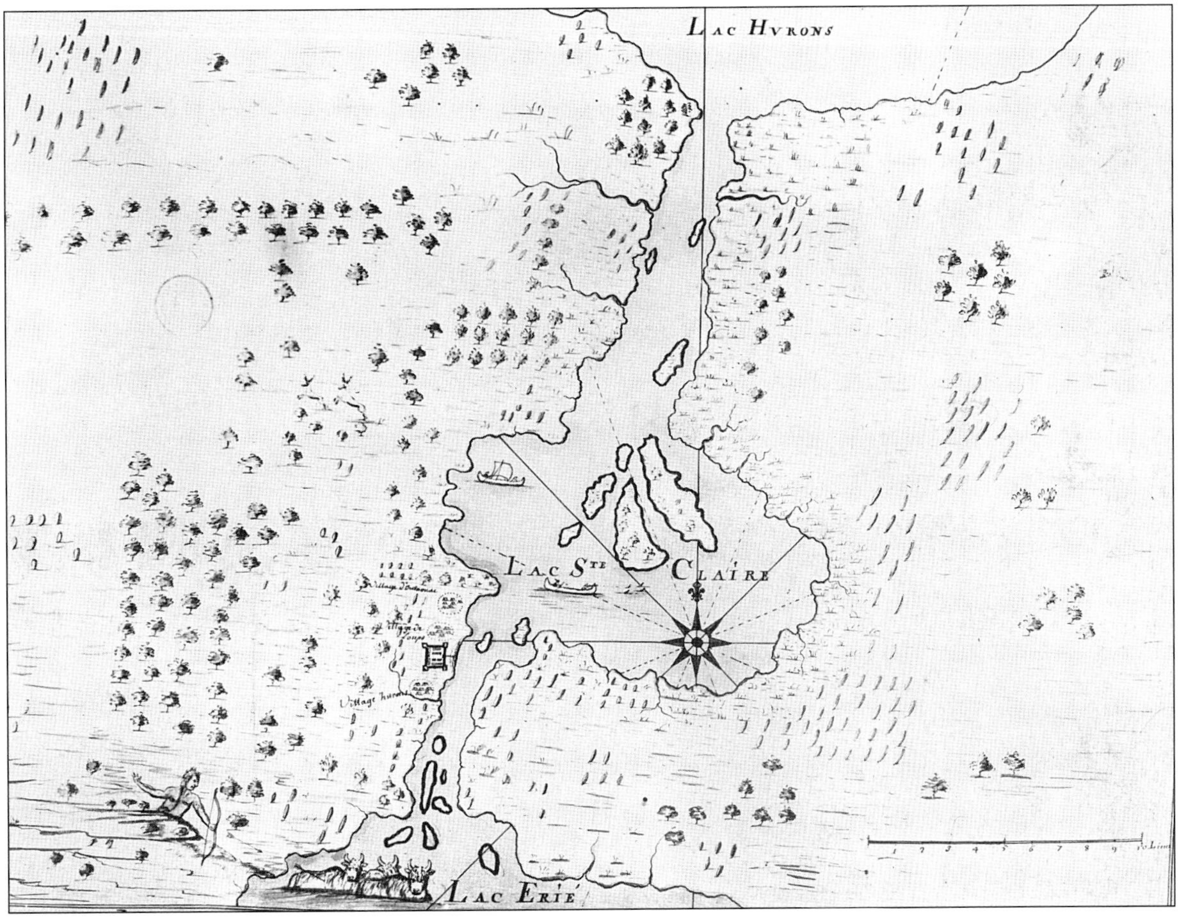

This map is probably the one enclosed with Cadillac's September 25, 1702, report to Count Pontchartrain. The map lacks a title and date but is sometimes called the "Buffalo Map" because of the image of a man shooting at a buffalo (at the lower left—the edge of Lake Erie near the site of present-day Monroe). Courtesy Burton Historical Collection, Detroit Public Library.

and in 1711 he left Detroit, never to return. In 1720 he returned to France and was given the governorship of Castelsarrasin, a small town near his birthplace. He filled that position until his death at age seventy-two on October 15, 1730.

At first, the farmers were granted house lots inside the fort while they farmed on the public domain outside the stockade walls. Beginning on March 10, 1707, the settlers, or "habitants" as they were then called, were awarded farms up and down both sides of the river. These farm grants, known as the private claims in today's land abstracts, consisted of river frontage of from one to four or five arpents (one arpent equals about two hundred linear feet), and in some cases extended back two or three miles. The rear line of most of the original grants that are not within the city of Detroit is somewhere in the vicinity of Holden and Harper Avenues. In this manner each property owner had access to the river. This was extremely important, since the river was a source for food and drinking water and was the highway on which farmers transported their goods to and from the marketplace. Eventually, these grants became known as ribbon farms because of their long and narrow shape, and their boundaries are marked in modern Detroit by streets that bear the names of the original owners, such as Beaubien, Riopelle, St. Aubin, Chene, Campau, and Livernois.

For nearly sixty years after Cadillac's founding of Detroit, it was a completely French town, socially as well as governmentally. And

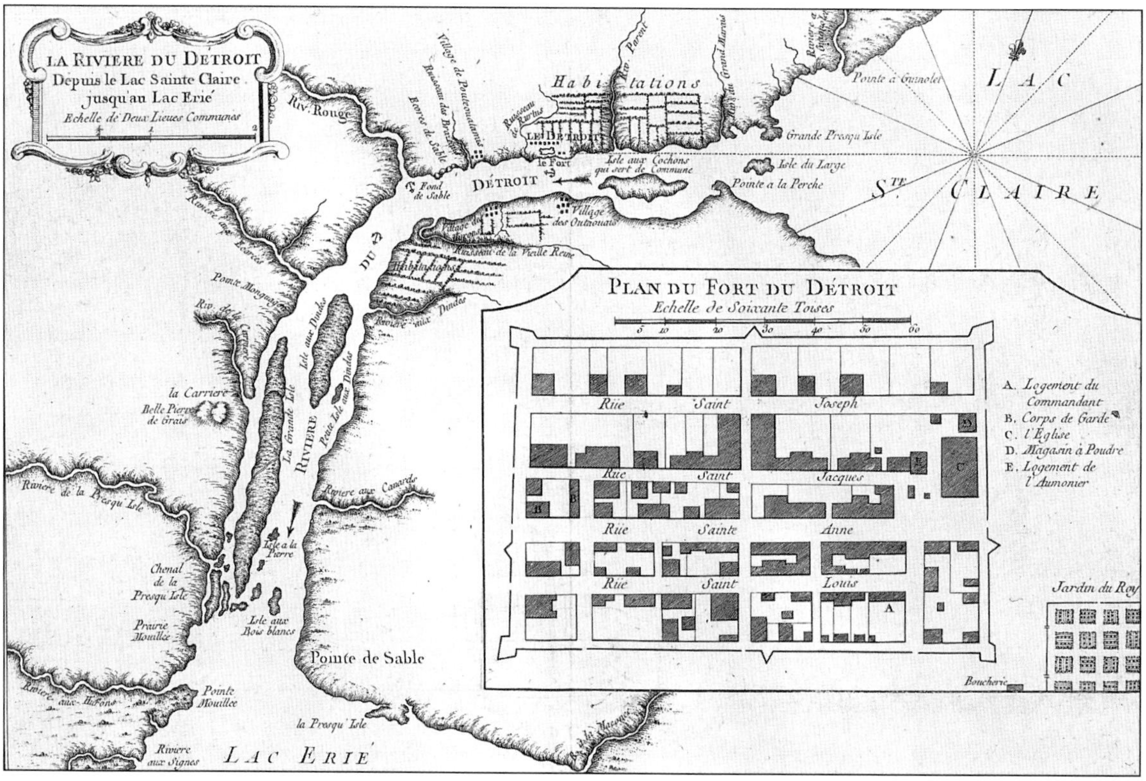

This first printed map of Detroit, which shows the fort and river as they appeared in 1749, is based on surveys made by Ensign Gaspard-Joseph Chaussegros de Lery. Courtesy Frank J. Kerwin Collection, St. Clair Shores Public Library.

In 1712 the Fox and Sac Indians laid seige to the fort at Detroit. Driven off by the French and their allies the Ottawas and the Hurons, the Fox and Sacs were defeated at a battle on Windmill Pointe (on the border of present-day Detroit and Grosse Pointe). From a painting by Frederick Remington. Courtesy Burton Historical Collection, Detroit Public Library.

except for a siege of the fort by the Sac and Fox Indians in 1712, and a few other occasional Indian troubles, life in the town was quiet and uneventful.

The fertile soil yielded good crops of wheat, oats, and some corn. Families consumed most of what they raised, and either sold the surplus or donated it for the support of the town, the garrison, and the church. Almost all of the farms had cattle, pigs, and chickens. The nearby forest supplied the family table with venison, birds, and muskrat, and the river at the front door was a never-failing source of sturgeon and whitefish. Each farm had its orchard of apple, peach, and pear trees. The apple crop made a superior cider, the peaches produced an excellent brandy, and both wild and cultivated grapes and berries were plentiful, so the wine crocks were always full.

The houses of the habitants became a little more livable as time went on, although they were never pretentious. The early rough log structures eventually were clapboarded over;

The farmhouse of the Navarre family of Monroe, much as it would have looked in the late eighteenth century, is similar in style to the homes of the French habitants of Fort Pontchartrain. Many of the furnishings found in a French farmhouse were locally made, like this chair, while others, such as this crystal goblet, were imported from Europe. Courtesy Monroe County Historical Museum.

For years, windmills could be found on both sides of the river up and down from the fort. This mill, as it might have looked in the 1750s, stood on a point that is now the foot of Lakepointe in Grosse Pointe Park. From a painting by Robert Hopkin. Courtesy Prismatic Club of Detroit.

lofts or second floors, lighted by dormer windows, became common. Many of the houses were whitewashed, and their Dutch doors were frequently painted apple green. Their yards, enclosed by picket fences, contained the usual bake ovens and wells with long sweeps. Similar houses can still be seen along the St. Lawrence River.

The habitants raised large families, and their sons and daughters married at an early age. While they were devoted to their church, they were also a merry lot, with their songs and dances. In the warmer weather there was cart racing. In the winter months, horse racing and sleigh riding up and down the frozen river were the most common sports. Schools were not regularly kept, and most habitants were illiterate. Newspapers were unheard of and unneeded. When the occasional traveler brought news of the outside world or an official announcement was to be made, the town crier called it out from the steps of Ste. Anne's after Sunday morning mass. Because there were no democratic institutions at this time, politics as we know it did not exist. Except for early trials such as a smallpox threat in 1752, it was an isolated and in many ways idyllic life that Detroiters lived during this period.

But there were clouds upon the horizon. Within a few short years, France and England would be at war.

Four

The British Fort

French rule came to an end in Detroit in 1760 when the village was given to the British as part of the spoils of the French and Indian War. Although part of a long European power struggle between France and England, the conflict was almost entirely a North American war. It grew out of the desire of the English seaboard colonies for the vast Ohio River and Great Lakes country, which were French property.

The war lasted from 1754 until 1760, but Detroit never came under direct attack from the British. The issue was settled elsewhere, on the Plains of Abraham just outside Quebec. On September 13, 1759, British General James Wolfe scaled the high bluff that appeared to make the city impregnable and decisively defeated the French defenders. Only Montreal was left, and it was surrendered to General Jeffrey Amherst on September 8, 1760. Detroit and all the remaining French possessions were included in the capitulation.

Detroit was still more of an area than a village when the British arrived. The entire population up and down both sides of the river was about two thousand, with fewer than five hundred people living in the village. The fort itself was considerably larger than the one Cadillac had built; its dimensions were about one hundred yards north and south by two hundred yards east and west. There were blockhouses at the corners and over the main gates, and these towers were armed with cannons of varying size. Inside the stockade the streets were much as they had been, though some of them had been extended beyond the walls, so the village actually included more than just the fort. In fact, more people lived outside the walls than inside.

Early in the spring of 1761, English traders began to arrive at Detroit, thus affording the Indians an opportunity to dispose of their winter's catch of furs and to trade for needed goods. To satisfy the wants of the Indians, the traders stocked their stores with snowshoes, large brass locks, pewter plates, ink powder, burning glasses (magnifying glasses used to start fires by concentrating the sun's rays), scalping knives, nightcaps, mounds of blankets, hair powder, candles, animal traps, Dutch ovens, tea, silver buckles, earrings, breastplates, powder, flints, shot, muskets, rolls of tobacco, mococks (baskets) of maple sugar, and barrels of rum.

As was the case under the French, large quantities of furs continued to be exported from Detroit. One such shipment consisted of the skins of 12,132 deer, 9,482 raccoons, 682 wildcats and foxes, 413 bears, and countless mink. Hard money, or specie, was scarce. In its place the settlers used furs, slaves (usually Indians, but occasionally blacks and whites), tobacco, and clam and oyster shells manufactured by the Dutch of New York and carried by the Indians as wampum.

Unfortunately, the English traders proved to be an unscrupulous lot, and hard bargainers as well. The Indians began to complain to Captain Donald Campbell, the fort's British commandant, about the high prices. The English were not as friendly as the French, and the Indians, who at first had welcomed the British takeover of Detroit, quickly became disillusioned. As time went on, the dissatisfaction grew. The officers at the fort, with the possible exception of Captain Campbell, were disdainful and suspicious, and they treated the Indians with a frosty arrogance. When General Amherst issued orders limiting the distribution of ammunition (and thus their ability to hunt), the Indians easily believed the rumor that the British were trying to starve them to death.

In the spring of 1763, the gathering tempest broke. Under a plan of confederation developed by the Ottawa Chief Pontiac, the British forts from Niagara and Fort Pitt to Michilimackinac and St. Joseph were to be simultaneously attacked. Pontiac summoned a war council, which was held in April on the Ecorse River below Detroit, and gave final instructions. For himself Pontiac reserved the principal city—Detroit. His first step was to move his village from the Canadian shore across from the lower end of Belle Isle to the American side. He set up his encampment on the farm of Baptiste Meloche on the east side of Parent's Creek. The location today is a short distance west of the Belle Isle Bridge.

Pontiac had a worthy foe, the British Commandant Major Henry Gladwin of the Eightieth Light Armed Foot, who had been sent to Detroit with a troop detachment in the

Although no portrait of Pontiac is known to exist, this sketch is believed to be an accurate representation of the famous Ottawa chief. Courtesy Burton Historical Collection, Detroit Public Library.

Major Henry Gladwin, of the Eightieth Light Armed Foot, arrived at Detroit as commandant with a detachment of British troops in the fall of 1761. Courtesy Burton Historical Collection, Detroit Public Library.

fall of 1761. Gladwin superseded Campbell, who remained as second in command. Pontiac made his first move in early May of 1763 when he asked for a meeting with Gladwin. At the appointed time, Pontiac, with about sixty warriors, arrived at the fort's east gate, known thereafter as the Pontiac Gate. Today the location is marked by a plaque at the corner of Griswold and Jefferson. It was Pontiac's plan that once inside the fort, he would deliver a speech. Then, if conditions seemed favorable, he would signal his warriors to bring out the muskets hidden under their blankets and massacre the British troops. If conditions did not seem right, the attack was to be postponed.

The British, however, were well aware of the plan. For years, Detroiters have cherished the legend that Gladwin learned of the scheme from a beautiful Indian woman. Actually, the "secret" was widely known. For several weeks the Indians had been asking local blacksmiths for hacksaws and files, and several people had reported seeing Indians cutting down their musket barrels. Many of the French farmers knew of the plot; in fact, Pontiac had actually tried to enlist their aid. There is also the story that a French girl warned her British fiancé, and that it was he who reported to Gladwin.

Whatever the facts, the British were ready and waiting. When the Indians entered the fort, they found the British troops in full battle dress. Pontiac asked why the soldiers were so heavily armed. Gladwin gave an evasive answer to the effect that he was merely drilling his troops. Realizing all hope of surprise was gone, the Indians stalked out of the fort, their plan a complete failure. A few days later, Pontiac returned to the fort but was not allowed to enter. Enraged, he turned his warriors loose. They massacred the Turnbull family on a nearby farm, and proceeded to Belle Isle, where they killed several members of the James Fisher family. On May 10, Captain Campbell and Lieutenant George McDougall went with several Frenchmen to the home of Antoine Cuillerier to discuss a truce with Pontiac. The chief's response was to hold the two officers as hostages for future bargaining.

Popular legend has it that Major Gladwin learned of Pontiac's plan from a beautiful Indian woman, but facts indicate that the plan was known by several people some time before its enactment. Courtesy Burton Historical Collection, Detroit Public Library.

Pontiac hands over his belt of wampum to Major Gladwin. Courtesy Burton Historical Collection, Detroit Public Library.

The next two months were spent in a state of siege. The Indians and British fired upon each other intermittently, neither making any headway. On July 4, a party set out from the fort to retrieve some lead from the home of Jacques Baby. En route they met an Indian warrior whom they scalped and then decapitated. Lifting the bloody head, they shook it in the direction of the Indian camp. Unfortunately, the warrior was the nephew of the Chippewa Chief Wasson. In retaliation, Captain Campbell was cut to pieces and devoured (McDougall had escaped two days earlier). As was the custom with prisoners, Campbell's heart, still raw and dripping with blood, was consumed by Wasson. This act was not simple cannibalism to the Indians, but was symbolic of taking on the courage of the enemy.

One by one the posts around the Great Lakes were attacked, and eventually every fort west of Niagara except Detroit was taken. Sandusky, St. Joseph, Fort Miamis, Presque Isle, and Michilimackinac were all captured

Following his meeting with Major Gladwin, Pontiac realized all hope of surprise was gone, and he and his warriors left the fort. From a painting by Frederic Remington. Courtesy Burton Historical Collection, Detroit Public Library.

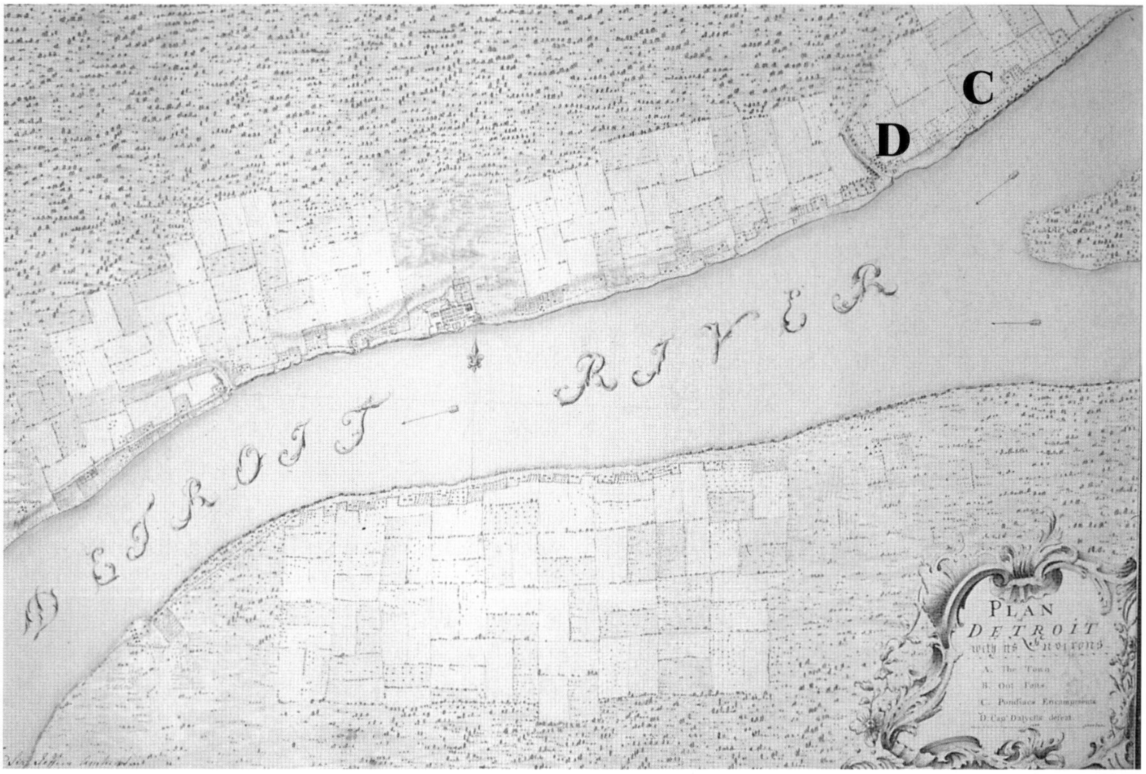

This painting is from a survey taken by Captain John Montresor, a British engineer who arrived in Detroit on October 3, 1765. The letter "C" *(upper right on map)* marks Pontiac's camp. The Battle of Bloody Run began at the bridge over Parent's Creek *(marked with "D" on map)*. Courtesy William L. Clements Library, University of Michigan.

and their garrisons either massacred or held prisoner by the Indians. At Detroit the stalemate continued until July 28, when Captain James Dalyell and Major Robert Rogers arrived with some three hundred reinforcements. Dalyell, an ambitious officer, persuaded Major Gladwin that a surprise attack on Pontiac's camp would defeat the Indians. Although he was urged to wait for more men, Dalyell felt determined to move at once. And so, one hour before daybreak on July 30, he led a column of 250 soldiers out of the fort and along the River Road, present-day East Jefferson Avenue.

When the soldiers reached Parent's Creek and began to cross the narrow footbridge, the waiting Indians, hidden in the bushes, opened

A huge whitewood tree that eventually became known as Pontiac's tree stood near Parent's Creek, at the site of the Battle of Bloody Run. The tree is seen here, a century after the battle. The road on the left is Jefferson, looking east. Courtesy Burton Historical Collection, Detroit Public Library.

fire. The lead troops were cut down before they could form a defense. One of those who fell was the overzealous Dalyell. Luckily, Major Rogers reached the nearby Campau house, from which he and his sharp-shooting rangers covered the retreat. In all, twenty British were killed and another thirty-seven were wounded, three of whom later died. So many dead and dying soldiers fell into Parent's Creek that its water ran red. From that time on the battle and the stream were known as Bloody Run.

The siege continued through the summer months and into the early fall. But then it had to end, for the Indians needed to set out for their winter hunting. Despite Pontiac's protestations, the Chippewa, Potawatomi, and Huron chiefs settled a weary peace with Gladwin and headed for home. Finally, on October 31, 1763, Pontiac sent a message to Gladwin offering to make peace. Without waiting for an official reply, Pontiac and his Ottawas left Detroit for their camp on the Maumee River. The siege was over, and of all the western forts, only Detroit had survived.

Following Pontiac's War, life in Detroit settled down to a peaceful and normal pattern that more or less continued for about a dozen years. But the peaceful days did not last. In 1775 Britain's Atlantic seaboard colonies rose up in armed rebellion.

Detroit played a key, though not decisive, role in the American Revolution. It served chiefly as a base from which expeditions were sent to attack American settlements in Kentucky, western Pennsylvania, and New York. Led by white partisan raiders, these bands of Indians struck terror into the hearts of the American settlers, and with good reason. It has been estimated that more than two thousand men, women, and children were killed, many of them scalped by these Detroit-based Indian war parties.

Behind all this border fury was Henry Hamilton, who had arrived in Detroit on November 9, 1775, to assume the duties of lieutenant governor. Although Hamilton was an army man, his duties as lieutenant governor were more those of a civil administrator. He determined overall policy, but he did not command the garrison, which for most of the war was in the capable hands of Captain Richard B. Lernoult. Because of Hamilton's part in planning and directing raids, particularly against Kentucky, the Americans hung the label "Hamilton the Hair-Buyer" on him. There is no real evidence that he paid for scalps; on the contrary, he frequently cautioned departing war parties not to make war against women and children.

In order to check the raiding parties from Detroit and capture the fort, the Americans

Lieutenant Governor Henry Hamilton, who arrived at Detroit in November 1775, was the senior British officer during the Revolutionary War. In later years he served as governor of Bermuda, where the city of Hamilton bears his name. Courtesy Burton Historical Collection, Detroit Public Library.

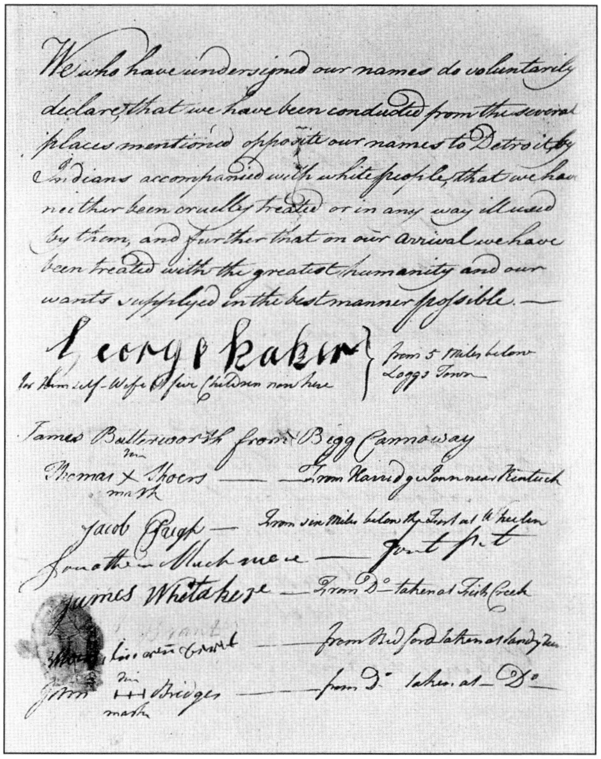
We who have undersigned our names do voluntarily declare that we have been conducted from the several places mentioned opposite our names to Detroit by Indians accompanied with white people, that we have neither been cruelly treated or in any way ill used by them, and further that on our arrival we have been treated with the greatest humanity and our wants supplyed in the best manner possible.—

George Baker } from 5 Miles below Loggs Town
for Himself - Wife & five Children now here

James Butterworth from Bigg Cannoway

Thomas his X mark Shoers —— from Harrodsburgh near Kentuck

Jacob Pugh — from six Miles below the Fort at Wheelen

Jonathan Muchmore —— fort pit

James Whitaker —— from Do taken at Fish Creek

Grant —— from Bedford taken at Sandy Run

John his H mark Bridges —— from Do taken at Do

Lieutenant Governor Hamilton, who was criticized for using Indians as allies during the Revolutionary War, obtained this certificate of humane treatment of prisoners. Courtesy Burton Historical Collection, Detroit Public Library.

organized an offensive in 1778 under Colonel George Rogers Clark. With a force of Virginia and Kentucky frontiersmen, Clark captured the distant posts of Kaskaskia and Cahokia and appeared ready to advance upon Detroit. Alarmed by the threat, Lieutenant Governor Hamilton gathered a small force of rangers and regulars and went to Vincennes, Indiana, to block Clark's advance. Clark, however, made an epic march across the flooded plains of southern Illinois and Indiana and surprised Vincennes; Hamilton, outnumbered and unprepared, surrendered.

Clark's planned advance toward Detroit was stalled by lack of manpower; meanwhile, a new threat was posed. Daniel Brodhead with a small army of Pennsylvanians marched from Pittsburgh into Ohio and built a fort about ninety miles south of Sandusky. To Captain Lernoult, an attack against Detroit appeared certain and imminent. Surveying his facilities for defense, Lernoult found much to be desired. Detroit was a tinderbox with its wooden buildings, and it was obvious that the old stockade could not withstand an attack by a properly armed enemy. From the height of land several hundred yards north of the town, enemy cannon could easily control the defenses and force a quick surrender. Lernoult decided that a new fort must be built as soon as possible on the strategic hill if Detroit were to be held by the British.

In the absence of the regular engineering officer, Lernoult picked Captain Henry Bird to design and construct the new fort. One late afternoon in November 1778, Bird paced off the outline of a new defense works, and the next day construction began. Placed on the rising ground north of town, the new fort covered an area of about three acres, its center being at the present-day intersection of Fort and Shelby Streets.

During the winter of 1778-79, Lernoult and Bird drove their men relentlessly. Lernoult also enlisted civilians from Detroit to help on the project, ordering all able-bodied men to work three days out of nine. The British citizens, mostly merchants, willingly consented to these demands, while the French farmers had to be coerced. Finally, in April 1779, the work, named Fort Lernoult in honor of the captain, was ready for action.

The completed fort had earthen ramparts eleven feet high, twenty-six-feet thick at the base, and twelve feet wide at the top of the parapet. The land surrounding the new fort was cleared so that the enemy would have no cover during an attack. There was only one gate, on the south or town side, and it was protected by a blockhouse and a drawbridge.

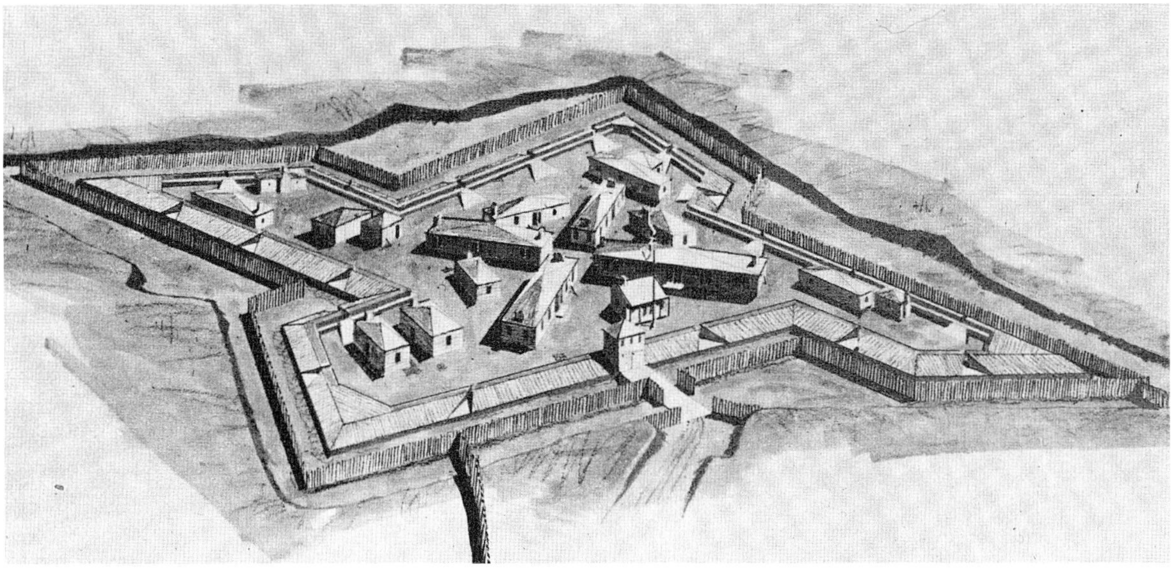

Captain Richard B. Lernoult had a fort built as a defense against an American attack that never came. Completed in 1779, the fort carried the names Fort Lernoult, Fort Detroit, and Fort Shelby until it was torn down in 1827. From Philip P. Mason, *Fort Lernoult and the American Revolution.*

Lernoult stripped the old fort and the naval vessels on the river of their guns and requisitioned more from Quebec. Inside the fort, a number of buildings were put up and a well was dug to ensure a supply of fresh water. Finally, pickets were erected to extend from the corners of the new fort down to the east and west walls of the town.

When construction was completed, the garrison moved into the fort and prepared for an attack. Captain Lernoult waited to hear of the movements of the American forces, but the threatened attack never came. The Americans were never able to muster a force sufficient for such a campaign.

The fort continued to be called Fort Lernoult as long as the British occupied Detroit. When the Americans took over it was renamed Fort Detroit, and so it was known until after the War of 1812, when it became Fort Shelby in honor of the Kentucky governor who led an army of Kentuckians to the relief of Detroit. In 1827, no longer needed, the fort was dismantled; the earth from the ramparts was used to fill in the land below Jefferson Avenue, and the ground where the fort stood was subdivided.

The Revolutionary War ended in 1781 with the surrender of Yorktown, and yet the war did not end for Detroit. A formal peace treaty was signed in 1783 that assigned all of the Northwest Territory to the United States. This, of course, included Detroit and Michigan. To assert its sovereignty over the area as well as to provide for its orderly development, Congress adopted the Ordinance of 1787, better known as the Northwest Ordinance. A notable charter, the ordinance provided for the territory's division into five states when the population warranted and laid down certain ground rules for a territorial form of government until the time for admission to the Union arrived.

But the transition was slow as far as Detroit was concerned. The British were loath to give Detroit up. Under pressure from local and Montreal merchants who did not want to lose the rich Indian trade, British occupation continued. The excuse was that the United States had not yet fulfilled all its 1783 treaty obligations. Consequently, Detroit existed in a sort of political limbo. Although legally it was a United States possession, the British continued to occupy it with troops and to govern it after a fashion. It continued to be the chief western base for the British Indian Department, and the British gave huge amounts of money in the forms of gifts and subsidies in an effort to maintain control over the midwestern tribes. War parties still harassed Ohio and Indiana, and the authorities at Detroit just turned their backs on what was happening. Merchants complained because what amounted to military government was bad for business, and a lack of civil courts made the collection of debts difficult. To placate the merchants, a semblance of civil law was established, and when the British established their Court of Common Pleas for the residents, they were careful to use buildings on the legally British side of the river for their proceedings. Then, in 1791 when Upper

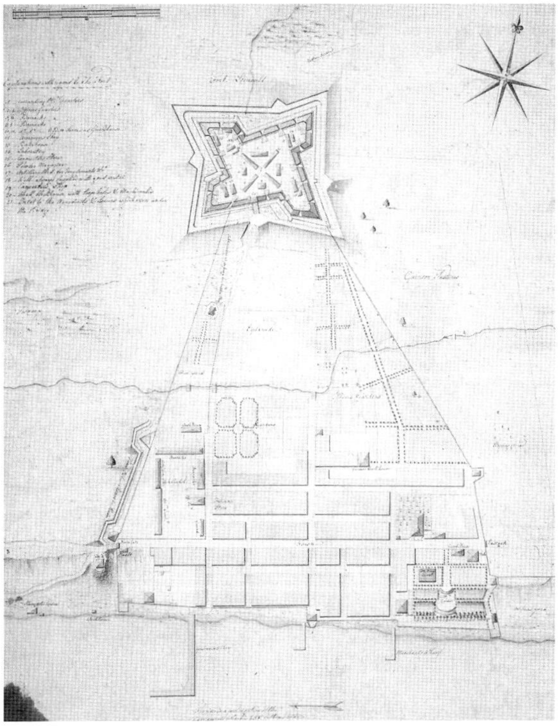

This 1797 map of Detroit was painted by Major Jacob Rivardi, a Frenchman serving in the Corps of Artillerists and Engineers of the U.S. Army. Rivardi was stationed in Detroit from 1796 to 1797. Courtesy William L. Clements Library, University of Michigan.

This view of Detroit in 1794 shows the southwest corner of the Citadel (now Congress and Jefferson), the small wooden houses of the town, British ships, Indian canoes, and the busy waterfront. Courtesy Burton Historical Collection, Detroit Public Library.

Canada, now Ontario, was separated from Quebec, Detroit, an American city, elected two representatives to the Canadian provincial council of Parliament.

Obviously, it was a situation the United States could not long tolerate. President George Washington sent an army into the Ohio country to subdue the Indians once and for all. After a couple of abortive campaigns, General "Mad Anthony" Wayne defeated the confederated tribes in 1794 at the Battle of Fallen Timbers near present-day Toledo. This victory placed a well-trained and effective American army on the doorsteps of Detroit. The British position was untenable, and when Chief Justice John Jay negotiated a peace and commercial treaty with the British government in November 1794, he had no difficulty securing an article that provided for the evacuation of Detroit. In the spring of 1796, the garrison of Detroit was withdrawn across the river and the new British base, Fort Malden, was established at Amherstburg at the mouth of the Detroit River. Only a small detail of British troops remained at Detroit.

On July 11, 1796, a detachment of sixty-five American troops under the command of Captain Moses Porter arrived at Detroit. The fort was turned over to them and the Stars and Stripes were hoisted. Detroit became an American town at last.

General "Mad Anthony" Wayne led the troops who won the Battle of Fallen Timbers (1794), which ended the British hold on Detroit. Courtesy Burton Historical Collection, Detroit Public Library.

Five

The American Town

TWO DAYS AFTER CAPTAIN PORTER arrived at Detroit, the remainder of the first American troop contingent reached the town. The American army at this time was known as the Legion of the United States, and Anthony Wayne was its commanding general. The legion was divided into four sub-legions corresponding to regiments. The First Sub-Legion was commanded by Lieutenant Colonel John Francis Hamtramck and was assigned the duty of taking over Detroit. Canadian-born but of Luxembourgian and French ancestry, Colonel Hamtramck had served with distinction in the American army during the Revolutionary War. Hamtramck settled in Detroit and purchased a farm east of the town. Eventually the area grew into Hamtramck Township, and later a northern section became the city of Hamtramck.

General Wayne arrived in Detroit on August 13 and set up his headquarters. However, he remained here only until November, when he left for his home near Philadelphia. Unfortunately, he never made it. At Erie, Pennsylvania, Wayne became seriously ill, and he died on December 15.

The arrival of the Americans at Detroit caused serious problems for some of the town's

When he became commandant at Detroit, Colonel John F. Hamtramck purchased the old Campau farm, just east of Detroit, and in 1802 he built this house on the river. The building was demolished in 1898. Courtesy Burton Historical Collection, Detroit Public Library.

residents, especially those who were unwilling to relinquish their British citizenship. These included several of the more prosperous and influential merchants who wanted to retain their close trade connections with Montreal. Some solved the dilemma by packing up their possessions and moving across the river to Canada, where they were already large landowners. Among those who made this move were the families of John Askin and Angus MacIntosh.

The move was not too difficult for Askin. His daughter had married Elijah Brush. The Brushes remained on the old Askin farm where downtown Brush Street is now. Thereafter known as the Brush farm, it was the first one east of the town. A sister-in-law of Askin's was married to Commodore Alexander Grant, who commanded His Majesty's Royal Navy on the upper Great Lakes. Grant had a palatial house at Grosse Pointe and did not want to leave it. He settled the problem by ignoring the change in government and staying. Detroit was amused by the anomaly of having the British naval commander directing his fleet from the United States. Grant continued to do so until his death in 1813.

Not all the merchants moved away, however. Families such as the Macombs, Campaus, Abbots, and Mays accepted American citizenship, retaining their businesses and, in some cases, their slaves. Of the latter there were about 175 in the town when the Americans arrived. About half of them were Indians (called Panis), but the rest were blacks who had been brought to Detroit from raids into Kentucky during the Revolution. There were a few Germans and a few Dutch in Detroit as well. Added to the French, English, Scotch, and Irish, they gave the town a cosmopolitan flavor that it has always retained.

Accompanying General Wayne when he arrived in Detroit was Winthrop Sargent, secretary of the Northwest Territory. Two days after Sargent came to town, on August 15, 1796, he issued a proclamation organizing Wayne County. At that time the county consisted of a huge part of this region, including all of Michigan's lower peninsula, part of its upper peninsula, and parts of present-day Wisconsin, Illinois, Indiana, and Ohio. Later, of course, boundaries were revised, and in 1815 Wayne County was reduced to its present dimensions.

For the next decade, the population of this region grew slowly. But grow it did, and in 1805 the Territory of Michigan was established with Detroit as its capital. To govern this new territory, President Thomas Jefferson appointed Revolutionary War veteran William Hull of Massachusetts as governor and

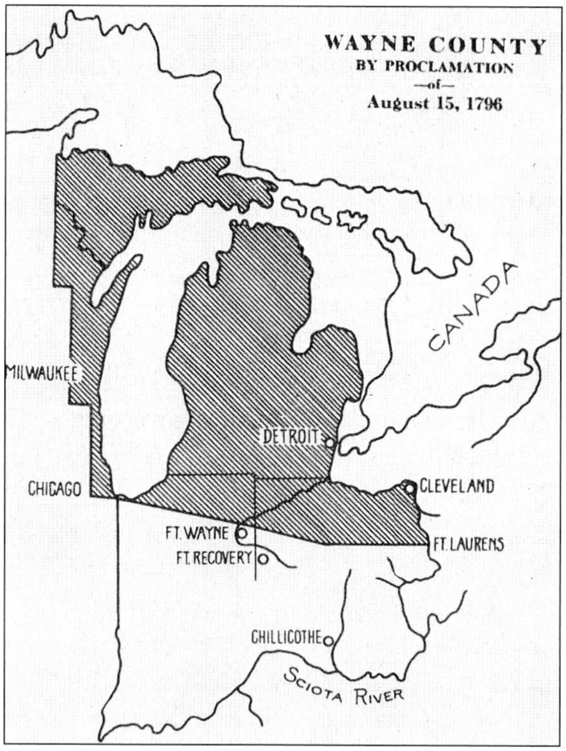

On August 15, 1796, a proclamation was issued that organized Wayne County. The region's first county, it covered a large part of the Northwest Territory. Boundaries were later revised, and in 1815 the area of the county was reduced to its present dimensions. From Clarence M. Burton, *History of Wayne County.*

In 1805 President Jefferson appointed Revolutionary War veteran William Hull the first governor of the Territory of Michigan. Courtesy Burton Historical Collection, Detroit Public Library.

Stanley Griswold of New Hampshire as secretary. The remainder of the new governing board, known as the Governor and Judges, was made up of Judge Augustus B. Woodward, a native of New York who at the time of his appointment was living in Washington, D.C.; Judge Frederick Bates of Virginia, who had been serving since 1802 as Detroit's first postmaster; and Judge Samuel Huntington of Ohio. Huntington, however, declined his appointment, and Judge John Griffin of Virginia was made his replacement.

On January 18, 1802, prior to these developments, an act had been adopted for the incorporation of Detroit. The act also called for a slate of municipal officers that included a board of five trustees, a secretary, an assessor, a tax collector, and a marshal. The first meeting of the trustees was held in February 1802 in the tavern of John Dodemead on Jefferson Avenue near Washington Boulevard. At this time the town's population numbered about five hundred, not counting the soldiers at the fort. In all the town contained about three hundred buildings, including homes, sheds, stores, outhouses, barns, and sties. There were probably no more than one hundred dwelling places, and the entire town, exclusive of government structures, was owned by sixty-nine proprietors.

One of the first official acts of the new board of trustees was to adopt better ordinances for fire protection. The threat of fire was a constant worry, since the old frame houses that crowded on top of each other were tinder dry and made the town a veritable fire trap. Each householder was required to keep a ladder on his roof, to have fire buckets, and to cover his hearth fire every night. The town watch was instructed to report any house in which candles were seen burning later than usual. The town had a fire engine of sorts, a pump kept in a shed adjoining Dodemead's tavern.

The morning of June 11, 1805, dawned clear. It was a Catholic feast day as well as market day, so the French farmers had come to town early to attend mass at Ste. Anne's before setting out their produce for sale. Elsewhere the town was bustling as usual, with people going about their business. One of the town bakers, John Harvey, had set out to replenish his supply of flour. Climbing into his cart, he rapped his clay pipe against his boot. A live coal fell onto a pile of straw and set it afire. In a matter of seconds, the blaze engulfed Harvey's barn and began to spread to adjoining buildings. The dreaded call of "Fire!" was sounded and a bucket brigade was formed. The townspeople carried buckets of

This watercolor by British army surgeon Dr. Edward Walsh dated June 22, 1804, is a view of Detroit from the Canadian shore. The Huron church in the foreground is the current site of the Canadian approach to the Ambassador Bridge. Courtesy William L. Clements Library, University of Michigan.

water from the river and tried to dampen the flaming thatched roof with swabs at the end of long poles. The fire engine was hauled out, but its suction hose was dropped into a cistern next to a hatmaker's shop and it became clogged with bits of felt. Householders and merchants scurried back and forth with armloads of possessions, trying to get them safely to the commons or onboard boats. Soldiers rushed down from the fort to lend a hand, but the flames got past them.

The day was almost windless, but the fire created its own draft and swept across the town in all directions. The Citadel and the government store were consumed. The flames raced down Ste. Anne Street (now Jefferson Avenue), devouring Dodemead's tavern, the stores of merchants, the church, and the council house. John Askin, looking out the door of his home across the river, saw a huge pillar of black smoke rising from the town. He called his sons and servants and pushed off in a boat to give what help he could. But Detroit was beyond help. In less than three hours, nothing remained of the town except a warehouse near the river, a blockhouse, and a few blackened chimneys. Everything else was gone, and from the fort, which remained untouched, observers gazed on a scene of indescribable desolation. People took refuge where they could find it—in the farmhouses up and down the river, in the fort, and in tents and hastily constructed bowers of branches on the common. Fortunately, no one was seriously injured. Father Gabriel Richard, the beloved aristocratic Sulpician priest who had been part of Ste. Anne's since 1798 and who had barely escaped the Reign of Terror after refusing to take the oath of loyalty to the French Republic, set to work at once organizing relief and gathering food and clothing for the homeless. Surveying the scene, he was heard to murmur: "Speramus meliora; resurget cineribus": "We hope for better things; it will arise from the ashes." Years later, these words would be incorporated into the city's seal and become Detroit's official motto.

For the first few days after the fire, little was done. The people were in a state of shock, overwhelmed with despair and uncertainty. Left to themselves, Detroit's citizens would have rebuilt the town as before, with its narrow streets and small clustered lots. Fortunately, wiser heads prevailed. Governor Hull and the other newly appointed territorial officials arrived in Detroit on June 30 and immediately set to work. They rejected the idea of rebuilding the town within its former crowded area. Instead, they persuaded Congress to donate the commons east of the fort, plus an additional parcel known as the Ten Thousand Acre Tract to the north of the fort, so that the area of the town could be expanded. It was decided that one new lot would be given to each person seventeen years of age or older who had been a resident of the town at the time of the fire. The location of each property was determined by a drawing, and included in this drawing were eleven of the city's free blacks. The Ten Thousand Acre Tract was to be offered for sale in parcels of eighty acres or more, the proceeds to be used to build a jail, a courthouse, and other public buildings.

It was left to Judge Woodward to decide how the new town was to be laid out. Born in New York City in 1774 and a graduate of Columbia College, Woodward had practiced law in Virginia and Washington, D.C. He had formed a close friendship with Thomas Jefferson, from whom he derived many of his ideas. These ideas, quite advanced for a fairly primitive frontier society, caused him to be regarded by many Detroiters as an eccentric. While living in Washington, he had observed Major Charles L'Enfant lay out that capital city, and he would adopt many of L'Enfant's ideas for the new Detroit.

The Woodward Plan, as it came to be known, called for a system of north-south and east-west boulevards 200 feet wide which, at regular intervals, would intersect at extensive circular plazas or circuses. From these would also radiate, like the spokes of a wheel, a series of secondary avenues 120 feet wide. Then two boulevards and four avenues would be linked together by a network of 60-foot-wide streets, in effect creating three concentric circles around each circus. Each of these circus-oriented systems would be a hexagonal unit, and each hexagon was composed of twelve triangular units of eight blocks. In the center of each, one block—or one-ninth of all the land—was to be reserved for public buildings, churches, and schools. Each of these hexagonal units could be repeated and tied into others just like it so that the town could be expanded in any direction as the population grew. Lots of no less than five thousand square feet each would provide for spaciousness. Actually, these large lots established a traditional characteristic of Detroit; with plenty of land available, it became a city of single-family homes. For years, in fact, Detroit led the nation's major cities in the number of homes occupied by single owners. On the other hand, no row houses, which would have led to a greater concentration of population, were ever built. This ultimately produced problems from which Detroit still suffers acutely, such as a lack of effective transportation.

Within a short time, Woodward's plan was adopted. Several new streets were laid out according to his ideas, while some of the old

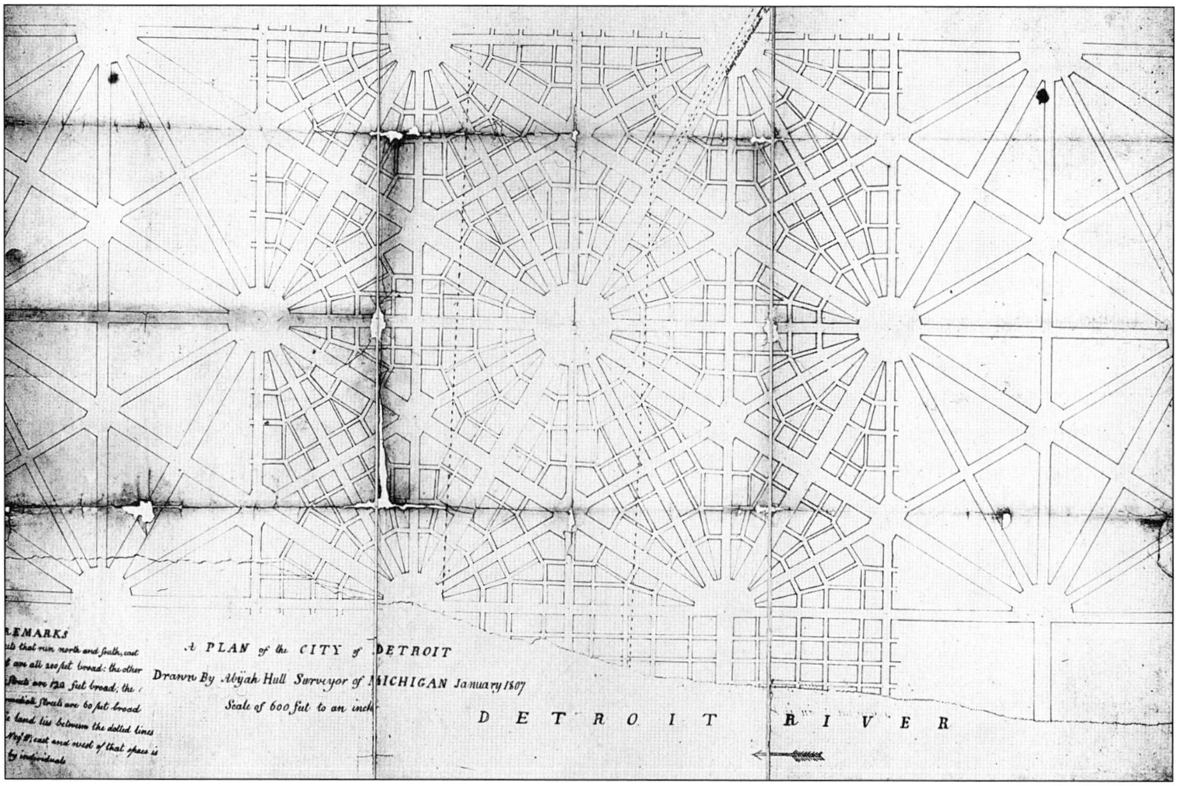

Judge Woodward's plan for the city of Detroit called for a system of interlocking hexagons, bisected by broad avenues and studded with plazas and circuses. This copy of his plan was drawn by surveyor Abijah Hull in January 1807. Courtesy Burton Historical Collection, Detroit Public Library.

ones were widened and renamed. For example, Ste. Anne's Street, Detroit's earliest street, became Jefferson Avenue. The center of the town was now located between the river and Larned Street to the north. The major north-south streets became Wayne (now Washington Boulevard), Shelby, Griswold, Bates, and Randolph. Construction west of Griswold was discouraged by the federal government, which wanted to keep a clear field of fire for the fort. A few families built their homes as far north as Grand Circus Park, but the area north of Campus Martius was largely open, unsettled country. Woodward's original plan called for Washington Boulevard to be the city's main street, but the location of the fort prevented its extension south to the river. The avenue that eventually did become the main street was named Woodward—not in his honor, the judge coyly observed, but because it ran "towards the wood, or woodward."

Although by 1818 the decision was made to abandon the Woodward Plan and to adopt the more familiar checkerboard pattern, remnants of the Woodward Plan can still be seen in the central part of downtown. Campus Martius, which marked a corner of the original hexagon, is one of the open plazas, with streets such as Woodward, Michigan, Cadillac Square, Fort, and Monroe radiating from it. Continuing up Woodward to Grand Circus Park, one can find a dramatic example of half of one of Woodward's projected circuses, and his radiating boulevards (Madison and Washington) and avenues are clearly discernible.

Tall and angular with piercing eyes, Judge Woodward continued to be one of Detroit's most influential citizens and the head of Michigan's judicial system until 1824, when he was appointed to a district judgeship in Florida by President Monroe. Some may question whether he was an eccentric or a genius years ahead of his time, but there is no doubt that Augustus Brevoort Woodward was a remarkable man who left his mark on Detroit.

Following Detroit's rebuilding, the major business interest of the town continued to be furs. Although the trade prospered, it did so in most cases at the expense of the Indians. Many independent traders were dishonest in their dealings with the Indians, and some of the government agents were little better. Dissatisfaction with the government's fur-trading policies and encroachment on their hunting lands by American settlers caused the Indians to look to the British for aid and comfort. Fort Malden, headquarters for the Canadian Indian Department, became a

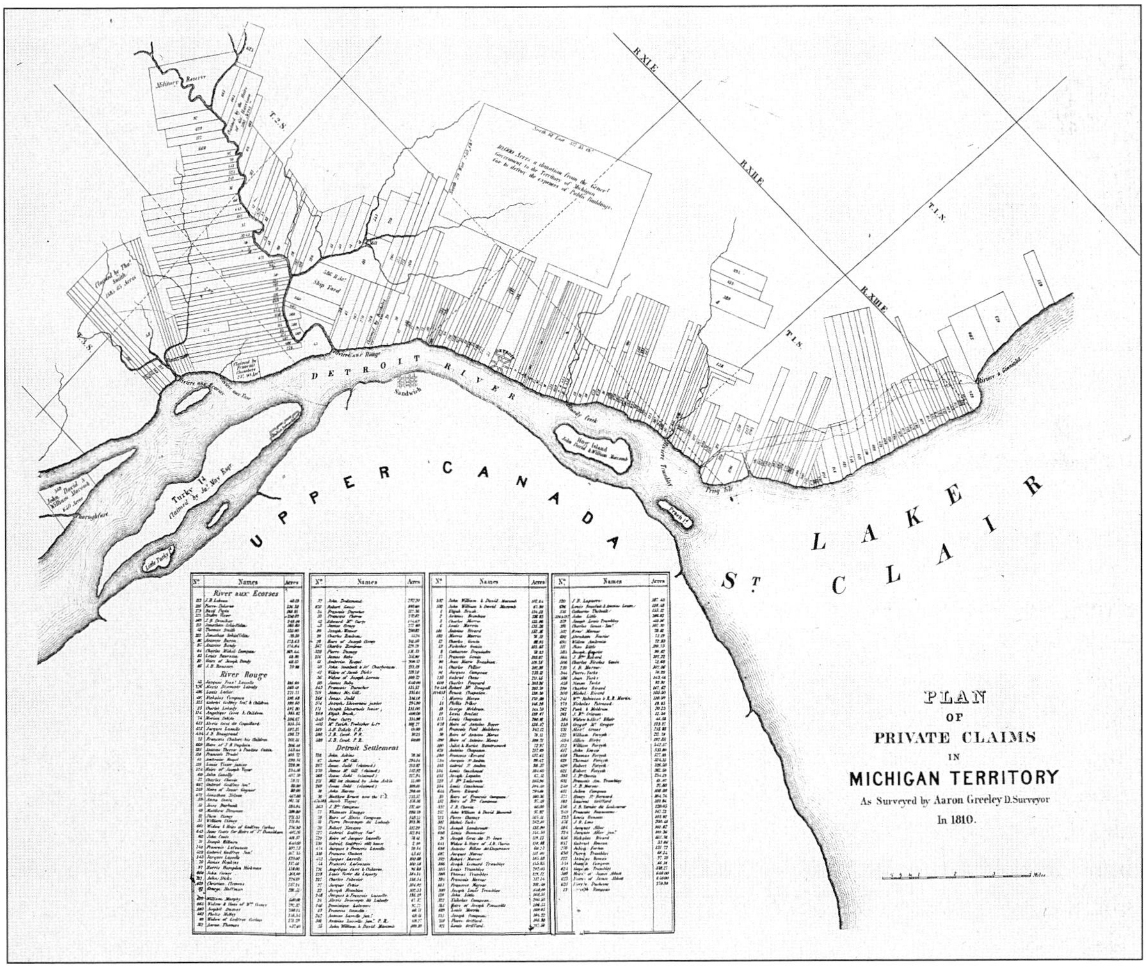

This "Plan of Private Claims in Michigan Territory as surveyed by Aaron Greeley in 1810" clearly illustrates the early French ribbon farms that stretched up and down the river from the fort. Courtesy Burton Historical Collection, Detroit Public Library.

This view of the Detroit River, Fort Malden, and the town of Amherstburg dates from about 1813. On the left is Bois Blanc Island (Bob-Lo); to the right is Fort Malden and the dockyard. From *View of Amherstberg 1813* by Margaret Reynolds. Courtesy Parks Canada, Fort Malden National Historic Site.

major center for Indian subsidies for tribes from all over Michigan and the Midwest. British traders—some say they were actually British agents—traveled throughout Michigan and kept the Indians supplied with weapons and encouragement. The Americans in turn distrusted both the Indians and the British.

These Indian problems continued to grow, and while not the only cause, they were major factors contributing to the War of 1812. The portents were there for all to read, however, long before hostilities erupted. Fearful of attack as early as 1807, Governor Hull strengthened the town's defenses and partially mobilized the militia. The Indians, on the other hand, were again raiding frontier settlements, and the Shawnee Chief Tecumseh was trying to form an alliance of the various tribes of the region. He was aided by his brother,

In an effort to settle differences, the Shawnee Chief Tecumseh met with General William Henry Harrison. The meeting was unsuccessful; the Indian village of Tippecanoe was destroyed, and Tecumseh allied himself with the British. Courtesy St. Clair Shores Public Library.

Tensquatawa (the Prophet), who was preaching a holy cause to the Indians. In November 1811, Governor William Henry Harrison of Indiana led an army that destroyed the Prophet's village at Tippecanoe, and Tecumseh openly allied himself with the British. War became inevitable.

The War of 1812 marked a period of real suffering for the people of Detroit. In June 1812, Governor Hull reluctantly accepted command of a force of twenty-five hundred U.S. Army regulars, Ohio volunteers, and local militia. After an abortive assault on Fort Malden, Hull retreated to Detroit and prepared for an attack. He did not have to wait long. On August 13, General Isaac Brock, commander of British forces in Upper Canada and a most able military officer, sent Hull a demand for surrender. When Hull rejected the demand, Brock began a cannon bombardment of Detroit from the Canadian shore. Realizing that his supply lines were cut off and fearing Indian atrocities if he put up a fight, Hull decided to surrender. In this fashion, Detroit won the dubious distinction of being the only major American city ever to be surrendered to a foreign foe. Altogether it was one of the most dreary military fiascoes ever

British Indian agent Matthew Elliott's red coat, apparel typical of a British army officer of the Detroit River region during the War of 1812. Courtesy Fort Malden National Historic Site, Parks Canada.

U.S. Militia coat, waistcoat, and chapeau, apparel typical of an American officer during the War of 1812. Courtesy Fort Malden National Historic Site, Parks Canada.

On August 13, 1812, with his supply lines cut and fearing Indian atrocities, Governor William Hull surrendered to British General Isaac Brock, and Detroit thus became the only major American city ever to be surrendered to a foreign foe. Courtesy Burton Historical Collection, Detroit Public Library.

suffered by American troops. It was made more so by the fact that despite a numerically superior and well-armed force at Hull's command, not a single shot was fired in defense of Detroit. For his action, the aging Hull was court-martialed and sentenced to be shot for cowardice. At the last minute, however, President James Madison pardoned him in view of his Revolutionary War services, but Hull lived out his life in disgrace.

The British occupation that followed Hull's surrender lasted just over one year. During that time, the people of Detroit were forced to live under semi-martial law. Indians were allowed free access to the town, and most of the merchants had their stores broken into and their merchandise carted away. Fearful of antagonizing his Indian allies, British Commandant Colonel Henry Proctor did nothing to prevent the plundering. But Proctor's days were numbered as far as Detroit was concerned. On September 10, 1813, Commodore Oliver Hazard Perry with his naval squadron met and defeated the British flotilla off Put-in-Bay Island in Lake Erie. This allowed General Harrison to immediately invade Canada. His troops captured Fort Malden, and he sent a brigade across the river to reoccupy Detroit on September 29. Proctor and his British forces retreated toward Niagara, but Harrison caught up with him on October 5 near Chatham, Ontario, and totally defeated the British forces in the Battle of the Thames. During the battle, Chief Tecumseh was killed and Proctor fled ignominiously. Although the war would continue for another year, Detroit was never again seriously threatened.

The year 1814, however, marked a low point in Detroit's history. Even though a large number of troops were stationed in the town, the citizens lived in constant fear of another attack by the British and their Indian allies. In addition, the countryside had been ravaged by war. Indians and British and American troops had vied with each other in destroying fields, tearing down fences and barns for firewood, and stealing livestock. The war had also interrupted the planting of crops, and the townspeople and soldiers were constantly hungry. The situation became so serious that in some outlying areas people were reduced to eating boiled hay. Judge Woodward wrote: "The desolation of this territory is beyond all conception [with] more than half of the population destitute." Then, during the winter, an epidemic swept through the town and several hundred people died. No one was certain what the disease was; it was simply called a plague.

The war finally came to an end in late December 1814 with the signing of the Treaty of Ghent. The following February, word reached Detroit that the peace pact had been ratified by Congress. To celebrate the ending of the war, the leading citizens of the town gathered at Ben Woodworth's Steamboat Hotel, located at the northwest corner of Woodbridge and Randolph Streets, and staged an all-night party billed as the Grand Pacification Ball. To show that there were no hard feelings, the Detroiters invited the British officers from Fort Malden and civilian dignitaries from the town of Amherstburg to attend. The fiddles played late into the night, glasses were filled and emptied time after time, and huge quantities of food were consumed. It is reported that the party was a great success, and that it indeed did much to pacify the ill feelings of the war.

Shortly after the Americans reoccupied Detroit in September 1813, a combined British and Indian force was defeated by American troops at the Battle of the Thames. During the battle, Indian leader Tecumseh was killed. Courtesy Burton Historical Collection, Detroit Public Library.

To celebrate the ending of the War of 1812, Detroit officials invited British officers from Fort Malden and civilian dignitaries from Amherstburg to a Grand Pacification Ball at Woodworth's Steamboat Hotel. Courtesy Burton Historical Collection, Detroit Public Library.

Six

The Road West

DURING THE TWO DECADES THAT followed the War of 1812, Detroit was to experience its first dramatic growth. This prosperity can be largely attributed to one man—Lewis Cass. A man of extraordinary talents, Cass probably had a greater influence on the growth and development of Detroit and Michigan than did any other single individual.

Born in New Hampshire in 1782, Cass moved to Ohio as a young man. There he studied law and served in the Ohio legislature. He arrived in Detroit in 1812 as a colonel of Ohio volunteers. After the city's surrender, Cass was sent back to Ohio on parole. Later he was exchanged and returned to Detroit in 1813 with General Harrison's army. Because of Cass's services, both military and political, President Madison appointed him governor of the Michigan Territory on October 29, 1813. Cass proved to be a most able administrator, and he served as governor of the territory for eighteen highly successful and progressive years. When he finally relinquished the position in 1831, he went on to

Territorial governor, secretary of war, ambassador, U.S. senator, secretary of state, and presidential nominee, Lewis Cass had a greater influence on the growth and development of Detroit and Michigan than did any other individual. Author's collection.

become Secretary of War, minister to France, United States senator from Michigan, presidential nominee of the Democratic Party in 1848, and finally Secretary of State on the eve of the outbreuak of the Civil War. Cass died in Detroit on June 17, 1866, at the age of eighty-three.

At the end of the War of 1812, Detroit had a population of about 850, with the Territory of Michigan at something less than 5,000. But with the war now over and the threat of Indian attack no longer serious, a great migration to the West began. However, the rush of settlers bypassed Michigan, pouring instead into Ohio, Indiana, and Illinois. One reason for this was that Detroit and Michigan had gained a poor reputation from adverse government surveyors' reports, one of which stated that Michigan was "an interminable swamp." Another reason for the lack of public enthusiasm for Michigan was its inaccessibility. To reach Detroit, one had to travel across Canada or across Ohio, a most difficult journey that included crossing the Black Swamp. The only other way to reach Michigan was by slow, uncertain, and expensive passage across the lakes on a sailing vessel.

Thus, throughout the East, Michigan was given—however understandably—an undeservedly poor image. Governor Cass took note, and took action. He began a publicity campaign. A most capable writer, Cass wrote articles for major eastern publications and urged residents of the territory to write letters extolling Michigan's virtues to friends and relatives back home. He invited visitors and

Originally built facing the river in the 1740s, the Cass House—Lewis Cass's longtime home—was moved to Larned between Fort and Second Streets in 1836. After Cass was appointed territorial governor, the house was known as the White House of the Northwest. James Monroe, the first president to visit Detroit, stayed here. Courtesy Burton Historical Collection, Detroit Public Library.

tourists to come and see Michigan for themselves. In 1817, President James Monroe was persuaded to visit Detroit, and other distinguished citizens came from time to time as well. Their visits received considerable publicity in the East and helped change the unappealing image of Michigan.

Three national events also influenced this situation and were major factors in determining Detroit's growth. First was the development of the steamboat. In 1811, Robert Fulton sailed his *Clermont* up the Hudson River from New York, and almost immediately people began to think in terms of steam navigation. At Black Rock, near Buffalo, shipbuilders laid the keel of a 135-foot side-wheeler. Launched on May 28, 1818, she was named *Walk-in-the-Water*. As the first steamboat on the upper Great Lakes, she caused considerable enthusiasm in the West. *Walk-in-the-Water*'s maiden voyage was to be to Detroit, and under the command of Captain Job Fish she sailed from Buffalo on August 23, 1818, carrying twenty-nine passengers. Detroit prepared for her arrival by building a new wharf at the foot of Bates Street. After a number of stops along the way at Dunkirk, Erie, Cleveland, Sandusky, and Venice, Ohio, she arrived at the mouth of the Detroit River late on August 26 and dropped anchor for the night. The following morning she picked up a welcoming delegation of distinguished Detroiters at Fighting Island, including Judge Woodward, and headed upstream. Lacking a whistle, *Walk-in-the-Water* signaled her approach to Detroit by firing a small signal cannon carried on her forward deck. Everyone in town turned out to greet her, and wild cheering erupted as she headed into her berth with the not-so-dignified Judge Woodward astraddle her bowsprit, waving a bottle.

Walk-in-the-Water continued in operation for three years. She charged a fare between Buffalo and Detroit of $18.00 first class and $7.00 steerage. She was capable of accommodating one hundred passengers and was soon on a biweekly schedule that continued until

Walk-in-the-Water, the first steamboat to operate on the upper Great Lakes, arrived in Detroit from Buffalo on August 27, 1818, ushering in a new era of transportation. From Samuel Ward Stanton, *Great Lakes Steam Vessels*.

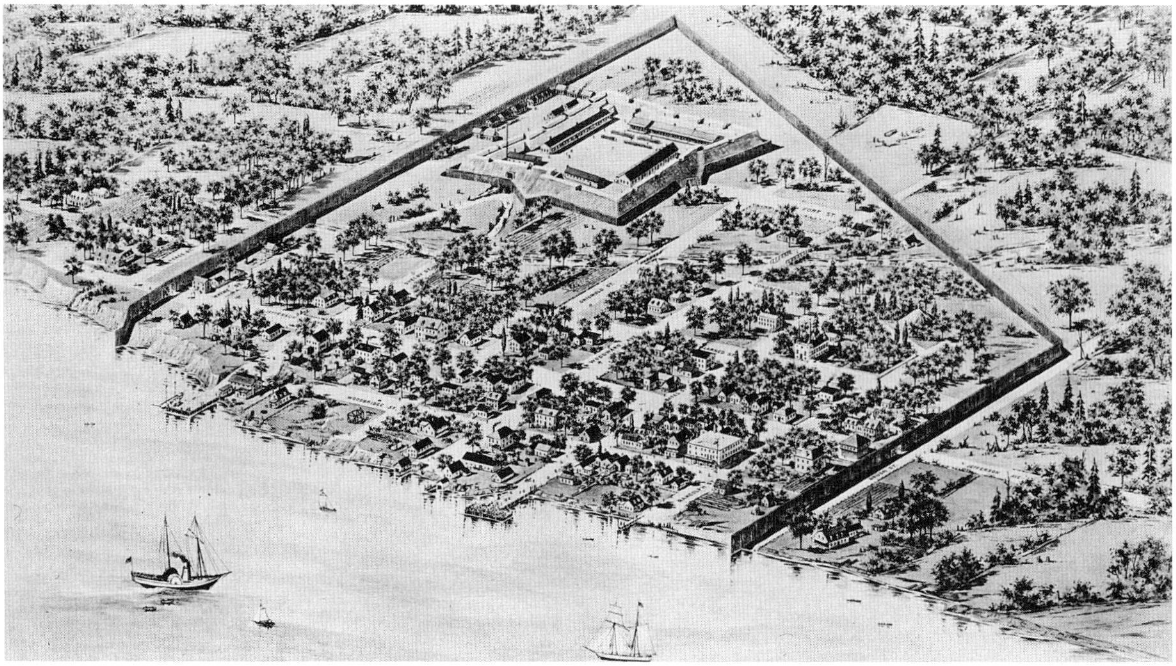

Detroit only had about one thousand inhabitants when the *Walk-in-the-Water* arrived in 1818. At the time this bird's-eye view was painted, it was considered "historically correct in every detail." Courtesy Burton Historical Collection, Detroit Public Library.

1821, when she foundered in a gale near Buffalo. But she set the pattern for what was to come, for before long many more steamships were built. Among the most famous in the 1820s and 1830s were the *Charles Townsend, Superior, Henry Clay, William Penn, Niagara, Peacock,* and *Enterprise.* By 1831 Detroit could expect daily arrivals during the navigation season, and in 1833, Oliver Newberry, an enterprising Detroiter, launched the *Argo,* the first steamboat built in the city.

The second factor affecting Detroit's growth was the sale to settlers of public land in Michigan. Again the important figure was Lewis Cass. As governor, one of the first things Cass did was to negotiate a series of treaties with the Indians, who called him "Big Belly" in friendly tribute to his ample girth. As a result of these negotiations, the Indians ceded most of the land in what is now Michigan to the federal government.

Steam navigation became big business in the 1820s and 1830s. Built in Detroit in 1833 by Oliver Newberry, *Michigan* was at the time the largest steamboat on the Great Lakes. From Samuel Ward Stanton, *Great Lakes Steam Vessels.*

On August 7, 1679, French explorer La Salle set sail across Lake Erie aboard this ship, the *Griffon*. On August 11 he entered the Detroit River, and the *Griffon* became the first sailing ship to traverse these waters. From a painting by James Clary. Courtesy St. Clair Shores Public Library.

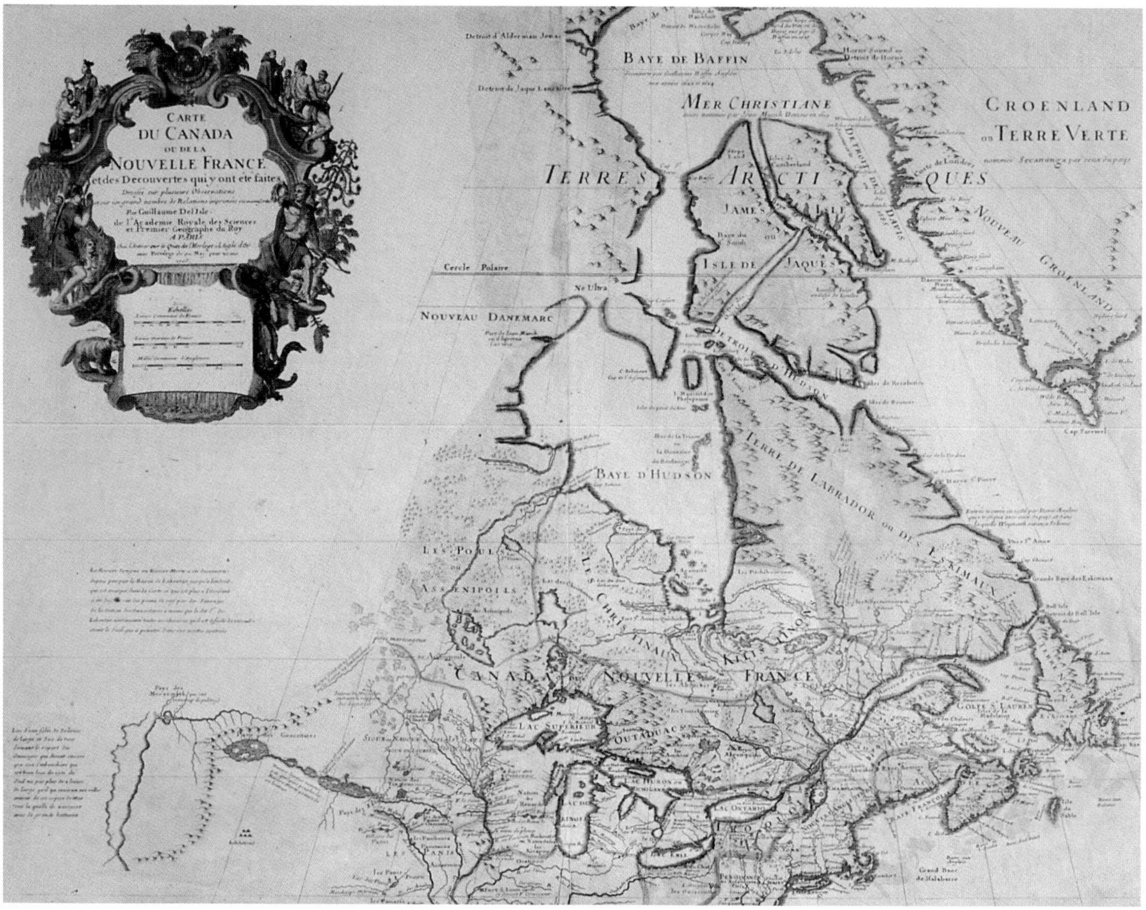

This 1703 map is the earliest known map of the Great Lakes region showing the location of Detroit.
Courtesy Burton Historical Collection, Detroit Public Library.

Sainte Claire of Assisi, for whom Lake St. Clair is named, a voyageur, and a coureur de bois, as depicted in this mural by Gari Melchers. Courtesy Burton Historical Collection, Detroit Public Library.

Madame Cadillac and Madame Tonty, the latter the wife of Cadillac's second in command, arrived at Fort Pontchartrain in September 1701. They were the first women to join the garrison at Detroit. Courtesy Burton Historical Collection, Detroit Public Library.

For years, windmills could be found on both sides of the river up and down from the fort. This mill, as it might have looked in the 1750s, stood on a point that is now the foot of Lakepointe in Grosse Pointe Park. From a painting by Robert Hopkin. Courtesy Prismatic Club of Detroit.

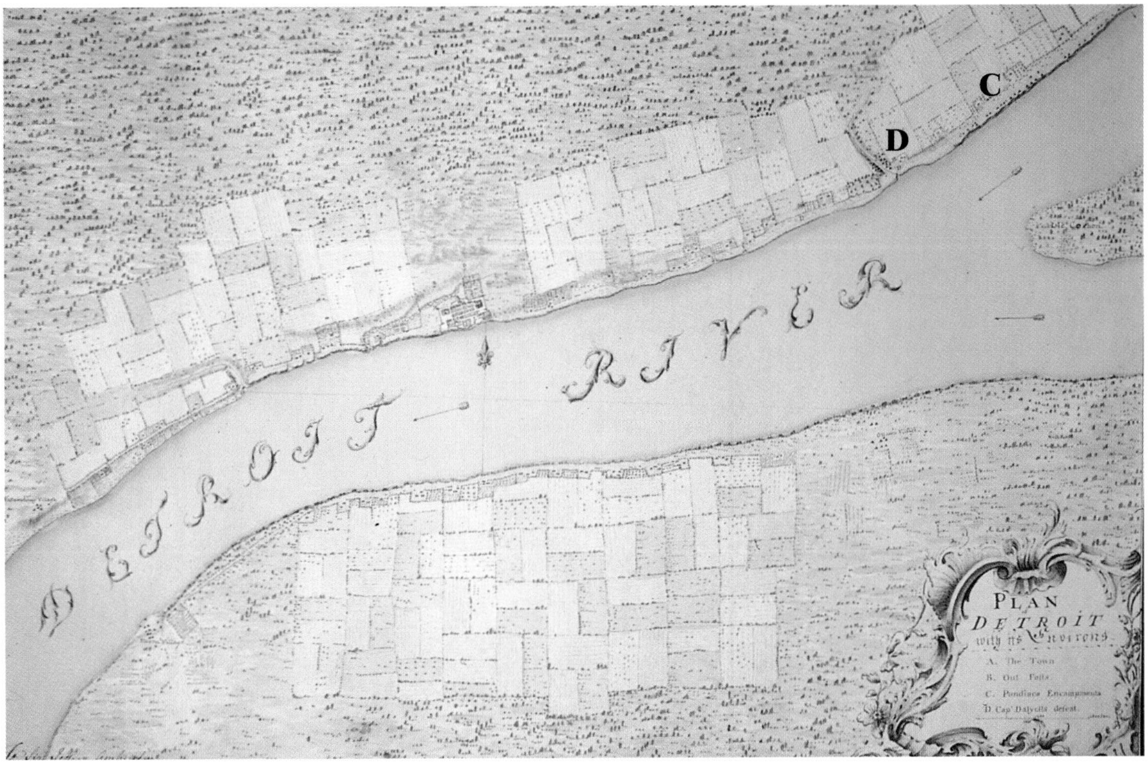

This painting is from a survey taken by Captain John Montresor, a British engineer who arrived in Detroit on October 3, 1765. The letter "C" *(upper right on map)* marks Pontiac's camp. The Battle of Bloody Run began at the bridge over Parent's Creek *(marked with "D" on map)*. Courtesy William L. Clements Library, University of Michigan.

Popular legend has it that Major Gladwin learned of Pontiac's plan from a beautiful Indian woman, but facts indicate that the plan was known by several people some time before its enactment. Courtesy Burton Historical Collection, Detroit Public Library.

Pontiac hands over his belt of wampum to Major Gladwin. Courtesy Burton Historical Collection, Detroit Public Library.

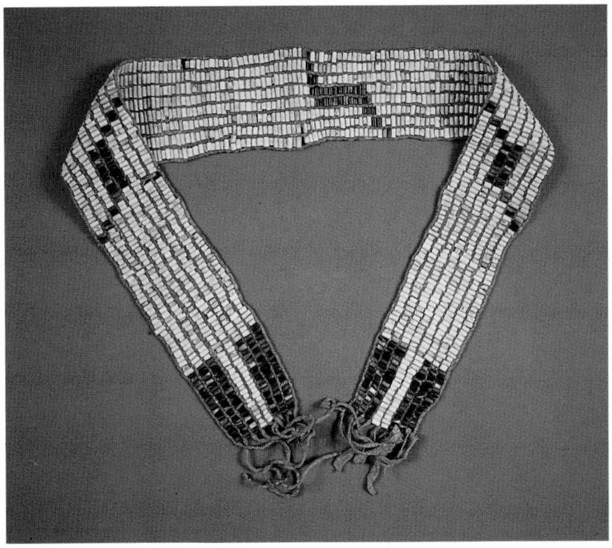

Wampum belts were used by both Indians and Europeans for a variety of purposes. This belt, Pontiac's Hog Island wampum belt, was used as part of the agreement by the British in May 1768 to purchase Hog Island from the Ottawas and the Chippewas. The sale price of the island, in trade goods, was $194.00. Today Hog Island is known by its much more familiar name—Belle Isle. Courtesy Burton Historical Collection, Detroit Public Library.

This view of the Detroit River, Fort Malden, and the town of Amherstburg dates from about 1813. On the left is Bois Blanc Island (Bob-Lo); to the right is Fort Malden and the dockyard. From *View of Amherstberg 1813* by Margaret Reynolds. Courtesy Parks Canada, Fort Malden National Historic Site.

This portrait of Keesheewaa, a noted Fox warrior and medicine man, first appeared in Thomas McKenney's *Sketches of a Tour to the Lakes.* McKenney describes him as a man "of good character" and as a "firm, onward, fearless chief." From James D. Horan, *North American Indian Portraits.*

Territorial governor, secretary of war, ambassador, U.S. senator, secretary of state, and presidential nominee, Lewis Cass had a greater influence on the growth and development of Detroit and Michigan than did any other individual. Author's collection.

This watercolor by British army surgeon Dr. Edward Walsh is dated June 22, 1804. The Huron church in the foreground is the current site of the Canadian approach to the Ambassador Bridge. Courtesy William L. Clements Library, University of Michigan.

This view of Detroit from the Canadian shore shows the busy waterfront town in the spring of 1838. In this scene, the Detroit-to-Cleveland packet *Sheldon Thompson,* is passing downstream from Port Huron en route to Cleveland. From a painting by John Stobart. Courtesy the artist.

This humorous painting shows a Democratic rally on the grounds of the capitol at the first state election in 1837. In the foreground, Governor Mason pays a local citizen a dollar for his vote. From a painting by Thomas Mickell Burnham. Courtesy Burton Historical Collection, Detroit Public Library.

The First Michigan Colored Regiment, raised through the efforts of Detroit's black leaders, was entirely made up of volunteers. A regimental band was formed during training that toured southern Michigan in 1863 to recruit additional enlistments. From a painting by Steward Ashlee. Courtesy Michigan Department of History.

In 1876 the steam tug *Champion* enters the Detroit River from Lake St. Clair with a tow of five sailing vessels. To the left is the Windmill Point Lighthouse; to the right is Belle Isle. From a lithograph by Seth Arca Whipple. Author's collection.

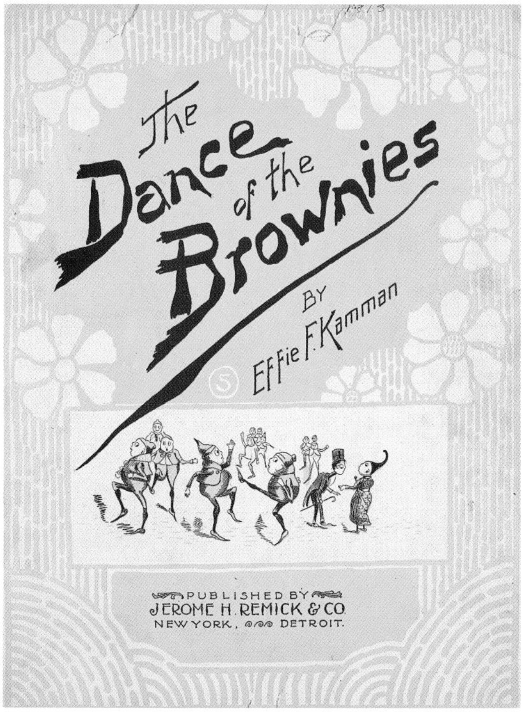

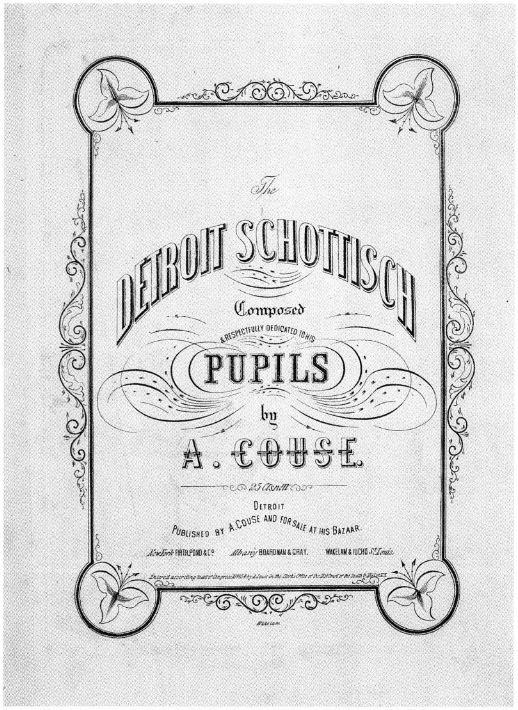

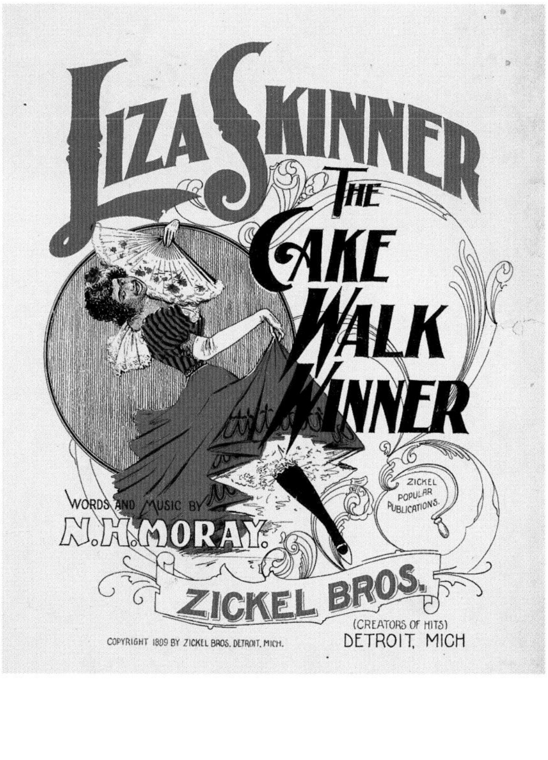

During the last half of the nineteenth century and the early years of the twentieth, Detroit was a leader in the music-publishing business, second only to New York City. Hits included "The Dance of the Brownies," "The Detroit Schottisch," and "The Cake Walk Winner." Courtesy Music and Performing Arts, Detroit Public Library.

The first horseless carriage to appear on the streets of Detroit was built by Charles B. King, shown here at the tiller with his young assistant, Oliver Barthel. Courtesy Burton Historical Collection, Detroit Public Library.

This 1913 postcard shows the waiting room for the Belle Isle ferry and a steamer ready to leave for the island. A ferry ride to Belle Isle was a popular pastime for Detroiters. Ferries served Belle Isle on and off from 1882 until the service was permanently discontinued in 1957. Courtesy Cynthia Bieniek.

1823.

NEW LAKE ERIE STEAM-BOAT

SUPERIOR,

JEDEDIAH ROGERS, Master,

Will sail from Buffalo for Detroit, on or about the twenty-fourth day of April next, if the Lake is then clear of ice; and thereafter will sail from Buffalo and Detroit on the following days.

From Buffalo at 9 o'clock A. M.	*From Detroit at 4 o'clock P. M.*
May 3, 12, 21, 30,	May 7, 16, 24,
June 7, 16, 25,	June 3, 11, 20, 28,
July 5, 14, 23,	July 9, 18, 26,
Aug. 1, 9, 18, 27,	Aug. 5, 13, 22, 30,
Sept. 5, 13, 22,	Sept. 9, 17, 26,
Oct. 1, 10, 18, 27,	Oct. 4, 14, 22, 31,
Nov. 5.	Nov. 8.

The Trips in November to depend on the state of the weather. Passengers will be landed and received at Erie, Grand River, Cleaveland and Sandusky, as usual, unless prevented by stress of weather. If a Trip should be made to the Upper Lakes this season, due notice will be given. Great pains have been taken since the last season to put the Boat and machinery in ample order, and duplicate wheels have been provided, so that it is believed there will be no delay in the regular sailing of the Boat during the season. With respect to accommodations, stores and attendance, it is only necessary to say, they will be as usual.

NOTICE.

Pursuant to a resolution of the Board of Directors of the Lake Erie Steam-Boat Company, notice is hereby given, that all goods, wares and merchandize, furniture, plate, jewels and specie, which may be shipped or transported on board of the Steam-Boat Superior, shall be at the risk of the respective owners or shippers thereof; and the said Company, or the stockholders, will not pay nor hold themselves, either individually or as a Company, liable or responsible for any loss or damage which may happen in the shipment, transportation or delivery of any of the articles aforesaid; and that the Captain of the said Steam-Boat is to receive no freight, excepting on the conditions in this resolution mentioned.

Albany, February 23, 1823. J. I. OSTRANDER, *Sec'ry.*

☞ *Notice by Davis & Center.*—Goods or Packages forwarded by the above Boat, or destined to go by her, directed to the care of Davis & Center, will receive particular attention from them.

Packard & Van Benthuysen, Printers, Sign of Franklin's Head, 435 South Market-st. Albany.

The *Superior* was one of the most popular of the early Great Lakes steamers. Built near Buffalo, she first arrived in Detroit on May 25, 1822. Courtesy Burton Historical Collection, Detroit Public Library.

A federal land office had been opened in Detroit as early as 1804, but at that time there just was not much land to sell. Beginning in 1820, however, when the first treaties were signed, that all changed. In that year, Congress passed a new land act permitting individuals to purchase a minimum of eighty acres for cash at $1.25 an acre; a settler with $100 could purchase a family-size farm. Sales began to increase, and by 1826 the land office was moved into larger quarters in a building at the northwest corner of Jefferson and Randolph. Sales for land soon became so brisk that on some days Jefferson Avenue was thronged with hundreds of men queued up waiting to file their claims. It is from such a situation that the expression "a land office business" evolved.

The third factor to affect Detroit's growth was the Erie Canal. Opened in late 1825, this great inland waterway connected the eastern seaboard with the Great Lakes. The canal stretched 363 miles across New York State. Its eastern outlet was on the Hudson River between Albany and Troy, and its western terminus was at Buffalo. It took eight long years to complete the canal, which had an average width of forty feet and a depth of four feet. It cost the then staggering sum of $20,000 per mile to dig, but it was a financial success almost from the beginning. Huge barges, capable of hauling heavy loads and many passengers, were pulled by horses at a rate of "a cent and a half a mile; a mile and a half an hour." At Buffalo the westward-bound passengers or cargo could be placed aboard one of the new lake steamers and be in Detroit in a matter of hours. Hailing the canal's opening, the *Detroit Gazette* proudly reported: "We can now go from Detroit to New York in five and a half days. Before the war, it took at least two months more."

This combination of improved transportation and cheap land brought thousands of settlers to Michigan from New England and New York. And it was through Detroit that most of these settlers passed on their way to their new Michigan farms. In fact, during the 1820s and 1830s the reception and outfitting of these new settlers was Detroit's most important business. Many stopped in Detroit only long enough to refresh themselves and get a line on some good land before pushing on into the oak clearings of the interior. Some did not go far. They established settlements where the land was fertile and the streams would turn millwheels. Scores of new Michigan towns like Birmingham, Royal Oak,

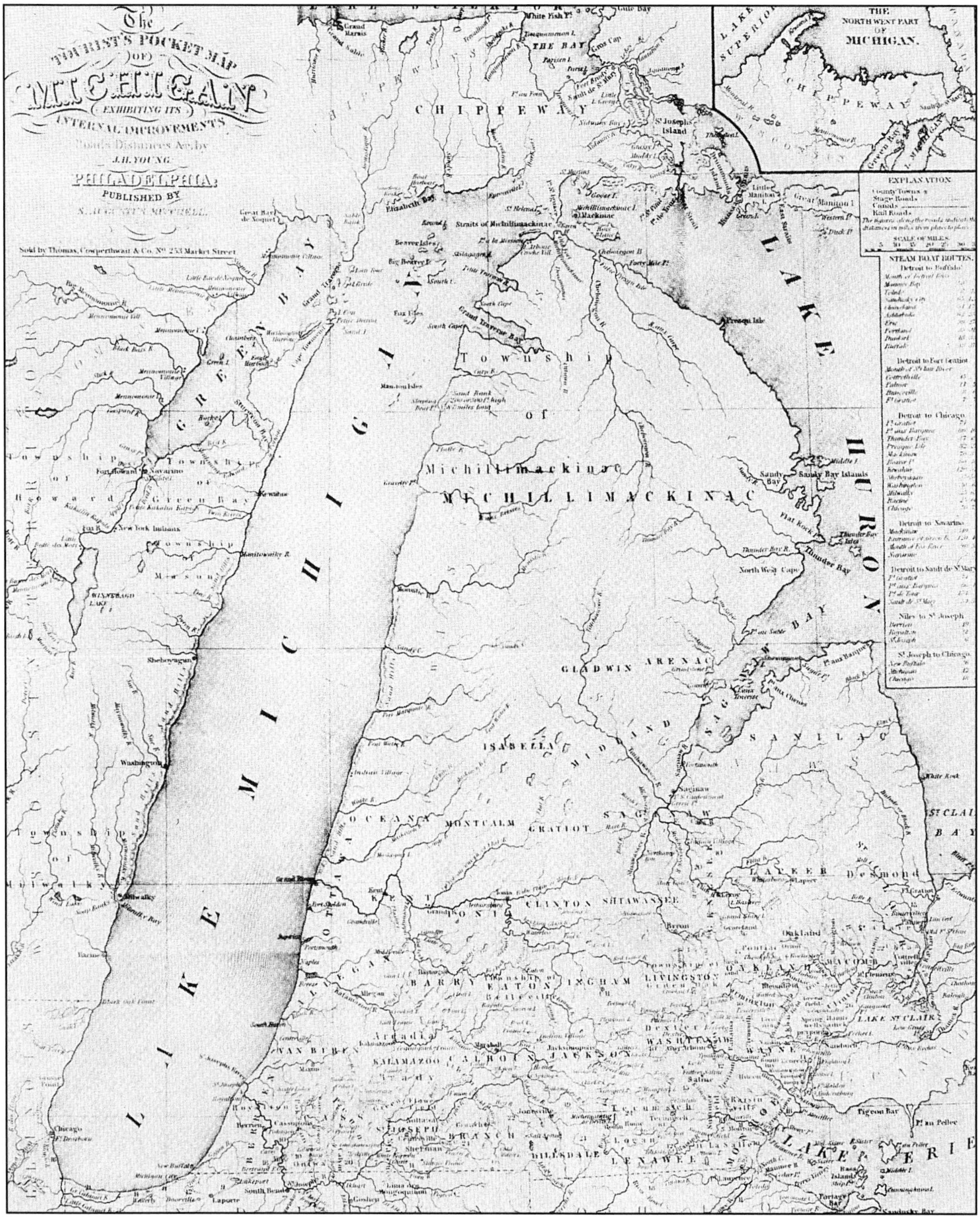

Tourists' pocket maps, such as this one from 1839, helped to promote Michigan by showing improvements and detailing roads. They were circulated throughout the East. Courtesy Burton Historical Collection, Detroit Public Library.

Plymouth, Northville, Troy, Utica, and Romeo bore the names of New England places from which their first settlers came.

On a single day in May 1836, more than twenty-four hundred settlers poured into Detroit, and the daily arrival of seven to ten steamboats was not uncommon. Observing this hustle and bustle, Charles C. Trowbridge, mayor of Detroit in 1834 and a longtime friend of Cass's, wrote to Lewis Cass, who was then in Paris: "The opening of navigation has brought us immense crowds of old fashioned immigrants with their wives and babies and wagons and spinning wheels, and a hundred dollars to buy an eighty acre lot for each of the boys. I have never seen more crowded boats. Yesterday (May 28, 1837) our arrivals were eight steamboats, one ship, three large brigs and nineteen schooners. The day before, seven steamboats arrived."

The new transportation and the Erie Canal affected Detroit and Michigan in another important way. The immigrants—mostly farmers—had produce to sell from their farms, and the canal opened up a market for Michigan crops in the East. Even as the canal was being opened, newspapers reported the "singular first" of the arrival in Detroit of a wagonload of flour from a mill in Pontiac. It was the first ever from the

Commercial fishing became an important business along the Detroit River. By 1830 seven vessels were engaged in shipping salted fish to the East. Here fisherman are seen harvesting whitefish from the shallow waters around Grassy Island. Courtesy St. Clair Shores Public Library.

interior. Two years later, the first bag of flour was loaded onto a boat for export. It was not long before regular shipments of Michigan corn, wheat, and pork were on their way to eastern cities.

The vast fishing grounds of the Great Lakes could now also be commercially exploited. A typical catch might include pike, pickerel, perch, bass, bullheads, and sturgeon, some weighing up to 125 pounds. In a single day in the fall of 1824, roughly thirty thousand whitefish were caught at the fishery on Grosse Ile just south of Detroit. By 1830, seven vessels were engaged in shipping salted fish to the East. Others carried products such as ice and cider, returning with oysters and manufactured goods.

Detroit's growth, while not spectacular at first, was nonetheless steady. In 1819 the population was only 1,110, not much more than at the end of the war. By 1830 it had doubled to 2,222, and by 1840 it reached 9,124. The New England families who settled in Detroit and Michigan brought with them their Yankee characteristics and colloquialisms, as well as their independence of mind. Along with household belongings and farm implements that the new transportation facilities permitted them to carry, they also brought their moral sensibility, thrift, religion, and desire for education. Within a matter of two decades, they transformed Detroit from a French wilderness outpost into a model of a New England town.

Detroit had no schools during the French and British regimes, so it was left to the Yankee settlers to introduce this somewhat revolutionary notion. In 1816, Reverend John Monteith arrived from Princeton and immediately founded a common school. It came to

This view of Detroit from the Canadian shore shows the busy waterfront town in the spring of 1838. In this scene, the Detroit-to-Cleveland packet *Sheldon Thompson,* is passing downstream from Port Huron en route to Cleveland. From a painting by John Stobart. Courtesy the artist.

Reverend John Monteith started a common school in 1816, but it closed when the teacher threw a knife at one of the students and was chased out of town. Courtesy Burton Historical Collection, Detroit Public Library.

an untimely end, however, when the teacher, a Mr. Danforth, hurled a knife at one of his obstreperous scholars and was thereupon chased across the river by the vexed parents. Father Gabriel had even less luck in bringing education to the community. In 1804 he had started a church school, and five years later he had imported the first printing press into the territory. The French citizens of the town showed little interest in either. He also had worked diligently to promote an Indian school to prepare Indian children for life in the rapidly changing culture. But this school also failed when its federal funding was withdrawn.

In 1817, Judge Woodward became seriously engaged in the field of higher learning when he organized the "Catholepistemid, or University of Michigana." Thirteen *didaxiim* (professorships) were established. Reverend Monteith was appointed to seven of these and Father Richard to six, their combined annual salary set at $181.25. In 1837 the school was moved to Ann Arbor, where it became, and prospered as, the world-renowned University of Michigan. Several other attempts were made at establishing public schools in Detroit, but they too met with little success. In 1842, however, a new law was passed that created a city-wide board of education and gave the city the power to levy a school tax. To provide a place of learning for its new students, the board of education purchased its first schoolhouse the following year. Located at Park Place (now Times Square) near Grand River, the building cost the grand sum of $540.

Along with their lack of interest in books, the early French had little interest in newspapers. It was Father Richard who published the town's first newspaper, called the *Michigan Essay or, the Impartial Observer*—a title almost as big as the paper itself. The first issue appeared August 31, 1809, with articles in

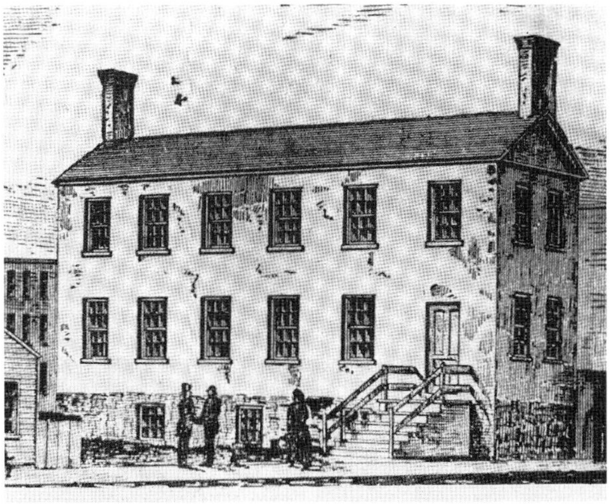

This first University of Michigan building was constructed in 1817–18 on the west side of Bates Street near Congress. In 1837 the university was moved to Ann Arbor. Courtesy Burton Historical Collection, Detroit Public Library.

Detroit's first public school was on Woodbridge Street near Shelby. Occupied from 1838 to 1842, the schoolroom was on the second floor, and the grocery store of N. Prouty was on the ground floor. Courtesy Burton Historical Collection, Detroit Public Library.

both French and English. But this undertaking could hardly be called a success, for as far as is known there was never a second issue. Fortunately, the next newspaper venture was better received. At the urging of Governor Cass, a new weekly called the Detroit *Gazette* began publication on July 25, 1817. Although crude when compared with today's journals, the *Gazette* was a lively and informative paper. As Detroit's first real newspaper, it remained in business until its plant on Atwater near Wayne was destroyed by fire in 1830. During the next several years, a number of other papers began publication. By far the most successful of these published its first issue on May 5, 1831, as the *Democratic Free Press and Michigan Intelligencer,* a name that was soon shortened to the *Detroit Free Press.*

During Michigan's formative years, Detroiters had almost as much trouble going to church as they did going to school. Except for the Catholics, that is, who were well provided for by Ste. Anne's and by new parishes as the city grew. The British garrisons usually had chaplains, but there was no settled Protestant minister in Detroit until Reverend Monteith arrived in 1816. The following year, the Protestants banded together and formed the First Evangelical Society. In 1821 its name was changed to the First Protestant Society. As the society grew, the various Protestant denominations broke away to form their own churches: the Methodists in 1823, and the Episcopalians in 1824. In 1825 the remaining members of the society formed the First Presbyterian Church. During the next decade, other Protestant churches were formed. The First Baptist Church was organized in 1830, and the Second Baptist Church, Detroit's first black church, was established in 1836. The city's first Lutheran church was established in 1833 following the initial wave of German immigrants into Detroit. The

Construction of Ste. Anne's Church was begun in 1818, Seen here, on Larned between Bates and Randolph Streets, Ste. Anne's served parishioners until 1886. Courtesy Burton Historical Collection, Detroit Public Library.

In this view of the east side of Woodward between Congress and Larned in 1849, the Methodist church is to the left, St. Paul's Episcopal Church is in the center, and the First Presbyterian Church is to the right. Courtesy Burton Historical Collection, Detroit Public Library.

Congregationalists moved into their first church in 1844. It was also around this time that Detroit's Jewish community began to grow. Within a few short years, there were enough members to form Congregation Beth El, organized in 1850.

The New England settlers who poured into the Michigan Territory quickly found that they had little liking for the autocratic rule of the Governor and Judges, a form of government in whose affairs they had no voice. Governor Cass, aware of this discontent, made plans to do something about it. The first change came in 1819, when the Michigan Territory was granted the right to elect a delegate to Congress. The first man to represent the territory was William Woodbridge, a close friend of the governor's. In 1825, Father Richard was elected representative and became the first Roman Catholic priest ever to sit in the halls of Congress. In 1824 the rule of the Governor and Judges came to an

Detroit's first mayor was John R. Williams, for whom John R. Street is named. Courtesy Burton Historical Collection, Detroit Public Library.

end, replaced by an elected legislative council. Detroit reorganized its city government that same year, and the people elected a mayor, a clerk, and a board of five aldermen. The first man to be elected mayor was businessman John R. Williams. Several years later, Detroiters honored their first mayor by naming two streets after him. The first, Williams Street, has long since disappeared, but the second, John R. Street, is still one of our region's major thoroughfares.

So that the new legislative council would have a place to meet, a capitol was built. Under the Woodward Plan of 1807, such a

Michigan's territorial capitol was built in Capitol Park in 1828. It served as the seat of government until 1847, when Lansing became the state capital. In later years the building was used as the city's high school. Courtesy Burton Historical Collection, Detroit Public Library.

building was supposed to have been erected in Grand Circus Park, but that was still too far out in the country in 1824. Another site was selected, the small triangular plot of ground fronting on State Street at the head of Griswold, today known as Capitol Park. Finally completed in 1828 at a cost of $21,000, this beautiful building could easily have passed as a New England church. The building served as the capitol until 1847, when Lansing—because of its location near the center of the state—became the capital city. After Detroit ceased to be the center of government, the Old Capitol, as the building eventually came to be known, was used for a variety of purposes. In 1893, while serving as the city's high school, it was destroyed by fire.

When Lewis Cass resigned as governor in 1831 to go to Washington as Secretary of War, he was succeeded by George B. Porter. Not known for his diligence, Porter was frequently absent from Michigan. As a result, Stevens T. Mason, the young territorial secretary, was called upon to serve as acting governor. It was while Mason was serving as acting governor in 1832 that the state militia had to be called out. The troops were sent to Chicago to help quell the Indian uprising in northern Illinois known as the Black Hawk War. The war itself never touched Detroit directly, but one incident connected with the war did, and with disastrous results.

On its way to Chicago from Buffalo with more than three hundred soldiers, the steamer *Henry Clay* stopped off at Detroit on July 4, 1832. After the ship docked, local health officials were called aboard to identify the illness that had struck down several of the soldiers. Their findings could not have been worse: the disease was the dreaded cholera, and the vessel was ordered to cast off at once. The disease spread so quickly among the troops, though, that the *Henry Clay* was forced to stop at Port Huron. There, about 150 of the soldiers deserted the ship and headed back to Detroit on foot. Many were able to reach the city, but many others died along the way. The disease spread rapidly among the townspeople of Detroit, who, living close to the waterfront, drew their water and passed their water indiscriminately along the riverbank. On July 6, Detroit recorded its first death. Cows, pigs, goats, and other domestic animals spread the epidemic. Many citizens fled the city in fear for their lives, but when they tried to enter nearby towns they found the roads barricaded and were turned back by armed guards. Those who were able did what they could for those who contracted the disease, but in truth, there was little that could be done. Father Richard made a daily circuit of the town in a cart to collect the

One of early Detroit's most important citizens, Father Gabriel Richard, beloved priest of Ste. Anne's Church, was also an educator, publisher, and politician. He died nursing the sick during the cholera epidemic of 1832. Courtesy Burton Historical Collection, Detroit Public Library.

dead for burial. He also nursed the sick until, with the epidemic already on the wane, he contracted cholera himself and died on September 13, 1832. He was one of ninety-six to die of the disease that summer.

Cholera struck again in 1834, but this time with added horrors. During a three-week period in August, 122 people—7 percent of the city's population—died of the disease. The custom of ringing the church bells to announce a death was abandoned, for the ceaseless tolling only added to the panic of the residents. With bells, horses' hooves, and hawkers' cries stilled, the town was eerily peaceful. The streets were choked from the smoke of pitch, which people burned in the belief that it warded off the disease. The capitol and Most Holy Trinity Church were turned into hospitals. Father Martin Kundig tore out the pews and set up litters, and the men and women of the parish served as nurses. Altogether, Detroit suffered four cholera outbreaks. The third was in 1849, and the fourth and last epidemic occurred in 1854.

It was during the city's second outbreak of cholera, in July 1834, that Governor Porter died. As a result, Stevens T. Mason became acting governor on a full-time basis. He did such a creditable job that in 1835, when Michigan declared itself a state, he was

Father Martin Kundig turned the Most Holy Trinity Roman Catholic Church into a hospital during the cholera epidemic of 1834 and used parishioners as nurses. The church was located at the northwest corner of Bates Street and Cadillac Square. Courtesy Burton Historical Collection, Detroit Public Library.

This humorous painting shows a Democratic rally on the grounds of the capitol at the first state election in 1837. In the foreground, Governor Mason pays a local citizen a dollar for his vote. From a painting by Thomas Mickell Burnham. Courtesy Burton Historical Collection, Detroit Public Library.

elected the first governor, though he was only twenty-four years old. The citizens of the territory also adopted a constitution, although because of a boundary dispute with Ohio, it was not until January 26, 1837, that Michigan was officially admitted to the Union as the twenty-sixth state.

The two decades following statehood were a time of continued growth for Detroit and Michigan. After 1830, fur was no longer a major factor in Detroit's economic life. The commercial center of the city remained concentrated near the riverfront, the principal streets being Atwater, Woodbridge, and Jefferson. Above Jefferson was the residential district extending north to about Adams, with Third the western boundary and St. Antoine the eastern. Gradually, some of the more prosperous citizens moved out East Jefferson, and a few of the old houses dating from the 1830s and 1840s may still be seen there. Others moved up Woodward, and as business encroached north of Jefferson, the residential area pushed north of Grand Circus Park. In 1836, Detroit's population was 6,927. By 1840 it had reached 9,124, and by 1850 it had taken a significant jump to 21,019. By the mid-1840s Detroit had lost most of its characteristics of a riverfront trading post. It had become a town of businessmen and shopkeepers, of busy commercial houses and of quiet, tree-lined residential avenues.

The first Michigan state fair was held in 1849 on a site west of Woodward between Columbia and Vernor. Here, at that first state fair, Secretary Holmes announces the premium awards to the Board of Managers. The open window allows a glimpse of the fairgrounds. From a painting by Frederick E. Cohen. Courtesy Burton Historical Collection, Detroit Public Library.

SEVEN

The Civil War

DURING THE 1840s AND 1850s, a zealous wave for reformation swept across the United States. It began in western New York State in the 1820s, and one of its most important goals was the abolition of slavery. Because many Detroit settlers in the 1820s and 1830s were from western New York, it is understandable that a strong anti-slavery and pro-abolition sentiment developed in the city.

Slavery had existed in Detroit since the city's earliest days and had persisted well into the nineteenth century. The first mention of black slaves in Detroit dates back to 1736. As late as 1830, slaves were still owned by those who had lived in the city during the British period. A provision in the Jay Treaty of 1794 allowed settlers to keep "all their property of every kind," and since slaves were considered property, those residents who owned slaves were allowed to keep them. Records show that 175 slaves were in Detroit when the Americans arrived in 1796. There were also a number of free blacks living in the town at this time. One William Lee worked on the Macomb farm, and a free woman known as Black Betty worked as a cook for several of the town's well-to-do families. After 1796, no new slaves were brought to Detroit and the anti-slavery movement took hold. Finally, in 1835, when the new state constitution was signed, the institution of slavery was at last abolished in Michigan. Just prior to this, however, Detroit was jolted by a serious racial incident.

In 1831 a slave named Thornton Blackburn and his wife, Ruth, escaped from Kentucky and made their way to Detroit. In the summer of 1833 they were traced by slave hunters and claimed by their owner. The Blackburns were arrested and held in the city jail pending their return to the South. A large crowd, made up mostly of blacks, stormed the jail on Gratiot between Farmer and Library Streets and demanded the Blackburns' release. A woman obtained permission to visit Mrs. Blackburn, and once inside she changed clothes with her, thus enabling Mrs. Blackburn to escape to Canada. A couple of days later, while her

In 1833, from the city jail (*left*) on Gratiot between Farmer and Library Streets ("A" on map above) ex-slaves Thornton and Ruth Blackburn were to be transported to the boat dock at the foot of Randolph Street and returned to their former owners in the South. Fortunately, with the help of friends, the Blackburns were able to escape and make their way to Canada. Courtesy Burton Historical Collection, Detroit Public Library.

husband was being escorted to a boat to start his journey back south, the crowd rushed the sheriff, John M. Wilson, and severely beat him; in the melee that followed, Blackburn was spirited away. It appeared that Blackburn and his rescuers had made good their escape in a cart by way of the post road, but when a posse overtook them some miles from town they found the cart empty. Blackburn had joined his wife in Canada.

During the year following the Blackburn riot, Erotius Parmalee Hastings organized the first anti-slavery society in Detroit. Two years later, in 1836, a group of Quakers, Methodists, Congregationalists, and Presbyterians met in a Presbyterian church in Ann Arbor and established the Michigan Anti-Slavery Society. This was all at a time when the local Detroit newspapers were still publishing advertisements for the recapture of fugitive slaves.

Because of its location across the river from Canada and its accessibility from the border states, Detroit became an important last station on the Underground Railroad. Thousands of slaves escaping from the South were passed along the "Railroad" through Ohio, Indiana, and Illinois into Michigan and on to Detroit. The slaves were hidden during the day by sympathetic townspeople and farmers in barns, attics, haystacks, cellars, and church steeples and transported at night from one station to the next. In Michigan these stations were located about every fifteen miles. Seven main routes were in operation by 1840, with the Detroit River as route No. 1.

Once in Detroit, many fugitives were hidden in the livery barn of Seymour Finney's Temperance House. The hotel was at the corner of Woodward and Gratiot, which today is the site of the park area known as the Kern Block. The stable was a block away at the northeast corner of State and Griswold, across the street from the Old Capitol. A

The livery barn of Seymour Finney's Temperance House at the northeast corner of Griswold and State Streets was one of the important stations on the Underground Railroad. Courtesy Burton Historical Collection, Detroit Public Library.

Michigan state historical marker on the wall of the Comerica Bank branch office now marks the location. Legend has it that many fugitives lay hidden in Finney's stable while the men who owned and pursued them dined in Finney's hotel.

Another important station was the Second Baptist Church, located at the corner of Monroe and Beaubien. On any night of the week, the church could expect the arrival of passengers on the "Railroad." The pastor, Reverend William C. Munroe, would receive a note from one of his members which might read: "Pastor, tomorrow night at our 8:00 meeting, let's read Exodus 10:8." In Underground language, that meant "Conductor No. 2 will be arriving at 8:00 P.M. with ten slaves, eight men and two women."

At each of these stations, the stationmaster would hide, feed, and instruct the passengers during the day, then take them to waiting boats during the night and send them across the river to Canadian sanctuary. As a result, a sizable and energetic black community developed in Windsor, and from there Henry

Located at the corner of Monroe and Beaubien Streets, the Second Baptist Church was founded in 1836 by thirteen ex-slaves. Reverend William C. Monroe, who taught the first classes for black children in Detroit in the church's basement, was also the first pastor. The city's first celebration of the Emancipation Proclamation was held here on January 6, 1863. Courtesy Burton Historical Collection, Detroit Public Library.

Bibb's *Voice of the Fugitive* eloquently advanced the anti-slavery cause. Passengers also traveled through Detroit to Amherstburg, Colchester, New Canaan, Gosfield, Chatham, Shewsburg, Dresden, and London. Today, large numbers of blacks in southwestern Ontario trace their ancestry to passengers on the Underground Railroad.

The Civil War was to bring to an end a need for the Underground Railroad, although the movement remained active by helping freed slaves relocate in the North. On April 7, 1870, Detroiters celebrated the ratification of the Fifteenth Amendment to the U.S. Constitution, which guaranteed all citizens the right to vote regardless "of race, color, or previous condition of servitude." George DeBaptiste, a local leader in the railway movement, displayed a sign on his store that read: "Notice to Stockholders of the Underground Railroad: This office is closed. Hereafter all stockholders will receive dividends according to their merits."

In 1854, a group of prominent Detroiters including Zachariah Chandler, a wealthy dry goods merchant, decided that some political action was needed to offset the obnoxious Fugitive Slave Law of 1850 and other governmental measures "truckling to the southern slavocracy." Chandler and his supporters held an informal conference in the newspaper office of the *Tribune* and then called a mass meeting at City Hall. The latter meeting issued a call for all interested parties to attend a rally of similar committees from around the state at Jackson on July 6, 1854. The result was the organization "under the oaks" of the Republican Party.

On March 12, 1859, Detroit was to experience a meeting of quite a different sort. On that date the noted black orator and abolition-

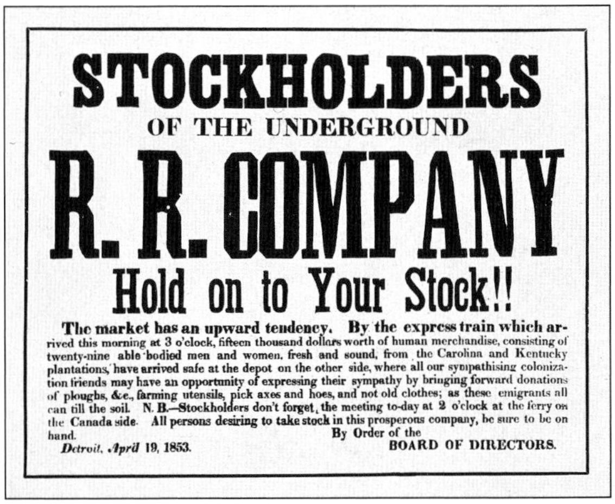

STOCKHOLDERS
OF THE UNDERGROUND
R. R. COMPANY
Hold on to Your Stock!!

The market has an upward tendency. By the express train which arrived this morning at 3 o'clock, fifteen thousand dollars worth of human merchandise, consisting of twenty-nine able bodied men and women, fresh and sound, from the Carolina and Kentucky plantations, have arrived safe at the depot on the other side, where all our sympathising colonization friends may have an opportunity of expressing their sympathy by bringing forward donations of ploughs, &c., farming utensils, pick axes and hoes, and not old clothes; as these emigrants all can till the soil. N. B.—Stockholders don't forget, the meeting to-day at 2 o'clock at the ferry on the Canada side. All persons desiring to take stock in this prosperous company, be sure to be on hand.

By Order of the BOARD OF DIRECTORS.

Detroit, April 19, 1853.

This handbill from April 19, 1853, reports on the successful arrival in Canada of twenty-nine escaping slaves and of the next meeting of the Detroit "stockholders" of the local Underground Railroad. Courtesy Burton Historical Collection, Detroit Public Library.

ist Frederick Douglass was in Detroit to give a lecture at City Hall. That evening he talked about the moral dilemma of slavery and its negative effect upon master and slave. That same day, the fiery, fanatical abolitionist John Brown arrived in town with fourteen escaping slaves from Missouri. After the passengers had been safely delivered to conductors for transfer to Windsor, Brown went to the home of William Webb, a local black leader with whom Douglass was staying. There, by candlelight, in the quiet, two-story frame house on East Congress Street, Brown outlined his plan for the organization of simultaneous armed slave uprisings all across the South. George DeBaptiste, one of the men attending the meeting, suggested that the rebellion include the wholesale elimination of planters. Douglass, however, was far too discerning to commit himself to such a course. Brown did receive promises of help, though, from some of the others present; he then moved on to Chatham, Ontario, to recruit a band of followers. His next and most historic stop was at Harpers Ferry in 1859. The Webb house, where the Detroit meeting took place, was on the north side of Congress near St. Antoine, and today the site is indicated by a nearby state historical marker.

On April 12, 1861, a Detroit telegraph operator received the news that Fort Sumter had been fired upon. Five days later, President Lincoln announced a state of war. The next day, a citizens' mass meeting was held in front of the newly built post office and customs house at the northwest corner of Griswold and Larned Streets, and a wave of patriotic fervor swept the city. The first to answer Lincoln's call for volunteers was the First Michigan Infantry, composed of militia companies drawn from Detroit and several other Michigan towns. Orders for the formation of the First Michigan were issued April 24, and on May 2 the regiment was mustered into service. The

On March 12, 1859, during a lecture visit to Detroit, abolitionist Frederick Douglass (*left*) met the fiery John Brown (*second from left*) at the home of William Webb on East Congress Street (*third from left*). William Lambert (*right*), owner of a clothes cleaning shop at Bates and Larned, and one of Detroit's leading abolitionists, listened with others as Brown outlined his plan of armed uprising throughout the South. Others there that night were Reverend William C. Monroe, George De Baptiste, and Henry Bibb. America would later hear of John Brown at Harper's Ferry. Courtesy Burton Historical Collection, Detroit Public Library.

troops were trained at Fort Wayne, located south of Detroit on the riverfront in Springwells Township. Construction of the fort, which covered sixty-six acres, had been begun in 1841 because of the fear of invasion during Canada's Patriot's Rebellion. Completed in 1851, Fort Wayne never fired a shot in anger, though it was garrisoned almost continuously until World War II. On May 11 an impressive ceremony was held in Campus Martius in which the ladies of the city presented the First Michigan with its colors. Two days later, the regiment left for Washington to become the first troops from west of the Alleghenies to reach the nation's capital. Their arrival reassured President Lincoln that the western states would remain loyal. He is said to have exclaimed, "Thank God for Michigan." In all, Detroit would send about six thousand soldiers to the battlefields during the four

On April 12, 1861, a Detroit telegraph operator received news that Fort Sumter had been fired upon. Six days later, a citizens' mass meeting was held in front of the newly built post office and customs house on the northwest corner of Griswold and Larned Streets. The old state capitol can be seen in the distance, at the head of Griswold. Courtesy Burton Historical Collection, Detroit Public Library.

On May 11, 1861, the First Michigan Infantry, in an impressive ceremony, received its colors in Campus Martius. The First Michigan departed for Washington on May 13 and was the first western regiment to arrive in the nation's capital. Courtesy Burton Historical Collection, Detroit Public Library.

years of the Civil War. Michigan would send over ninety thousand. Of this number, nearly fifteen thousand never came home.

Another distinguished Michigan regiment was the Twenty-fourth Infantry, composed almost entirely of Detroit and Wayne County volunteers. It trained at the old fairgrounds, then at Woodward and Canfield Avenues, and arrived at the front in time to take part in the Battle of Antietam. Later it was incorporated into the famous Iron Brigade. It opened the Battle of Gettysburg on July 1, 1863, and was almost completely destroyed while holding up the Confederate advance until the mass of the Army of the Potomac could get into position. Its casualty rate was the highest of any Union regiment in the battle.

As it became obvious that the war was going to be a long and painful struggle, the call went out for more volunteers. To encourage local enlistments, Detroit officials decided in July 1862 to pay a bounty of $50 for each single man and $100 for each married man who volunteered. In all more than $200,000 was paid by the city during the war. In addition to these funds, a number of organizations also made contributions of money and materials to the various societies that provided special services to the city's soldiers and sailors. These included the Michigan Soldiers' Relief Organization, which gave aid to the sick and wounded, the Ladies Aid Society, which packed and shipped supplies for the men at the front, and the Michigan Christian Commission, which ministered to the soldiers' spiritual needs.

In addition to its young men, Detroit supplied munitions and food for the Union army throughout the war. The city, in fact, was a principal distribution point for supplies from Michigan towns and farms. In 1862 a new cantonment was built on Clinton between Joseph Campau and Elmwood Avenues just opposite the present entrance to Elmwood Cemetery. Barracks for ten thousand men were erected. The cantonment was used as a recruiting and replacement depot, and later for the discharge of returning soldiers. Toward the end of the war it was used for the care of slightly wounded convalescents. The post was

Troops of the Second Michigan Infantry muster at Fort Wayne in 1861. To encourage local enlistments, in 1862 Detroit officials decided to pay a bounty of $50 for each single man and $100 for each married man who volunteered. Courtesy Burton Historical Collection, Detroit Public Library.

The Twenty-fourth Michigan Infantry, recruited in Detroit and Wayne County, belonged to the famous Iron Brigade. It was one of the first Union regiments in action at the Battle of Gettysburg, July 1, 1863. The Twenty-fourth Michigan suffered the highest casualty rate of any Union regiment in the battle. Courtesy Dearborn Historical Society.

known as Camp Backus and was dismantled soon after the war ended.

Unfortunately, Detroit's Civil War record was tarnished in March 1863 by a deplorable race riot. The city's unskilled Irish and German immigrants were incensed over the newly passed national conscription law because the affluent could escape the draft by paying a $300 fee. The white immigrants associated this with the kind of discrimination that had caused them to leave their homelands. Most of these immigrants had relatively little interest in the war to preserve the Union. They were more concerned about the competition of black laborers for unskilled and service jobs. As a result, race relations in the city were severely strained. The incident that touched off the riot occurred when William Faulkner, a black man, was arrested, tried, and convicted of raping two nine-year-old girls, one black, the other white. An angry mob attempted to lynch Faulkner as he was being taken to jail from the courthouse on the morning of Friday, March 6. Held back by Federal troops, the crowd turned and started down to Beaubien Street, where most of the city's blacks lived. Armed with guns, clubs, axes, and a rope, the mob swept through the area. A large part of the district was damaged, and some thirty dwellings occupied by blacks were burned. Looting and vandalism were extensive. Scores of blacks were beaten, and two men were killed. Others were forced to flee their homes, and some escaped across the river to Canada. Among the blacks who sought ought temporary refuge in Canada were Robert and James Pelham. Robert Pelham, a mathematician, bricklayer, mason, and contractor, had left the South during the hysteria that followed John Brown's raid on Harpers Ferry. In 1862 the family arrived in Detroit and rented a house on Congress Street. During the next hundred years, the Pelhams were to become one of Detroit's leading families. The riots continued throughout the day on Friday. Order was not restored until nightfall, when additional troops from Fort Wayne and Ypsilanti arrived. Ironically, William Faulkner was later proven innocent when the two girls confessed that they had perjured themselves.

It is also important to note that the First Michigan Colored Infantry was mustered into service and left Detroit just a few months after the riots. The regiment, which had been raised through the efforts of Detroit's black leaders, was made up entirely of volunteers from Canada and Detroit. The regiment was organized at Camp Ward, which was located on Macomb Street east of Chene. A regimental band was formed during training, and it toured southern Michigan to recruit additional volun-

The First Michigan Colored Regiment, raised through the efforts of Detroit's black leaders, was entirely made up of volunteers. A regimental band was formed during training that toured southern Michigan in 1863 to recruit additional enlistments. From a painting by Steward Ashlee. Courtesy Michigan Department of History.

This view is a staged photograph of Fourth Michigan soldiers with a young black contraband—a slave who escaped to the Union lines. Courtesy Jackie Napoleon Wilson.

teers. In all about fourteen hundred blacks enlisted, and of these some one thousand had been born in slave states. In the spring of 1864 the regiment became the 102nd United States Colored Infantry. This unit saw service in South Carolina, Georgia, and Florida and took part in several engagements. Mustered out in Charleston on September 30, 1865, the soldiers returned to Detroit shortly thereafter.

As the Civil War continued for four long years, Detroiters took pride in the fact that the Union's most famous general had once lived in the city. From 1848 to 1851, Lieutenant and Mrs. Ulysses S. Grant made their home in Detroit while Grant was commanding officer of the Detroit Barracks, which were built in 1838 at Gratiot and Mt. Elliott and remained in use until about 1855. The Grants lived in a small frame house typical of the workingman's house of the day. It was on the north side of Fort between Russell and Rivard Streets. During the 1930s the house was donated to the state of Michigan by the Michigan Mutual Liability Company and moved to the Michigan State Fair Grounds. While living in Detroit, Lieutenant Grant was twice in the public notice. He once slipped and fell on the icy sidewalk in front of Zachariah Chandler's dry goods store. He unsuccessfully sued the merchant, who later became a leader in the Republican Party and his Secretary of the Interior when Grant was elected president. On the other occasion, Grant was fined for riding his horse too fast through the city's streets.

The Civil War ended on Palm Sunday, April 9, 1865, when Lee's armies surrendered at Appomattox Courthouse. The Union was preserved. The wreckage was surveyed, and the task of rebuilding began. The United States faced the future uncertainly, little knowing that it stood on the threshold of an industrial expansion which, in little more than half a century, would make it the richest and strongest nation in the world. Detroit was to play a vital role in this industrial growth.

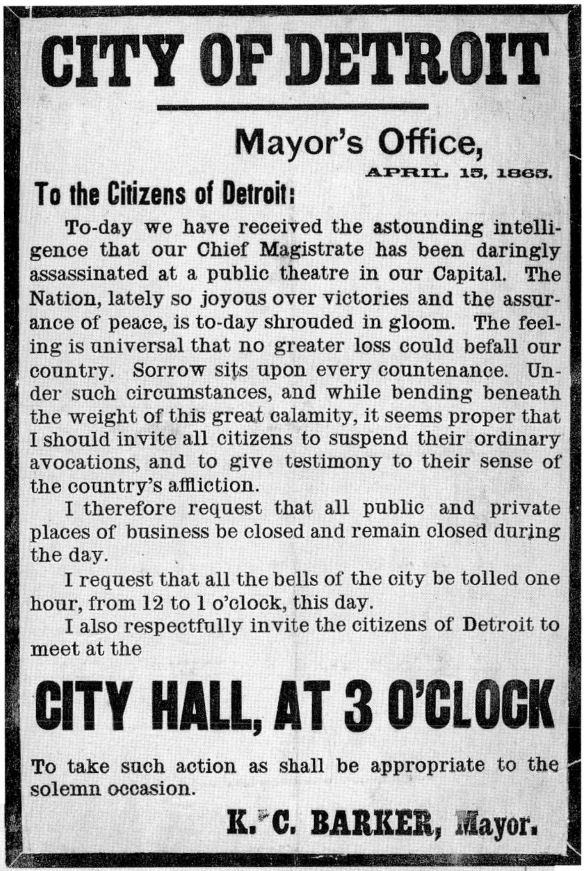

CITY OF DETROIT

Mayor's Office,

APRIL 15, 1865.

To the Citizens of Detroit:

To-day we have received the astounding intelligence that our Chief Magistrate has been daringly assassinated at a public theatre in our Capital. The Nation, lately so joyous over victories and the assurance of peace, is to-day shrouded in gloom. The feeling is universal that no greater loss could befall our country. Sorrow sits upon every countenance. Under such circumstances, and while bending beneath the weight of this great calamity, it seems proper that I should invite all citizens to suspend their ordinary avocations, and to give testimony to their sense of the country's affliction.

I therefore request that all public and private places of business be closed and remain closed during the day.

I request that all the bells of the city be tolled one hour, from 12 to 1 o'clock, this day.

I also respectfully invite the citizens of Detroit to meet at the

CITY HALL, AT 3 O'CLOCK

To take such action as shall be appropriate to the solemn occasion.

K. C. BARKER, Mayor.

This announcement *(top)* of President Lincoln's assassination was issued by Mayor K. C. Barber on April 15, 1865. Ten days later, a memorial service *(above)* was held in Cadillac Square at Campus Martius on Woodward Avenue. Courtesy Burton Historical Collection, Detroit Public Library.

On April 9, 1872, the residents of Detroit dedicated this grand Soldiers' and Sailors' Monument to honor those who had served their country in the Civil War. To this day it stands in Cadillac Square at Campus Martius on Woodward Avenue. Courtesy Burton Historical Collection, Detroit Public Library.

In 1866, Civil War veterans formed the Grand Army of the Republic. The G.A.R. quickly attained a preeminent place among veterans organizations that formed at the end of the war. By 1890 its membership had reached more than four hundred thousand. Here, stalwart veterans from Detroit march down Woodward past Grand Circus Park in the city's Memorial Day parade, May 30, 1909. Courtesy Burton Historical Collection, Detroit Public Library.

Eight

An Industrial Center

THE GROWTH THAT DETROIT was to experience following the Civil War had its beginnings in the 1840s. The source of this expansion was the natural resources of Michigan—specifically from copper, iron, and lumber. Copper had been known to exist in Michigan's Upper Peninsula from the earliest days. The French had learned of it from the Indians, and the exploration of the upper Great Lakes was due in part to the desire to locate these deposits. It was not, however, until after the discovery of rich copper deposits in Michigan's Upper Peninsula by young Douglass Houghton that the extraction and refining of copper ore began on a commercial basis. A need for metals used in the manufacture of steamship and logging engines caused copper and brass to become important factors in Detroit's economy in the 1850s.

In 1844, about the time the copper industry was beginning to grow, substantial deposits of iron ore were also discovered in the Upper Peninsula. Then, in 1855, the new canal at Sault Ste. Marie was completed, and soon thereafter great shipments of iron ore were on their way down the lakes. With iron ore and limestone—the necessary materials for the production of pig iron and steel—now readily available, Detroit was gradually becoming a center for heavy industry. A number of foundries and machine and boiler works were built in which boilers and engines for the new mining industries, ships, and sawmills were produced.

There were always a number of sawmills in Detroit, but the city never became a major lumbering center as did Bay City, Saginaw, Muskegon, and a number of other Michigan towns. Nevertheless, large amounts of Detroit capital went into lumbering, and several Detroiters amassed great fortunes from the industry in the latter part of the nineteenth century. Included were such men as Russell A. Alger, John S. Newberry, William H. Murphy, Eber B. Ward, and David Whitney, Jr.

In addition to these natural resources, the railroad and railroad equipment were also to play an important part in Detroit's growth at this time. The first railroad out of the city was the Detroit and Pontiac Railway, which began

Woodward Avenue looking north from Jefferson in 1869. To the right is the Russell House (with the cupola) at Cadillac Square. The spire of the Central Methodist Church at Grand Circus Park is in the distance. Courtesy Detroit Historical Museum.

This engraving of the Michigan Central Railroad roundhouse and freight yard shows the city shortly after the Civil War. The railroad, and the railroad equipment industries, were to play a major part in Detroit's growth as an industrial center. Courtesy Dossin Great Lakes Museum, Detroit.

operations on May 19, 1838, with twelve miles of track completed to the vicinity of Royal Oak. The cars were drawn by horses for the first year, but in 1839 a steam locomotive was obtained. The line ran out Dequindre on the same right-of-way the Grand Trunk uses today. The original depot was at Dequindre and Jefferson, but it was soon moved to Gratiot and Farmer, the line being extended from Dequindre to Gratiot. Behind the depot facing Campus Martius was Andrews' Railroad Hotel, which was connected with the station.

Residents of the east side opposed having the rails on Gratiot with trains running past their homes, so in 1852 the route was changed. The trains ran from Dequindre to Atwater and then west to Brush Street, where a new depot was built. The Detroit and Pontiac gradually reached out to Pontiac and eventually to Grand Haven, where it had car ferry connections with Milwaukee. Ultimately it became part of the Grand Trunk system.

The Michigan Central was the second railroad. Organized in 1837 as the Detroit and St. Joseph, it began operations in 1838 when the line was completed to Dearborn and then to Ypsilanti. Kalamazoo was not reached until 1846. That same year, track was laid through to New Buffalo on Lake Michigan and ferry service was available from there to Chicago. The Michigan Central finally entered Chicago in 1852.

The Michigan Central line ran down Michigan Avenue to Griswold Street. Its first depot was on the site later occupied by the City Hall (now Kennedy Square). A spur track was extended down Woodward to Atwater to serve the businesses in that area. However, the citizens objected to the nuisance, just as they did to the Detroit and Pontiac on Gratiot, and in 1848 a new depot was built near the foot of Third Street.

The great desire of the people of Detroit during the 1840s and 1850s, and particularly of the business community, was for closer connections with the East. The Michigan Central built and operated a fleet of luxurious lake steamers that carried passengers and freight between Detroit, Cleveland, and Buffalo, but the fleet was useless during the winter shutdown of lake navigation. So in 1854, partly with the help of Detroit capital, the Great Western Railroad was built across the lower Ontario peninsula with its western terminus at Windsor. That opened the East, and a traveler from Chicago using the Michigan Central could make connections on the Great Western to the Niagara River, where he or she could board the New York Central for Albany and New York. Other lines were built into Detroit later. Among the more important were the Wabash, Pere Marquette, and Pennsylvania. They used the Fort Street or Union Depot at Fort and Third, which was built in 1893.

During the early years of the railroad, when there were no rail connections beyond Michigan's borders, most of what was needed in the way of rolling stock and equipment had to be produced locally. Thus it was that Detroit's first heavy industry was the manufacture of railroad cars, wheels, and other railway equipment.

The first major production of rail equipment began here in 1853 when a physician, Dr. George B. Russel, organized a firm that became the Detroit Car and Manufacturing Company. Starting with a small plant on Gratiot, operations soon expanded to larger shops at the foot of Beaubien and then on Monroe Street. Competitors entered the field, such as the Michigan Car Company, founded in 1865 by James McMillan and John S. Newberry. In 1872 their plant was located at the Grand Trunk Railway Junction in Springwells. Then there was the Peninsular Car Works, founded in 1879 by Frank J. Hecker and Charles L. Freer.

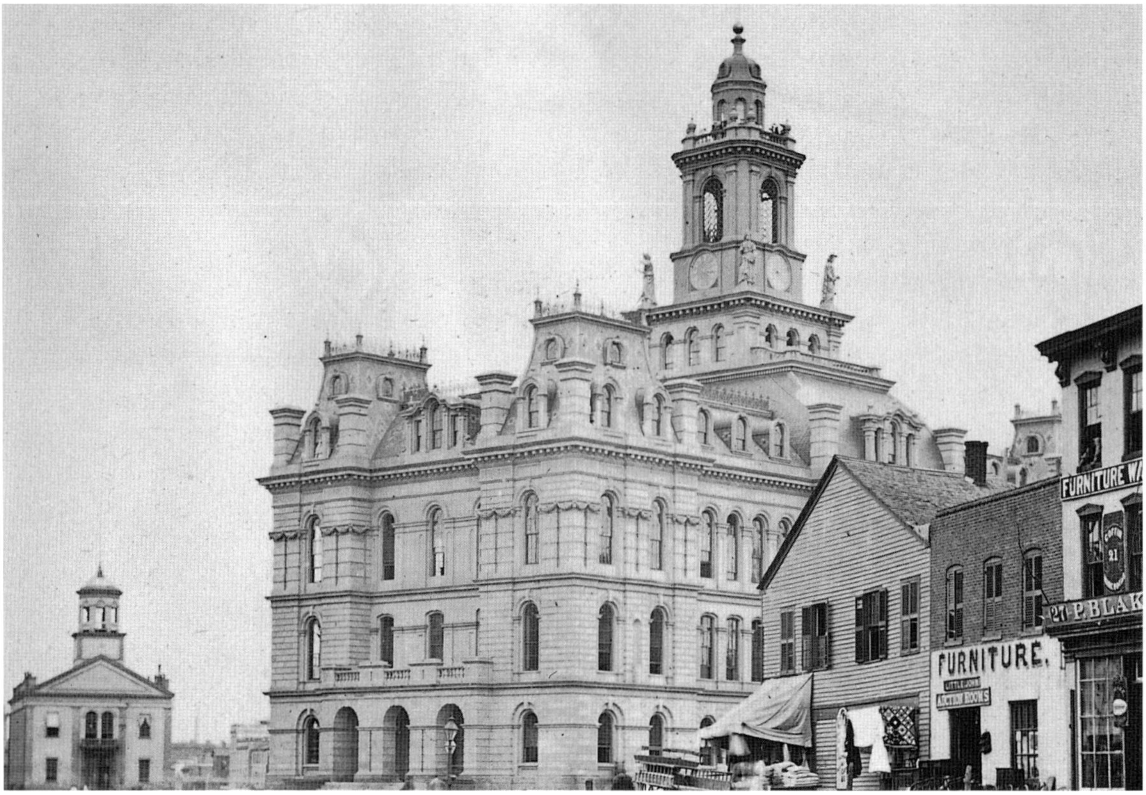

The new City Hall, as it was then called, was completed in 1871, in what is now Kennedy Square. The old City Hall, built in 1835, was located in Cadillac Square across the street from the new building. Courtesy Burton Historical Collection, Detroit Public Library.

The Peninsular shops were on Ferry between Riopelle and Dequindre at the Detroit and Milwaukee Railroad Junction. In addition to freight cars, the Peninsular works turned out wheels and axles for both cars and locomotives. In 1892 several of these concerns merged, including the Russel interests and Michigan Car, and in 1899 they were taken over by the American Car and Foundry Company.

In 1871 George Pullman bought a plant in the area bounded by Monroe, St. Aubin, Macomb, and the railroad, and for eight years Detroit was the main center for the manufacture of the Pullman sleeping car. In 1879 chief operations were moved to Chicago, but cars continued to be built here until 1893. In 1868, Detroiter William Davis perfected his

On July 18, 1871, the mayor and city council, attired for the occasion, marched across Woodward Avenue from the old City Hall to formally occupy the new one. Courtesy Burton Historical Collection, Detroit Public Library.

refrigerator car and persuaded local meat-packer George H. Hammond to provide the needed capital to set up his business. The first shipment by refrigerator car was made from Detroit to Boston in 1869. These industries naturally encouraged other inventions, and many new railroading ideas and mechanical improvements came out of local shops. One of these was the railroad track cleaner and snowplow, the invention of August Day.

Another major contribution was made by a mechanical engineer named Elijah McCoy. McCoy's invention, the automatic lubricating cup, allowed railroad engines to be lubricated automatically while the train was moving, thus preventing the problem of overheating. Prior to this it was necessary to stop trains every so often to lubricate them—a process that took considerable time. In all, McCoy is credited with more than eighty inventions and some fifty-seven patents. Because of the quality of McCoy's workmanship, railroad men would insist on his design when buying a lubricator. From then on people referred to the genuine article as "the real McCoy." In 1975 the site of McCoy's home on Lincoln Avenue near Hobart Street was designated a historic site by the Michigan Historical Commission and commemorated by the erection of a historical marker.

Railroad equipment and other metal products that rolled out of Detroit factories in increasing quantities required a basic metals industry that Detroit was quick to provide. Behind this local enterprise was the figure of a most remarkable man—a real giant of industry. He was Eber Brock Ward, born in 1811 in Ontario of Vermont stock. The Ward family settled at Marine City soon after the War of 1812, and when Eber was twelve or thirteen years old he shipped as a cabin boy and deckhand on the river trading schooner of his uncle Captain Sam Ward. Through shrewdness and hard work, Eber Brock Ward prospered and became one of the developers of Michigan industry. His interests were broad.

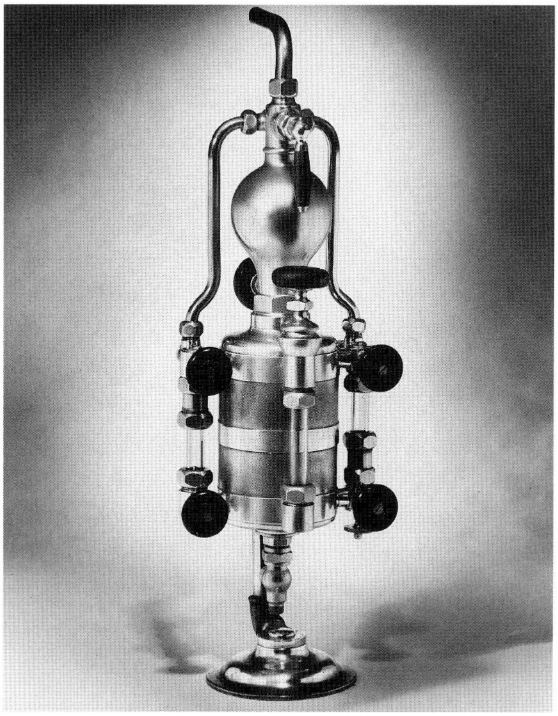

Detroit was the site of several important innovations dealing with the railroads. One of the most significant of these was the automatic lubricator —"the real McCoy" *(right)* made by Elijah McCoy *(above)*. Courtesy Burton Historical Collection, Detroit Public Library.

They included the ownership of timber and ore lands, newspapers, railroads, steamship and insurance companies, glass manufacturing, and banking. He was one of the promoters of the Soo Canal and one of the first to take advantage of it.

With a group of local financiers, Ward organized the Eureka Iron and Steel Works in 1853 on a 2,200-acre site in Wyandotte. There a big furnace and a tremendous plant were erected. It was an ideal location: northern ore and limestone could be brought in cheaply by water—mostly in Ward's bottoms; extensive beech forests were nearby to supply the charcoal with which most steel was then made; and it was close to a growing market that eventually became nationwide. It was in the Eureka furnace in 1864 that the first commercial steel was produced in the United States by the Bessemer process.

The company prospered, and Ward with it. He was probably Detroit's richest man and its first millionaire. He lived in a palatial home at Fort and Nineteenth (now Ste. Anne) Streets, then a suburban area. After Ward's death in 1875, the steel plant declined and eventually closed. In the early 1890s the Eureka works were razed except for part of the furnace and the administration building. They remained for many years as a reminder of how close the Detroit area came to being the steel-producing center of the United States.

Another industry that had an early start in Detroit was the manufacturing of stoves, which began locally in the 1830s. At that time, most stoves were made either in Albany or Troy, New York. Because it took so long to get a replacement part from the East, the Hydraulic Iron Works in Detroit began making parts for the local market. The company was successful enough to branch out into the production of complete stoves. In 1861, Jeremiah Dwyer, who had worked in an

Detroit was the nation's leading stove manufacturing center in the late 1800s. As the symbol of the city's importance to the industry, this giant stove was constructed for the Chicago Columbian Exposition in 1893. Located for many years on the grounds of the Detroit-Michigan Stove Company at Jefferson and the Belle Isle Bridge, it may be viewed today, beautifully restored, at the Michigan State Fairgrounds. Courtesy Burton Historical Collection, Detroit Public Library.

Albany stove works and as an apprentice with Hydraulic, opened his own stove company in Detroit. He did well, and three years later two Detroit industrialists, George Barbour and Charles A. Ducharme, put up the necessary capital for expansion. First called the Detroit Stove Works, Dwyer's operations grew and in 1871 the firm became the Michigan Stove Company. During the 1870s and 1880s other firms began operations, such as the Peninsular Stove Company. As a result, for more than fifty years the manufacturing of stoves and kitchen ranges was Detroit's leading industry.

The drug and pharmaceutical industry, another business venture of great importance to Detroit, grew from the activities of a number of local druggists who began to manufacture their own medicines. The industry was to include not only the manufacture of over-the-counter "patent medicines," but a large wholesale pharmaceutical business as well. The industry developed to a point where Detroit was the second-largest producer of pharmaceuticals—the largest being New York City.

The industry got its start in Detroit in 1845 when Jacob Farrand began to manufacture pills in his grocery and drugstore on Woodward near Jefferson. Before long his business grew, and Farrand, Williams and Company became one of the leading wholesale drug firms in the Midwest. In 1865, Frederick Stearns opened a drugstore on Jefferson near Brush Street, and soon he too was manufacturing pharmaceuticals. As his business grew, Stearns moved to a number of locations, finally building a large factory and laboratory on East Jefferson at Bellevue. Today the building has been converted into lofts and apartments.

Detroit's largest pharmaceutical concern, Parke, Davis and Company, dates to 1867. Its founder, Dr. Samuel Duffield, a member of a distinguished local family, began making pharmaceuticals in a drugstore at Cass and Henry. It was not long before the entire building was

This first Parke Davis plant was located on the corner of Cass Avenue and Henry Street. Founded in 1867, the firm moved from this site in 1873 to a new plant on the river near the foot of Joseph Campau. Courtesy Burton Historical Collection, Detroit Public Library.

turned into a factory, and Duffield was joined by partners Hervey C. Parke and George S. Davis. A short time later, Duffield left the business and the firm became Parke, Davis and Company. In 1873 the firm moved to a new plant on the river near the foot of Joseph Campau. This complex was later expanded, and today the buildings house a luxury hotel, a fine restaurant, and a complex of apartments.

Not all druggists went into the business of manufacturing pills. For example, Theodore Eaton, who had begun a wholesale drug business in 1855, eventually went into the production of chemicals and dyes. There were other firms in the field as well, including F. A. Thompson and Company, which specialized in making insect poison from nicotine extracted from tobacco. Another druggist, James Vernor, liked to mix soft drinks in his store and produced a very fine ginger ale. It was not long before the soft drink business outgrew the drugstore, and for well over a century Vernor's Ginger Ale has been enjoyed by millions.

Along with railroad equipment, steel, stoves, and drugs, several other important

On the southwest corner of Woodward and Clifford was James Vernor's store. It was in this store in 1876 that he made the first batch of his famous ginger ale. Courtesy Burton Historical Collection, Detroit Public Library.

industries were established in Detroit about the time of the Civil War. These included paints and varnish, soap, shoes, seeds, and tobacco. The great company names were the Berry Brothers, Detroit White Lead and Color Works, Queen Ann Soap, D. M. Ferry Seed, American Eagle Tobacco Company, and the Pingree-Smith Shoe Factory. The men who made these and other companies prosper and grow included John J. Bagley, Daniel Scotten, Henry R. Baldwin, Richard H. Fyfe, Hazen S. Pingree, Dexter M. Ferry, and James McMillan.

It was also at this time that Detroit became a major shipbuilding center. Two significant events were to influence this development. In 1852, O. M. Hyde erected a floating dry dock in the Detroit River, and the Detroit Dry Dock Company built a huge dry dock at the foot of Orleans Street. Before

During the last half of the nineteenth century, Detroit was a major shipbuilding center. Here, workmen at one of the city's shipyards pause from their work. Courtesy Dossin Great Lakes Museum, Detroit.

In 1876 the steam tug *Champion* enters the Detroit River from Lake St. Clair with a tow of five sailing vessels. To the left is the Windmill Point Lighthouse; to the right is Belle Isle. From a lithograph by Seth Arca Whipple. Author's collection.

In the 1880s and 1890s, the corner of Michigan and Woodward was the site of Fred Sanders's confectionery. In 1875 Sanders served the first ice cream soda. Courtesy Burton Historical Collection, Detroit Public Library.

long, the east-side waterfront in the neighborhood of Hastings and Orleans was lined with boiler and engine works, shipyards, and ship suppliers and chandlers. Then, in 1879, Detroit Dry Dock bought an extensive shipyard previously established in Wyandotte by Eber Brock Ward. In 1902 the Great Lakes Engineering Works acquired the Riverside Iron Works, makers of marine engines, and then built a second major shipyard in Ecorse. By 1905 Detroit accounted for half the tonnage of all vessels built on the Great Lakes.

In addition to this heavy industry, there was Bernhard Stroh, grandson of a German innkeeper who brewed his own beer. Young Stroh immigrated to Detroit in 1850 and set up his first brewery. In 1875 he expanded operations and opened the Lion Brewing Company, which in 1885 became the Stroh Brewery Company. About 1870, R. L. Polk and Company was incorporated and issued its first directory. Roehm and Wright established a jewelry firm, and when Roehm decided to leave the business, John Kay became Wright's partner and they moved into a new store at Woodward and Campus Martius. Fred Sanders opened his confectionery on Woodward Avenue in 1875 and served the country's first ice-cream soda. Ira and Clayton Grinnell opened their music store and several years later began manufacturing pianos.

For their shopping needs, Detroiters of this period could choose from a number of excellent department stores, including Mabley's (the city's first big department store), the Newcomb-Endicott Company, the Ernst Kern Company, People's Outfitting, and Partridges, which in 1908 became the Crowley-Milner Company.

Without a doubt, though, the leading merchant of the day was Joseph Lowthian Hudson. In 1877, Hudson moved to Detroit as manager of Mabley's clothing department.

Four years later he opened his own store, establishing the J. L. Hudson Company in the Opera House on Campus Martius. In 1891, Hudson moved into a new building at the corner of Farmer and Gratiot. Over the years, the building was expanded and enlarged until, in 1946, it filled the entire block bounded by Woodward, Farmer, Gratiot, and Grand River. Carrying everything from grand pianos to spools of thread, designer dresses to jasmine tea, original oil paintings to electric trains, Hudson's grew into the third-largest department store in the United States. In its heyday, Hudson's downtown store was *the* shopping place for Detroiters. Its twenty-five stories made it the tallest department store in the world, and its nearly two million square feet made it second only to Macy's New York store in space under one roof. Hudson's had the largest sales force, the biggest switchboard (second only to the Pentagon's), and the world's largest American flag, which covered six stories of the Woodward side of the building when it was displayed each Flag Day.

In 1897, just down Woodward from Hudson's, the notions business of Kresge and Wilson was established. When Sebastian S. Kresge bought out his partner a short time later, the business was moved across Woodward to the corner of Grand River. Offering a wide variety of merchandise in the attractive price range of five to ten cents, this store became number one in the billion-dollar nationwide Kresge (later renamed K-Mart) chain.

Detroit's banking system did not develop until well into the nineteenth century. The

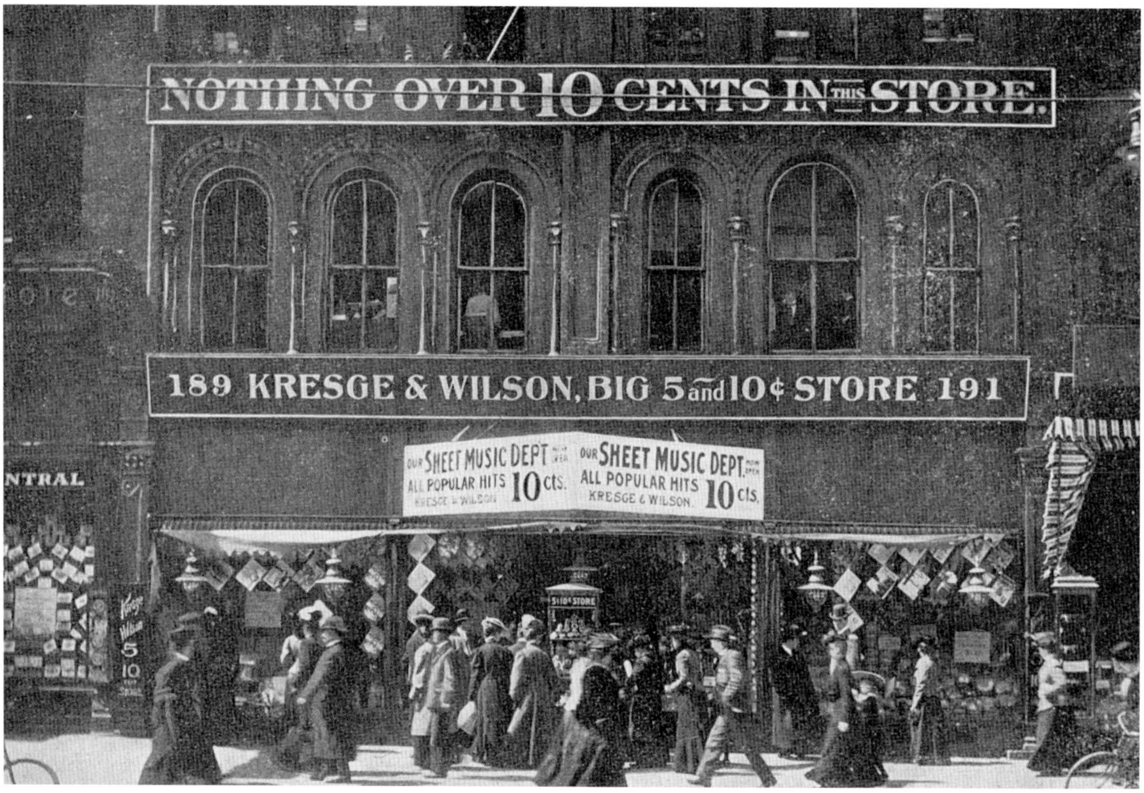

This Kresge and Wilson Big 5 and 10¢ Store on Woodward Avenue opened in 1897 and eventually became the first store in the nationwide Kresge chain. Courtesy Burton Historical Collection, Detroit Public Library.

In 1881, Joseph L. Hudson opened his clothing store on Campus Martius, on the first floor of the Opera House. Next door was the jewelry firm of Roehm and Wright, later known as Wright Kay and Company. Hudson's would become one of the nation's great department stores. Courtesy Burton Historical Collection, Detroit Public Library.

first, the Bank of Detroit, opened in 1806, but its capital of $10,000 disappeared with the cashier. The next attempt at a bank did not come until 1818, when the Bank of Michigan was lawfully chartered. It served the community well, and when its charter expired in 1842 it closed its doors, but with no losses to the depositors. Since then a large number of banking institutions have been established in Detroit. One of the most sound was the Detroit Savings Fund Institute. This bank began operations in 1849 at the northwest corner of Griswold and Woodbridge, on property that is now part of the civic center. After a few years it changed its name to the Detroit Savings Bank, then to Detroit Bank and Trust, and today it thrives as Comerica. In general, however, the city's current banking structure dates from the Depression. Several new banks were organized to replace others closed in the 1930s by government proclamation; that story will be told later.

The growth of Detroit's industrialization in the nineteenth century was aided by a major expansion of public utilities and other services. When only two thousand residents lived in the village along the river, people simply drew their water supply by hand. A private waterworks that opened in 1827 pumped river water into a reservoir on Randolph Street, and from there it went through a system of hollow tamarack logs. The city took over the system in 1836 and built a new waterworks at the foot of Orleans. After the state legislature created the Detroit Board of Water Commissioners in 1853, a new reservoir was built on Wilkins Street between Riopelle and Dequindre. As the city's population grew following the Civil War, a new pumping plant at Waterworks Park out East Jefferson was

The Detroit Savings Bank building at Griswold and Larned was erected in 1878. Known as the Bank Chambers, it was the home of the Detroit Savings Bank (today Comerica Bank) until 1906. Courtesy Burton Historical Collection, Detroit Public Library.

opened in 1878. The plant served as the primary source for the city's water system for many years.

Detroit's streets were first lighted by gas in 1851, with homes and other private buildings following soon after. The first supplier was the Detroit Gaslight Company. A competitor, the Mutual Gaslight Company, was established in 1871, but after a brief period of ruinous competition the two firms simply divided the city, using Woodward Avenue as the boundary. Political pressures forced them to merge in 1893 to form the Detroit City Gas Company, the predecessor of today's MichCon. The first gasworks were on Woodbridge between Fifth and Sixth Streets.

In 1882 the Brush Electric Light Company generated the first electricity in Detroit (for street lighting); electricity for home lighting began in 1893. The present Detroit Edison was incorporated in 1903, although its predecessor, the Edison Illuminating Company, had been operating for several years prior to that. The first Edison office and generating plant, Station A (the first plant in the country actually built for this purpose), was a two-story brick building constructed in 1886 on the corner of Washington and State (a replica of this building, operated by retired Detroit Edison employees, can be seen at Greenfield Village). In that building a young stationary engineer was employed at the turn of the century. His name was Henry Ford.

Other services also contributed significantly to the growth in the city's population and industry. Four streetcar lines (Jefferson, Woodward, Gratiot, and Michigan Avenues) began operations in 1863, all using horse-drawn cars. By 1886 there were thirteen lines extending a total of forty-two miles, with 155 cars and 1,470 horses. But then, in 1893, the system was converted to electrical operation. Shortly thereafter, high-speed interurban lines began to connect Detroit with other towns in Michigan and Ohio. The interurban terminal long stood on Bates Street just south of Jefferson. The telegraph had reached Detroit in 1847, the first line running to Ypsilanti. The local telegraph office then was in the rear of a building at the northeast corner of Jefferson and Cass. The telephone came in 1878; the first exchange was in the basement of a building on Griswold near Jefferson. As the number of subscribers increased, the telephone company erected a building on Clifford at Washington.

Industrial development before and after the Civil War required a substantial labor force. Although many who found jobs in the shops, factories, and stores were native-born Americans, there was a great increase in immigration. The Germans and Irish were the first to immigrate en masse to Detroit. Many Germans fled the political unrest of their homeland in the early 1830s. Most were educated, and many came with some capital. They settled on the city's near east side around Gratiot, where they established small shops and businesses, as well as religious, social, and cultural institutions. Many were skilled tradesmen and found a ready market for their crafts.

The Irish came shortly after. Forced to flee their native island because of the potato famine and political troubles, large numbers began to arrive in Detroit in the 1840s. It is estimated that more than a million people fled Ireland between 1845 and 1850. Unlike the Germans, the Irish arrived in Detroit lacking professional skills. Of necessity they became laborers, working in factories and on public projects such as road and rail construction. Many of the young women became domestics, and the men, who traditionally had a way with horses, manned the livery stables. The Irish settled on the lower west side around Most Holy Trinity Church at Porter and Sixth Streets. They called the area

Corktown because many had emigrated from County Cork. By 1850, one of every seven Detroiters was Irish.

The largest ethnic group to adopt Detroit as its new home was the Poles. A few Poles had arrived at a relatively early date, but the heavy influx began in the mid-1870s. Unlike the Germans and Irish, the Poles were actively recruited through immigration offices or bureaus the state of Michigan maintained from 1869 to 1885. Agents of the commission also met the immigrant ships at eastern seaports and channeled the new arrivals to the city. They were greatly needed at the time as common labor in the railroad shops and stove works. Some among the first arrivals in Detroit settled close to the German community, but as their number grew they formed their own community around St. Albertus Church on St. Aubin Street, which was founded in 1872. Later, about 1910, other citizens of Polish descent began to settle in Hamtramck. That suburb, with as many as fifty-six thousand residents, was for years more a Polish than an American city, and to this day it retains much of its Polish character.

After the Germans, the Irish, and the Poles arrived, immigrants from all over the world began descending upon Detroit. Most settled in areas with others of the same nationality for support, for companionship, and to retain their ethnic heritage. This was necessary in a society that recognized them as little more than a tool for getting the job done, instead of appreciating the richness of culture and tradition they brought to their new land.

In 1860, Detroit's population stood at 45,619. By 1870 it had grown to 79,577, and by 1880 it reached 116,340. A large percentage of this growth came from the new immigrants, and indeed, they came from everywhere. Census records from 1880 showed the following breakdown of countries represented in Detroit's foreign-born citizenry: British America, 10,754; Germany, 17,292; Ireland, 6,775; England, 4,200; Scotland, 1,783; Poland, 1,771; France, 721; Bohemia, 557; Switzerland, 421; Holland, 275; Italy, 127; Russia, 77; Wales, 71; Hungary, 64; Sweden, 55; Norway, 27; Austria, 15; China, 11; India, 9; Spain, 8; Mexico, 6; Malta, 3; Cuba, 3; Africa, 2; Gibraltar, 2; Greece, 1.

Another segment of Detroit's population that was experiencing considerable change at this time was the city's African American community. Following the Civil War, most of Detroit's black businessmen continued to turn their services and skills into small businesses serving white clientele. These included barbershops, clothes-cleaning stores, construction firms, tailor shops, delivery services, carpentry shops, and grocery stores. In the early 1880s, however, an important change found black businessmen turning from serving the white population to serving the black community. As the city's black population grew and settled along the lower east side (in 1880 Detroit's black community numbered 2,921, nearly 2.5 percent of the city's total population), the number of black businesses grew and diversified. During the next two decades, black businessmen were to be found as owners of moving companies, coal and lumber yards, drugstores, groceries, funeral homes, news dealerships, restaurants, hotels, and saloons—all largely serving the black community. The period was also to witness the rise of the city's first black financial and realty agencies.

One of the major forces in this change was the city's first successful black-owned newspaper, the *Plaindealer.* Organized in 1883 by Robert A. Pelham, Jr., Walter H. Stowers, William H. Anderson, Benjamin B. Pelham, and Byron G. Redmond, the *Plaindealer* was an important landmark in the history of black Detroit. During its eleven years of publication, the paper was a champion of racial unity, a promoter of black business, and a leading force in local politics. The offices of the paper were located at the southwest corner of Shelby and State Streets.

By 1890, Detroit had lost most of its small-town characteristics and had become a city, big and bustling. The population had grown to 205,876, ranking it fifteenth among United States cities. Some city boosters were predicting that almost any time now Detroit would surpass Cleveland in population and wealth. The city's boundaries had been pushed out north to Grand Boulevard, east to Baldwin Avenue (near Mt. Elliott), and west to Livernois, and the new residential sections were developed in what only a short time before had been open countryside. Huge elm, maple, and chestnut trees shaded the streets. Homes, most of them frame and painted either white or dark green, gave the newer residential areas an air of comfort and well-being.

Although Detroit was indeed a big city by 1890, it would be the motorcar that would transform its destiny to that of one of the world's major urban centers.

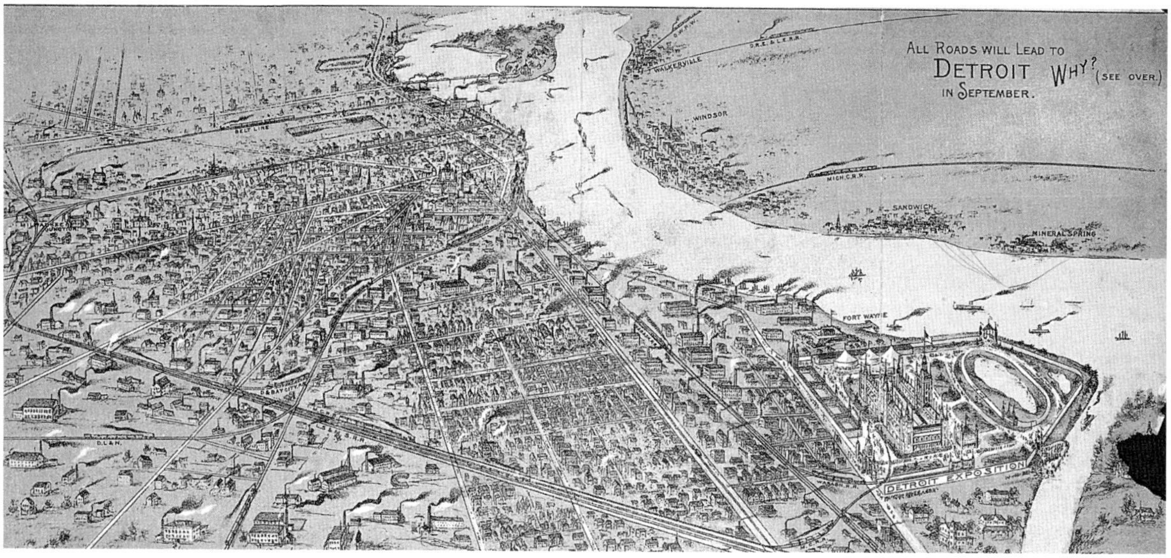

From 1889 to 1892 a grand international exposition and fair was held on a seventy-acre tract downriver from Detroit at Delray. The main exposition building, which was also the entrance to the fairgrounds, was described as "the largest of its kind in the world." The property was later sold to the Solvay Process Company. From a tourists' pocket map published by the Calvert Lithograph Company. Courtesy Dossin Great Lakes Museum, Detroit.

NINE
The Automobile

IT ALL BEGAN ON THE COLD, SNOWY evening of March 6, 1896. The time was about 11 P.M. There was a last-minute bustle of activity in John Lauer's machine shop on the east side of St. Antoine Street just south of Jefferson Avenue. A couple of husky men opened the large doors to the shop and helped roll a carriage-like contraption out into the street.

Charles Brady King, a young man wrapped up in a short coat for protection against the cold, with a muffler around his throat and a derby perched on his head, climbed into the vehicle and grasped the steering tiller. Someone spun the crank, the engine snorted and popped, King threw in the clutch, and the first automobile to appear on the streets of Detroit moved uncertainly up St. Antoine toward Jefferson.

At Jefferson, King steered west and went to Woodward, where he turned north and chugged up to the Russel House at Cadillac Square. There the motor died, and there is no account of how King got his machine back to Lauer's shop. Epochal as that short trip was, it stirred only casual public interest. The following day the *Free Press* carried only a brief account, buried on its back page: "The first horseless carriage seen in this city was out on the streets last night. The apparatus seems to

The first horseless carriage to appear on the streets of Detroit was built by Charles B. King, shown here at the tiller with his young assistant, Oliver Barthel. Courtesy Burton Historical Collection, Detroit Public Library.

work all right, and it went at the rate of five or six miles an hour at an even rate of speed." The longest account of King's feat was a quarter column on an inside page of the *Journal*. The *Tribune* gave it only three lines.

Charles King was not the only local mechanic working on a horseless carriage in 1896. A young man named Henry Ford was also building a machine. Ford was the night-shift engineer at the Edison Illuminating Company (the present-day Detroit Edison Company), where he earned $125 a month. In his spare time he worked in a small brick shed at the rear of his Bagley Avenue home. Ford completed work on his machine on June 4, but he discovered too late that to get it out onto the street he had to knock out part of the shed's wall. The building was removed from its original site many years later and is now at Greenfield Village. So is the machine.

Ford cranked up his quadricycle, as he called it, and nobody was more surprised than he was when it started. "The darn thing ran!" exclaimed Ford. At the time, neither Ford nor King had any idea they were launching a great industry, and neither one would be

The first automobile plant in Detroit was the Olds Motor Works located on East Jefferson at the Belle Isle Bridge. Olds began operations here in 1899, but when this plant burned to the ground in 1901, Olds moved to Lansing. Courtesy National Automotive History Collection, Detroit Public Library.

In this painting, Ford is seen bringing his first auto, the quadricycle, out of the shed at the rear of his Bagley Avenue home in 1896. From Milo M. Quaife, *This Is Detroit, 1701–1951*.

the first to begin the production of automobiles in Detroit.

The first to open an automobile plant in Detroit was Ransom E. Olds. Working in his hometown of Lansing, Olds had built what he called the Oldsmobile, but to produce his car in quantity he needed capital. He came to Detroit and met Samuel L. Smith, who had made a fortune in lumber and copper. Smith agreed to back Olds (as long as his two sons would be given jobs in the company), and as a result, the Olds Motor Works was founded. The first Oldsmobiles were good machines. They ran well on paved streets and the company sold all it could make, which was not many. An Olds cost $2,382, so only the wealthy could afford them.

Then, on March 9, 1901, a fire completely destroyed the Olds plant, including all the plans and machinery for producing the Oldsmobile. Only a small experimental model car with a curved dash was saved. Olds decided not to rebuild in Detroit and moved back to Lansing, where he began production of his smaller car. But the ties with Detroit were not broken. Olds was no longer able to machine parts in his own factory, and

In this shop on Trombley at Dequindre, Henry M. Leland began building motors for Olds. Leland would later organize the Cadillac Motor Car Company. Courtesy National Automotive History Collection, Detroit Public Library.

the manufacture of his cars became essentially an assembly process. Work was farmed out to a dozen suppliers, most of them Detroit shops. The Leland-Faulconer machine shop on Trombley at Dequindre, headed by Henry M. Leland, built the motors; John and Horace Dodge, who had recently been making bicycles in Windsor, supplied transmissions; the Briscoe Manufacturing Company produced radiators; and Bryson F. (Barney) Everitt went to Norwalk, Ohio, and hired a young fellow named Fisher, one of seven brothers, to help make the bodies. Consequently, the Olds was produced more economically, and the price of the curved-dash car was drastically reduced to $625. Within a year the company was turning out the first popular low-priced car and making 25 percent of all the autos built in the United States.

During this time, Henry Ford continued to make improvements on his machine. Charles King, on the other hand, decided to follow other interests. Ford's major thrust, though, was not in producing cars but in racing them. He induced driver Barney Oldfield to race his cars, and in 1901 Oldfield set a record of sixty miles per hour on the Grosse Pointe track. Ford personally drove a race on the ice of Lake St. Clair in 1904, setting a new world speed record of ninety-three miles per hour.

Finally, Ford decided to begin producing cars in quantity, and after several unsuccessful starts he was able to obtain financial backing for a new company. On June 16, 1903, the Ford Motor Company was incorporated, beginning operations in a factory on Mack Avenue at Bellvue (a replica of the building can be seen today in Greenfield Village). Among those who furnished the money (actually only $28,000 in working capital was paid in) were Alexander Y. Malcomson, a coal dealer; John S. Gray, a banker; and Horace H. Rackham, an attorney. John and Horace Dodge, who contracted to make parts for Ford in their shop on Beaubien at Fort and later in larger quarters on Monroe at Hastings, were given shares of stock in payment. When a loan was later made to keep

Henry Ford's first interest was in racing cars, not building them. Here he is seen with Barney Oldfield at the wheel. In 1901 Oldfield set a record of 60 mph on the Grosse Pointe racetrack. Courtesy Henry Ford Museum and Greenfield Village Research Center.

the company afloat, one banker protested that he had never seen a worse investment. Malcomson's bookkeeper, James S. Couzens, put up $2,500 and joined the Ford Motor Company as its business manager. In 1919, Ford bought him out for $29,308,857, a substantial part of which Couzens returned to the community in philanthropy.

Ford's plan was to build a car that would provide basic transportation for farmers and small-town residents as well as for city dwellers. He envisioned a mass-produced, low-priced automobile so simple in construction that any handyman could repair it. The idea paid off from the start, and in 1906 Ford moved to a larger plant on Piquette Avenue at Beaubien. It was in this plant in 1908 that Ford began production of probably the most famous automobile of all time—the Model T. The car was so popular that the company was soon unable to meet the demand. Within just two years, Ford was six months behind in deliveries. So the decision was made to move again, this time far out Woodward Avenue to the city of Highland Park. There, on sixty acres of land, famed Detroit architect Albert Kahn was called upon to design a radically new plant. Kahn pioneered in industrial architecture for Ford, utilizing reinforced concrete and glass as structural elements and providing facilities that brought the work to the man instead of sending the man to the work. Ground was broken in 1909, and by January 1, 1910, the Highland Park factory was in partial operation. For the time being the Piquette plant was retained.

With production well under way at the new plant, Ford introduced a revolutionary procedure. In 1913 the first automatic assembly line was put in operation. Ford had already perfected the standardization of parts at the plant, and now these parts were made to flow in a continuous stream to the moving line. The required part reached the line just as it was needed by the worker, who now performed only a single task. At the end of the line, the body of the car slid down an incline just as the completed chassis arrived. The two were bolted together, and the finished auto was driven away under its own power. With this system, production was far more economical and efficient, yielding an almost unlimited quantity potential. This extraordinary change in the technique of manufacturing allowed Ford to produce 146 Model T's per hour in 1913. By comparison, in 1908, initial Model T production was, at best,

At this Highland Park plant, Ford built his Model T, introduced the first moving assembly line, and announced his $5-a-day pay for workers. Designed by famed Detroit architect Albert Kahn, this plant, seen here in the 1950s, was the largest automobile factory in the world when it opened in 1910. Courtesy National Automotive History Collection, Detroit Public Library.

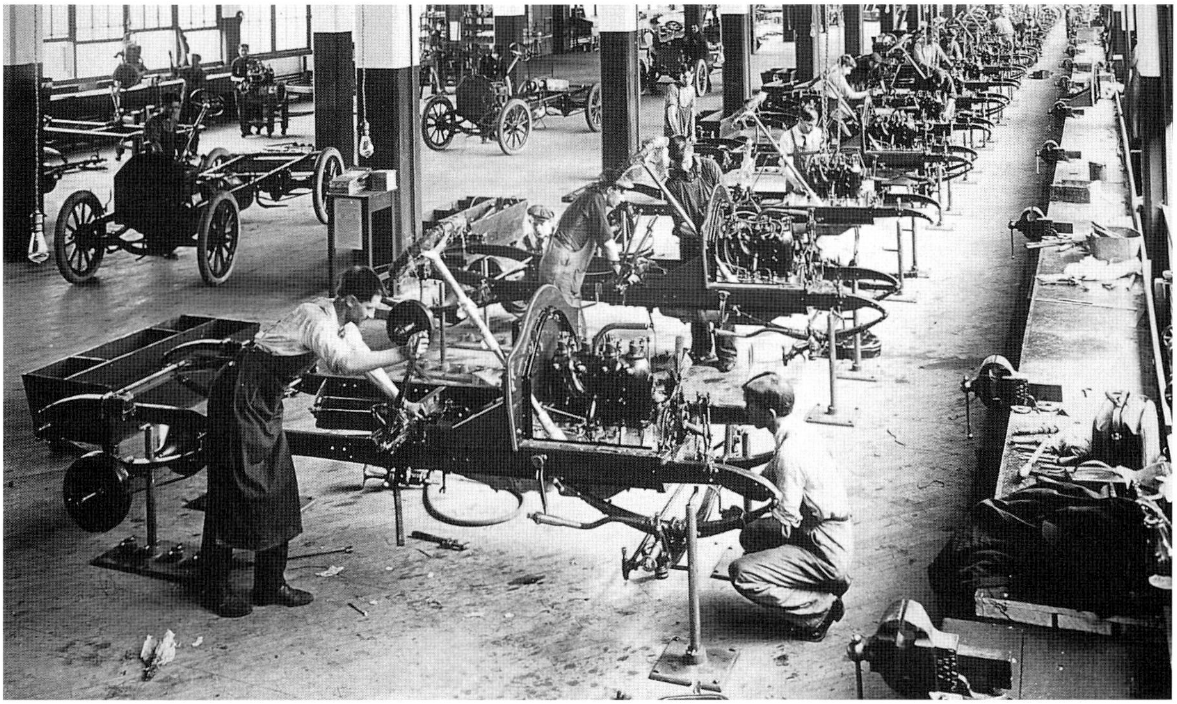

Before Ford introduced the moving assembly line, autos were built individually and components were brought to the frames, as seen here at the Chalmers plant, ca. 1910. Courtesy Henry Ford Museum and Greenfield Village Research Center.

When Ford introduced his moving assembly line in 1913, each required part reached the worker just as it was needed. At the end of the line, the body of the car slid down an incline just as the completed chassis arrived. Courtesy National Automotive History Collection, Detroit Public Library.

only 7.5 per hour. In 1910, before the moving assembly line, the price of a Model T was $780. By 1916, after the introduction of the assembly line, Ford was able to reduce the price to $380.

While the assembly line was an important milepost, Ford's next innovation staggered the competition. On January 12, 1914, Ford announced that henceforth each production worker in his plant would be paid $5.00 for an eight-hour shift. To workers for whom $2.75 or less for a ten-hour day was standard pay for unskilled or semi-skilled labor, this sounded like a new gold strike. Men from all over Michigan left the lumber camps and farms and headed for Detroit. Job seekers came from other states as well, and even from Europe. Thousands lined up at the Highland Park plant gates. So dense was the throng of job applicants that it was necessary on one occasion to use fire hoses to disperse them. In 1904 the Ford Motor Company had thirty-one workers, but by 1920 it employed fifty-six thousand, with two-thirds of them working at the Highland Park plant.

In 1904 this first Buick model was test-driven from Flint to Detroit by chief engineer Walter Marr, the driver, and David Buick's son, Tom. Courtesy National Automotive History Collection, Detroit Public Library.

In 1902, the year before Ford and his backers launched their company, another Detroit industrialist entered the automotive field: Henry M. Leland and his associates put their first car on the market under the name of Cadillac. In 1905 they changed the name to the Cadillac Motor Car Company. When the firm lost its first plant to a fire in 1904, they rebuilt a new factory in reinforced concrete at Cass and Amsterdam.

Olds, Ford, and Leland were not alone, though. There was engineer David D. Buick, who had met with considerable success in the plumbing supply business. He became interested in automobiles and in 1903 built a car that he named for himself. Unfortunately, he depleted his resources in doing so and was forced to sell out. His company was purchased by wagonmaker William C. Durant and moved to Flint.

With Buick as his base, Durant formed the General Motors Company on September 16, 1908. In the next two years he bought in quick succession Cadillac, Oldsmobile, Oakland (which was manufactured in Pontiac and was the forerunner of the Pontiac car), and several other smaller auto producers. Financial difficulties, however, forced Durant out of General Motors in 1910, so he joined forces with Swiss-born mechanic and race car driver Louis Chevrolet and launched the Chevrolet Motor Car Company in Detroit in 1911. In 1915 Durant was able to regain control of General Motors, and he brought with him the Chevrolet. With the Chevrolet, which he moved to Flint, Durant had the inexpensive auto that could compete with Ford's "Tin Lizzie." Other firms, particularly companies making parts and accessories, were also added to the corporation. With its headquarters in Detroit and its production sites widely scattered, Durant had General

The first Chevrolet was manufactured in 1912. Seen here admiring the car are Louis Chevrolet (*at left without hat*) and William C. Durant (*far right with derby*). The firm turned out 2,999 cars that first year. Courtesy National Automotive History Collection, Detroit Public Library.

Motors well on its way to becoming the giant of all American industrial enterprises.

The year 1903 was to witness the beginnings of another car in Detroit. It was the Packard, which had originally been produced in the town of Warren, Ohio. While on a trip to New York, two wealthy Detroiters, Henry B. Joy and Truman H. Newberry, saw a new Packard parked on the street. While they were inspecting the car, a fire engine went by. The owner dashed out of a nearby building, started the motor with one spin of the crank, and went off in pursuit. Joy and Newberry were impressed, and shortly thereafter they purchased the Packard Company and moved it to Detroit. Henry Joy became president of the new company and engaged Albert Kahn to serve as the firm's architect. The first nine buildings Kahn designed for Packard on East Grand Boulevard near Mt. Elliott were of the standard mill construction, but in 1905 he designed Building No. 10 in reinforced concrete, the first such building in Detroit, the forerunner of a new type of industrial architecture.

The year following Packard's move to Detroit, Jonathon Maxwell obtained financial backing to build his new car, which he called, not surprisingly, the Maxwell. A former Olds factory manager, Maxwell soon had his automobile in production at a factory at East Jefferson near Connors. During the depression that followed World War I, however, the company fell on hard times. To help get the firm back on its feet, onetime railroad master mechanic Walter P. Chrysler was called in. Chrysler, who had previously worked for Buick as plant superintendent, reorganized the company, and in 1925 the last of the Big Three was born.

During the years prior to World War I, a number of other cars were produced in Detroit: Hupp and Paige; Krit and Saxon; Liberty and Rickenbacker. In 1909 the Hudson Motor Car Company was organized by Roy D. Chapin, a former Olds employee, who obtained his financial backing from department store owner J. L. Hudson. In 1911 the Studebaker Brothers Manufacturing Company of South Bend, Indiana, merged with a Detroit firm, the Everitt-Metzger-Flanders Company, to form the Studebaker Corporation, which built cars in plants on Piquette Avenue and out West Jefferson. But the life of these early automobile companies was precarious. Of the 202 different makes of automobiles being produced in 1910, only four remain today: Buick, Cadillac, Ford, and Oldsmobile. Chevrolet and others would follow.

Railroad master mechanic Walter P. Chrysler was hired to reorganize the failing Maxwell Motor Car Company, and in 1925 the last of the Big Three was born. From a 1929 sketch by John Copin. Courtesy National Automotive History Collection, Detroit Public Library.

When Henry B. Joy formed a syndicate that brought the Packard Company to Detroit in 1903, he wanted to construct a fire-resistant factory. This reinforced concrete building on East Grand Boulevard, designed by Albert Kahn, introduced a new era in industrial architecture. Courtesy National Automotive History Collection, Detroit Public Library.

In 1914 the Dodge brothers left Ford and organized their own company, producing their automobile in a new plant in Hamtramck. The Dodge Brothers Company grew with a line of well-built, moderately priced cars and durable trucks. In 1920, however, with the tragic deaths of both brothers, the company began to falter. The situation continued to deteriorate until April 30, 1925, when a New York banking interest headed by Dillon Read and Company bought the Dodge properties for $146 million. At the time, this was the largest cash transaction in the history of American industry. Three years later, with his eye on the success of General pitals, Walter Chrysler obtained control of

Horace Dodge (*left rear*) and John Dodge (*right rear*) take delivery of the first Dodge automobile, November 14, 1914, in front of the John Dodge estate, 75 East Boston Boulevard. Courtesy National Automotive History Collection, Detroit Public Library.

the company and it became the Dodge Division of the Chrysler Corporation.

In addition to automobile manufacturing, the years prior to World War I witnessed the mushrooming of the parts and accessories industry. Many of these companies started as small shops, but by obtaining contracts from the auto manufacturers they grew and prospered along parallel lines. Typical of these early shops was the Rands Manufacturing Company, founded in 1904 by William C. Rands. Originally in the bicycle business, Rands turned to building windshields, cloth tops, lamp brackets, and other auto equipment. The company prospered and in 1916 became the Motor Products corporation. One of the largest firms, the Timken-Detroit Axle Company, was founded in 1909 in Canton, Ohio, but later moved to Detroit, where it soon employed 4,500 workers. Then there was Morgan and Wright, the predecessor of Uniroyal, which employed over 4,000 at their tire plant on East Jefferson near the Belle Isle Bridge. Other major producers included the C. R. Wilson Body Company, Briggs Manufacturing, the Murray Body Company, Budd Manufacturing, McCord Manufacturing, and the Kelsey Wheel Company. There were dozens of other specialized firms manufacturing engines, transmissions, wheels, brakes, springs, radiators, belts and hoses, gears, frames, lights, and electrical systems. By 1917 Detroit had twenty-three automobile companies providing jobs for almost 93,000, and 132 parts firms employed an additional 44,000 workers.

Thus, within a relatively short time Detroit had become the heart of the automobile industry. There were several reasons for this. First, for several years the city had been the center of the marine gasoline engine industry. Second, Detroit was also the center of the malleable iron manufacturing industry. It had plants that could turn out springs, copper and brass parts and fittings, and paints and varnishes. Third, the lumber era was coming to an end in Michigan and a supply of unemployed labor was at hand. Fourth, there was money here, and lots of it. During the second half of the nineteenth century, fortunes had been made in lumber, mining, and shipping. Wealthy Detroiters had capital they could afford to risk in ventures that gave promise of being economically sound. And finally, there were also several key individuals who had a significant impact during the early years of development, particularly Olds and Ford. Thus it was that Detroit, more than any other city, possessed all the necessary elements at just the right time.

Now that Detroit was producing better cars, local motorists began to demand better

Early motorists had their problems with muddy roads, flat tires, and weather—from which they had little protection. A major step toward improving roads was taken in 1909 with the laying of the first mile of concrete highway in the United States, on Woodward Avenue between Six and Seven Mile Roads. Courtesy Burton Historical Collection, Detroit Public Library.

Here, at Woodward and Congress, a patrolman directs traffic using a hand-controlled signal. Just visible in the center of this photo is the overhead suspended light (the nation's first) that was controlled from the tower at Woodward and Michigan. Courtesy Burton Historical Collection, Detroit Public Library.

The Central Oil Company built in 1910 what may have been the first drive-in gas station with an island. Here is the company's second such facility, at the corner of Woodward Avenue and High Street (now Vernor), in 1915. Courtesy Burton Historical Collection, Detroit Public Library.

roads. Rural roads were muddy and difficult most of the year, and people were no longer satisfied being restricted to city driving. In response, the Wayne County Road Commission laid the world's first stretch of concrete highway in 1909 on Woodward Avenue between Six and Seven Mile Roads. In 1911, County Road Commissioner Edward H. Hines had the world's first white center line painted on the River road near Trenton. To control all the traffic on the new roads, young Detroit police patrolman William L. Potts invented the electric red-amber-green traffic light. The first unit was installed on a high tower at the corner of Woodward and Michigan Avenues in October 1920. Detroit's first stop signs went up in 1923, installed by the Detroit Automobile Club, forerunner of the Automobile Club of Michigan, founded in 1916.

By 1916 the automobile was big business in Detroit, and the city was well on its way to becoming the Motor Capital. Yet Detroit was not a one-industry town. Industrial production rose from $600 million to $900 million between 1915 and 1916, and while automotive products accounted for the largest portion of this figure, the manufacture of stoves, furnaces, paints, pharmaceuticals, marine equipment, and tobacco continued to be important. For example, in 1916 more than a million cigars a day were being produced in the city.

Detroit's supply of skilled labor attracted other industries to the city. In 1904 the Arithmometer Company of St. Louis moved to Detroit, opened a plant at Second and Amsterdam, and began producing adding machines. The following year it was incorporated as the Burroughs Adding Machine Company, later to become the Burroughs Corporation. The salt mining, steel production, and chemical industries also helped to produce many of the city's new jobs. To coordinate and stimulate business activity, the Detroit Board of Commerce was organized in 1903.

Detroit was in high gear.

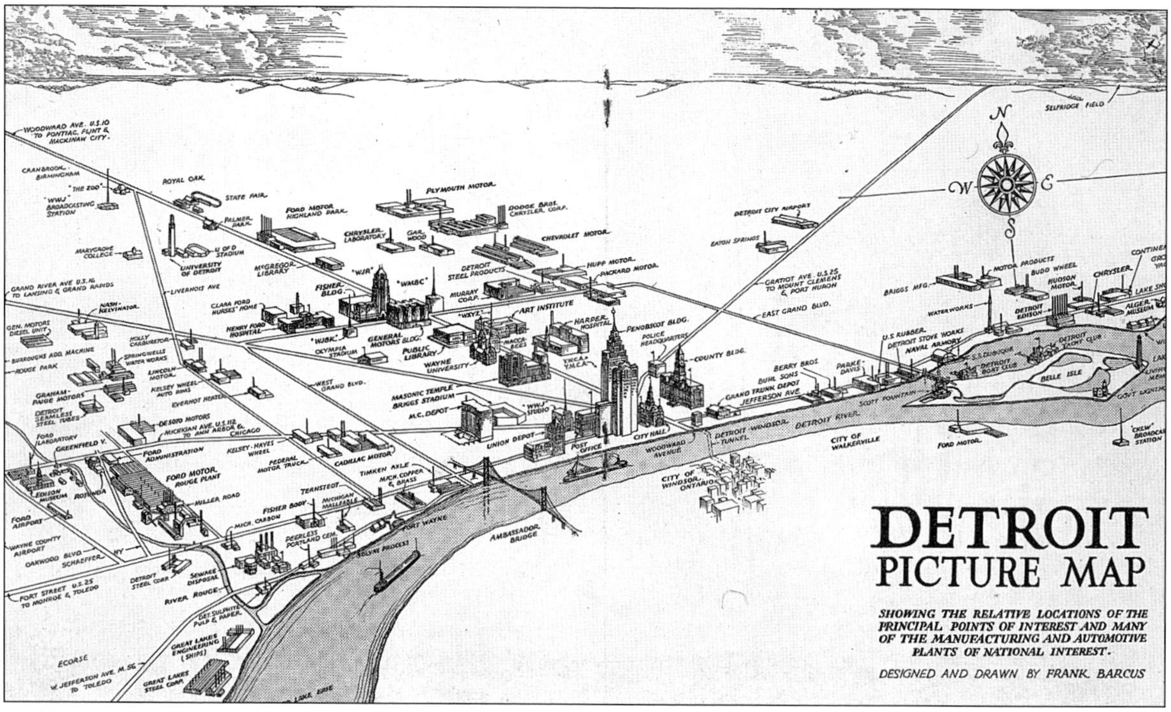

Within a relatively short time, Detroit became the heart of the automobile industry—the Motor Capital. From Frank Barcus, *All Around Detroit*.

Ten

World War

THE UNITED STATES, ON APRIL 6, 1917, officially joined the war against Germany, which had been raging in Europe since 1914. Detroiters had taken an active interest in the war long before 1917, however. Because Canada had been involved since 1914, many Detroiters crossed the river and entered the Canadian army and air force.

In 1915, Henry Ford had tried to settle the European conflict himself by chartering a "Peace Ship" and transporting a group of "peace delegates," technical staff, newspaper reporters, and students across the ocean for the purpose of "getting the boys out of the trenches by Christmas." Ford accompanied the party to Norway, but he returned promptly

Taken from the old City Hall, this view of Woodward Avenue at West Fort Street in 1912 shows a busy downtown with horse-drawn vehicles still much in evidence. Courtesy Burton Historical Collection, Detroit Public Library.

This 1913 postcard shows the waiting room for the Belle Isle ferry and a steamer ready to leave for the island. A ferry ride to Belle Isle was a popular pastime for Detroiters. Ferries served Belle Isle on and off from 1882 until the service was permanently discontinued in 1957. Courtesy Cynthia Bieniek.

when he sensed the futility of the effort. The expedition, needless to say, came to nothing. In fact, no informed person ever gave it a chance to succeed.

Following the declaration of war, the Michigan National Guard was called into service to form the Thirty-second Division. The troops from Detroit, the Thirty-first Infantry, became part of the Sixty-third Brigade. They were joined by a medical detachment, a headquarters unit, the 119th Field Artillery, a machine gun company, and part of a cavalry squadron. Two base hospitals were also organized; No. 17 was made up of doctors and nurses from Harper Hospital, and No. 36 represented the Detroit College of Medicine. In addition to these Detroiters, thousands of others volunteered and went into the regular army, navy, and marine corps.

Guardsmen and volunteers, however, did not provide the total manpower needed. On June 5, 1917, all Detroit men between the ages of twenty-one and thirty went to voting booths, schools, and other public places to register for the draft. Two later registrations were necessary before the war ended. Many of the men drafted from Detroit and Michigan trained at Camp Custer near Battle Creek and became part of the Eighty-fifth Division.

Ladies and gentlemen dressed in their finery stop for lunch at the self-serve restaurant in the basement of the Majestic Building in 1914. Courtesy Cynthia Bieniek.

One regiment of the Eighty-fifth had a most strange adventure. The 339th Infantry, with a substantial representation of Detroiters, was sent to Archangel in northern Russia in 1918 to fight the Bolsheviks and provide what it was hoped would be a rallying point for non-Communist Russians. Poorly armed and equipped, the regiment, along with several other military units, served through the extremely severe winter of 1918–19. Finally brought home in July 1919, they were given the name Polar Bears. Altogether, Detroit sent about 65,000 men and women to serve in the armed forces during World War I. Of those, 1,360 would not survive the conflict.

On the home front, the civilian population also was mobilized to support the war effort. With the departure of the Michigan National Guard, a home guard was organized. Known as the Michigan State Troops, two regiments, the 551st and 552nd, were raised in Detroit and the surrounding area. In addition, a full-time unit was created. This was the Michigan State Constabulary, patterned after the Royal Canadian Mounted Police. After the war the constabulary became the Michigan State Police. In Detroit they were kept busy guarding railroad yards, the waterfront, and other strategic places. A careful watch was kept on the Michigan Central Railroad tunnel connecting Detroit and Windsor. Federal authorities had knowledge of an enemy spy and sabotage ring operating in Detroit and Canada. The Detroit group was directed by Karl Kalschmidt, who, along with several others, was arrested and convicted. Some prominent German American Detroiters were interned on farms in the Oscoda region. Unfortunately, these activities, plus the nationalistic tensions that existed, also led to the persecution of several loyal German American families. Yellow paint was splashed on their houses, and they were threatened with physical violence and ostracized by their neighbors.

Detroiters also served in the Red Cross, the YMCA, the Knights of Columbus, and the Salvation Army, all of which provided aid and

Thousands of Detroiters lined Woodward Avenue at Campus Martius for this "Liberty Bond Drive" parade. With most soldiers and sailors at the front, city police and firemen made up the bulk of the marchers in this 1918 parade. Courtesy Burton Historical Collection, Detroit Public Library.

comfort to servicemen with their canteens and other efforts at home as well as overseas. Locally, liberty bond drives were organized and well subscribed to. Food and fuel supplies also caused grave concern, and serious shortages were felt. High school students and women were recruited in Detroit and sent out to work on farms in the state, particularly at harvest time. Breadless and meatless days were proclaimed, unessential businesses were encouraged to close on Mondays to save coal, and early in January 1918 the fuel shortage became so acute during a prolonged spell of bitterly cold weather that all businesses except hotels, restaurants, and drugstores were required to close down for five days. During February the city's public schools were closed.

The harsh winter, the lack of fuel, and the crowding of workers contributed to the outbreak of an influenza epidemic in 1917. Particularly virulent during 1918, the epidemic was worldwide and took millions of lives, both civilian and military. Detroit suffered severely; nearly everyone was stricken to some degree by the Spanish flu, as it was called, and hundreds died. For weeks many Detroiters went about wearing gauze masks in the belief that such devices would give protection. Unfortunately, they did not.

Along with its citizens, Detroit's automobile industry also went to war in 1917. And, for the first time in history, the industry became a principal factor in the production of war materials. In fact, it was the industry's production capacity that helped to bring about the Allied victory. Even before the United States entered the war, some auto plants held contracts with the Allies, so the conversion was not an immediate thing. Nor was it ever a complete one. Unlike in World War II, production of cars for the domestic civilian market was not halted, although it was slowed down.

To support the war effort, the automobile industry turned out a variety of military equipment. Guns, ammunition, and even the tin helmets of the doughboys were produced in huge quantities. Detroit also supplied thousands of trucks, ambulances, and staff cars. Not only did these motorized vehicles help defeat the German army, they also brought an end to the use of cavalry and horse artillery. In addition, Detroit produced the famous Liberty aircraft engine. It was built by Ford, Packard, Cadillac, and the recently organized Lincoln Motor Company at its new plant at Warren and Livernois. Ford also produced Eagle boats, small but fast submarine chasers, at the new Rouge plant, using a revolutionary new

Detroit's automobile industry played a major role in the Allied victory of World War I. Here are two-ton White trucks in a convoy somewhere in France *(left)*. At the Ford Highland Park plant on July 17, 1918, Red Cross workers were trained using Ford-built ambulances *(center)*. Also at the Highland Park plant, Ford tested a new type of war machine, the Whippet tank *(right)*. Courtesy National Automotive History Collection, Detroit Public Library.

moving assembly line technique similar to the one the company had already pioneered. At the Highland Park plant, Ford was building a newly designed armored tread-operated vehicle called the Whippet tank. To test it Ford built some artificial hills on the ground just north of the plant on Woodward Avenue, and because of very minimum security, the public could easily watch the Whippet being tested.

In the late summer of 1918 the German armies began to collapse, and on November 11 the armistice was signed. When word reached the city, Detroiters poured into downtown to celebrate.

The war left many marks on Detroit, the most obvious being a serious housing shortage. The result was a building boom, and to obtain lots it was necessary to expand the city's boundaries. Small annexations had been made from time to time before the war, such as Delray in 1906 and Fairview on the east side in 1907. In 1916 a large area on either side of Woodward extending roughly from the Highland Park city limits to Eight Mile Road was annexed. Then, beginning in 1922, sizable sections were added in the Livernois area, in 1924 and 1925 huge parcels on the northwest and northeast perimeters were taken in, and in 1926 the last major annexation occurred when Redford became part of Detroit. With this last addition, Detroit's area had grown to 139 square miles—the size it has remained to this day.

It was also during the era of World War I that Detroit's municipal government was modernized. It began in 1890 when Hazen S. Pingree was elected mayor. Pingree, or Ping as his fellow citizens fondly called him, served six years and gave Detroit one of its most productive administrations. He cleaned up the graft-ridden city departments and laid the foundations for the relatively clean nonpartisan form of municipal government that was later to be adopted. He cleaned out the notorious red-light district on the lower east side and fought the entrenched combine that controlled the street railway franchises, forcing them to reduce fares under threat of munici-

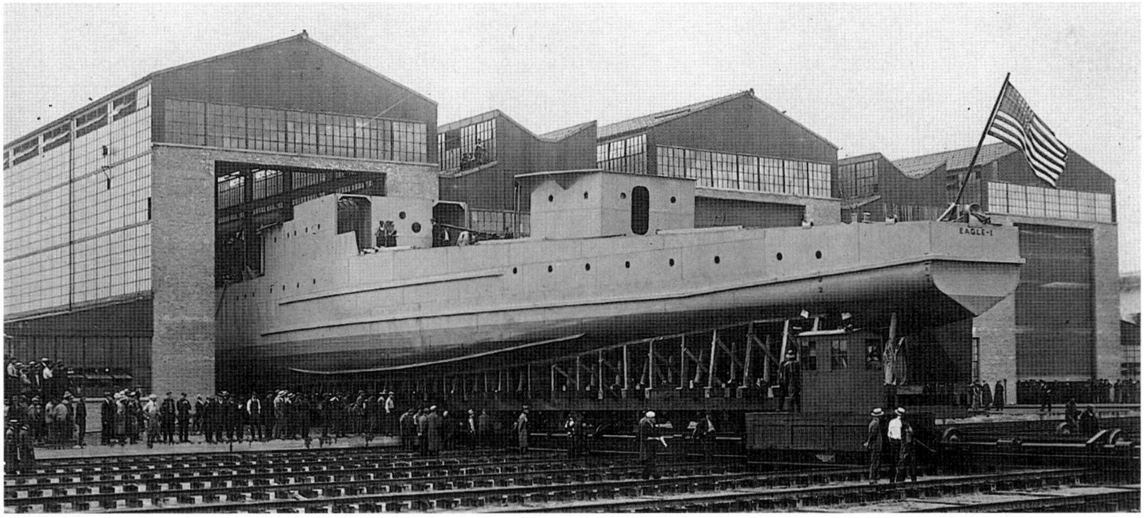

Not only did Ford diversify his automobile production during the war, but his company also constructed Eagle boats at the new Rouge plant. Mass-production techniques enabled workers to build Boat No. 59 in just ten days. Here work is completed as a boat is moved out of the assembly building. Courtesy Dossin Great Lakes Museum, Detroit.

The Progressive Era and the modernization of Detroit's municipal government began with the election of Hazen S. Pingree as mayor. Here, on August 10, 1891, the mayor loads a shovel of dirt into a wagon to formally begin the construction of Grand Boulevard. Courtesy Burton Historical Collection, Detroit Public Library.

pal ownership. When he felt the conservative newspapers were not stating his position fairly, Ping refused to talk to reporters. Instead, he posted his own bulletins on the door of City Hall and the citizens flocked downtown to read them.

When the Depression of 1893 struck, causing widespread unemployment (during the winter of 1893–94, more than twenty-five thousand men in Detroit lost their jobs), Pingree sought to relieve the hardship by having the City Hall lawn, public parks, and other vacant land plowed up and turned into vegetable gardens on which Detroit's poor families could grow their own food. They were known as Ping's Potato Patches, and while it may be doubted that they actually saved anyone from starvation, the people loved him for them. He was elected governor of Michigan in 1896 and was reelected in 1898. He died while on a trip to England in 1901. His appreciative fellow citizens raised the necessary funds, much of it in pennies from schoolchildren, for a seated statue of Pingree that was placed in Grand Circus Park in 1903, a perpetual monument to one of Detroit's foremost public servants.

During the first two decades of the twentieth century, Detroit's population grew at an unprecedented rate. In 1900 the city's population was 285,704. By 1910 it had reached 465,766, and by 1920 it had mushroomed to 993,678. Detroit was becoming too big and too complex to operate with an inefficient municipal government. In 1912 the Detroit Citizens League was organized. One of those responsible for its formation was Henry M. Leland, thus marking one of the first instances when the automotive industry demonstrated its concern about civic improvement. One of the league's first projects was the publication of the *Civic Searchlight,* a journal that became the standard for the independent voter. As a result of pressure by the Citizens League, aided by church groups, the Detroit Board of Education was reorganized in 1916. A school board of seven nonpartisan members elected from the city at large—instead of from wards, as in the past—was provided for, and public education was largely removed from the arena of partisan politics.

On June 25, 1918, Detroit voters approved, by a large margin, a new city charter that embodied several unusual features. The forty-two-member council (two elected from each ward) was replaced by a nine-member council chosen at large. The power of the mayor was spelled out in detail and enlarged. All of the officials, including judges, were to be chosen on a nonpartisan basis. James Couzens, Henry Ford's former associate, became the first nonpartisan mayor under the new charter, and in 1920 the reform movement was further advanced by the reorganization of the municipal courts.

On June 25, 1918, Detroit voters approved a new city charter by a wide margin. James Couzens, Henry Ford's former associate, became the first nonpartisan mayor elected under the new charter. Courtesy Burton Historical Collection, Detroit Public Library.

Mayor Couzens was elected on a platform of ending the streetcar monopoly, and the issue of municipal ownership became a lively and bitter one during his term of office. Couzens dramatized the question in 1918 by boarding a streetcar, refusing to pay the full fare, and having himself thrown off. In office he sought to smash the combine by using city funds to build the St. Jean line, in reality a belt line that circled the city and crossed Woodward at Clairmont Avenue. Once this line went into operation in 1921, private ownership was doomed. In 1922 the question of municipal ownership was placed before the people and was approved. The old Detroit United Railways, which had been privately operated under city-awarded franchises, now became the municipal Department of Street Railways (DSR).

The DSR, however, was little more successful in providing adequate streetcar service than the privately owned system had been. It still was taking too long to lay tracks and extend lines to meet the needs of the rapidly growing city. To provide more facilities, the Detroit Motorbus Company was organized in 1920 and eight double-decked buses were purchased. The new service soon proved very popular, and additional buses were purchased. The competition hurt the DSR, however, and in 1932 the city took over the Detroit Motorbus Company and made it part of the municipal system. The DSR continued to operate both streetcars and buses until the decision was made to completely motorize the system, and on April 7, 1956, the last Detroit streetcar made its run on Woodward Avenue.

In 1925 Detroit was to experience the beginnings of a reform movement of a very different nature—improved housing for its black

Dr. Ossian Sweet and his wife, Gladys, were both charged with conspiracy to commit murder after defending their home on Detroit's east side. Courtesy Walter P. Reuther Library, Wayne State University, Detroit.

The NAACP hired renowned defense attorney Clarence Darrow (*far right*) to help the Sweets. Darrow stands here with his defense team after winning an acquittal for Henry Sweet (Ossian's brother) during a second trial. Courtesy Walter P. Reuther Library, Wayne State University, Detroit.

citizens. At this time African Americans were by and large restricted to purchasing homes in several well-defined areas. These included the East Side District, bounded by the river, Mt. Elliott, Mack, and Brush; the Warren-Tireman District; the Holbrook-Clay District; and the North Detroit or Carpenter Avenue area. In the fall of 1925, Dr. Ossian Sweet, a black gynecologist who had graduated from Howard University and who later studied under Madame Curie in France, purchased an $18,000 two-story brick home at Garland and Charlevoix, a comfortable east side middle-class neighborhood in which there had been some racial mixing. But the Sweet family was not welcomed. In fact, they received threats from their new neighbors even before they moved in. On September 8 the Sweet's moving van pulled up under police escort, but that night a crowd gathered, and during the next two days it became menacing. Several friends and relatives joined the Sweets to help them defend their home. Ten policemen were assigned to keep the crowd away, but despite their presence, rocks were thrown at the windows. At one point, the crowd surged toward the home and panic swept over those inside the house. Suddenly there was a blast of gunfire from an upstairs window, and a white man sitting on his porch across the street was struck and instantly killed.

Dr. Sweet and ten of his companions, including his wife, were arrested and tried for murder. The case not only united the middle-class black community but brought to Sweet's defense famous trial lawyer Clarence Darrow—a defense financed largely by the National Association for the Advancement of Colored People (NAACP). The judge to whom the case was assigned was Frank Murphy. The trial was lengthy, and its sensational aspects, together with the presence of Darrow, attracted front-page attention across the country. The first trial resulted in a hung jury, but the retrial jury deliberated only briefly before bringing in a verdict of acquittal. The trial prompted Mayor John Smith to appoint an interracial committee, the first in city's history, to find jobs and housing for blacks. This was really the first major breakthrough in both of these areas for Detroit's black citizens.

Shortly after the war Detroit experienced a short recession, but by 1923 the worst was over and the economy was again on the upswing. Unfortunately, the good times became somewhat too good. Serious inflation began, and people began complaining about HCL—the high cost of living. Wild speculation in the stock market and in real estate, as well as considerable overspending, caused no particular widespread concern. Inflation continued, speculation continued, spending continued, and Detroit, along with the nation and much of the world, was heading toward the crash of 1929.

Ford's Model A—the successor to the Model T—on the assembly line in 1928 at the Rouge complex. Courtesy Henry Ford Museum and Greenfield Village Research Center.

It was during Detroit's postwar years that the automobile industry reached maturity. During the 1920s the domestic production of cars and trucks rose steadily until 1929, when the milestone of five million units was passed for the first time. Not until 1948 would that figure again be attained.

Several factors contributed to this growth. Millions of soldiers had learned to rely on the automobile during the war, so it was one of the first things they wanted when they returned to the States. The industry was now producing cars that were safer, faster, and more comfortable. Millions of dollars were spent on researching such innovations as clear, unbreakable safety glass and more dependable brakes. The invention and perfection of the self-starter—thereby eliminating the crank—made the automobile available to those without strong right arms, and by 1920 it was standard equipment on virtually all cars. Also during the 1920s, the closed car, originally regarded as a luxury model, became the standard, and in 1925 the sale of closed cars passed the sales of the open models for the first time. Despite production increases, however, fewer automobile companies were able to survive. Difficulty in obtaining the financing necessary to adjust to new marketing conditions and to technological changes forced many companies to close their doors. By the late 1920s, Ford, General Motors, and Chrysler had become the "Big Three," although Hudson, Packard, Hupp, and Graham-Paige were still in production.

This period did see the end of one best-selling car, however—Henry Ford's Model T. For nearly twenty years the Model T had remained substantially unchanged, but the American public was looking for something new, and they found it in the Chevrolet. Chevrolet, which had been outsold fifteen to one in 1921, was selling more than half as many cars as Ford in early 1927. And so the decision was

Although the moving assembly line had been in use for more than ten years, these workers at Fisher Body still painted one auto body at a time by hand. Courtesy Henry Ford Museum and Greenfield Village Research Center.

made. On May 30, 1927, the last of 15,007,003 Model T's rolled off the assembly line. In 1928 the Model A made its appearance and Ford was back in competition, but the company never again had the field to itself as it did during the heyday of the Model T.

Gradually the automobile industry began to decentralize. The companies found it more economical and efficient to assemble cars in plants close to the consumer. Before long, Detroit proper was producing relatively few complete automobiles. But the major offices remained in the city, and Detroit continued to be the industry's nerve center.

It was also just before World War I that Detroiters developed a serious interest in aviation. On July 14, 1910, local residents saw their first airplane. The pilot was a barnstormer, Arch Huxey, and he flew his biplane at the Michigan State Fair Grounds. Huxey's flight and others like it were little more than exhibitions, but the war changed all that. In 1917, Selfridge Field was established near Mount Clemens through the efforts of men like Henry B. Joy, president of Packard, and

William B. Mayo, Ford's chief engineer, both aviation enthusiasts. When the auto plants began to turn out Liberty engines and other aircraft parts for the war effort, Detroit awoke to the fact that the air age had dawned.

In 1920 the first airmail was flown into Detroit, and in 1922 a seaplane service began operating from a ramp just above the Belle Isle Bridge to carry passengers to Cleveland. In that same year a young genius, William B. Stout, who had been a Packard engineer, designed an all-metal plane powered by a Liberty engine. Stout attracted the attention of Henry Ford, who saw possibilities in the airplane and laid out the area's first real civilian airport on Oakwood just south of Michigan Avenue in Dearborn. From that field Ford operated the world's first air freight service, ferrying parts from Dearborn to his plants in Cleveland and Buffalo. In the shops adjoining the airport, Stout built a trimotor plane that was taken over by Ford in 1925. This was the famed Ford trimotor transport, capable of carrying twelve passengers.

This cartoon of "Miss Detroit—an Ambitious Young Lady" appeared in the October 16, 1922, issue of *Aviation Magazine.* Courtesy John Bluth.

William B. Stout's air pullman *Maiden Detroit,* built in 1922, was a forerunner of the famous Ford trimotor. Courtesy Burton Historical Collection, Detroit Public Library.

Until 1927 the Ford airport, now the company's proving ground, was the center of Detroit's aviation activity. Besides serving as the terminal for passenger and mail service, it was also used for aircraft shows, reliability tours, air sightseeing, and other activities. The field was something of a scientific base as well, because in 1926 a Stout-Ford trimotor was built and equipped for South Pole exploration by Admiral Richard E. Byrd. An earlier plane, a Fokker, was donated by Ford for North Pole exploration. Named the Josephine Ford, it is on view today in the Henry Ford Museum.

In May 1927 aviation was given tremendous impetus by Charles A. Lindbergh's nonstop flight from New York to Paris. This was of particular interest to Detroit because Lindbergh was born here at a home on West Forest Avenue near the Wayne State University campus. Although he lived there only a short while, his mother, Evangeline Lindbergh, a teacher at Cass Tech High School, was a Detroit resident at the time of his famous flight.

With the upsurge in aviation interest, resulting in large part from Lindbergh's feat as well as the 1927 around-the-world flight of two other Detroiters, Billy Brock and Ed Schlee, Detroit began to think of itself as the emerging aviation capital of the world. Enthusiasts pointed out that the same elements of skill, know-how, and material that made the city the center of automobile production were applicable to aircraft. Companies were formed, notably the Buhl Aircraft Company, the Verville Aircraft Company, and the Stinson Aircraft Company. Each one produced excellent planes, but with the exception of Stinson, which was absorbed by the Cord Corporation, they did not survive the depression of the 1930s. Several aircraft engine and parts companies were established as well. Among the better known were the Warner Aircraft Corporation and Continental Motors.

Following his famous flight, aviator Charles Lindbergh met with Henry Ford (*left*) and toured the Ford airport in August 1927. Courtesy Henry Ford Museum and Greenfield Village Research Center.

At one point a group of Detroit industrialists began thinking in terms of a General Motors Corporation of the air. In 1929 they organized the Detroit Aircraft Corporation, a holding company that controlled or sought to control several of the most active and successful companies in the aircraft industry. Among the organizers were William B. Mayo of Ford and Charles F. Kettering of General Motors. Detroit Aircraft acquired the assets of the Aircraft Development Corporation, the Ryan Aircraft Corporation (builder of Lindbergh's Spirit of St. Louis), a tool company, and a flying service, and it negotiated for the Lockheed Aircraft Company. In addition, it took over the Grosse Ile airport, which eventually became a naval air station. But the scheme was too grandiose, business was not forthcoming, and although many Detroiters bought stock in Detroit Aircraft, the Depression burst the bubble.

After Detroit City Airport was built at Gratiot and Conners Avenues in 1927, activities gradually began to shift away from the

During his visit to the Ford airport in August 1927, Charles Lindbergh taxied the first Ford *Flivver* airplane out of its hanger. At this time, the Ford airport was the center of Detroit's aviation activity. Courtesy Henry Ford Museum and Greenfield Village Research Center.

Ford airport. Commercial services as well as private fliers began to use the new municipal field, and before long it was claimed to be the busiest commercial airport in the United States. Until the end of World War II it was the area's principal passenger terminal. Both during and after the war, major operations centered at Willow Run Airport, the city airport being too small to handle the big jet passenger planes. Even Willow Run soon became inadequate, however, and Wayne County developed the huge Metropolitan Airport—an outgrowth of the old Wayne County Airport, long used for private flying and as a national guard air base. During World War II its facilities were improved to handle the bombers produced in the area. In 1966, the last commercial lines left Willow Run and all the major lines concentrated their operations at Metropolitan. Metropolitan Airport has been enlarged, and several facilities, including a huge international terminal, have been built, making it one of the nation's busiest airports. Today City Airport, amidst considerable neighborhood and suburban controversy, is also being expanded and is experiencing a resurgence as a small commercial passenger airport.

It was also almost immediately after the end of World War I that Detroit's skyline underwent a major facelift. After New York and Chicago, Detroit took third place nationally in building construction during the 1920s. Sumptuous new public buildings, hotels, and movie palaces gave the city an air of lush prosperity, but the most ambitious new architectural endeavors were the towering skyscrapers that transformed Detroit's downtown skyline. Included in this list of skyscrapers were the Penobscot Building (1928), the tallest in the city for nearly fifty years, the Buhl Building (1925), the Barlum Tower (now the Cadillac Tower) (1927), the David Scott Building (1929), and the Guardian Building (1929). The Book Brothers took the lead in transforming Washington Boulevard into a replica of New

York's Fifth Avenue. The Book-Cadillac Hotel at Michigan and Washington was the showplace of the new development. The magnificent new movie palaces included the Michigan (1925), the United Artist (1928), and the grandest of them all, the Fox (1928).

In 1919 General Motors began construction of its new headquarters, at the time the largest office building in the world. This marked the beginning of the New Center Area at Second and West Grand Boulevard. In 1928 the beautiful Fisher Building was completed across the street from the General Motors Building. The Detroit River was also the scene of great building activity. In 1929 the Ambassador Bridge was completed, providing motorists with an alternative to the antiquated and inadequate ferry service. The following year, the Detroit-Windsor Tunnel was opened to traffic.

During the 1920s Detroit's population grew nearly 58 percent, reaching 1,568,662 by 1930. By early 1929, industry in Detroit was also at a new high, providing employment for almost 330,000 workers. Although the automobile industry unquestionably ranked first, pharmaceuticals, tobacco, copper, steel, printing, meatpacking, and leisure goods industries all contributed to Detroit's phenomenal economic boom. Then on October 24, 1929, the New York Stock Exchange collapsed. The market continued its plunge until November 13, ushering in the greatest economic depression the United States had ever known.

During the 1920s, downtown Detroit experienced a major building boom. The most ambitious new buildings were the towering skyscrapers that transformed the city's skyline. Courtesy Dossin Great Lakes Museum, Detroit.

ELEVEN

The Great Depression

THE CAUSES OF THE GREAT Depression that followed the stock market crash of 1929 did not, of course, originate in Detroit. They were worldwide. They can be found in the aftermath of the war with its ensuing inflation and in the European financial and political collapses. The fall of the stock market itself was a devastating blow. Thousands lost their money in the market. Everything tightened up and people stopped buying. The era of good times, easy credit, and unprecedented prosperity was over.

At the time of the Depression and during the years immediately preceding it, Detroit had two major industries—the manufacture of automobiles and the distribution of bootleg Canadian liquor. The latter began in 1916, in that reform-minded period of World War I. That year, Michigan amended its constitution to prohibit the manufacture and sale of intoxicating liquor. On the night before the ban became law on May 1, 1918, many Detroiters gathered in their favorite saloons in an effort to consume a good portion of the remaining supply. Needless to say, they were unsuccessful but they made a valiant try.

For the next year and a half, most of Detroit's bootleg booze came from Ohio. Then on January 16, 1920, with the signing of the Eighteenth Amendment to the U.S. Constitution, Prohibition became national, Canada became the chief source of supply, and bootlegging began across the Detroit River. Within a short time, Canada became the source not only for Detroit but also for Chicago and much of the American Midwest. Syndicates—such as the one led by Al Capone—moved in, and the smuggling of beer and whiskey from the Windsor area became a well-organized business. No one really knows the value of the liquor carried across the Windsor-Detroit border in the 1920s and 1930s, but it was in the hundreds of millions of dollars. It is said that 85 percent of all the liquor smuggled into the United States from Canada crossed at Detroit. At times the business amounted to 500,000 cases a month.

There was, in fact, no place along the St. Clair and Detroit Rivers where smuggling was not carried on. Each night, fast, high-powered boats made runs to the Canadian shore and back, all in a matter of minutes. After the Ambassador Bridge and the Detroit-Windsor Tunnel were opened, booze came across by the truckload. Individuals brought in single bottles hidden under their coats or in the upholstery of their cars. Women, safe from search by authorities, tucked bottles inside their girdles and waddled blithely through customs. This contraband was known as girdle or panty whiskey.

Every sort of ingenious device was used to get liquor across the border and to distribute it. A bank vault in St. Clair Shores was used as a storage place. It had more cases of whiskey than currency and securities. In at least two instances windlasses were rigged on

A bootlegger awaits a signal to cross the Detroit River from Windsor and land a shipment of liquor at Seventeenth Street, April 27, 1929. Courtesy Dossin Great Lakes Museum, Detroit.

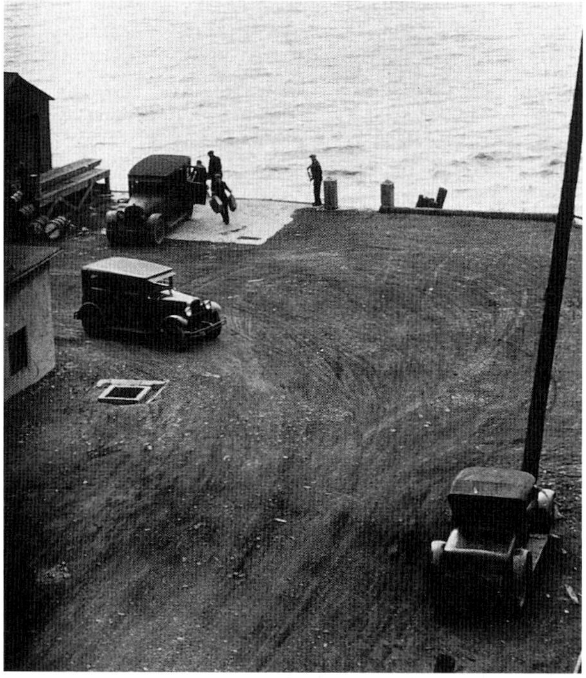

Rumrunners at the foot of Riopelle Street on April 15, 1929. This photo was taken by a *Detroit News* photographer hidden in a warehouse loft. Courtesy Dossin Great Lakes Museum, Detroit.

the American shore and sledlike contraptions were hauled over the riverbed. When customs or enforcement patrols were known to be out on the prowl, rumrunners were alerted by a system of signals tooted by locomotive engineers in the railroad yards along the riverfront. The Detroit-Windsor Tunnel was referred to as the Detroit-Windsor Funnel. There was even a rumor that a pipeline connecting a Canadian distillery with a Detroit bottling plant had been laid across the river.

With beer and liquor no longer legally available from their friendly neighborhood tavern, Detroiters turned to the speakeasy—or as they were more commonly called, blind pigs. This latter term, used to described an illegal establishment where alcoholic beverages were sold, dates to the 1870s. In those days, in an effort to evade the law, a store or saloon owner would advertise that he owned a pig

Detroit police raided this speakeasy and confiscated the distilling apparatus, along with a huge supply of liquor. Courtesy Dossin Great Lakes Museum, Detroit.

Customs agents confiscate a truckload of supplies at the border. Courtesy Dossin Great Lakes Museum, Detroit.

Federal Prohibition agents check a cache of Canadian beer produced at the Riverside Brewery in Windsor. Courtesy Dossin Great Lakes Museum, Detroit.

that was blind and that for a ten-cent admission charge he would allow a customer to view his pig. There was, of course, no sightless farm animal to be seen, and upon payment of his dime the customer was handed instead a glass of whiskey. It has been estimated that there were once as many as twenty-five thousand blind pigs in Detroit during Prohibition. In downtown Detroit, many different storefronts were used to disguise the illegal drinking spots. For example, one was located in a well-equipped radio store where several salesmen were ready to wait on customers. If one were a preferred customer, however, he or she was ushered into the stockroom and through an unmarked door that opened into a completely furnished barroom. There was a similar setup in a luggage shop, another in a laundry. There is also the record of a blind pig in a funeral home where the liquor was stored in caskets.

While many blind pigs did nothing more unlawful than sell a little illegal booze, others expanded their operations into another business. Gamblers took advantage of police nonintervention, and several casinos were opened in and around Detroit. There was the Aniwa Club, for example, on Van Dyke just off East Jefferson, patronized by well-to-do Grosse Pointers. There were others such as the Blossom Heath Inn on Jefferson Avenue near Ten Mile Road in St. Clair Shores, the Chesterfield Inn, the Club Royale, Doc Brady's, and Lefty Clark's big dice parlor over a garage in Ecorse. With things on such a free and easy basis, prostitution also flourished. There were several notorious houses in Detroit. When jobs were scarce during the Depression, many out-of-work office girls operated out of their apartments in better-class neighborhoods.

Conditions continued to worsen, and there was a great deal of corruption among the local officials. This was finally disclosed by the post-Prohibition grand jury investigation conducted in 1940 by Circuit Court Judge (later U.S. Senator) Homer Ferguson. As a result of

When federal agents raided this still on Gratiot Avenue, they poured the illegal booze out of the third-floor windows. Courtesy Dossin Great Lakes Museum, Detroit.

One of the well-known night spots during Prohibition was Blossom Heath Inn located on Jefferson Avenue in suburban St. Clair Shores. Courtesy St. Clair Shores Historical Commission.

Ferguson's cleanup campaign, the mayor of Detroit, the county sheriff, the prosecuting attorney, several other officials, and scores of top-ranking police officers were indicted and eventually jailed.

As was noted, the illicit liquor traffic was, within a short time, under the complete control of the big city gangs. In Detroit, two principal gangs ran rampant during Prohibition—the Purple Gang and the Licavoli Gang. The exploits of these two groups of organized hoodlums left a bloody mark on the city. Murder became so commonplace that it would make newspaper headlines one day, only to be forgotten the next day when some new act of violence occurred.

The worst outbreak of gang murder in Detroit happened in 1930. During the first two weeks of July, ten men were gunned down by gangsters, and the month became known as Bloody July. Then, on the morning of July

These members of the Purple Gang were photographed in a Detroit police lineup on March 30, 1928. By 1933 most of these men were in jail or had been murdered by rivals. Courtesy Burton Historical Collection, Detroit Public Library.

22, one of the most sensational murders in Detroit's history occurred: the gangland-style shooting of prominent and popular radio commentator Jerry Buckley in the lobby of the La Salle Hotel at Woodward and Adelaide Street. Once a gangland hangout, the La Salle later became a respectable retirement home and was renamed Carmel Hall. Buckley's murder was never solved; no one was ever really certain of the motive, and no one ever went to jail. The police, however, believed they knew the identity of one of the triggermen—a member of the Licavoli Gang.

The death of Buckley, official corruption, and the boldness of the gangsters led to a public disillusionment with Prohibition, and a strong repeal sentiment began to grow. The Depression helped this cause because it was widely felt that by legalizing the liquor business many new jobs would be created. In 1931 a government study of the effect and effectiveness of Prohibition, known as the Wickersham Report, flatly stated that Detroit topped the nation in Prohibition law violations. Prominent Detroit business and social leaders, supported by some well-known clergymen, organized a repeal movement. In 1932 Michigan repealed its state Prohibition statutes, and the following year it became the first state to ratify the Twenty-first Amend-ment to the U.S. Constitution, which repealed the Eighteenth Amendment. The legislature created a state Liquor Control Commission and authorized the sale of beer and wine beginning April 7, 1933. Detroit celebrated when the lid was removed, and blind pig operators hastened to go legitimate by applying for liquor licenses. In many cases they were granted. On December 5, 1933, the Twenty-first Amendment was ratified and what President Herbert Hoover had once referred to as "the noble experiment" passed into history.

While Prohibition ended, the Depression did not. Due to its industrial makeup and heavy dependence on the automobile industry, Detroit had been one of the first cities to

On July 22, 1930, popular radio commentator Jerry Buckley *(left)* was gunned down in the lobby of the LaSalle Hotel. Before his funeral, close to thirty thousand Buckley admirers filed past his coffin as his body lay in state. Courtesy Burton Historical Collection, Detroit Public Library.

feel the Depression. In 1929 more than 5,337,000 vehicles had been produced. In 1930 production was down to 3,363,000 units, and in 1931 it fell to 1,332,000. By the end of 1931, General Motors had laid off 100,00 workers in Detroit out of its 1929 workforce of some 260,000 employees. In 1932, Ford Motor Company laid off more than two-thirds of its workers, and of those employees who remained on the payroll, many went on shorter hours. It has been estimated that perhaps one-third of all those employed in Detroit were working only part-time. All told, 223,000 workers were jobless and out walking the streets of Detroit by the winter of 1931–32.

On the eve of the Depression, Charles Bowles was elected mayor. His victory came as a surprise, since Bowles had been attacked with unsubstantiated charges that he had Ku Klux Klan endorsement and that he was going to create a "political machine" that would destroy the city's nonpartisan government. Unfortunately, Bowles was unable to carry out his campaign pledge of economy because of the Depression-caused welfare burden. The majority of his recommendations aroused intense opposition, and as a result, on July 22, 1930, less than seven months after his inauguration, Bowles was ousted by Detroit voters in a special recall election.

Bowles's successor, Frank Murphy, a judge of the city's Recorder's Court, became mayor at a time when the Depression was creating almost unsolvable problems for the city. A liberal and a humanitarian, Murphy took on the task of alleviating the widespread distress. It was obvious that to avert starvation and homelessness, public assistance in the form of a substantial welfare program was essential. The mayor adopted a middle-of-the-road policy in the heated controversies between welfare advocates and the proponents of rigid economy. While maintaining the financial integrity of the municipal government, he ordered the public welfare officials to meet the steadily rising relief needs of the unemployed. Murphy's program for Detroit attracted national attention, and in 1933 President Roosevelt appointed him governor general of the Philippines. In 1936 Murphy successfully sought the office of governor of Michigan, and subsequently he served as U.S. Attorney General and as a justice of the U.S. Supreme Court.

During the Depression, Detroit families, like millions of other Americans, gathered around their radios every Sunday to listen to the inspiring and hypnotic voice of Father Charles Coughlin. Coughlin was a Roman Catholic priest and pastor of the Shrine of the Little Flower in suburban Royal Oak, and his

Frank Murphy became mayor at a time when the Depression was creating almost unsolvable problems for the city. Courtesy Burton Historical Collection, Detroit Public Library.

During the Depression millions of Americans gathered around their radios every Sunday to listen to the inspiring and hypnotic voice of Father Charles Coughlin. Courtesy Burton Historical Collection, Detroit Public Library.

first programs were of a religious nature. A persuasive and eloquent speaker, he soon began to talk about the social, economic, and political problems of the day. He quickly gained a tremendous influence by his attacks on international bankers, at whose doorstep he placed all the world's problems. Before long, Coughlin was the number one radio personality of the day. Along with his radio programs, he began to publish a magazine called *Social Justice,* for which he claimed 600,000 subscribers. But then, apparently carried away by his own eloquence and sense of power, Father Coughlin's speeches began to deteriorate into bitter and abusive anti-Semitic and isolationist remarks. He was finally silenced by his superiors in the church, and his magazine was barred from the mail early in 1942 because of its opposition to the U.S. war effort.

Another voice focusing on the problems of the day was that of Reverend Gerald L. K. Smith, a Protestant evangelist who had been allied with Senator Huey Long of Louisiana. Father Coughlin and Reverend Smith represented the extreme Right. On the opposite side was the U.S. Communist Party, more active in Detroit than in many other cities, working to make converts among the unemployed and welfare recipients.

Detroit's most explosive event of the Depression occurred on March 7, 1932. A Communist-inspired demonstration, it has become known as the Ford Hunger March. The march began peaceably enough as the demonstrators, about three thousand strong, assembled in downtown Detroit, intending to go to Dearborn and present Henry Ford with a list of demands that included union recognition, fuller employment, and better working conditions. As the marchers attempted to enter Dearborn, however, they were stopped by a squad of Dearborn police. The marchers were met by a barrage of tear gas, and during the melee that followed shots were fired. Four marchers were killed and a hundred were injured. The marchers finally dispersed when Detroit police arrived on the scene; they never reached the Ford plant.

The next few days saw a series of Communist demonstrations, and an estimated fifteen thousand walked in the four-mile funeral procession for the slain members. At graveside, thirty thousand gathered to hear the band play "The International" and the funeral march of the 1905 Russian revolutionaries. Observers said later that the affair had all the ingredients for the start of a Communist revolution. That it did not come off may be attributed to the fact that most of Detroit's workers had more innate confidence in the U.S. Constitution than in the red banner. But as one writer said in retrospect, "It was the best chance the Communists ever had in the United States."

At the height of the Depression in March 1932, three thousand demonstrators attempted to march to Dearborn to present Henry Ford with demands for union representation, fuller employment, and better working conditions. Here marchers cross the Rouge River Bridge on Fort Street. Courtesy Walter P. Reuther Library, Wayne State University, Detroit.

Another dramatic incident of the Depression occurred on February 14, 1933, when Detroit and Michigan banks were closed by decree of Governor William A. Comstock. In 1933 Detroit's banking system was dominated by two large holding companies, the Guardian Detroit Group, established in 1929, and the Detroit Bankers Company, founded in 1930. Each of these organizations was based upon a major Detroit bank, along with trust companies and other financial institutions acquired by purchase or merger. The two central banks were the Guardian National and the First National. By early 1933, unknown to the public, the two banking groups were in serious trouble—their condition a reflection of the speculative days of the 1920s and the economic setbacks of the 1930s. The banks held mortgages on which jobless borrowers could not keep up their payments. They had also granted large loans and now found that the collateral they had accepted—most of it in stocks and bonds—had shrunk to a fraction of its original value.

In addition to the two big banks, Detroit had four independent banks. These were smaller, more conservatively managed, and in relatively good shape. It was feared that if the two large banks collapsed, sound banks in Detroit and outstate might be pulled down as well. Efforts were made to bolster the Guardian with a large government loan; this proved to be insufficient, however, and a still larger one was sought. The government, unable to find security for such a loan, made a counteroffer. It proposed putting up part of the needed money if the large depositors such as Ford, General Motors, and Chrysler would guarantee the balance. General Motors and Chrysler agreed, but Henry Ford, who had long carried on a feud with the banks, refused to participate.

The outlook was bleak, and on Sunday, February 12, New York and Chicago bankers hastened to Detroit to meet with Detroit bank officials, industrialists, and government representatives to see if the situation could be salvaged. After a two-day conference it was agreed that the condition of the Guardian and First National appeared hopeless and that they should not be permitted to open on Tuesday, February 14, Monday being a legal holiday. Fearing that the failure of the two big banks to open would cause a run on the smaller banks, drastic measures were advocated. Governor Comstock was called in and asked to issue a bank holiday proclamation, closing all banks in the state effective February 14. He agreed, and the proclamation was written out at the Detroit Club during the night of February 13. Shortly before midnight, Comstock and his press secretary left the Detroit Club, walked around the corner to the Detroit Free Press, and made the announcement.

On the morning of February 14, Detroiters were in a state of shock and disbelief. People who transacted their business by check found they had no funds. Merchants could not pay their bills, and employers could not meet their payrolls. Business operations throughout the city and state were suddenly at a standstill. The only money that was available was that which people had in their pockets, in cash registers, or in safety deposit boxes. The large corporations, with banking connections outside the state, had currency shipped in to them, but even this source disappeared on March 6 when President Roosevelt declared a national bank holiday.

By March 21 all the solvent banks had reopened, although under tight restrictions. The two large Detroit banks, however, with their more than 800,000 depositors, were not allowed to reopen and were put through the process of liquidation. The large depositors waived their claims so that the smaller ones could be paid off, and the remaining good assets were sold to two new banks, the Manufacturers National and the National Bank of Detroit. Fortunately, by 1934 sufficient recovery had been made so that

EIGHT-DAY HOLIDAY FOR ALL BANKS IN MICHIGAN

CITY EDITION — DETROIT TIMES — EXTRA

330 YEAR, NO. 137 — DETROIT, MICHIGAN, TUESDAY, FEBRUARY 14, 1933 — 24 PAGES — THREE CENTS

Proclamation Closing Banks to Protect State

Whereas, in view of the acute financial emergency now existing in the city of Detroit and throughout the state of Michigan, I deem it necessary in the public interest and for the preservation of the public peace, health and safety, and for the equal safeguarding without preference of the rights of all depositors in the banks and trust companies of this state and at the request of the Michigan Bankers' Association and the Detroit Clearing House and after consultation with the banking authorities, both national and state, with representatives of the United States Treasury Department, the Banking Department of the State of Michigan, the Federal Reserve Bank, the Reconstruction Finance Corporation, and with the United States Secretary of Commerce, I hereby proclaim the days from Tuesday, February 14th, 1933, to Tuesday, February 21st, 1933, both dates inclusive, to be public holidays during which time all banks, trust companies and other financial institutions conducting a banking or trust business within the state of Michigan shall not be opened for the transaction of banking or trust business, the same to be recognized, classed and treated and have the same effect in respect to such banks, trust companies and other financial institutions as other legal holidays under the laws of this state, provided that it shall not affect the making or execution of agreements or instruments in writing or interfere with judicial proceedings. Dated this 14th day of February, 1933, 1:32 a. m.

WILLIAM A. COMSTOCK, Governor of the State of Michigan.

ERNIE SCHAAF SUCCUMBS TO BRAIN OPERATION AFTER KNOCKOUT

NEW YORK, Feb. 14.—Ernie Schaaf, Boston boxer knocked unconscious in his bout with Primo Carnera Friday night, died at Polyclinic Hospital at 4:20 o'clock this morning.

Mortgage Holiday Asked in Nebraska

War Supply Bill Hiked $24,000,000

Banking Holiday Here Ties Up 720 Million

Prisoner Is Slain By Fellow Convict

Utility Chief Took Life, Coroner Says

Lay $230,000 Theft To High School Boy

STATEMENTS BY OFFICIALS

GOVERNOR COMSTOCK

Crisis Caused by Threatened Withdrawals and Frozen Assets

Gives Federal Agencies Time To Work Out Stabilizing Plans

Under Secretary of Treasury Pledges Fullest Aid of U. S.

All Detroit Banks and Trust Companies to Close for Holiday

Appeal From Detroit Bankers For Eight-Day Breathing Spell

UNION GUARDIAN TRUST CO. DIFFICULTY CAUSES ORDER; BRINGING U. S. AID

Governor William A. Comstock at 3 o'clock this morning issued a proclamation closing all banks, trust companies and all other financial institutions in Michigan for an eight-day period from February 14 to February 21 inclusive.

This action, ties up for at least a week, $650,523,979 in deposits in Detroit banks alone. In addition, $71,567,808 of trust deposits are impounded.

About 500 banks and trust companies are affected by the bank holiday.

Governor Comstock, in a signed statement, announced the bank holiday in Michigan was due to difficulties in which the Union Guardian Trust Company found itself.

"It was the consensus of opinion," the governor asserted, "that the difficulties might be ironed out, provided time could be had for negotiations."

The governor's statement said the Union Guardian Trust Company would have had to close its doors today, and it was in fear this step would cause disaster to other banking

On the morning of February 14, 1933, Detroiters awoke to these newspaper headlines. Without warning, they found all their banks closed. Author's collection.

Detroit's banking community was once again on a sound footing.

Just as the causes of the Depression were at work before the people became aware of them, so was the process of recovery. Following his inauguration in 1933, President Roosevelt presented Congress with a program of relief measures, among them the establishment of the Civilian Conservation Corps, the Civil Works Administration, the Works Progress Administration, and the Public Works Administration. Other relief included a federal agency created to enable distressed homeowners to refinance their mortgages, thus avoiding foreclosure on their homes. Detroit City Treasurer Albert E. Cobo also produced a beneficial plan that enabled local property owners to extend payments of delinquent taxes over a seven-year period. This freed them from the fear of losing their homes through foreclosure sales. Known as the Seven Year Plan, this arrangement won Cobo such public favor that in 1949 he was elected mayor. He later became one of the city's most progressive chief executives. Radical changes were also made in the tax system. The state property tax was abolished and a 3 percent state sales tax was adopted, part of the revenue being rebated to local communities. A 15-mil ceiling was also placed on the amount of taxes local units of government could levy.

Thus, gradually, a better financial base was built and purchasing power was restored. People's confidence returned, and with it came signs of prosperity. Just as Detroit was one of the first cities to feel the Depression, so it was one of the first to find the road to recovery. A car-hungry nation began again to buy automobiles, and in 1936 the auto industry produced nearly 4.5 million cars and trucks.

Unfortunately, in 1937, when it finally appeared that all was well again, there was another recession. The Great Depression had not yet run its course.

City Treasurer Albert E. Cobo devised a Depression-era plan enabling property owners to extend delinquent tax payments over a seven-year period. Courtesy Burton Historical Collection, Detroit Public Library.

On March 24, 1933, after the city's banks reopened, an apprehensive crowd fills the main floor of the First National Bank located on the east side of Woodward at the corner of Cadillac Square. Courtesy Burton Historical Collection, Detroit Public Library.

Downtown Detroit looking north up Woodward Avenue from Cadillac Square on October 21, 1930. The Soldiers and Sailors Monument is in the foreground. The old Detroit Opera House is across Campus Martius. Courtesy Dossin Great Lakes Museum, Detroit.

TWELVE

A City of Champions

IT WAS DURING THE TRYING TIMES of the Depression years that Detroit proclaimed itself the "City of Champions." It all began with Gar Wood when he successfully defended the Harmsworth Trophy—the most coveted international prize for unlimited powerboat racing—in a race on the Detroit River in 1931. Then Eddie Tolan, a young African American from Cass Technical High School and the University of Michigan, won two gold medals in the 1932 Olympics, capturing the 100- and 200-meter sprints. The Detroit Tigers won the American League pennant in 1934 and then again in 1935, when

In 1931 powerboat designer and driver Gar Wood successfully defended the Harmsworth Trophy in a race on the Detroit River. Here, Wood (*left*) is at the helm of one of his boats powered by four Packard engines. Courtesy Dossin Great Lakes Museum, Detroit.

they won the World Series. The Detroit Lions won the National Football League championship in 1935. The Detroit Red Wings won hockey's Stanley Cup that same year, and then again in 1937.

The claim "City of Champions" was topped off in 1937 when Joe Louis Barrow, known as Joe Louis—the Brown Bomber—defeated Jim Braddock to win the world's heavyweight boxing championship. Born on an Alabama sharecropper's farm, Louis moved with his family to Detroit in 1926 when he was twelve. Rising out of Brewster's East Side Gym, he became the pride of Detroit and heavyweight champion of the world. Louis reigned as champion for eleven years and eight months and defended his title twenty-five times, records unequaled by any heavyweight boxer before or since. In all, Louis won more than $4.6 million, but he spent it and gave it away as fast as he earned it. Following his retirement as undefeated champion on March 1, 1949, Louis was so heavily in debt for back taxes that he tried to make a comeback. But age had caught up with the Brown Bomber. He lost his two title challenges and retired permanently in 1952.

Though not a native Detroiter, Joe Louis was raised in the city, and once his professional career was established he retained

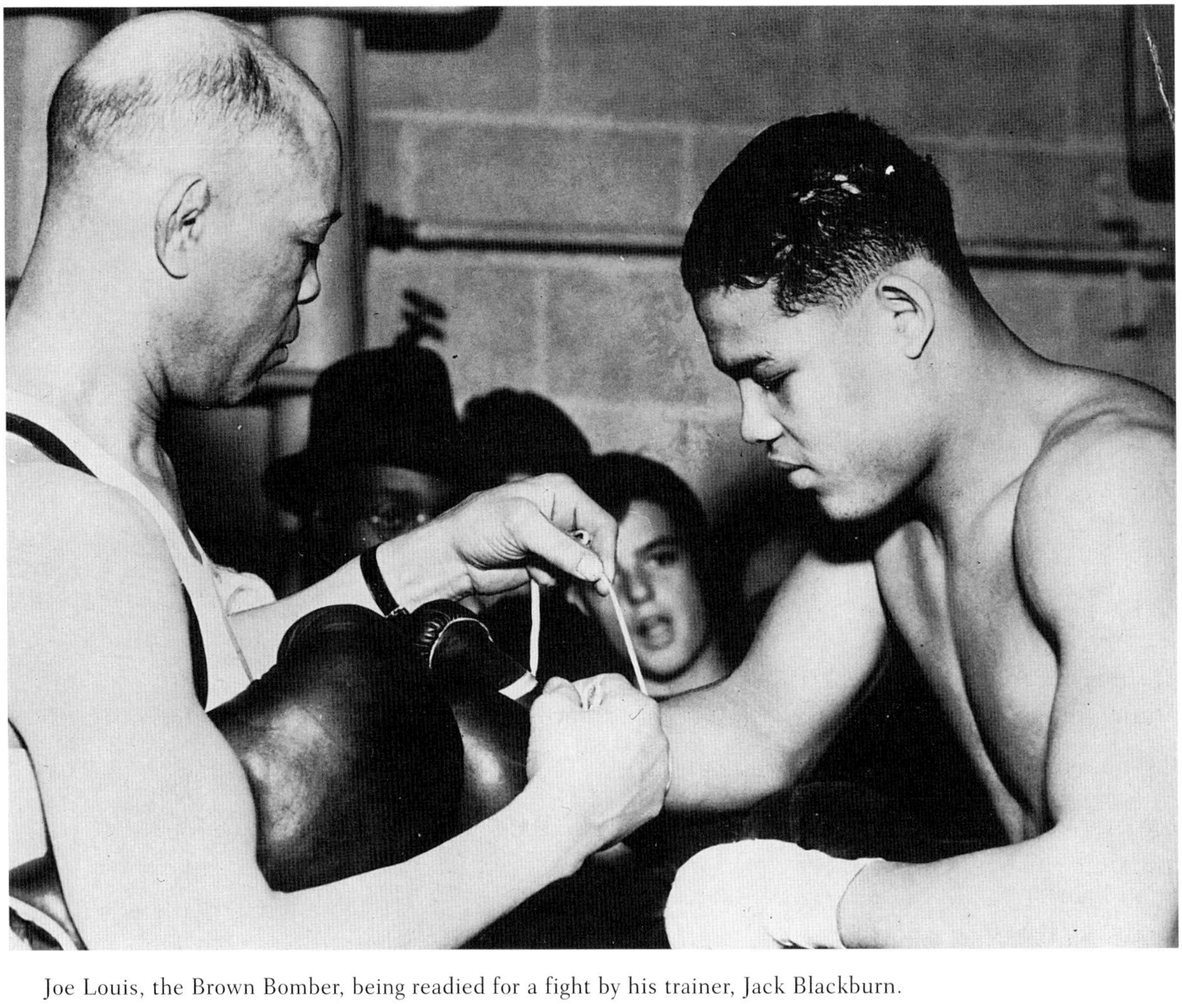

Joe Louis, the Brown Bomber, being readied for a fight by his trainer, Jack Blackburn. Courtesy Burton Historical Collection, Detroit Public Library.

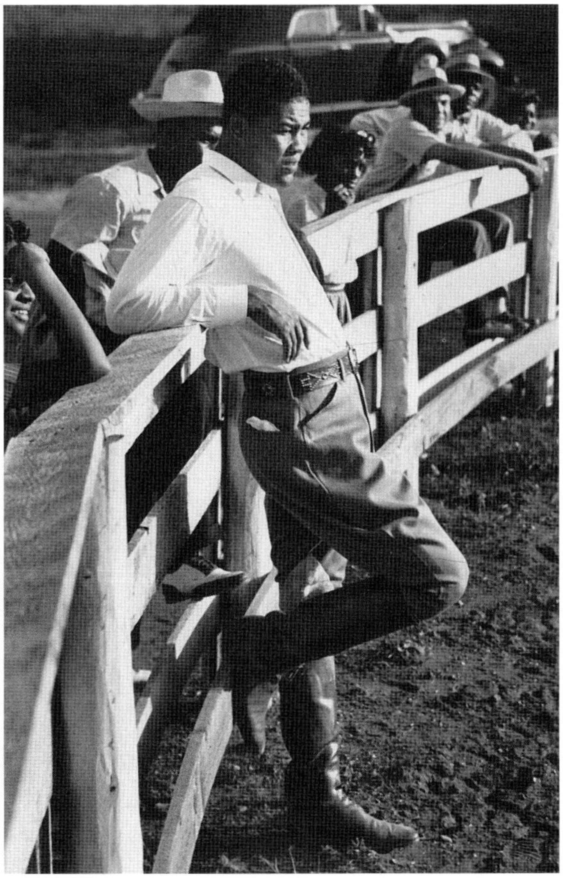

The champ at his Spring Hill Farm in suburban Utica watching friends riding horses. Photo by Tony Spina. Courtesy Walter P. Reuther Library, Wayne State University, Detroit.

close ties with Detroit. He lived in the city part of each year, bought a farm not far from the city, contributed to Detroit charities, and worked with the young people of the city. But Joe Louis was more than a citizen of Detroit. His major impact was on America as a whole. During the turbulent 1930s and 1940s, the Brown Bomber's public image was often ambiguous, reflecting the uncertainties of his age. But beneath the ambiguity was a clear message: Louis was a beacon of hope for his race as well as a champion admired and respected by white Americans.

Joe Louis was never forgotten. In tribute to this great Detroiter, the Detroit City Council on June 22, 1978, voted to name the new riverfront sports arena for Joe Louis. They could not have made a more fitting choice. Said old-timer Eddie Futch, a lightweight on the amateur boxing team on which Louis was the light-heavyweight: "He was the champion, is the champion and always will be the champion." Louis died in 1981 at the age of seventy-six.

Sports, of course, were nothing new to Detroit. Along with horse racing and sledding on the frozen river, boating was one of the earliest forms of organized sport enjoyed by the people of Detroit. In 1839, for example, the Detroit Boat Club was founded. Its members actively participated in rowing and sailing, and their first clubhouse was built in 1873 standing over the river at the foot of Hastings Street. In 1877 it was moved to the foot of Joseph Campau Street, and in 1891 the club built quarters on Belle Isle. Unfortunately, declining membership and increased operating costs forced the club into bankruptcy in 1992, and on March 2, 1996, the clubhouse on Belle Isle was turned over to the city of Detroit for nonpayment of rent and back taxes. Fortunately, however, the club's rowing team, funded by the Friends of Detroit Racing, continued to use the old Boat Club facility and is today the oldest rowing club in the United States. Many other boat clubs were organized in Detroit and in neighboring river communities. In order to provide regular competition, they formed what was known as the Detroit River Navy. Many great crews and oarsmen developed from this competition, and Detroit Boat Club crews regularly competed against the best universities and private clubs in the United States, Canada, and Great Britain.

Other river clubs concentrated more on powerboating and sailing, particularly the Detroit Yacht Club (DYC). Organized in 1868, the DYC bought the Michigan Yacht Club facilities on Belle Isle and moved from

Water sports have long been one of Detroit's most popular activities. Here the National Association of Amateur Oarsmen return from a four-oared shell race, August 16, 1877. At left is the clubhouse of the Detroit Boat Club. Courtesy Dossin Great Lakes Museum, Detroit.

Hydroplanes *Miss U.S.* and *Atlas Van Lines* roar past the Roostertail restaurant on the Detroit River during the 1976 Gold Cup races. From a painting by James Clary. Courtesy St. Clair Shores Public Library.

the mainland in 1895. That building burned in 1904, and a new facility was built. In 1923 the present DYC clubhouse was built just to the east of the old facility. Still a very active organization, the DYC sponsored the Gold Cup and Harmsworth Trophy races and was the home port of Gar Wood. For those interested strictly in sailing there was the Bayview Yacht Club, founded in 1915, with its clubhouse at the foot of Clairepointe Street opposite Belle Isle. Since 1925, Bayview has been the host of the famous Bayview to Mackinac Race. Racing up Lake Huron to Mackinac Island, this is today the premier sailing event on the Great Lakes.

Landsmen were also busy in Detroit. Cricket was in considerable vogue in the mid-1800s, and in 1858 the Peninsular Cricket Club was organized. It obtained use of a large field on Woodward at Canfield, then well out in the country, and held its matches there. The Peninsulars attained considerable standing and in 1879 played an all-England side, with rather unfortunate results for the local eleven.

After the Civil War the popularity of baseball began to rise, and as early as 1867 the game was being played at the cricket field, by that time known as Peninsular Park. Before long cricket began to be forgotten. In 1887 the Detroit Athletic Club (DAC) was organized, with baseball and track as the principal sports. In 1888 the DAC built a clubhouse facing Woodward opposite

The Detroit Athletic Club cricket team of 1890 poses at the entrance to the old clubhouse at Garfield and Woodward. Courtesy Burton Historical Collection, Detroit Public Library.

From 1896 to 1999, professional baseball was played in Detroit at the corner of Michigan and Trumbull. This view of Tiger Stadium dates from 1968, the year the Tigers united a city torn apart by racial and economic strife. The last game "at the corner" was played on September 27, 1999. Courtesy Burton Historical Collection, Detroit Public Library.

Garfield. The athletic field took in most of the land between Woodward and Cass and between Canfield and Forest. Although strictly amateur, the DAC's baseball teams were of championship caliber. The club also obtained the services of Michael C. Murphy, a renowned track and field coach from Yale. Under Murphy's direction, John Owens, Jr., became the first person known to have run the hundred-yard dash in under ten seconds. The DAC soon became a social center; the clubhouse and surrounding grounds were the scene of fine parties and concerts.

Coinciding with the rise of high school and college athletics, the DAC began to fall on lean times. In 1912 the old clubhouse was torn down, and some of the diehard members of the DAC resolved that the organization should have a new beginning. In 1913 the club was reorganized, and in 1915 a fine new Albert Kahn–designed clubhouse was built on Madison between Randolph and John R. Streets. Today this beautifully restored and completely renovated building continues to serve as a center of much of the city's social life.

Baseball was Detroit's first major professional sport. A team called The Detroits was formed in 1881, and after obtaining a franchise previously held by Cincinnati it became a member of the National League. The home grounds of The Detroits were at Recreation Park, located on Brady between Brush and Beaubien Streets. The park could seat five thousand fans. In 1887 Detroit beat St. Louis for the world's championship, and the following year the club's owner, drug manufacturer Frederick Stearns, sold off most of the players. The club lost its National

Ty Cobb slashes into third base to beat the tag in a 1909 game against the New York Highlanders (later known as the New York Yankees). Many consider Cobb the greatest Tiger of them all. Courtesy Burton Historical Collection, Detroit Public Library.

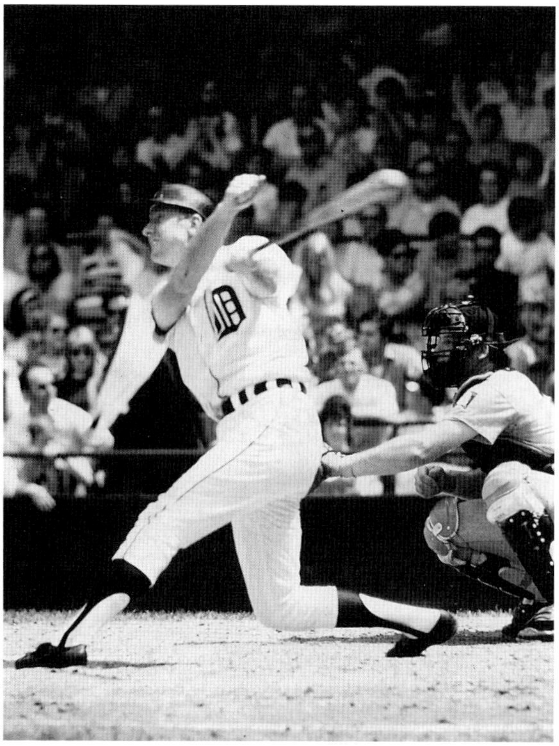

Hall of Famer Al Kaline at the plate at Tiger Stadium in 1971. One of the greatest right fielders of all time, Kaline was known for his fine hitting and his strong throws from the outfield. Courtesy Bruce Mugerian.

League franchise and became a member of the newly formed International League. A move was made from Recreation Park in about 1893 to build a new field at East Lafayette and Helen. In 1894 the Western League was organized and Detroit joined it.

With professional baseball drawing ever larger crowds, a bigger and more accessible field was needed. In 1896 the club owners acquired a new lot at Michigan and Trumbull. Part of the old William Woodbridge farm, this location—a popular picnic ground and the site of Detroit's first zoo—had long been known as the Woodbridge Grove. After the zoo was disbanded, Woodbridge Grove served for many years as a hay market. Here a grandstand was erected, and the site was named Bennett Field after the club's star catcher, Charley Bennett. The team was still called The Detroits, but shortly thereafter it was renamed the Tigers when the players appeared in black and orange striped stockings.

In 1901 the Western League became the American League, and Detroit has played in it ever since. Ownership of the Tigers was acquired by Frank Navin in 1903, and nine years later the field's name was changed to Navin Field. Later, when millionaire autobody manufacturer Walter O. Briggs bought the ball club, it became Briggs Stadium. When ownership passed to his successors, the name was again changed, this time to Tiger Stadium. In 1992 ownership of the team was acquired by the Mike Ilitch family, and on September 27, 1999, the last Tiger game was played in the old stadium at the corner of Michigan and Trumbull. With the 2000 season, the team moved into its new home, Comerica Park, whose story will be told later.

Some of Detroit's finest baseball was played by the Detroit Stars, pictured here in 1920. The team, part of the great Negro National League, played in Detroit from 1919 to 1929. Their games were held at Mack Park, "a cozy wooden park" at Mack and Fairfield Avenues. Courtesy National Baseball Hall of Fame Library, Cooperstown, N.Y.

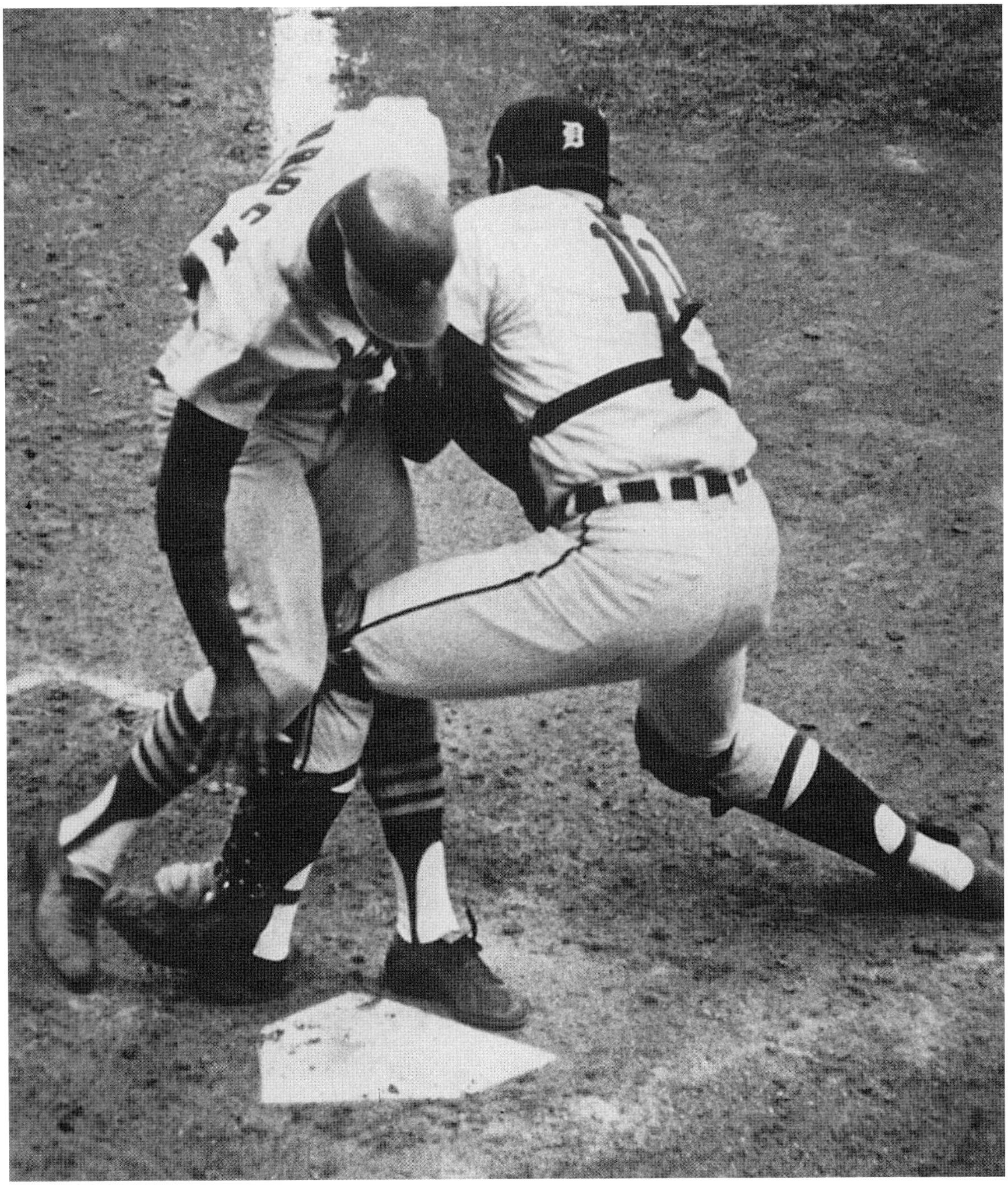

He shoulda slid! It was the 1968 World Series, and the Detroit Tigers were behind the St. Louis Cardinals three games to one. The Tigers won the fifth game after runner Lou Brock was called out at the plate on this play in the fifth inning at Tiger Stadium. Catcher Bill Freehan made the tag after catching a perfect throw from outfielder Willie Horton. Photo by Tony Spina. Courtesy Walter P. Reuther Library, Wayne State University, Detroit.

Detroit Lions star running back Barry Sanders on his way to a thousand-yard season on November 24, 1989. Before he retired in 1998 Sanders amassed the second-highest career rushing yardage in the history of professional football. Courtesy *Detroit News* Archives.

Joe Schmidt, Detroit Lions middle linebacker, number 56, stops running back John Henry Johnson of the San Francisco 49ers at the two-yard line, November 1956. Hall of Famer Schmidt is one of the greatest linebackers ever to play the game. Courtesy *Detroit News* Archives.

The Tigers won several league pennants in the early part of the century, but their golden era began in 1905 when a flashy young Georgian named Tyrus Raymond Cobb joined the team and began a twenty-four-year career that made him a legend. Throughout the succeeding years, others came to play at the corner of Michigan and Trumbull, players like Harry Heilmann and Micky Cochrane, Hank Greenberg and Charlie Gehringer, Hal Newhouser and George Kell, Al Kaline and Willie Horton, Alan Trammell and Lou Whitaker.

The growing auto town took to the club in its early years and supported it through good times and bad. Detroiters made local heroes out of anyone who donned the Tiger stripes, and celebrated in times of triumph such as 1940 and 1945 when the team posted World Series victories over Cincinnati and then Chicago. The sweetest victories, though, were without question in 1968, when the Tigers won an exciting come-from-behind World Series against the St. Louis Cardinals and united a city torn by civil strife, and then in 1984, when an incredible "wire-to-wire" season was capped by a World Series victory over the San Diego Padres.

Although there had been some professional football in Detroit as early as World War I, the city joined the big leagues in 1934 when a franchise was purchased from Portsmouth, Ohio, and the Lions entered the local arena. The Lions have produced some of Detroit's greatest sports moments with the glory years of Bobby Lane and Joe Schmidt during the 1950s. The Lions' first games were played at the old University of Detroit stadium. Later, games were played at Briggs Stadium. In 1964 the team was purchased by William Clay Ford, and in 1975 the Lions moved from Tiger Stadium to the huge 80,000-seat Silverdome in suburban Pontiac. During the 1990s, Lions fans watched one of the greatest running backs of all time, Barry Sanders. It was at this time as well that the Fords (son William Clay Ford, Jr., had joined the organization as the Lions' treasurer in 1980) made the decision to move the team back to the city. In 2002 the Lions will be playing in their new stadium, Ford Field, downtown next to the Tigers' new Comerica Park.

In 1926 the Detroit Hockey Club was organized and purchased the Cougars of Victoria, British Columbia. The team was moved to Detroit by a syndicate of investors that included Edsel Ford, *Detroit News* owner William E. Scripps, and Sebastian S. Kresge, founder of the S. S. Kresge store chain. The team was renamed the Falcons in 1930, and a short time later the Red Wings. The team's

The Detroit Red Wings won four Stanley Cups during the 1950s, led by one of the greatest players hockey has ever known—Mr. Hockey, number 9, Gordie Howe. From a painting by Joseph Maniscalco. Courtesy the artist.

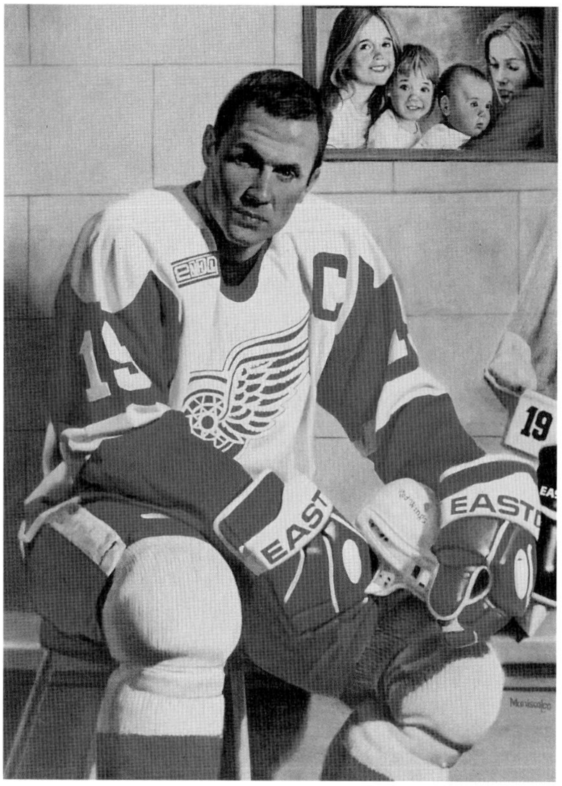

On June 7, 1997, the Detroit Red Wings, under the leadership of team captain Steve Yzerman, brought home the first of two consecutive Stanley Cups to Detroit. From a painting by Joseph Maniscalco. Courtesy the artist.

first home was the Border Cities Arena across the river in Windsor. Then, in 1927, the team moved to the newly built Olympia Stadium, located on Grand River between McGraw and Hooker Streets. Affectionately known as the "Big Red Barn," Olympia was the team's home until 1979. On December 27 of that year the team played its first game at the new Joe Louis Arena, located downtown on the city's riverfront just west of Cobo Center. Three years later, in June 1982, the team was sold by longtime owner Bruce Norris to Mike Ilitch, founder of Little Caesars Pizza.

One of the most successful hockey teams of all time, the Red Wings have given Detroit fans some unforgettable moments, including Stanley Cup victories in 1943, 1950, 1952, 1954, and 1955, as well as one of the greatest players the game has ever known—number 9, Gordie Howe. Then, on the night of June 7, 1997, the Red Wings, under the leadership of team captain Steve Yzerman, brought home the first of two consecutive Stanley Cups to "The Joe."

Professional basketball came to the city in 1957 when Fred Zolner brought the Pistons to Detroit from Fort Wayne, Indiana. The Pistons played their first four seasons at Olympia Stadium, then moved to Cobo Hall beginning with the 1961–62 season when exciting teams were led by Bob Lanier and the great Dave Bing. A few of the Pistons' earliest games were played at the University of

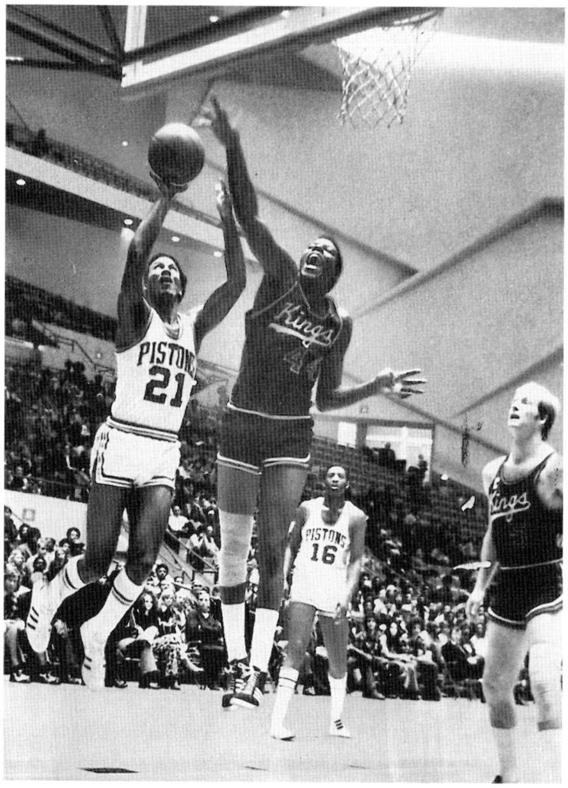

Detroit Pistons Hall of Famer guard Dave Bing, number 21, drives to the basket against the Kansas City–Omaha Kings, December 8, 1972, at Cobo Arena. Courtesy *Detroit News* Archives.

Detroit Field House, and they also had the distinction of playing one playoff game on March 12, 1960, at Grosse Pointe South High School. In 1974 industrialist Bill Davidson became majority owner of the team, and in 1978 the Pistons moved to the Pontiac Silverdome, where they played for the next ten seasons. In 1988 the Pistons moved once again, this time to the Palace, a fine new facility in suburban Auburn Hills. It was here that the Pistons enjoyed their finest seasons, with a team known as the "Bad Boys"—including Isiah Thomas, Bill Laimbeer, and Joe Dumars—winning back-to-back world championships in 1989 and 1990.

Since the earliest days of Henry Ford and Barney Oldfield, Detroiters have loved to race their automobiles. But it was not until 1982 that big-league professional motor racing, the Grand Prix, arrived in the Motor City. It was in that year that these finely engineered race cars first took to the streets of downtown Detroit. Since 1992 the event has been held on Belle Isle, where the world-class Grand Prix has become one of Detroit's premier sporting events.

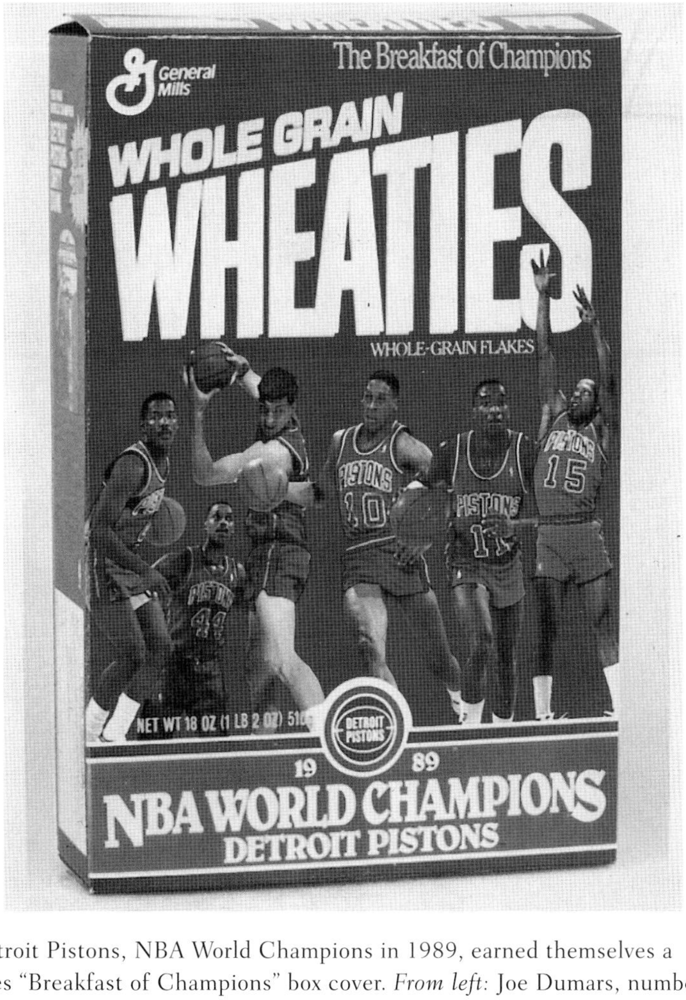

The Detroit Pistons, NBA World Champions in 1989, earned themselves a Wheaties "Breakfast of Champions" box cover. *From left:* Joe Dumars, number 4; Rick Mahorn, number 44; Bill Lambeer, number 40; Dennis Rodman, number 10; captain Isiah Thomas, number 11; and Vinnie Johnson, number 15. Courtesy *Detroit News* Archives.

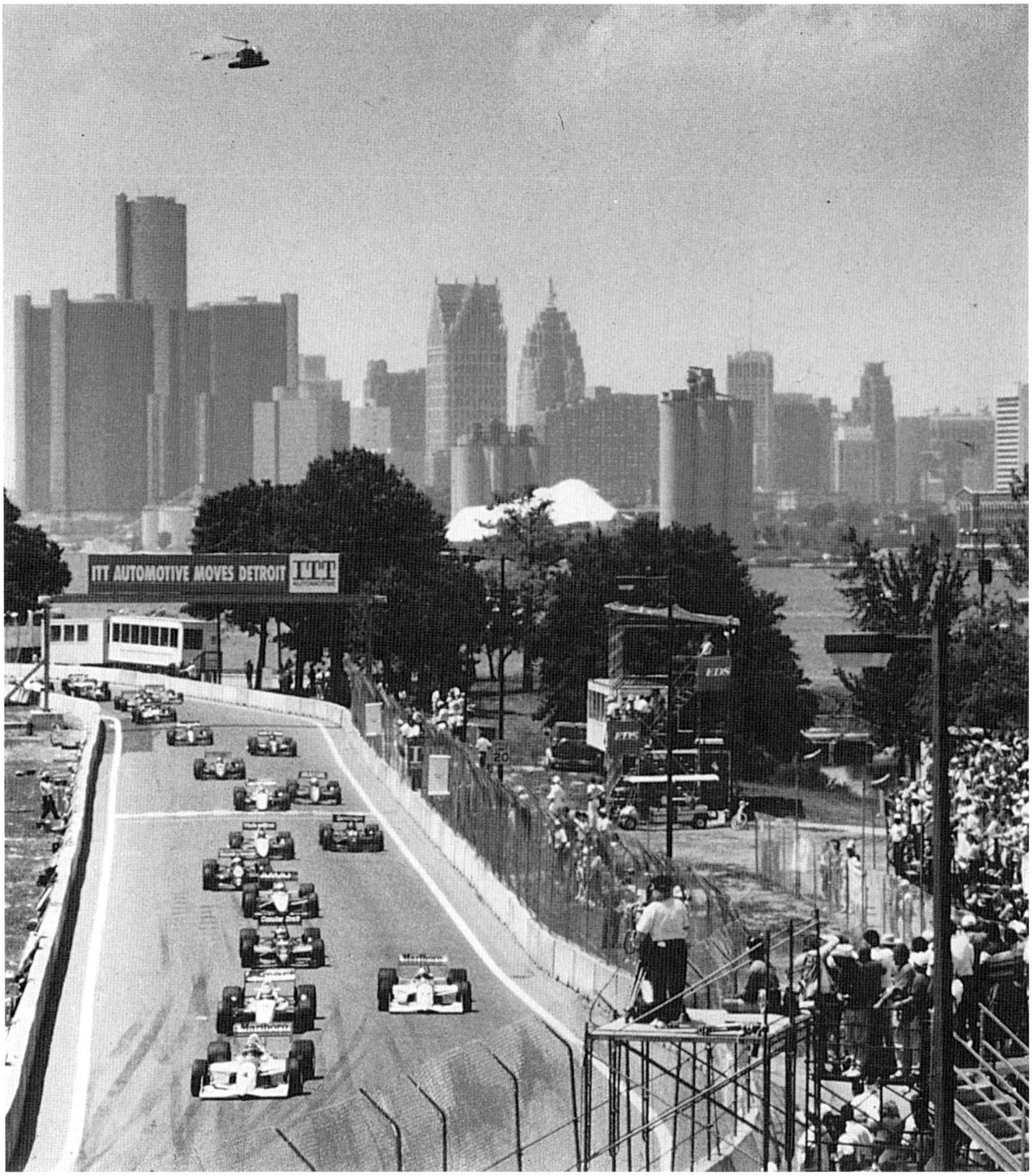

In 1982 big-league professional motor racing, the Grand Prix, arrived in the Motor City. Since 1992 the event has been held on Belle Isle. Photo by Tony Spina. Courtesy Walter P. Reuther Library, Wayne State University, Detroit.

Thirteen

The Rise of Labor

IT WAS OUT OF THE TURBULENT years of the Depression that a strong labor movement grew in Detroit. However, the history of the labor movement in the city began many years earlier. The Mechanics Society, an early type of labor union, was organized in Detroit as early as 1818, but the city's first real labor organization was formed by the printers in the 1830s. In 1839 they staged Detroit's first known strike. The strike's effectiveness is questionable, though, because as far as is known none of the affected businesses were forced to close. The group's structure at first was rather informal, but in 1848 the printers established the Detroit Typographic Union. Still in existence today, it is Detroit's oldest trade union.

The union movement itself began to grow in Detroit during the 1850s when a handful of local unions first became affiliated with national organizations. One apparent reason for the interest in unionization at this time in Detroit was the German immigrants. Many of the skilled German workers were union or guild oriented, and many were socialists who brought their ideas of craft organization to this country. The Civil War period saw further growth of unionism because of the wartime atmosphere of full employment, high wages, and still higher prices.

In 1860 the iron molders founded a highly successful union, and during the next four years the machinists, blacksmiths, carpenters, and plasterers also organized. In May 1863, Michigan Central Railroad workers went on strike after the locomotive engineers, meeting first in Marshall and then again in Detroit, organized what became the first of the railroad brotherhoods. In 1865 dockworkers at Buffalo went on strike and were joined by their Detroit comrades. By the end of the war the labor movement was large enough to form a separate division in the city's 1865 Fourth of July parade.

The first important local labor leader was Richard F. Trevellick, who was instrumental in establishing the Detroit Trades Assembly in 1864. This group, a coalition of most of the trade unions in the city, soon boasted a membership of five thousand—about 10 percent of

Detroit's population. However, the Depression of 1873 set the movement back and marked the end of the Detroit Trades Assembly. Although the assembly lasted only a few years, it was for a time a powerful force in Detroit. It served as spokesman for organized labor in economic matters and functioned effectively in city politics. Politicians actively sought assembly support at election time, and occasionally workingmen themselves ran for city office, often successfully.

In 1879 the Knights of Labor, which had been founded ten years earlier in Philadelphia, sent representatives to Detroit, and by the mid-1880s it had enrolled a large local membership. Yet many trade union people were frankly suspicious of the Knights (it had originally been a secret fraternal society), and by 1888 the organization was out of business. In 1881 the Detroit Council of Trades and Labor Unions was formed of representatives from each of the leading trade unions in the city (it became the Detroit Federation of Labor in 1906). It took an active interest in problems affecting workers, and on various occasions it even endorsed candidates for political office. In 1888 it assumed a major role in the formation of the Michigan Federation of Labor. One of the moving forces behind the council was Joseph Labadie, a printer of unusual literary talents and an outspoken advocate of reform. Along with Trevellick, Labadie was one of the outstanding champions of the labor cause in Detroit and Michigan.

By 1892 the Detroit Council of Trades and Labor Unions was made up of thirty-seven

The Detroit union movement began in the 1850s, but the first important labor leader was Richard F. Trevelick, who in 1864 led the organization of the Detroit Trades Assembly. Courtesy Walter P. Reuther Library, Wayne State University, Detroit.

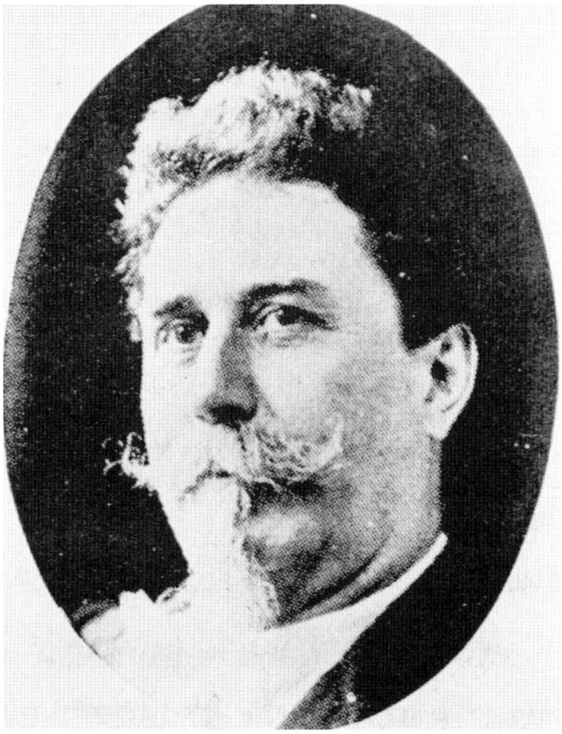

One of the leading forces in the formation of the Michigan Federation of Labor in 1888 was Joseph Labadie. A man of unusual literary talents, Labadie was an outspoken advocate of reform. Courtesy Walter P. Reuther Library, Wayne State University, Detroit.

local unions, many of which still thrive. Others, however, have been lost in the parade of progress, and their names and functions today leave a quaint sound, like the Horse-Collar Makers Union, the Cigar Packers Union, the Broommakers, and the Stove Mounters. Another that flourished at the time was the Florence Nightingale Union, whose membership was composed of women, most of whom were employed in the local shoe factories.

Between 1900 and 1910 the labor movement in Detroit seemed to lack the vitality of the era that had seen the formation of the Detroit Council of Trades. In fact, in the opinion of many labor leaders, Detroit at this time was a "poor union town."

The unusual growth of the city between 1910 and 1920 resulted in a large increase in membership of many craft unions. During the boom time of the 1920s, the highly specialized craft unions continued to grow. Throughout all this period, however, one group in Detroit remained largely unorganized—the factory workers, particularly the workers in the automobile plants. As early as 1903, the Detroit Council of Trades made some effort to organized automotive workers, but it met with little success. Other efforts were made in 1910 and 1916, but they too lacked results. One early attempt to organize Detroit auto plants took place at the Studebaker Corporation plant on Clark Street at West Jefferson, where the Industrial Workers of the World (IWW) helped launch a strike in June 1913. After some initial success, their efforts collapsed and the auto industry remained free of labor unions until the 1930s.

The unions had achieved little headway in the auto plants for several reasons. First of all, the auto industry was a high-wage industry. In 1918, for example, an autoworker in Michigan averaged $2.78 a day, while the statewide rate for men in general factory work was $2.19.

In the early years of the auto industry Detroit was considered a "poor union town." During the first World War women were employed in Detroit's auto factories to offset the shortage of men. Here, at Lincoln Motors, women machine-tool Liberty aircraft engine parts. Courtesy National Automotive History Collection, Detroit Public Library.

By the 1930s the assembly-line technique had been developed to the point where cars could be assembled as fast as a man could work. Courtesy Walter P. Reuther Library, Wayne State University, Detroit.

Then in 1914, Henry Ford announced his $5.00-a-day wage scale. In addition, the craft union leaders of organizations such as the American Federation of Labor (AFL) were simply not interested in organizing industrial workers. Autoworkers were fragmented by differences in language and culture, and the seasonal nature of the work, with long shutdowns for model changeovers, also discouraged union formation. Most importantly, though, autoworkers were essentially unskilled, and it was said that a new hire could be taught his job on the assembly line in just two or three days. The work was grindingly monotonous, the speed-up was commonplace, and workers were at the mercy of foremen who were sometimes corrupt and levied tribute as the price for holding a job. The industrial worker was not only easily replaceable but undoubtedly the most expendable tool in the auto plant. The workers themselves could see that with a large, untapped pool of easily recruited and cheap southern labor—both black and white—they were in no position to openly demonstrate an interest in organizing.

All this changed in 1932, however, with the election of Franklin Roosevelt and the passage of the National Industrial Recovery Act. This piece of New Deal legislation not only gave workers the right to organize, but even encouraged them to do so. It also required employers to bargain collectively with them.

As a result, a considerable amount of automotive union activity occurred in 1933, 1934, and 1935. In 1933 there were unsuccessful strikes against Briggs Manufacturing Company by the Auto Workers Union (affiliated with the Communist Party) and against the Murray Body Company by the IWW. The Mechanics Educational Society of America partially organized several Flint and Detroit plants in 1933 and 1934, but most of their members were tool and die makers. Then in August 1935, the AFL accepted the organization of a consolidated auto union, marking the beginning of the United Automobile Workers (UAW). At the outset the UAW was neither strong nor effective, and it lacked autonomy. The union was headed by a young Kansas City preacher, Homer Martin, who was described as an able agitator but a poor administrator. Seeking stronger leadership, the UAW turned for guidance to John L. Lewis, an AFL vice president and head of the United Mine Workers. Lewis provided the autoworkers with professional organizers, but more important, he walked out of the AFL and took the UAW with him. He formed the Committee for Industrial Organizations, which in 1938 became the Congress of Industrial Organizations (CIO).

The UAW, however, met with little success until the closing days of 1936, when workers staged a series of sit-down strikes in key General Motors plants—first in Flint, then at the Cadillac plant on Clark Street (Cadillac had combined operations at its new Clark Street plant in 1921). After several months of struggle, GM signed its first nationwide contract with the union on February 11, 1937. This was the first major breakthrough. Chrysler was the next target, and on March 8 the UAW launched massive sit-down strikes at the major plants, with 10,000 workers sitting down at Dodge Main in Hamtramck. Chrysler signed an agreement a month later, and by July 1937 the UAW had 370,000 members nationwide and 200,000 in Detroit.

Although the UAW now had contracts with General Motors, Chrysler, and the then-remaining independent companies, it still had its toughest customer to deal with: Henry Ford. Ford had announced that despite hell, high water, or the law, he would never recog-

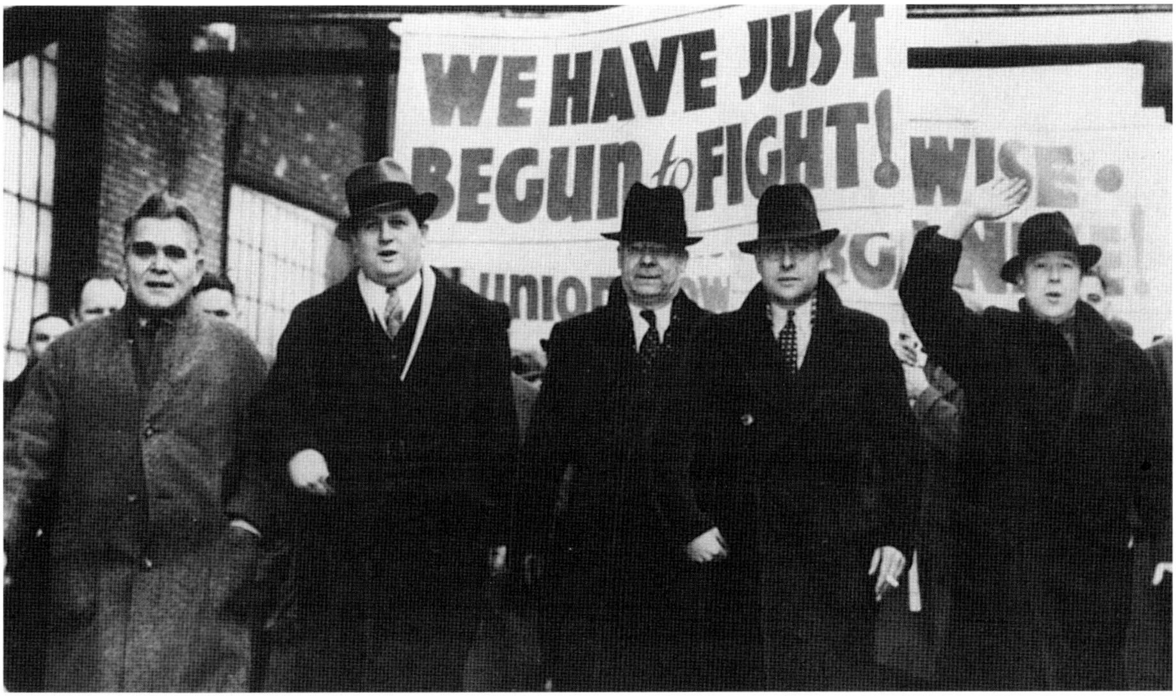

Union officials lead strikers out of the Clark Street Cadillac plant on January 17, 1937. From *left to right:* Julius Hochman, Richard Frankensteen, Leo Krzycki, Homer Martin, and Walter Reuther. Courtesy Walter P. Reuther Library, Wayne State University, Detroit.

The sit-downers at the GM-Flint plant in 1936 were never alone. Their comrades protected them from outside the buildings. Courtesy Walter P. Reuther Library, Wayne State University, Detroit.

nize the union. To enforce his policies, Ford called upon his special assistant, Harry Bennett, who directed the company's private army of Service Department men.

That the union was finally successful can largely be attributed to a blunder by Bennett. On May 26, 1937, a group of UAW people went to the Ford gates in Dearborn to distribute union leaflets. Among them were Walter Reuther and Richard Frankensteen. They were met at the Miller Road overpass to the Rouge plant by members of Bennett's Service Department, who gave the unionists an unmerciful beating and disrupted the women handing out leaflets at the gates. Two of the men were severely injured; the others, bloody and with their clothes half torn off,

Strikers at this Chrysler plant react to an injunction ordering them to leave the factory. Courtesy Walter P. Reuther Library, Wayne State University, Detroit.

Not all of the sit-down strikes were held in automobile factories. Here strikers sit on the lunch counter at the downtown Detroit Woolworth's store in 1937. Courtesy Walter P. Reuther Library, Wayne State University, Detroit.

were turned back, but not before press photographers recorded the entire disgraceful affair. The incident became known as the Battle of the Overpass, and from that moment the union, helped greatly by public opinion, gained the upper hand. After a long and bitter struggle Ford capitulated, and in May 1941 the UAW won out as the sole bargaining agent. Since then, the UAW has remained the unchallenged voice of labor in the automotive industry.

In 1939 the ineffective Homer Martin was voted out of office and replaced by R. H. Thomas. Thomas guided the union through World War II, a troublesome period for the UAW, which had difficulty holding its members in line and observing the wartime no-strike pledge. Then, in 1946, the UAW staged a bitter strike against General Motors that lasted 113 days. The strike proved the soundness of the new union strategy of striking only one of the Big Three at a time, thereby placing its target at a competitive disadvantage.

In 1946, Walter Reuther was elected president of the UAW and brought to the union a strong administration. It was not accomplished easily, however, and internal union friction sometimes took a violent turn. In 1948 Reuther was critically wounded by a would-be assassin, and an attempt was also made on the life of his brother Victor. The assailants were never apprehended, but they were believed to have been Communists whom Reuther had purged from the union.

In 1951 the UAW moved into Solidarity House, its new international headquarters on East Jefferson at Van Dyke on the site of a former home of Edsel Ford. Prior to the building of Solidarity House, UAW headquarters were located in the old Hyatt Roller Bearing Company building on the southwest corner of Cass and Milwaukee opposite the General

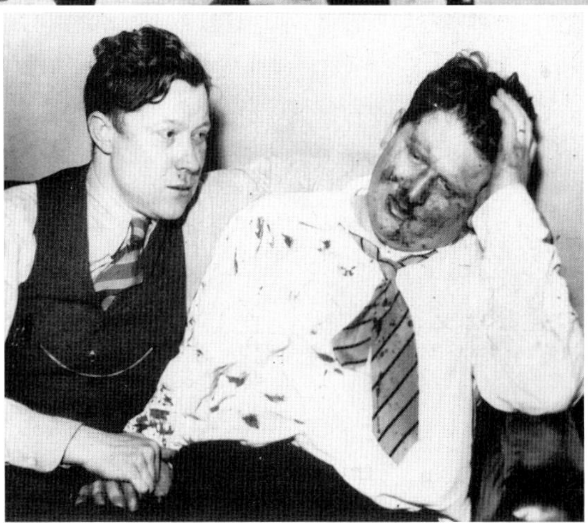

By early 1937 the UAW had contracts with GM and Chrysler, but Ford was adamantly opposed to union recognition. However, a blunder by Henry Ford's special assistant, Harry Bennett, caused the public tide to shift in favor of the union, when on May 26, 1937, a group of UAW women members, distributing leaflets at Ford's Rouge plant gates, were escorted off the premises *(top left)*. Press photographers recorded the rest: Robert Kantor, Walter Reuther, Richard Frankensteen, and J. J. Kennedy watching Ford Service Department men approach *(top right);* Richard Frankensteen with his coat pulled over his head *(center);* Reuther and Frankensteen after their beating *(bottom)*. Courtesy Walter P. Reuther Library, Wayne State University, Detroit.

In 1946 Walter Reuther was elected to the UAW's top office, and in 1949 a new labor contract was negotiated with Ford Motor Company. Reuther is on the right; Ford's John Bugas is on the left. Courtesy Walter P. Reuther Library, Wayne State University, Detroit.

Solidarity House, the international headquarters of the UAW on East Jefferson Avenue at Van Dyke, has been the union's home since 1951. Courtesy Walter P. Reuther Library, Wayne State University, Detroit.

Motors Building. During this time membership continued to grow, and in 1969 it reached its peak with more than 1.5 million members in the United States and Canada.

For twenty-four years after he was first elected president, Walter Reuther continued to head the UAW, playing a major role in the economic, political, and social affairs of the United States. On May 9, 1970, while traveling to northern Michigan, Reuther's light plane crashed and he was killed. Reuther was ably followed as president of the UAW by first Leonard Woodcock, then Douglas Fraser, Owen Bieber, and since 1995 by Stephen P. Yokich.

The Great Depression that witnessed the growth of the labor movement in Detroit was to last for more than ten long years. By the end of the 1930s a measure of prosperity had returned to Detroit, but full recovery was not to come from social legislation and financial pump-priming. Full recovery was to come with the onslaught of the blitzkrieg and the marching feet of invading armies.

Along with the UAW, the Teamsters had a strong influence on the labor movement in Detroit. Without question, the most recognized name was that of James R. "Jimmy" Hoffa. Hoffa joined the Teamsters in 1932 as a warehouseman and rose through the ranks to become president of the International in 1956. Here Hoffa addresses a meeting of Teamster officials, ca. 1960. Courtesy Walter P. Reuther Library, Wayne State University, Detroit.

FOURTEEN

The Arsenal of Democracy

THE DOMESTIC PROBLEMS OF THE Great Depression had tended to obscure the international scene for most Detroiters. Many had come to accept the theory that American participation in World War I had been a great mistake, and that the nation had been dragged into the war by British propaganda, by the munitions makers, and by the banks who wanted to secure the loans they had made to the Allies.

When the Nazis invaded Poland on September 1, 1939, many Detroiters felt that the United States should stay out of this new war and that military aid, given to the Allies, was all that would be needed to defeat the Axis powers. Others, however, were calling for direct American involvement. Then, on the morning of December 7, 1941, all speculation ended. With the Japanese attack on Pearl Harbor, the United States had no other alternative. The nation was once again at war.

As early as the fall of 1940, however, Detroit had begun to feel the impact of the war. On October 15 the Michigan National Guard was called into federal service after a summer of maneuvers. Once again, the Thirty-second Division was mobilized and other Michigan units were to follow, including the 210th Anti-aircraft Artillery Regiment and the 182nd and 177th Field Artillery Regiments. While the guard and reserve units

Before suburbia—Woodward Avenue, downtown Detroit in the 1940s. Courtesy Burton Historical Collection, Detroit Public Library.

With the advent of war, the auto industry went from building trucks for the domestic market to building trucks for the U.S. Army. Here trucks roll off the line at a General Motors plant. Courtesy Walter P. Reuther Library, Wayne State University, Detroit.

were being called up, more than half a million Detroit men registered beginning on October 16, 1940, for possible duty under the Selective Service Act. Altogether, 613,542 men and women from Michigan served in the armed forces during World War II, with Detroit furnishing about one-third of that number.

There was mobilization on the home front as well. The day after the attack on Pearl Harbor, army guards from Selfridge Field were posted at the entrance to the Detroit-Windsor Tunnel and the Ambassador Bridge to prevent sabotage, which was considered a very real danger. With the departure of the national guard, a new militia or home guard was organized, and Detroit had the strange experience of seeing anti-aircraft batteries installed in parks in defense against possible attack. As a precaution against air raids, a civil defense organization was created. Air raid warning sirens were mounted on public buildings, and people were taught the meaning of their wailing signals. More than 100,000 Detroit men and women were trained as air raid wardens, medical service volunteers, special police, and auxiliary firefighters. On May 3, 1942, a practice blackout was held and all lights in Detroit were extinguished for an hour. The city's air raid wardens, equipped with gas masks and wearing steel helmets, patrolled the darkened streets, enforcing the blackout regulations and requiring all unauthorized persons to stay indoors.

Thousands of military men and women, many of them aviators, were trained in the Detroit area at Selfridge Field near Mount Clemens and at the naval air base on Grosse Ile. Large military airports were also maintained at Romulus and at Willow Run. The Dearborn Naval School, in cooperation with Ford Motor Company, gave instruction to hundreds of mechanics. Fort Wayne was used as a Quartermaster Corps center for the reception and storage of military vehicles delivered from local auto plants. From Fort Wayne they were driven by civilians to various camps and embarkation points.

The declaration of war brought price controls and rationing to Detroit. To ensure enough material for the U.S. armed forces and its hard-pressed allies, rationing of gasoline and tires was ordered, thus severely limiting automobile travel. Later in 1942, shortages of commodities resulted in the rationing of meat, canned goods, shoes, clothes, and, unhappily for many, liquor and cigarettes. In addition, many Detroiters did their part by purchasing war bonds on a payroll deduction plan. Others participated in the activities of the Red Cross, the United Service Organizations, and other service and relief organizations. Many who stayed home cultivated victory gardens. Boys and girls collected scrap metal and milkweed pods, the floss from which was used to fill life jackets. Each evening, families gathered around the radio to hear the latest war news.

Behind the actual fighting front, the chief contribution to the war effort was made by American industry; in this, the role of Detroit's automobile industry was one of the most important. During the war the United States was called the "Arsenal of Democracy," and this designation came to be applied particularly to Detroit.

War production began in Detroit many months before the attack on Pearl Harbor. In 1940 the United States National Defense Council was created. William S. Knudsen, president of General Motors, was made its chairman, and in 1941 he resigned from his civilian job, was commissioned a lieutenant general in the army, and became the director of the Office of Production Management. It was apparent by 1941 what American and Allied war needs would be, and it was equally apparent to men like Knudsen that the automobile industry was best equipped to fill those needs. The problem was how to do it quickly and efficiently. Parts for tanks, planes, and guns were vastly different from parts for Fords, Chevrolets, and Packards, and yet the basic principles of engineering and production were much the same. It became necessary to find out which companies could most easily manufacture the new products of war—products they were then unfamiliar with.

Knudsen and his staff came up with the solution. Working with the newly created Automotive Council for War Production, they accumulated all the various parts that would be required and spread them out in a sort of museum display in the former Graham-Paige plant on West Warren at Wyoming. Then parts manufacturers, toolmakers, and everyone else with production capacity were invited to inspect the display. Representatives of more than fifteen hundred companies walked up and down the aisles looking at the samples. "We can make this," one would say, pointing to a part. "We can turn out these," said another. And so it went. As representatives found something their plant was equipped to turn out, they were given a contract or subcontract.

To build all these needed war materials, the government constructed new plants and turned them over to the auto companies to operate. Chrysler ran the great tank arsenal in Warren, Hudson Motor Car Company took over the navy gun arsenal in Center Line, and

New factories were constructed to build the needed war material. Chrysler ran the great tank arsenal in Warren where more than twenty-five thousand tanks were built. Here workers place a tarp over an M-3 tank at the arsenal in 1941. Courtesy Walter P. Reuther Library, Wayne State University, Detroit.

General Motors operated a tank arsenal near Flint. Ford assumed the responsibility for building B-24 Liberator bombers at its Willow Run plant, which was constructed at a cost of more than $100 million. The need to improve highway connections with these new war plants led to the beginning of Detroit's freeway system. The first segment was the 1.5-mile-long Davison Expressway, built in 1941–42 to relieve congestion in Highland Park and at the Ford plant. The Willow Run Expressway (now I-94) was built in 1942 and connected Detroit to Willow Run, some twenty-four miles to the west, thus enabling some twenty thousand workers to commute there from the city.

In August 1941 the production of automobiles and trucks for the civilian market began to be curtailed. On February 9, 1942, the last automobile was produced, and on May 31 the last truck rolled off the line. Production was not resumed until late 1945 and early 1946. All the industry's efforts were now concentrated on the production of war material.

The extent of the auto industry's involvement in the production of war material was evident in both variety and volume. The Chrysler tank arsenal turned out more than twenty-five thousand tanks, the rate of output sometimes reaching a thousand tanks a month. In addition, Chrysler plants turned out Bofors anti-aircraft guns, light ammunition, pontoons, aircraft engines, and aircraft fuselage sections and parts. At Willow Run, the first B-24 bomber came off the lines on September 10, 1942. A total of 8,685 of the huge aircraft were built there, more aircraft than were produced at any other U.S. plant. At its peak, the plant produced one aircraft every sixty-three minutes. Other Ford plants were producing aircraft engines, tank destroyers, amphibians, and gun directors. General Motors manufactured more than twenty-three hundred separate items, ranging from tiny ball bearings to thirty-ton tanks. The corporation also produced airplanes, airplane engines and parts, guns, shells, and marine diesel engines.

The plants of the other automotive companies were equally productive. Packard built thousands of Rolls-Royce aircraft engines and marine engines for PT boats; Studebaker produced Wright Cyclone aircraft engines; Nash

At Willow Run, the first B-24 Liberator bombers came off the line on September 10, 1942. A total of 8,685 of these huge aircraft were built here. Courtesy Walter P. Reuther Library, Wayne State University, Detroit.

turned out two-stage, supercharged, 2,000-horsepower Pratt and Whitney airplane engines; and Hudson built engine parts and suspension units for M-5 tanks. In addition, the companies turned out military vehicles of all types in a seemingly unending stream. At the Ford Rouge plant, a new kind of light vehicle was developed and tested; it was named the Jeep. Ford built them, and so did the Willys plant in Toledo. Both Ford and Willys were also producing jet buzz bombs near the end of the war.

During much of the war period Detroit bore the appearance of an armed camp, with uniforms of all the allied nations seen on the streets. The Guardian Building downtown was taken over by the army and turned into an ordnance center, a control point for all war production in the area and beyond. It was commanded by Brigadier General Alfred R. Glancy, another General Motors production expert turned soldier. By 1944 the metropolitan area had been awarded war contracts totaling $12,745,525,000, and there would be more. In September 1942, President Roosevelt made an unannounced visit to Detroit and toured some of the major war plants, including the B-24 bomber plant at Willow Run. It is reported that he was pleased with what he saw.

One of the most difficult problems facing the automobile industry during the war was that of securing enough labor. With so many men and women in the armed forces, the pool of skilled and unskilled workers was drained. To help meet this need, women were hired to fill jobs previously held only by men. It was the era of Rosie the Riveter, and it was soon

Most able-bodied men were called into the armed forces, and the industrial backup was handled by "Rosie the Riveter," as women who joined the workforce were called. Courtesy Walter P. Reuther Library, Wayne State University, Detroit.

apparent that women could indeed do this work and do it well. And so, a new social pattern was set, an outward symbol of which was the wearing of slacks by women. Previously unacceptable, slacks were a necessity in a factory. Thus the war and Detroit's automobile industry, in a real sense, promoted women's cause. When the war was over, many women did not return to their homes but remained in the labor force.

The need for additional workers, though, could not be filled by local women alone. It is estimated that between 1940 and 1943 more than 50,000 blacks from the South and 200,000 whites from West Virginia, Kentucky, and Tennessee—many of them Appalachian "hillbillies" who brought with them their undiluted racial prejudices—migrated to Detroit to work in the city's factories. As a result, Detroit faced a rapid deterioration of race relations.

Although Detroit's racial troubles had many roots, the one development that can best explain what happened in the early 1940s was the problem of housing for African Americans. By 1941 the housing situation had become intolerable. Blacks, crowded into segregated areas where they were forced to live under indescribable conditions, were victimized by unscrupulous landlords. Their resentment ran high, and whites in bordering neighborhoods feared them as a menace to their own somewhat precarious way of life.

It was not until the 1930s that Detroit's first public housing was built. However, none of the first projects were in black neighborhoods, nor were they intended for black occupancy. Officials were aware of the need for low-cost black housing and planned a project on the lower east side, but for some reason federal authorities changed the site location to an all-white, predominantly Polish neighborhood on the northeast side. It was named the Sojourner Truth Project, after the onetime slave woman who had been active in the emancipation movement. Detroit officials and black leaders objected to the change, pointing out that moving African Americans into that location would certainly lead to trouble.

The result was shameful vacillation and weakness on the part of federal officials. When white residents of the area protested, the National Housing Administration announced that the project would be occupied by whites. A month later, however, that decision was reversed and black occupancy was ordered. When blacks did begin to move in on February 28, 1942, a white mob gathered, wielding knives, bricks, and clubs. The mob was quieted with assurance that the policy had again been changed and that no blacks would be admitted. However, officials reversed their position again and the project went back to the blacks, who, protected by a

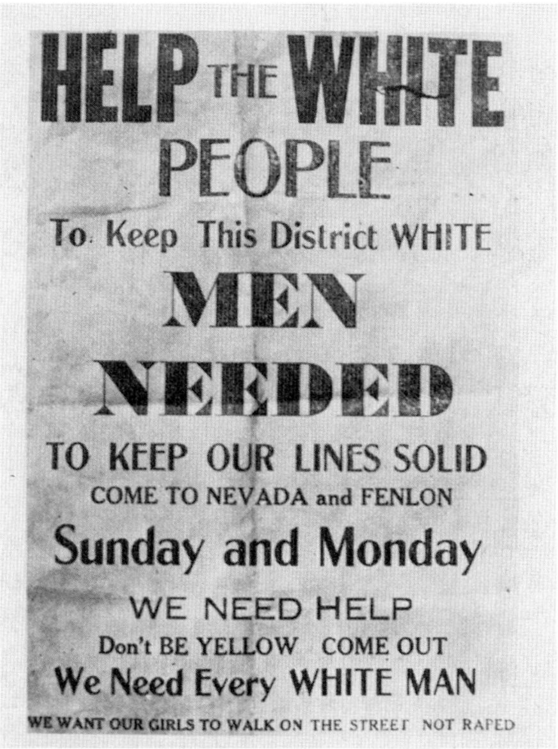

The Sojourner Truth housing incident produced hate literature such as this. Courtesy Walter P. Reuther Library, Wayne State University, Detroit.

cordon of 1,750 troops and police, finally moved in. If it was a victory over discrimination, it was also an example of how inept government could be in handling a difficult racial situation. Neither the white people in the area nor the black community would soon forget Sojourner Truth.

By mid-1943, racial tension in Detroit was tangible. Fights broke out almost daily, especially on packed buses and streetcars. In June more than twenty-five thousand Packard workers, protesting the upgrading of three black workers, staged a wildcat "hate strike," a common happening of that era. Many people predicted that Detroit was ready to explode.

The early summer of 1943 was extremely hot, and people sought relief from the heat in the city's parks. Because there were so few places for them to go, many blacks flocked to Belle Isle. It was on the island that the trouble started on the night of Sunday, June 20. No one knows what incident touched it off, but after sundown there was a series of fights, which were carried across the Belle Isle Bridge to the mainland. Then a fight broke out between African Americans and two hundred sailors at the nearby Brodhead Naval Armory. Before long, the mob had grown to an estimated five thousand and the police riot squad was called. Word of what was happening spread swiftly through the black districts. Wild rumors were circulated, and African Americans surged into the streets of the lower east side. Whites, unaware of what was happening, went to work as usual on Monday, some driving through riot-torn streets. Some were attacked and beaten, and at least one was killed.

As news of what was going on spread across the city, white mobs gathered and started to counterattack. General fighting broke out, the worst between Vernor and

Although members of the Detroit Urban League traveled to Washington, D.C., to protest the government's handling of the Sojourner Truth housing project, it did not prevent the riot of June 1943. Courtesy Walter P. Reuther Library, Wayne State University, Detroit.

Forest along Woodward and John R. Streetcars were stopped and blacks taken off and beaten; automobiles carrying blacks were tipped over and set on fire. Later in the day, a white mob of shouting men and boys, many of them in their early teens, moved downtown and gathered around City Hall. Blacks on their way home from work were caught in Cadillac Square as they transferred from one streetcar to another, and one was beaten to death on the Fort Street steps of the Federal Building.

Realizing that the police could no longer control the situation, Governor Harry F. Kelly proclaimed martial law and called for federal troop intervention. About 9:30 P.M. on Monday, June 21, the first contingent of twenty-five hundred troop arrived in the city. By nightfall order was restored, but for the next ten days Detroit was an armed camp. The troops remained until June 30, encamped on the lawn of the Main Public Library and at other strategic locations. No further major incidents occurred.

Altogether, thirty-four persons, twenty-three of them blacks, were killed during the riot. Hundreds were injured, eighteen hundred arrests were made, and property damage

The first major attempt to provide public housing for Detroit blacks turned into a battle between local and federal governments and eventually, in June 1943, into a black and white battle fought in the streets. Here a young black man is attacked by a group of whites *(above)*; a crowd watches an automobile burn on Woodward Avenue *(top right)*; and federal troops are called in to quell the riot *(bottom right)*. Courtesy Walter P. Reuther Library, Wayne State University, Detroit.

ran into the millions of dollars. Within a few short days, Detroit was back to its wartime pattern of life. Unfortunately, bitter feelings lingered and little was accomplished in attacking the many problems that had brought on that dreadful week of rioting.

On June 6, 1944, the great Allied armada landed on the beaches of Normandy. Gradually the enemy was pushed back, and on May 8, 1945, Nazi Germany surrendered. The war effort did not slacken, however, and on August 6 the United States crushed any last Japanese war hopes when the first atomic bomb was exploded over Hiroshima. With the dreadful destruction caused by the A-bomb, the Japanese realized that their cause was lost, and on August 14 the shattered and defeated Japanese Empire surrendered. When the news reached the city, a half million cheering, shouting Detroiters flocked into the downtown area for a great victory celebration, expressing their joy that at long last the war was finally over.

The years immediately following World War II were a time of prosperity for Detroit. True, there was a postwar period of adjustment as the sudden demobilization brought with it

In August 1945 the Japanese surrendered, and the citizens of Detroit poured into the streets to celebrate. Courtesy Walter P. Reuther Library, Wayne State University, Detroit.

equally sudden problems. There were shortages, inflation, and strikes. But the auto industry was booming and the first steps of urban renewal were being taken. The city's population was also on the rise. In 1940 Detroit's population stood at 1,623,452; by 1950 it reached its peak of 1,849,568.

On July 24, 1951, the city celebrated the 250th anniversary of its founding by Cadillac. At the corner of Woodward and Kirby the fine new Detroit Historical Museum was opened, a grand parade was held on Woodward Avenue, and that evening thousands of Detroiters gathered in Grand Circus Park to join in the lighting of a giant birthday cake. There was a feeling of optimism in the air. The future indeed looked bright.

On July 3, 1945, Ford produced its first postwar civilian automobile, a 1946 Super Deluxe two-door sedan. Here, with Henry Ford II at the wheel, the auto rolls off the line at the Rouge plant. Courtesy Henry Ford Museum and Greenfield Village Research Center.

President Harry S. Truman on the reviewing stand in front of the old City Hall for the big parade down Woodward. Truman came to Detroit on July 28, 1951, for the 250th anniversary of the city. Michigan Governor G. Mennen Williams introduced the president to the crowd. Photo by Tony Spina. Courtesy Walter P. Reuther Library, Wayne State University, Detroit.

FIFTEEN

A City of Change

As Detroit entered the 1950s and 1960s, it was to undergo a number of important changes. Some of the most important of these changes were to occur within the automobile industry.

During the first week of April 1947, the Rouge River, flooded by spring rains, overflowed its banks. Water from the river poured into the powerhouse on the Ford estate "Fairlane"—which still relied solely on its own facilities for generating electricity—and the lights and furnaces in the mansion flickered out. There, on April 7, just before midnight, in a house now heated by wood fires and lighted by candles and oil lamps, eighty-three-year-old Henry Ford died, and an automotive era came to an end.

In 1919, Ford's only son, Edsel, had become president of the company, but when Edsel died in 1943 the elder Ford resumed control. In actuality, the corporation was now run by Harry Bennett, head of the company's Service Department; as a result of some of Bennett's decisions, operations began to suffer. In 1945, Mrs. Edsel Ford and other

In 1945 the Ford family took control of the company from the aging Henry Ford, and young Henry Ford II was named president. Here, in 1953, in the front seat of a new Lincoln convertible are the three grandsons of the company founder. *From left:* William Clay Ford, Benson Ford, and Henry Ford II. Photo by Tony Spina. Courtesy Walter P. Reuther Library, Wayne State University, Detroit.

members of the family gained control of the company, and young Henry Ford II, Edsel's son, became president. Bennett was forced out, and major changes were made at the corporation's executive level. A staff of able, vigorous, and enthusiastic young men was brought in, including Robert S. McNamara (future U.S. Secretary of Defense) and Arjay Miller (future Ford president). Known in the industry as the "Whiz Kids," they overhauled every aspect of the company's operations. Within months the Ford Motor Company once again had a sound management structure and a promising future.

Another important change occurred in 1954 when Nash, a Wisconsin-based company, became American Motors and absorbed the Hudson Motor Car Company. Shortly thereafter, the Nash and Hudson lines were discontinued, and American Motors turned to the production of the smaller Rambler automobile. The year 1954 also saw the Packard Motor Company taken over by the Indiana-based Studebaker Corporation. In 1956 the Detroit Packard plant was closed, and the last Packard was built in 1958. According to one estimate, these plant closings, all on Detroit's east side, cost the area over seventy thousand jobs. Then, in 1963, Studebaker ended all auto production in the United States and built cars only in Canada. But the move was short-lived; three years later the final Studebaker was built, and the company closed its doors for the last time.

In 1946 Detroit celebrated the fiftieth anniversary of the automobile with a series of special events and parties and a grand parade down Woodward Avenue. That same year a new line of automobiles was introduced to the American public when Kaiser-Frazer began production in the old bomber plant at Willow Run. In 1953 the company merged with the

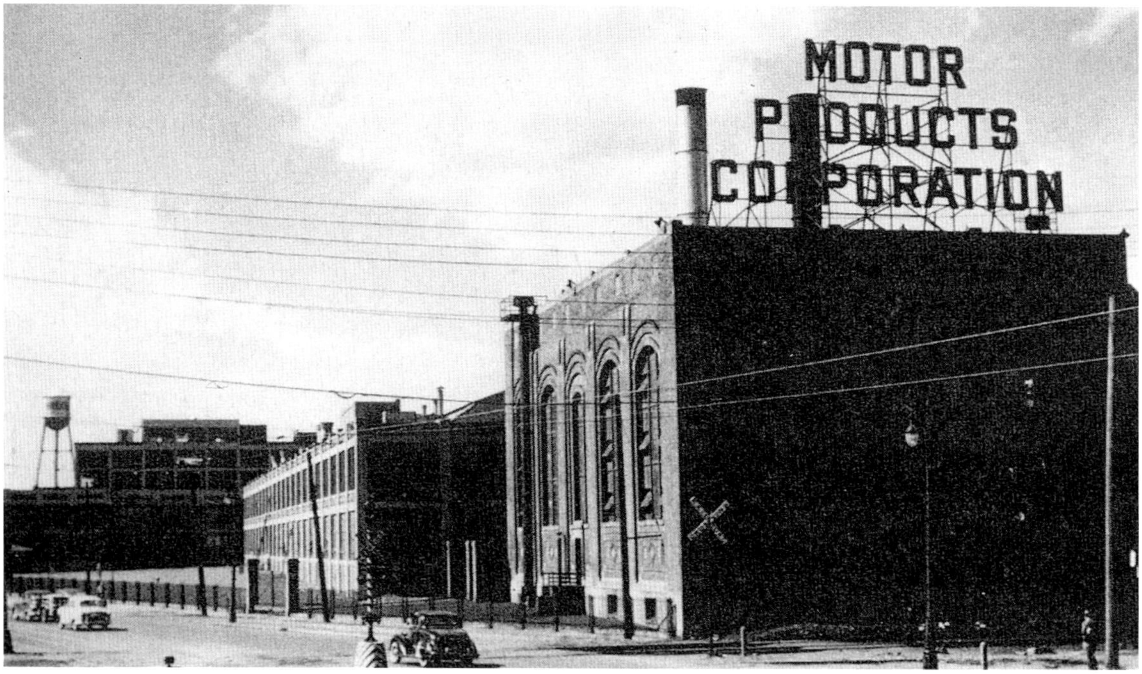

Two of the several plants that closed on Detroit's east side in the 1950s were the Motor Products and Briggs factories. Altogether, the east side lost more than seventy thousand jobs between 1954 and 1960. Courtesy Walter P. Reuther Library, Wayne State University, Detroit.

The Kaiser-Frazer Corporation assembly line at its Willow Run plant. The company ceased automobile production in 1955. Courtesy National Automotive History Collection, Detroit Public Library.

Willys Corporation of Toledo, then ceased passenger car production in 1955 while continuing to manufacture trucks and jeeps. In 1970 the company merged with American Motors, which dropped the production of trucks while expanding the production of the jeep line. By this date, the manufacturing of passenger cars in the United States was down to the Big Three and the much smaller American Motors.

The 1950s and 1960s marked several production milestones for the auto industry. In 1955 production passed the 9 million mark at 9,169,292, with nearly 8 million passenger cars and more than 1.2 million motor trucks and buses manufactured. Ten years later, another all-time one-year production record was set when 11,057,366 motor vehicles were produced. Then, in 1967, General Motors turned out its 100 millionth unit, a Chevrolet, and a few days later Ford passed the 70 million mark. The following year, the U.S. automotive industry manufactured its 250 millionth motor vehicle.

Along with these changes in the automobile industry, Detroit was to see a major change in the roads upon which these cars and trucks were to travel. These were the city's freeways—or expressways, as they were first called. It began in 1950 when the first portion of the north-south John C. Lodge was opened. The existing Willow Run Expressway was gradually extended eastward toward Mt. Clemens and renamed the Edsel Ford Expressway (I-94) in the process. With the passage of the Federal Highway Act of 1956, when the interstate highway system was initiated, the city's freeway network was expanded. During the next twenty years, the Detroit expressway system grew to include the Chrysler (I-75 northbound), the Fisher (I-75 southbound), the Jeffries (I-96), and the Reuther (I-696). By the early 1970s, almost two hundred miles of freeway were

Detroit's freeways began accommodating the automobile in 1950, and in the next twenty-five years, 265 miles of freeways were either built or under construction. Here is the Lodge Freeway looking south toward downtown. Courtesy Dossin Great Lakes Museum, Detroit.

completed in the Detroit metropolitan area, with another sixty-five miles under construction or scheduled for construction. This gave Detroit one of the most extensive freeway networks in the country.

These giant roadways created some problems as they solved others. While they allowed the rapid movement of vast numbers of cars and trucks across the city, they dislocated the thousands of people who lived in their path. By 1970 an estimated 20,400 homes in the Detroit metropolitan area had been demolished for freeway construction. In addition, the freeways divided or destroyed many of the city's neighborhoods. This was particularly true in Detroit's inner city, because most of the freeways converged upon the downtown area. For example, a predominantly Mexican American neighborhood west of the central business district became practically inaccessible.

As the freeways provided easy access to the plentiful land to the east, west, and north, Detroit's population began to seep outward. The city's lack of natural boundaries or nearby cities promoted this movement, and Detroiters discarded inner-city property as if it were a three-year-old car. White ethnic groups tended to move out along the nearest radial. African Americans also gained mobility and access to more desirable neighborhoods.

In 1950 the city's population was at an all-time high of 1,849,568, and the population of the suburban area was 1,166,629. By 1960 the city's population had fallen to 1,670,144, while the suburban area had almost doubled to 2,092,216. In 1970 these figures stood at 1,511,482 and 2,688,449, respectively.

The move to the suburbs has been almost exclusively a move by Detroit's white population, resulting in a dramatic shift in the city's racial composition. During the 1950s and 1960s, between 7,000 and 9,000 Detroit households changed from white to black each year. In 1950, 300,506 blacks lived in the city—16.3 percent of the total population. By 1960 there were 482,229 blacks, accounting for 28.9 percent of the residents, and by 1970 the number reached 660,428, or 43.7 percent of the city's population.

In the past, integrated neighborhoods were few. Normally, whites accepted a few black families in their neighborhoods, but when a critical proportion was reached an exodus of white homeowners followed. In many instances this was prompted and encouraged by such tactics as blockbusting, harassment of homeowners, and steering of black families in and white families out of target neighborhoods. This transition often brought on instability and turmoil, leaving a legacy of neighborhood depreciation and blight. During the 1970s this situation changed somewhat as local community groups tried to combat the more adverse effects of the transition process. These groups recognized the need for neighborhood stabilization and realized that this stabilization could only come about through ethnic integration.

The change in the makeup of Detroit's population also resulted in a change in leadership of the city government. In the mayoral election of 1961, a young, unknown lawyer, Jerome P. Cavanagh, challenged the incumbent, Louis Miriani. Mayor Albert E. Cobo had died in September 1957 and was succeeded by Council President Miriani; two months later Miriani was elected to a four-year term as mayor (the city charter had been changed in 1953 to extend the mayor's term from two to four years). Miriani represented the establishment, while Cavanagh took his campaign to the people, particularly to the black neighborhoods. When the votes were counted, Cavanagh was the new mayor. For the next eight years, he would bring a progressive administration to city government.

In 1961 Jerome P. Cavanagh took his campaign to the people, propelling the previously little-known attorney into the mayor's office. Courtesy Walter P. Reuther Library, Wayne State University, Detroit.

Cavanagh's first job was to tackle the city's growing fiscal problems. To assist him with this task he called upon Alfred Pelham to become city controller, the most important position next to that of mayor. It marked the first time an African American had been named to a major post in city government. One of Detroit's most distinguished citizens, Pelham had long served as county budget director and later as associate professor of political science at Wayne State University. Few had as good a grasp of the intricacies of urban government and its finances as did Pelham.

To balance the city's budget, Cavanagh succeeded in having a municipal income tax enacted—1 percent on residents and .5 percent on nonresidents working in the city. For the first time since the Depression, Detroit was on such sound financial footing that its bonds were accorded a prime rating.

Major changes came also to Detroit's downtown skyline in the 1950s and 1960s. For many years, the area between Jefferson Avenue and the river had consisted of dilapidated warehouses, lofts, and dock structures that cut off public view of the water. In the belief that the river was one of the city's principal assets, plans were made to tear down these old buildings and develop a civic center where Detroiters could enjoy the view of their waterfront. In the early 1950s, the civic center was begun as the area between First and Randolph Streets south of Jefferson Avenue was cleared. The first building, the Veterans' Memorial, dedicated June 14, 1950, stands at the foot of Shelby Street, about where Cadillac landed in the summer of 1701.

Next came the Henry and Edsel Ford Auditorium. Constructed just east of the foot of Woodward Avenue, the building was opened in 1956 as the new home of the

One of the most popular pastimes for generations of Detroiters was a trip to Bob-Lo Island aboard the *Columbia* or her sister steamer the *Ste. Claire.* Sadly, the amusement park on the island closed in 1994, and the two steamships were decommissioned and put up for auction in 1996. From a painting by William Moss. Courtesy Dossin Great Lakes Museum, Detroit.

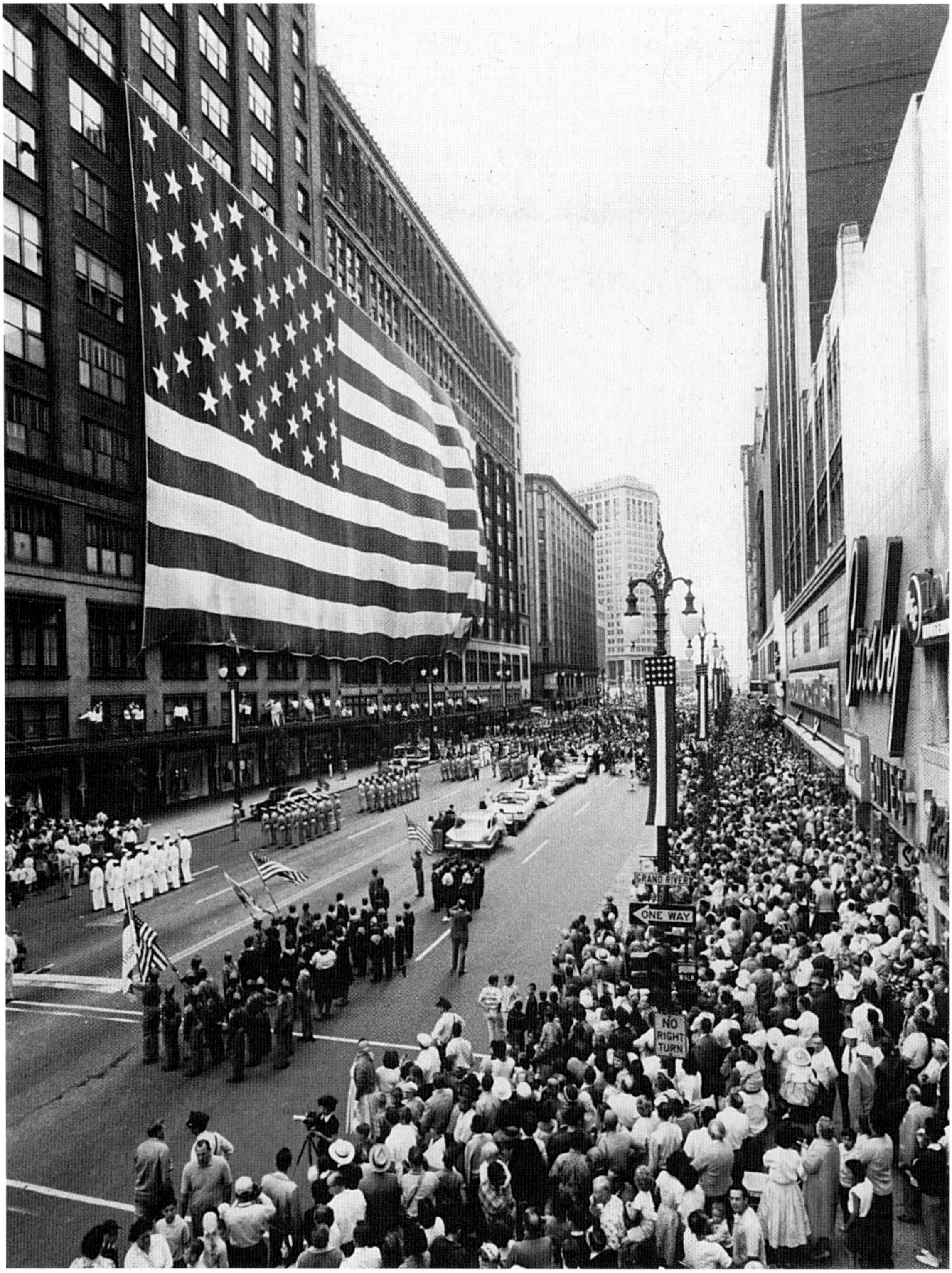

The world's largest flag was annually unfurled from the J. L. Hudson Building on Woodward Avenue, an event fondly remembered by many Detroiters. Photo by Tony Spina. Courtesy Walter P. Reuther Library, Wayne State University, Detroit.

In 1959 the St. Lawrence Seaway was opened and Detroit became an important center for international shipping. Courtesy Dossin Great Lakes Museum, Detroit.

Detroit Symphony Orchestra. The auditorium was the gift of the Ford Motor Company and the Ford and Mercury auto dealers of America as a memorial to the two Fords. The initial phase of the civic center development was completed in 1960 with the opening of the giant Cobo Hall and Arena. Built at the western end of the center, they were one of the nation's leading accommodations for conventions and exhibits.

The unique feature of the civic center is, without a doubt, old Mariners Church. Built in 1849 on the west side of Woodward Avenue between Jefferson and Woodbridge, it stood directly in the path of the civic center. Over the years the church had deteriorated into a run-down building used primarily for commercial purposes. The question now became, should it be torn down, or could it be saved? Preservation won. The church was saved, then moved from its original location to the eastern end of the civic center. A long and slow process, the move was begun on December 13, 1954, and completed on April 12, 1955—four months to move 880 feet. Once in place, this venerable old Episcopal church was beautifully restored. Today it stands as one of Detroit's outstanding historic sites.

As the civic center began to take shape, other new buildings began to rise in the downtown area. These included the City-County Building, the Pontchartrain Hotel, the National Bank of Detroit Building, and the Howard Johnson Motor Lodge. These were followed by the headquarters of Detroit Bank and Trust Company, Michigan Consolidated Gas Company, the First Federal Savings and Loan Association, and the Blue Cross/Blue Shield of Michigan Building. These were the first buildings to be erected in downtown Detroit since the Depression. Construction continued into the late 1960s

Old Mariners Church, seen here in the nineteenth century, was saved from demolition by being moved 880 feet in the 1950s. Courtesy Burton Historical Collection, Detroit Public Library.

One of the major buildings in Detroit's new civic center was the City-County Building. On September 23, 1955, Mayor Cobo and city officials marched down Woodward from the now old City Hall to occupy their new government home. Photo by Tony Spina. Courtesy Walter P. Reuther Library, Wayne State University, Detroit.

and 1970s and included the Frank Murphy Hall of Justice, the Manufacturers National Bank Building, the Edison Plaza, and the McNamara Federal Building. Along with all this new construction, several older but structurally sound offices and stores were remodeled and refurbished.

The revitalization of Detroit was not limited to the downtown area. With the aid of federal funds, the city began a massive urban renewal program. With some exceptions, the areas selected for urban renewal were located within Grand Boulevard and comprised the worst of Detroit's housing; virtually all of it was residential. The areas also made up some of the most vital and colorful of Detroit's ethnic and working-class communities—Black Bottom, Paradise Valley, Bagley, Corktown, and

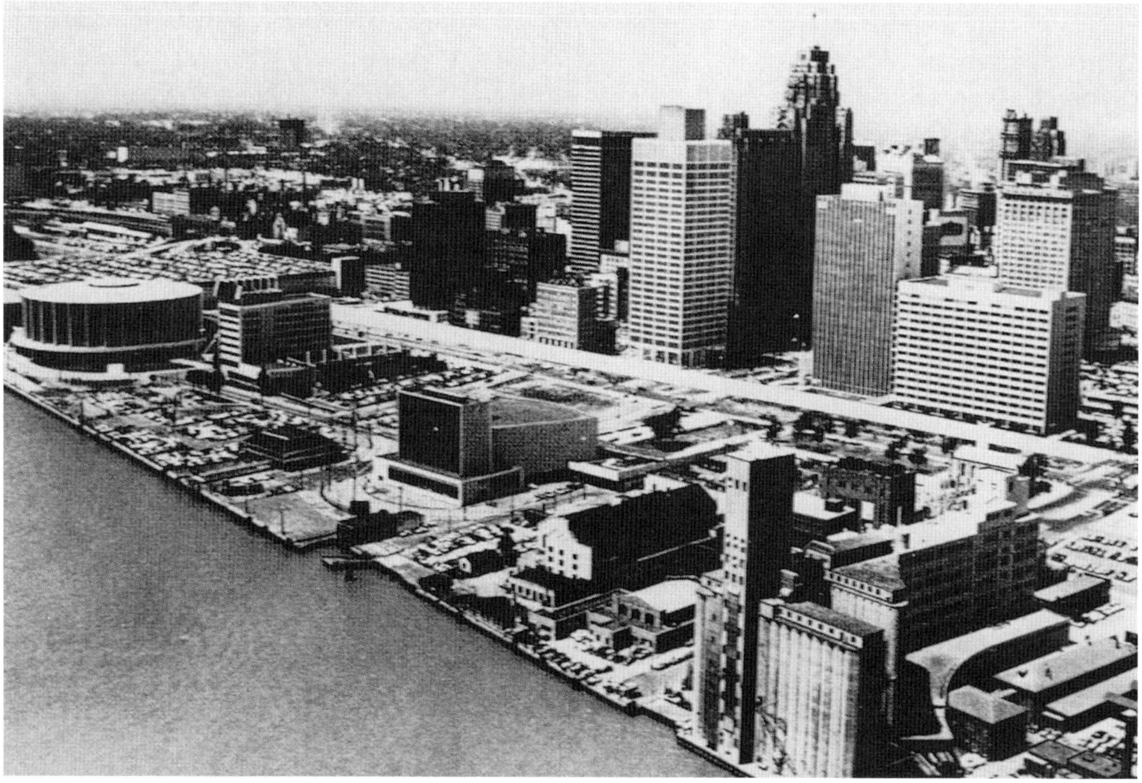

This view of Detroit's civic center, with Cobo Hall, Veterans Memorial, Ford Auditorium, and City-County Building, dates from the 1960s. Courtesy Burton Historical Collection, Detroit Public Library.

Thousands of Detroit residents were displaced by the clearance of land for urban renewal. Shown here is the area around Gratiot and Orlean Streets in the heart of Black Bottom. Courtesy Walter P. Reuther Library, Wayne State University, Detroit.

Chinatown—all important parts of Detroit's heritage. In all, the urban renewal program of that area accounted for more than 1,500 acres of land which at one time contained more than 17,000 housing units and nearly 2,000 businesses. More importantly though, an estimated 7,660 families and 6,730 single individuals had to be relocated.

In some areas, the urban renewal process proved to be highly successful. On the lower east side, for example, several high-rise luxury apartments were built, and Lafayette and Elmwood Parks—residential areas of tree-lined, spacious apartments and condominiums—lured people back to the central city. Several areas were renewed for industrial use, while others, notably in the University City and Detroit Medical Center areas, were designed for institutional use.

As in most other American cities, the urban renewal process in Detroit during the 1960s was long, complicated, and bureaucratic. Much of the land planned for renewal stood vacant for long periods of time. As a result, vacant land became (and continues to be) a pervasive and accepted part of the Detroit inner-city landscape. This land took on various hues and physical characteristics, from bare earth and weeds, to green, rural-like tranquillity, to western sagebrush, and to a Detroit specialty, white wooden fences, which gave vacant blocks in the heart of the city the appearance of Kentucky horse farms.

Unfortunately, when the urban renewal program began there was little real attempt made to understand the plight of the residents involved. Projects were discussed and planned with little local participation. Residents felt themselves to be at the mercy of a frightening combination of federal officials, city government, and the institutions that would benefit from development. Then, fortunately, an important change took place. Local resident organizations gained greater control of what was happening in their neighborhoods. This was brought about by federal revenue-sharing stipulations, model neighborhood examples, the growing power of citizen councils, and a changing attitude on the part of city officials as to what constituted "development."

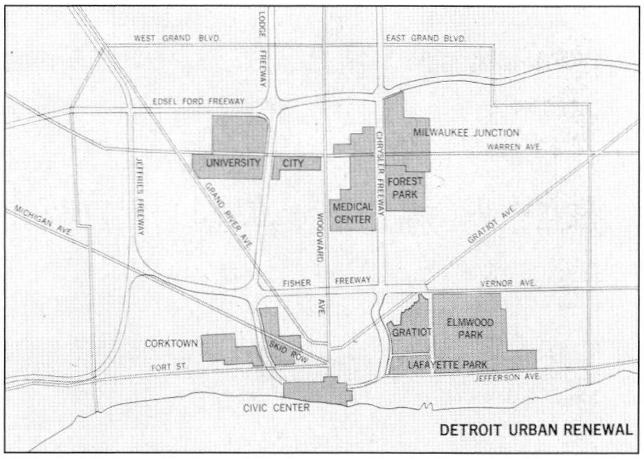

This map shows the location of the city's major urban renewal projects of the 1950s and 1960s. From Robert Conot, *American Odyssey.*

This concept of citizen involvement also spread beyond the urban renewal areas. Throughout the city, residents joined together in associations and block clubs to work for improvements. Included were such neighborhoods as Boston/Edison, Green Acres, Jefferson/Chalmers, Palmer Woods, Sherwood Forest, Rosedale Park, Grandmont, Berry Subdivision, Chandler Park Drive/Cadieux, Harmony Village, and two of the most historically interesting neighborhoods, West Canfield and Indian Village.

The West Canfield Historic District encompasses one block of West Canfield Avenue between Second Boulevard and Third Street just south of the Wayne State University campus. Originally part of the farm owned by Governor Lewis Cass, the land was first subdivided in 1869. All of the houses here were built in the 1870s, 1880s, and 1890s. With their ornately carved wood and stone trim, these elaborate homes reflect a variety of architectural styles, including Gothic Revival, Italianate, Second Empire, and Queen Anne. Many of Detroit's most prominent attorneys, physicians, and architects owned these homes. In the 1880s the area became commonly known as Piety Hill because of the alleged social and moral character of its residents. Through the years the houses were being destroyed by neglect, and in 1969 the Canfield West–Wayne Preservation Association was organized to promote their purchase and restoration. The area became Detroit's first local historic district in 1970, and it was listed on the National Register of Historic Places in 1971. Today, West Canfield, with its beautifully restored homes, is one of Detroit's most unique historic neighborhoods.

Located out East Jefferson Avenue about three and one-half miles from downtown, the area known as Indian Village was purchased by Abraham Cook from two French farmers, Gabriel St. Aubin and Francois Rivard, during the first decades of the nineteenth century. The vicinity, known as the Cook Farms, was a racetrack from 1836 to 1893. In 1894, Cook's heirs subdivided the property and named it Indian Village. The first home was built in 1895, and Indian Village developed into a distinctive single-family residential community of more than three hundred homes representing a diversity of popular styles of the late 1800s and early 1900s. Due to the unique combination of social and architectural history, Indian Village is one of the most significant neighborhoods in present-day Detroit. Beautifully restored and maintained, it was listed in the National Register of Historic Places in 1972.

Unfortunately, some areas did not fare as well because of one of the most detrimental aspects of the urban renewal process—the destruction of whole neighborhoods. Two of the best-known of these communities were Black Bottom and Paradise Valley.

During the 1920s, Detroit's African American population increased from 41,000 to 120,000, largely as a result of the expansion of the automobile industry. These new residents found plenty of jobs, but housing was a different matter. There were only a few neighborhoods into which they could move, and one of these was on the near east side close to downtown between Woodward and Chene. The area was originally inhabited by Italians, Greeks, Jews, and Poles. Within a short time, though, it became the predominantly black residential section commonly known as Black Bottom, so named for the rich, dark soil on which early settlers farmed.

Within Black Bottom, in an area roughly bounded by Vernor on the north, Madison on the south, Hastings on the east, John R. on the west, and with Gratiot cutting through it, was the area's business district. It contained shops, music stores, grocery stores, bowling alleys, hotels, restaurants, policy offices, and seventeen nightclubs—all owned by African Americans. It was known as Paradise Valley.

Although Paradise Valley was black-owned, its nightclubs during the 1930s and 1940s were true melting pots. Blacks and whites drank, danced, and were entertained side by side without undue tension or incident. The atmosphere, in fact, was cordial and happy, and violent crime was practically nonexistent. Black policemen assigned to patrol the Valley partied with the night crowd, but they set absolute rules forbidding criminal disorder.

Paradise Valley attracted all of the best black entertainers in the country. Many aspiring young singers, dancers, and musicians got their first big break at the Club Plantation, the 606, the B&C Club, Club 666, and the Forest Club. They all played the Valley—Earl Hines, the Inkspots, Ethel Waters, Pearl Bailey, Billie Holliday, Dinah Washington, Ella Fitzgerald, Bojangles, and many more. Even those established entertainers who performed at the Greystone Ballroom or the Michigan Theater, such as Duke Ellington, Lena Horne, and Cab Calloway, frequented the Valley's nightclubs after their acts. Here they relaxed and entertained at jam sessions, playing into the early hours of the morning. In those days, the downtown hotels would not accept black guests, so they stayed at the hotels in the Valley—the Dewey, the Biltmore, the Norwood, and the Mark Twain.

Along with the nightclubs, Paradise Valley was the home for a number of other well-known establishments. Long's Drug Store was the information center. The best restaurant was Perkins, and Brosche's was known for its

From the 1920s, Detroit's principal predominantly black residential neighborhood was known as Black Bottom. The main street of Black Bottom was Hastings, seen here in the 1970s. Courtesy Detroit Historical Museum.

At the 606 Horse Shoe Lounge owner William T. Johnson visits with a table of guests. Author's collection.

biscuits. In the basement of the Biltmore was "The Hole," the place to go for soul food. Another very popular spot was the Paradise Bowl, owned in part by Joe Louis, with a restaurant stocked from his Utica farm. This was a favorite stop for the "flyboys," black airmen stationed at Selfridge Field who bused into the city to come to the Valley. Also located within Paradise Valley's boundaries were the offices of the *Michigan Chronicle,* the *Detroit Tribune,* St. Antoine YMCA, Lucy Thurman YWCA, and St. Matthew's Episcopal Church. And nearby were the offices of the Detroit Urban League.

Another important aspect of the Valley's economy was gambling, particularly the policy operation (a southern black gambling game that originated in St. Louis) and later the numbers racket. For many years they flourished here, but they also marked the beginning of the end for Paradise Valley. In 1939 a woman committed suicide and left a note implicating police and city officials in

The 107-foot bar at the Forest Club was the longest bar in Paradise Valley. From Sunnie Wilson, *Toast of the Town.*

The Ruby Lee Beauty Salon. Courtesy Burton Historical Collection, Detroit Public Library.

Paradise Valley Distributors. Courtesy Burton Historical Collection, Detroit Public Library.

these illegal activities. A grand jury investigation followed in 1942, and the next year came Detroit's race riot. Many whites were now afraid to visit the Valley. Investigations following the riot also revealed the substandard, crowded conditions under which blacks were forced to live. This eventually brought about opportunities for blacks to move out of the area. Many club owners also left for more suburban locations.

Black Bottom and Paradise Valley survived until the 1950s, but the final blow came with urban renewal and the building of the expressways. The Chrysler Freeway obliterated Hastings Street, Stroh Brewery took St. Antoine Street, and Hudson's Warehouse took Brush and Beaubien. Finally, Black Bottom was transformed into Lafayette Park. When the construction of I-75 destroyed Paradise Valley, many of Black Bottom's families resettled around Twelfth Street, buying property from the Jewish population. In fact, some of the area's black churches were originally synagogues.

Detroit was committed to the progress of expressways and urban renewal. But it was progress with a price. Today, Black Bottom and Paradise Valley are only memories.

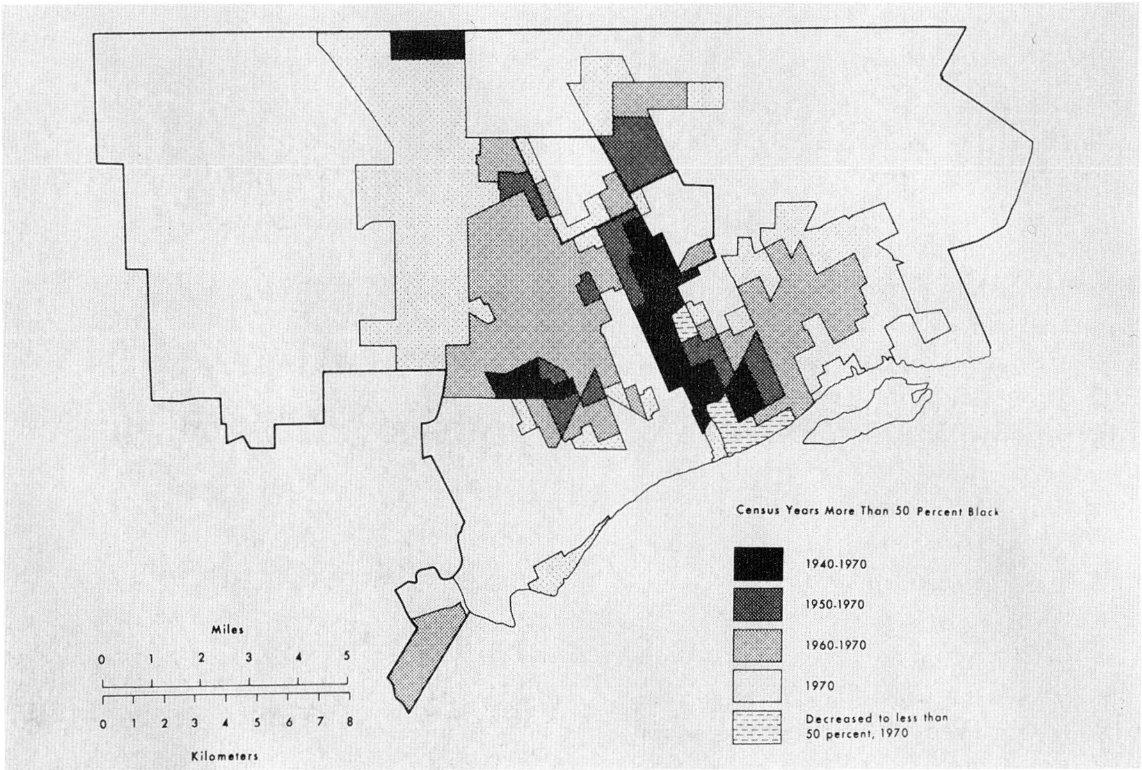

The location of Detroit's black population from 1940 to 1970. From Robert Sinclair, *Metropolitan Detroit.*

SIXTEEN

Civil Rights and Civil Strife

AFTER THE RIOT OF 1943, DETROIT experienced a period of racial calm and considerable progress in the area of race relations. The city was fortunate in having a strong black middle class with such men as the Urban League's John C. Dancy, who worked closely with responsible white organizations. Dancy's role in improving conditions for Detroit's black citizens had been a long and active one. He began his work in Detroit as executive director of the Detroit Urban League in 1918, a position he held until his retirement in 1960. The Detroit Urban League was founded in 1916 with Forrester B. Washington as its first executive director. The organization's initial purpose was the improvement of the social, moral, and marital status of the large number of blacks who migrated to Detroit during and directly after World War I. Dancy was succeeded by Francis A. Kornegay, who had joined the league in 1914 as head of the Vocational Services department. Kornegay later served as the league's assistant director, and he retired as executive director in 1978.

For more than forty years, John C. Dancy, the executive director of the Detroit Urban League, was one of Detroit's most influential citizens. Courtesy Burton Historical Collection, Detroit Public Library.

Headquarters of the Detroit Urban League on Mack Avenue and John R. Street. Founded in 1916, the league continues to actively serve Detroit's African American community. From W. Hawkins Ferry, *Buildings of Detroit.*

Today the league is most ably administered by President/CEO N. Charles Anderson.

It was also during the late 1940s that another barrier against open housing was brought down. Orsel McGhee, an African American, bought a house in an all-white neighborhood on Detroit's west side in the area of Grand River Avenue and Grand Boulevard. But once he had purchased the home, McGhee was told that a clause in the deed stated that it could not be owned by anyone other than a Caucasian. Whites in the neighborhood sued to have the clause enforced, and the local court found it to be valid. The case was appealed, however, and on May 3, 1948, in a unanimous decision, the U.S. Supreme Court ruled that the clause was in violation of the Fourteenth Amendment. It was a landmark decision, for this ruling was to have a significant effect not only for Detroit, but for the nation as well.

Although advances in education, housing, and job opportunities had indeed occurred, many African Americans were growing impatient with how slowly these changes were coming about. As a result, in the late 1950s and early 1960s moderate organizations such as the NAACP and the Urban League—which had been in the civil rights movement for decades—were suddenly considered contemptible and obsolete. Now activist groups such as the Southern Christian Leadership Conference and militant organizations such as the Student Non-Violent Coordinating Committee, the Congress for Racial Equality, the Republic of New Africa, and the Black

Panthers advocated confrontation instead of negotiation and litigation.

In 1955 a new era in the civil rights movement was ushered in when a young black woman, Rosa Parks, refused to give up her seat on a Montgomery, Alabama, bus to a white passenger. Her steadfastness eventually led to a successful boycott of that city's bus system, and slowly but surely the black struggle for equal rights spread. In 1957 Mrs. Parks and her family moved to Detroit, where she continued to work in support of the civil rights movement. In recognition of her efforts, President Bill Clinton presented Rosa Parks with the Medal of Freedom in 1996, and in 1998 she received the International Freedom Conductor Award. Then, in December 1999, Mrs. Parks was awarded the Congressional Medal of Honor by Vice President Al Gore during a tribute held at Detroit's Orchestra Hall.

Another Detroiter who played an important role in the civil rights movement was Viola Liuzzo. In 1965, Liuzzo, a housewife, mother, and student at Wayne State University, traveled to Montgomery, Alabama, to participate in a voting rights march. On the evening of March 25, as she was driving from Selma back to Montgomery, she was gunned down by a group of Ku Klux Klan members. In recognition of her sacrifice, Viola Gregg Liuzzo's name was inscribed on the Civil Rights Memorial in Montgomery, the only white woman to be so honored.

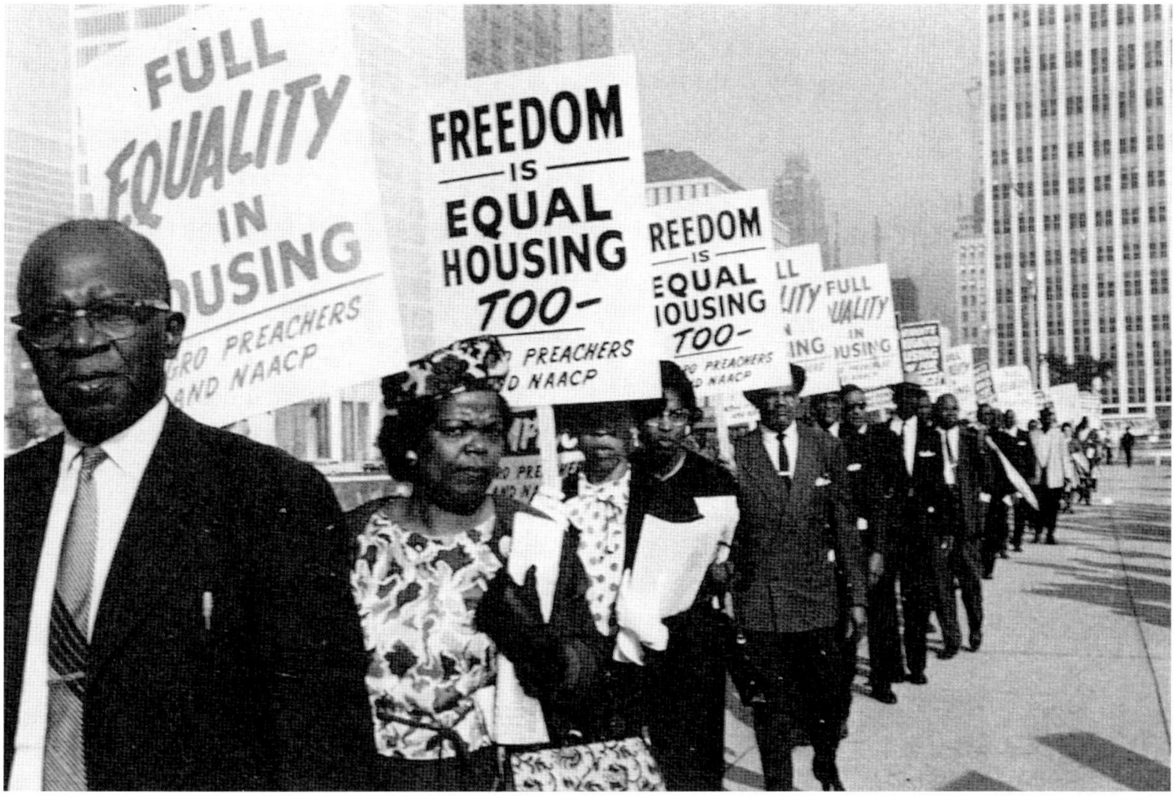

In the late 1950s and early 1960s, civil rights activists made neighborhood integration a central political issue in Detroit. In 1963 Detroit NAACP members and church leaders picketed in the civic center in favor of open housing. Courtesy Walter P. Reuther Library, Wayne State University, Detroit.

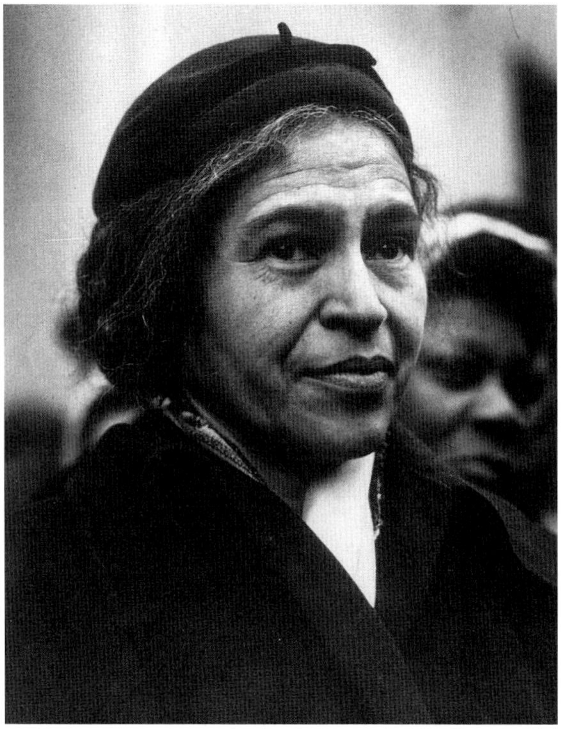

In 1955 a new era in the civil rights movement was ushered in when a young black woman, Rosa Parks, refused to give up her seat on a Montgomery, Alabama, bus to a white passenger. Courtesy Walter P. Reuther Library, Wayne State University, Detroit.

In the spring of 1963, the Detroit Council for Human Rights began plans for a march to commemorate the twentieth anniversary of the Detroit riot. Asserting that "the same basic, underlying causes for the disturbance are still present," the council's chairman, Reverend Clarence Franklin, scheduled the "Walk to Freedom" for Sunday, June 23, 1963.

On that hot, summer Sunday afternoon, 125,000 Detroiters—mostly black, but some white—marched about a mile down Woodward Avenue to the riverfront. Not since the days of the Depression had the city seen a demonstration like it. At Cobo Hall and Arena, 26,000—all the two buildings could hold—flocked inside, and the rest of the crowd remained outside where loudspeakers were set up. From the podium inside, Reverend Franklin introduced the main speaker of the afternoon, Dr. Martin Luther King, Jr. There, in his resonant voice, Dr. King revealed "a dream." In that dream, white men and black had been "walking together, hand in hand, free at last, free at last." King's speech lasted forty-eight minutes—long enough that an entire city of people, noted one observer, began to "feel and see and sense our power and our unity."

King's speech in Detroit foreshadowed, two months later, his famous "I Have a Dream" speech given on the steps of the Lincoln Memorial in Washington, D.C., on August 28, 1963. Tragically, Dr. King, the unquestioned leader of the nation's civil rights movement, was shot and killed in Memphis, Tennessee, on April 4, 1968.

In 1965 Detroiter Viola Liuzzo was gunned down by a group of Ku Klux Klan members. Her name was inscribed on the Civil Rights Memorial in Montgomery. Courtesy Walter P. Reuther Library, Wayne State University, Detroit.

Hydroplanes *Miss U.S.* and *Atlas Van Lines* roar past the Roostertail restaurant on the Detroit River during the 1976 Gold Cup races. From a painting by James Clary. Courtesy St. Clair Shores Public Library.

The Detroit Red Wings won four Stanley Cups during the 1950s, led by one of the greatest players hockey has ever known—Mr. Hockey, number 9, Gordie Howe. From a painting by Joseph Maniscalco. Courtesy the artist.

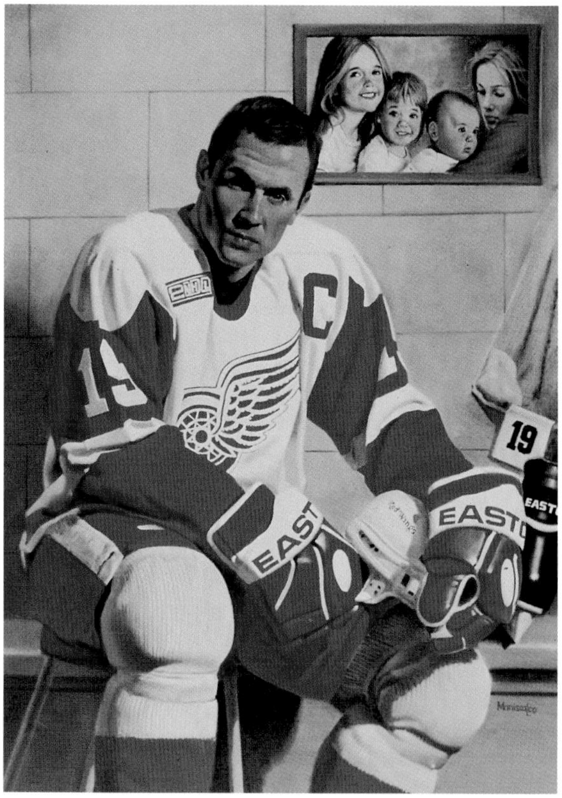

On June 7, 1997, the Detroit Red Wings, under the leadership of team captain Steve Yzerman, brought home the first of two consecutive Stanley Cups to Detroit. From a painting by Joseph Maniscalco. Courtesy the artist.

Hall of Famer Al Kaline at the plate at Tiger Stadium in 1971. One of the greatest right fielders of all time, Kaline was known for his fine hitting and his strong throws from the outfield. Courtesy Bruce Mugerian.

The new ballpark features stainless-steel statues of six Tiger greats. Included is the sculpture of power-hitting outfielder and 1968 World Series star Willie Horton. Photo by Deborah R. Kingery. Courtesy the photographer.

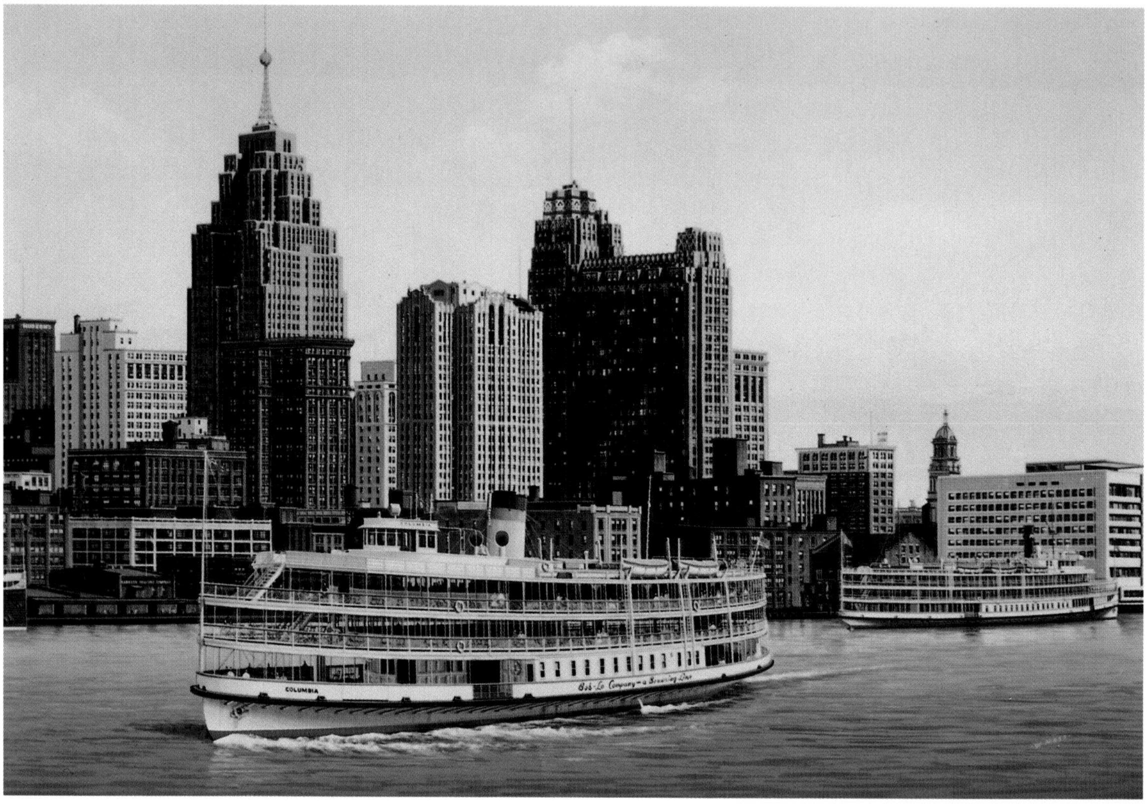

One of the most popular pastimes for generations of Detroiters was a trip to Bob-Lo Island aboard the *Columbia* or her sister steamer the *Ste. Claire.* Sadly, the amusement park on the island closed in 1994, and the two steamships were decommissioned and put up for auction in 1996. From a painting by William Moss. Courtesy Dossin Great Lakes Museum, Detroit.

George Martin, Ojibwe/Eastern Shawnee Native American, is an elder, Midewin, and beadwork artist. Native Americans from many tribes, including descendants of the original People of the Three Fires, live in Metropolitan Detroit today. Photo by S. Kay Young. Courtesy the photographer.

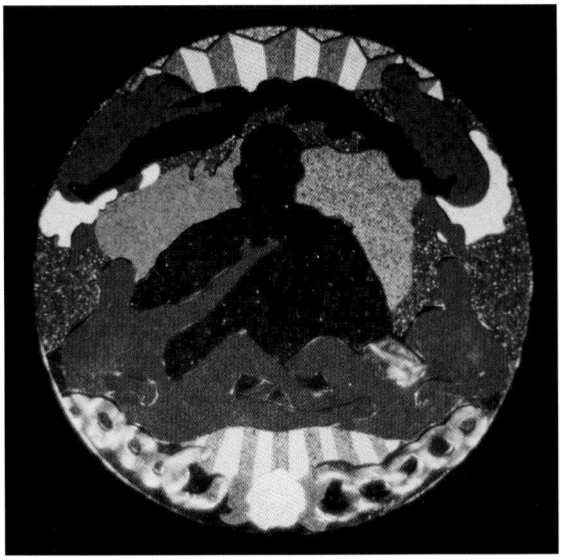

At the Charles H. Wright Museum of African American History the rotunda's impressive terrazzo floor, designed by artist Hubert Massey and titled "Genealogy," features historic figures who symbolize the struggles of African Americans in this country. Courtesy Charles H. Wright Museum of African American History and Felecia Hunt-Taylor, photographer.

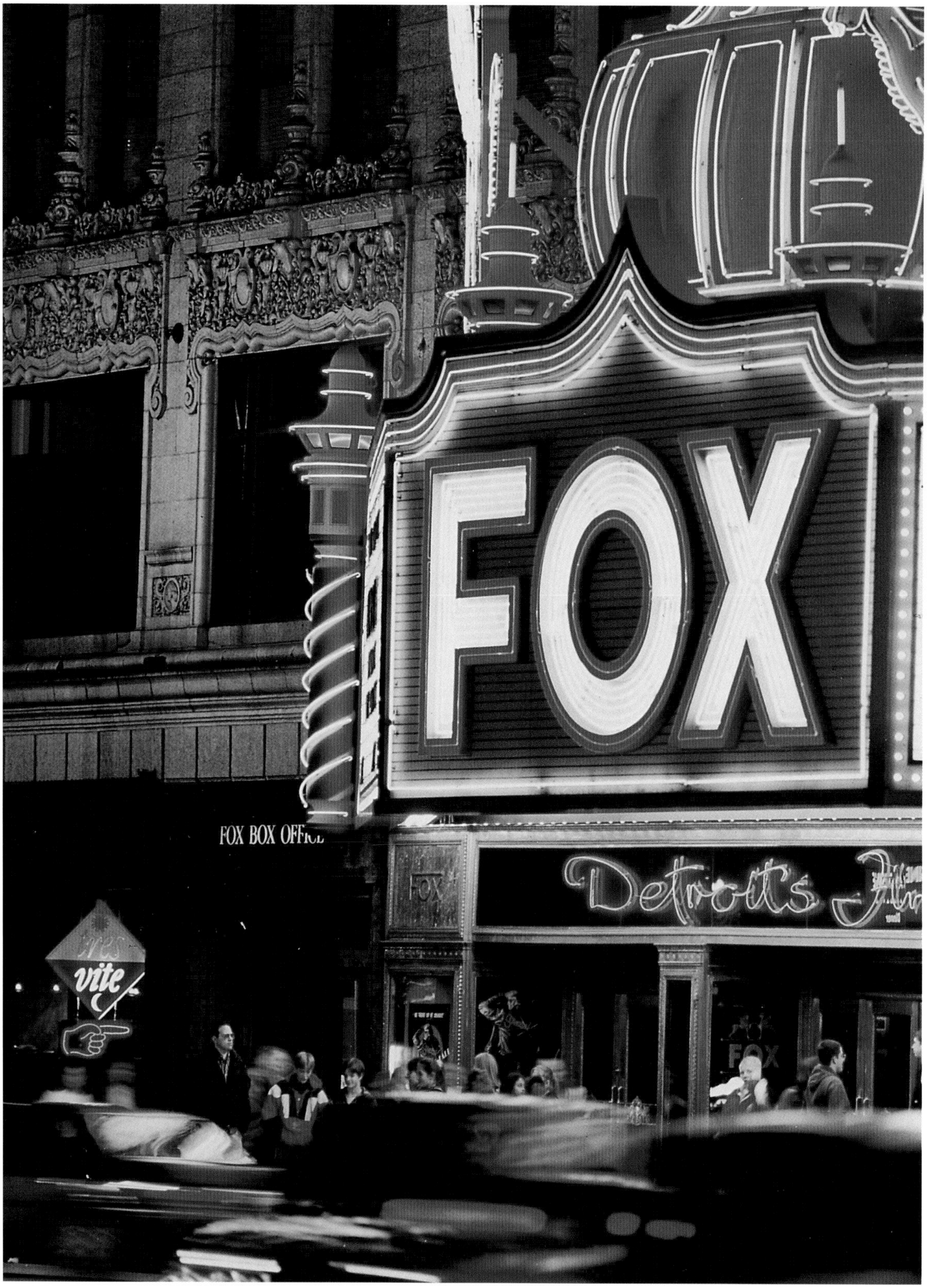

A multimillion-dollar restoration project culminated in the gala reopening of the Fox Theater on November 19, 1988. Courtesy the Fox Theater.

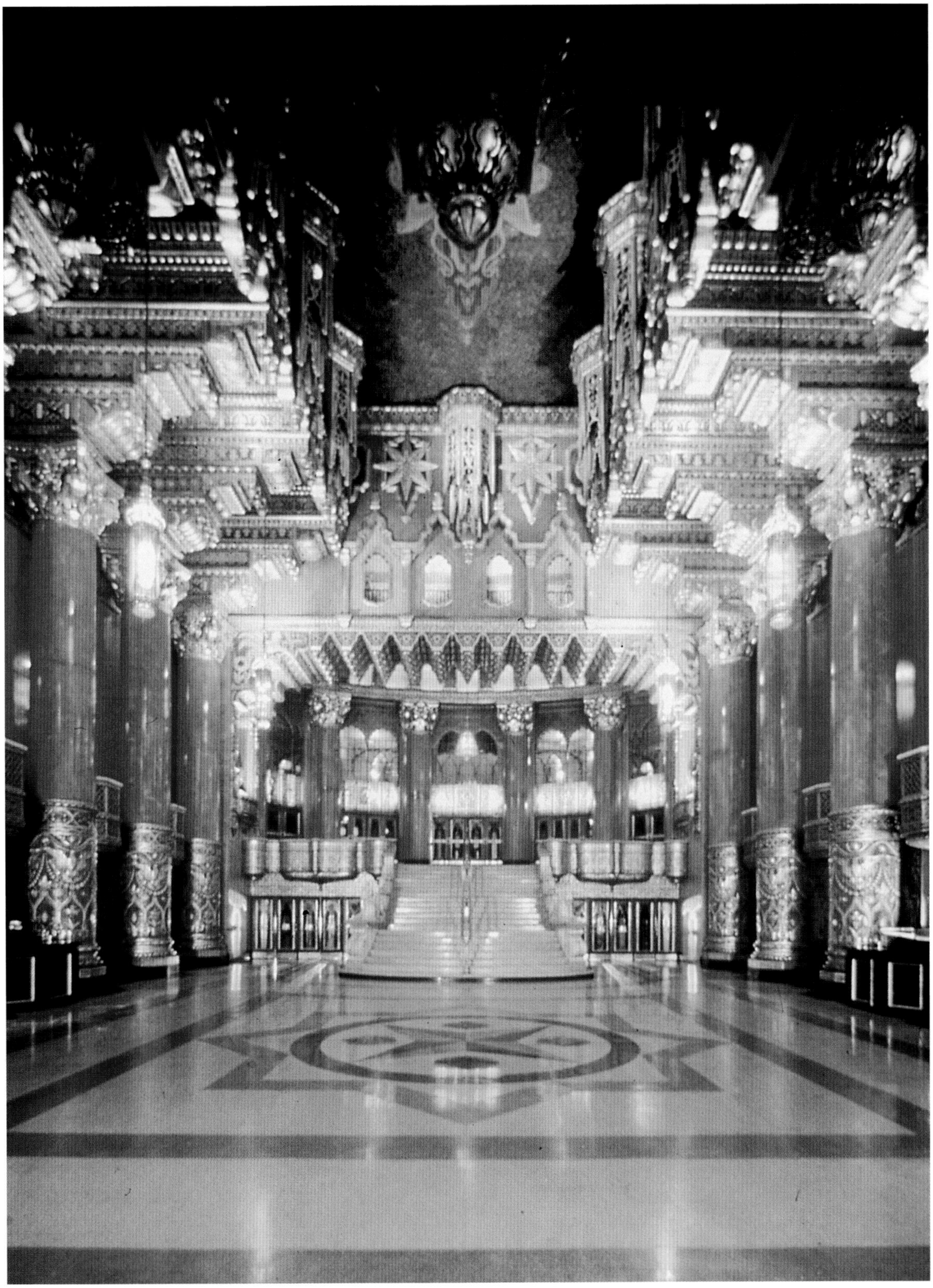

After nearly a year-long restoration, the Fox Theater was completely renovated; more than 80 percent of its original interior finish was preserved. Courtesy the Fox Theater.

Since 1979 Hart Plaza has been center stage for the world-renowned Ford Detroit International Jazz Festival. Held annually for four days over the Labor Day weekend, the festival brings together the region's finest jazz musicians. Courtesy Jazz Festival.

The first Detroit Electronic Music Festival, the largest in the world, was held in Hart Plaza in May 2000. Detroit is considered the birthplace of Techno music. Courtesy Pop Culture Media.

On October 29, 1998, demolition experts turned a switch and in a matter of moments the old J. L. Hudson Building on Woodward Avenue imploded into a pile of shattered brick, concrete, and twisted steel. Photo by Tom Sherry. Courtesy the photographer.

The beautiful old Michigan Theater, one of Detroit's grand movie palaces, now serves as a parking garage. Copyright Camilo Jose Vergara.

Detroit Industry, north wall, 1932–33, Diego M. Rivera. This view of the north wall of the court at the Detroit Institute of Arts shows one of the four frescoes by Rivera. The north wall depicts the automobile industry, along with the medical, pharmaceutical, and chemical industries. Photograph copyright 1991 Detroit Institute of Arts, Gift of Edsel B. Ford.

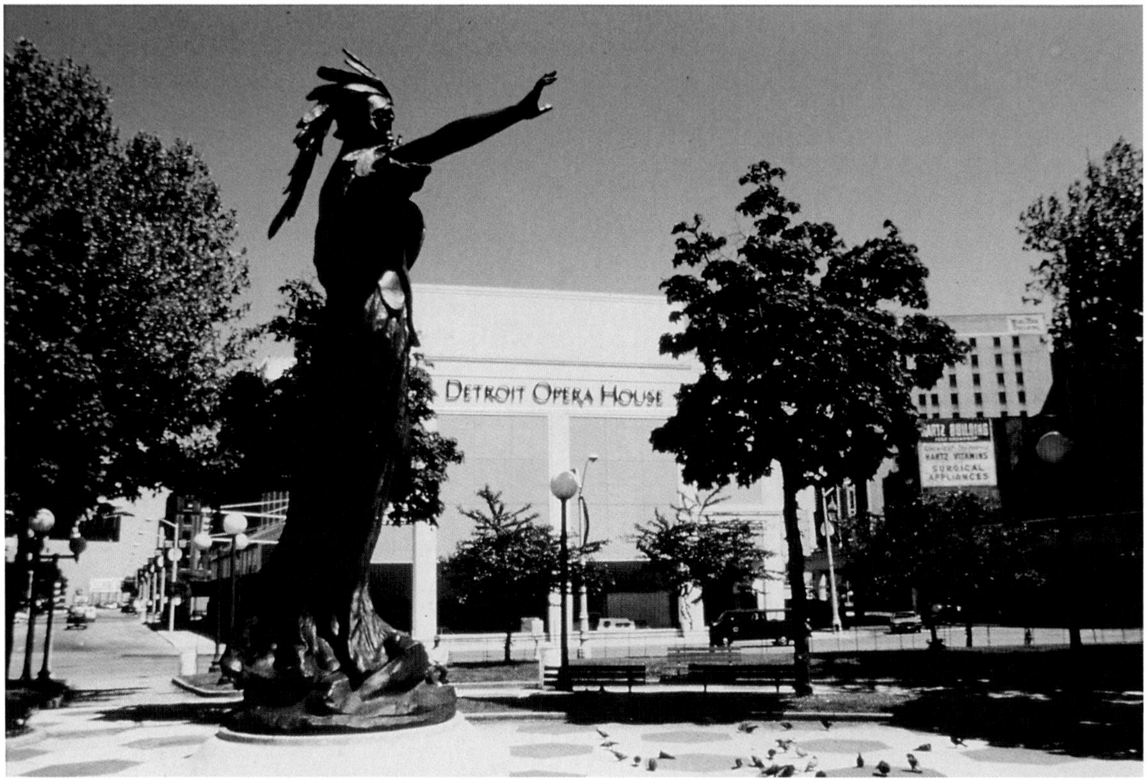

On April 22, 1996, the beautifully renovated theater was opened and Detroit once again had a magnificent opera house. Courtesy Michigan Opera Theatre.

On opening day, April 11, 2000, Tiger fans streamed through the main entrance of their new baseball stadium, Comerica Park. Photo by Deborah R. Kingery. Courtesy the photographer.

Phase one of the impressive new Orchestra Place, located on Woodward Avenue next to Orchestra Hall, was completed in 1999. © Glen Calvin Moon. Courtesy the photographer.

In 2000, after twenty-five years in suburban Pontiac, the Detroit Lions announced their move back to downtown Detroit. Their new stadium—Ford Field—will be completed by the 2002 football season. Courtesy Detroit Lions.

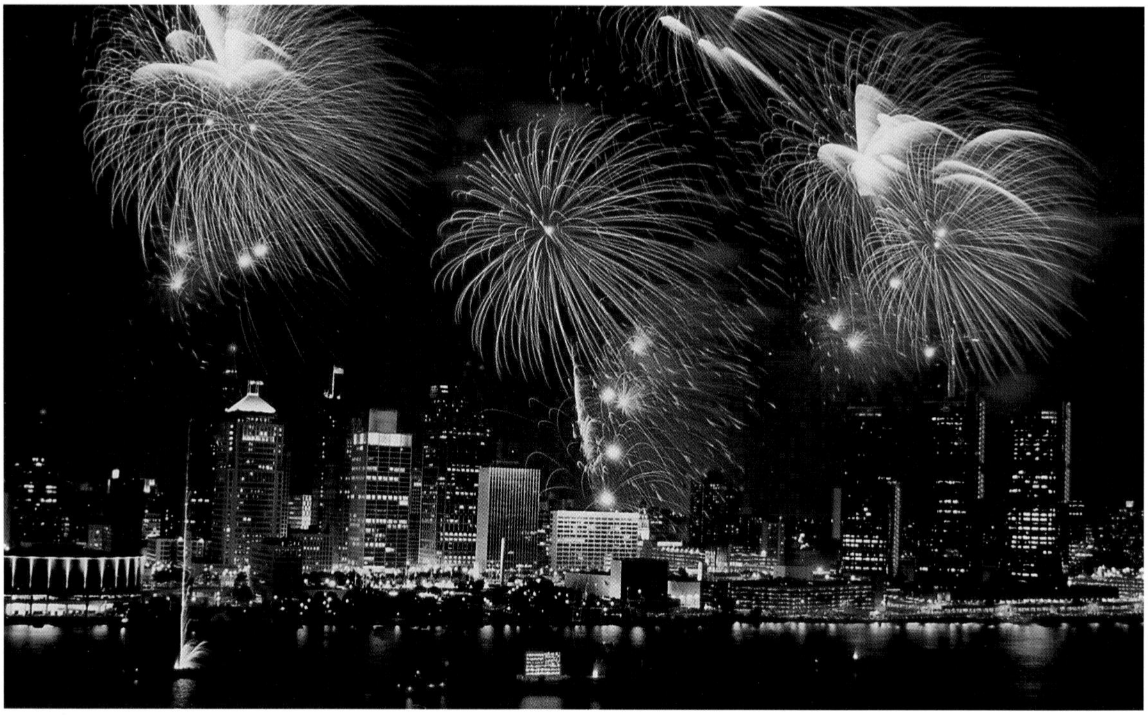

One of the region's most popular events is the annual fireworks display held on the Detroit River for the International Freedom Festival. Cosponsored by the cities of Windsor and Detroit, the event honors July 4th, Independence Day in the United States, and July 1st, Dominion Day, in Canada. Photo by Robert L. Stewart. Courtesy the photographer.

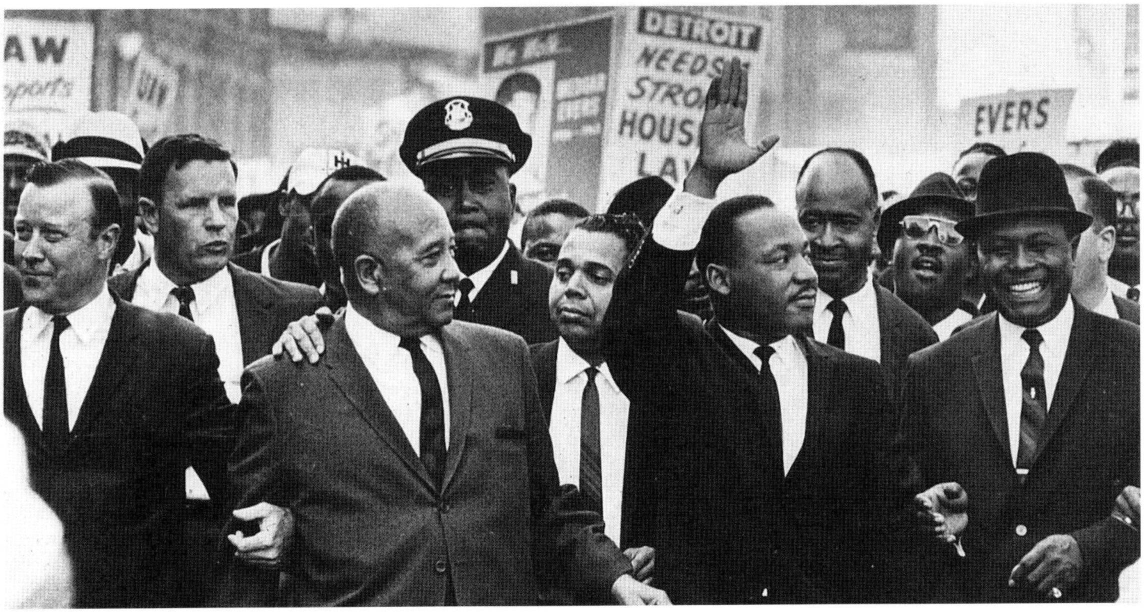

On June 23, 1963, civil rights leader Dr. Martin Luther King, Jr., led the "Walk to Freedom" down Woodward Avenue. More than 125,000 people participated in the march. With Dr. King in the front row are Walter Reuther, Benjamin McFall, and Reverend C. L. Franklin. Photo by Tony Spina. Courtesy Walter P. Reuther Library, Wayne State University, Detroit.

In 1968, two weeks before he was assassinated, Dr. King was in Detroit to give a speech at Grosse Pointe High School. Before his talk, Dr. King took time for a moment of prayer. Photo by Tony Spina. Courtesy Walter P. Reuther Library, Wayne State University, Detroit.

During the early 1960s, marches similar to Detroit's were held in many of the nation's other large urban centers. But it seemed that little progress was being made, and in the summers of 1965 and 1966 many militant blacks turned from marching and non-involvement to rioting. In the Watts district of Los Angeles, blacks rioted in the summer of 1965; thirty-four died and property losses ran to $40 million.

In Detroit, the feeling of most civic leaders was that a riot such as that which had occurred in Watts could not possibly happen here, and it seemed a reasonable enough expectation. Fully 40 percent of the black family heads owned their own homes. No city had waged a more massive and comprehensive war on poverty. Under Mayor Cavanagh, the city had obtained more than $42 million in federal funds for its poverty programs. "We learned our lesson in 1943," said the city fathers. They were to find, however, that there was more to learn.

The blind pig on Twelfth Street—where it all began. Courtesy Walter P. Reuther Library, Wayne State University, Detroit.

In the early-morning hours of Sunday, July 23, 1967, Detroit police led a raid on a blind pig on Twelfth Street near Clairmont. As those arrested were being taken from the building, a crowd of about two hundred African Americans gathered and began taunting police. A bottle was thrown, a brick was tossed, a fire was started, a store was looted. The crowd turned into a mob.

Patrol cars immediately began arriving on the scene, but police made no effort to beat back the mob—a decision that was to be bitterly denounced by black and white moderates alike. When this policy became evident, the looters ran rampant. As the riot spread, U.S. Representative John Conyers, Jr., one of the city's two black congressmen, and Reverend Nicholas Hood, the city's only black councilman, arrived at the scene hoping to talk the mob into dispersing. But the rioters would not listen to reason.

In late afternoon, when sporadic sniping was reported, Governor George Romney proclaimed a state of emergency and called in 400 state police and some 7,300 national guardsmen. But the riot was now spreading almost unchecked, and by evening Detroit's inner city was out of control. Although police and national guardsmen were now on the scene, it was soon obvious that they could not control the rioters. So at 3 A.M. on Monday, July 24, Governor Romney called for federal troops. However, there were several delays, so it was not until early Tuesday morning that the first of 4,700 airborne troops in full battle dress arrived in the riot area.

During the day on Monday, the number of fires reached its peak when the fire department received a staggering 617 alarms. Yet when they arrived at a fire, the firefighters were driven off by the rioters. By week's end, more than 1,600 fires were reported and damage from fire and looting edged past $50 million. Monday was also to witness the riot's first victim. A white man was killed by gunfire while running from a looted store. He was the first of forty-four killed.

By Tuesday night federal troops (many of them veterans of the Vietnam War) had brought a tense calm over the east side, yet the riot still raged out of control on the west side. On Wednesday more than 3,000 arrests were made (7,331 arrests were made by the time the riot was over). This resulted in prisoners being housed in Jackson State Prison, Milan Penitentiary, county jails, city buses, police garages, the police gymnasium, and even the public bathhouse on Belle Isle. Early on Thursday the riot finally began to subside, and on Friday the last major fire was reported.

As the fearful city began to return to some form of stability, the people of Detroit were left to talk about what had happened. They had not endured a battle between white and black like that which had torn the city in 1943. What they had been a part of was a new type of rioting, a battle against authority, whatever its skin color.

Although Detroit had endured a horrible disaster, there was one tentative answer—a

Twelfth Street on the first day of the riot, July 23, 1967. Courtesy Walter P. Reuther Library, Wayne State University, Detroit.

A young national guardsman watches as the city burns. This photo was used all over the world and was part of the entry that won the Pulitzer Prize for the *Detroit Free Press.* Photo by Tony Spina. Courtesy Walter P. Reuther Library, Wayne State University, Detroit.

new beginning. As Father Richard was heard to have spoken 162 years earlier, "Speramus meliora; resurget cineribus": "We hope for better things; it will arise from the ashes."

On Thursday, July 27, the first step toward the new beginning was taken. That afternoon, Mayor Cavanagh and Governor Romney invited five hundred Detroiters—a cross-section of the community including block club leaders, militant blacks, union officials, the heads of major companies, and a special committee from the Detroit Chamber of Commerce—to meet in the auditorium of the City-County Building. Never before had the city seen such a gathering. The leaders of the automobile industry were there: Henry Ford II; James M. Roche, president of General Motors; Lynn Townsend, president of Chrysler; and Roy Chapin, Jr., president of American Motors. UAW President Walter Reuther pledged the help of his huge union in the cleanup task, and Roche offered the "facilities, skills, resources, and people" of the giant General Motors.

Out of the meeting came the decision to establish a "New Detroit Committee," composed of all the elements of the community, to channel private resources into the city and to chart its future. Its staff would come largely from manpower loaned by various corporations. Department store president Joseph L. Hudson, Jr., was chosen chairman. William

During the riot whole city blocks were destroyed, and more than sixteen hundred fires were reported. Courtesy Walter P. Reuther Library, Wayne State University, Detroit.

T. Patrick, who had been the city's first black councilman, was named executive director. Hence, Detroit became the first city to organize an "urban coalition."

Over the next ten years, more than $28 million would be allocated for the various programs of New Detroit. These special program areas included education, employment and economic action, housing and neighborhood stabilization, health, drug abuse, community self-determination, minority economic development, public safety and justice, anti-racism, and the arts. During this same period, Detroit's black community would wage epic battles for their rightful places in the city's factories, courtrooms, police cars, schools, office towers, and City Hall. By the mid-1970s Detroit would be the largest city in America with a black majority. It would have a black mayor, a black police chief, and affirmative-action plans to give African Americans more city jobs, contracts, and power.

A meeting of the Board of Trustees of New Detroit, the nation's first "urban coalition." *From left:* Walter Douglas, Stanley Winkelman, William T. Patrick, Jr., Reverend Malcolm Carron, Lawrence Doss, and Max M. Fisher. Courtesy Walter P. Reuther Library, Wayne State University, Detroit.

SEVENTEEN

A City of Many Tongues

OUT OF THE UNREST OF THE 1960s and the civil rights movement came a renewal of interest in ethnic American culture. This was particularly important for Detroit, as it has the largest multi-ethnic population of any metropolitan area in the United States. The Detroit tri-county region has the largest Arabic-speaking population outside the Middle East, the second-largest Polish population in America (only Chicago has more), and the largest concentration of Belgians, Chaldeans, and Maltese. Detroit's largest ethnic group is, of course, African Americans, and their story will be found throughout the pages of this book. Here we turn to the story of the city's other ethnic groups.

Detroit has had an ethnic flavor since its earliest days, but between 1880 and 1930 it became truly cosmopolitan—a city of many tongues. In the mid-nineteenth century, the first wave of immigrants came to the city—Germans, Irish, Poles—but the big influx of immigrants arrived in the early years of the twentieth century to work in the automobile factories. They came by the thousands from Armenia and Syria, from Greece and Hungary, from Belgium and Italy, from Russia and the Ukraine. When Henry Ford announced his $5.00-a-day wage, the waves of immigrants grew to the tens of thousands, and Detroit was to see the arrival of Austrians, Bulgarians, Croatians, Finns, Lithuanians, Norwegians,

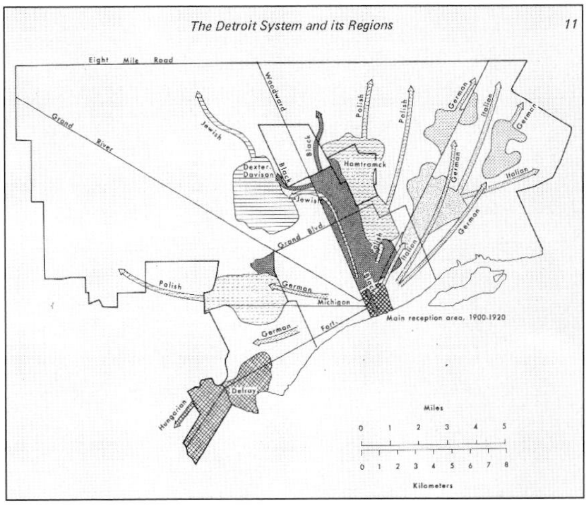

Detroit's ethnic communities in 1950 and migration path since 1900. From Robert Sinclair, *Metropolitan Detroit*.

Many Polish women found employment in the city's cigar factories. Shown here is the San Telmo Cigar Factory around 1913. Courtesy Burton Historical Collection, Detroit Public Library.

Romanians, Serbians, Slovaks, and Swedes. From 1900 to 1910 Detroit's foreign-born population grew from 96,503 to 157,534, and then nearly doubled again to 290,884 by 1920. This growth continued at such a rate that by 1925 the foreign-born accounted for nearly 50 percent of the city's population of 1,242,000. In 1904, on the eve of Detroit's manufacturing boom, there were 13,000 Poles, 1,300 Russians, and 900 Italians living in the city. By 1925 there were 115,000 Poles, 49,000 Russians, and 42,000 Italians. Detroit, which in 1900 had ranked as the thirteenth-largest city in the United States, had risen to fourth.

The first Finns to arrive were skilled metal workers from Massachusetts who came to make auto bodies for Packard Motor Company. When Ford announced his high wage, many Finns moved to Detroit from upper Michigan's copper country. A small group of Dutch also arrived at this time, and the auto industry is indebted to one of these immigrants, Jan Reef, for developing a gear process that was widely used by early carmakers.

One of the largest groups to settle in Detroit at this time was Hungarians. They first began to arrive in the late 1890s and settled in the Delray area on the city's southwest side. In 1905 a Catholic parish was established there, and by 1925 Holy Cross Hungarian Catholic Church was built with the help of immigrant craftsmen. By this time the Delray-Springwells area of Detroit was known as "Little Hungary" and was considered the center of Michigan's Magyar (Hungarian) culture.

The Armenian community that first grew in Detroit differed from the other ethnic settlements in that it was made up almost entirely of single young men. They lived in boardinghouses, and their social life was centered around local coffeehouses. The men worked in the auto plants, and when they were able they sent for their wives and intended brides back home. Many took their savings from their factory jobs and went into business for themselves: rug retailing, restaurants, shoe repair, dry cleaning, and hotels. The largest influx of Armenians to the Detroit area came after World War I, while fleeing the Turkish massacre (1915–18) during the Ottoman Empire. So many Armenians settled in the West Jefferson and South Solvey area of Delray that streetcar conductors on the West Jefferson line would call out "Armenian Boulevard" for the South Solvey stop. Other important Armenian communities grew in Highland Park and on Detroit's east side. Further immigration took place after World War II. Others came during the civil war in Lebanon in the 1970s, which was followed by the abdication of the Shah of Iran, and after the disintegration and collapse of the USSR.

The first Belgians began to arrive in Detroit about 1890, settling on the east side where they found employment in area brickyards. Many had come to Detroit after first settling in Buffalo, New York, and the term Buffaloes, now seldom heard, was applied to them. When World War I began in Europe, immigration from Belgium to the Motor City increased substantially. By that time, "the city," as they called Detroit, had become the largest community of Belgians in the United States.

During the early 1900s, Detroit's Jewish community, made up largely of Russians who were fleeing the pogroms and persecutions of their czarist homeland, was located on the lower east side along Hastings Street. In 1907 a Yiddish directory listed the names, addresses, and occupations of more than twenty-three hundred Jews living in Detroit.

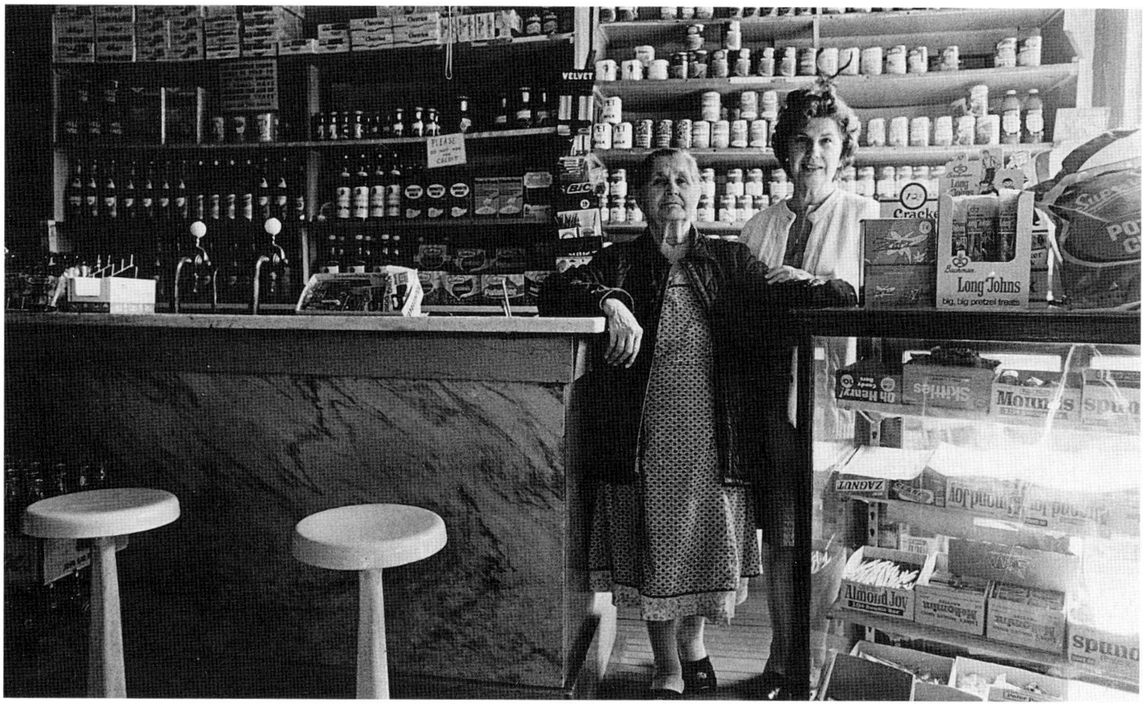

Hungarian grocery in Delray, 1973. Photo by Terry Yank. Courtesy Detroit Historical Museum.

One of the early Belgian businesses on Van Dyke Avenue was the Cornillie Bros. Moving and Storage Co., shown here with their horse-drawn wagon. Courtesy Genealogical Society of Flemish Americans.

Belgian children were brought to Detroit during World War I as refugees. Courtesy Walter P. Reuther Library, Wayne State University, Detroit.

The demographics changed little for the next thirty years, with the exception of a large influx of Jews fleeing Hitler's Germany in the 1930s. By the 1940s the Jewish community was to be found in the Twelfth Street, Linwood, and Dexter area. Later it transferred to the Livernois–Seven Mile area, then into the suburbs of Oak Park, Southfield, and West Bloomfield. The 1980s saw another influx of Russian Jews to the Detroit (primarily Oak Park) area, due in part to the relaxation in the Soviet Union's travel restrictions in 1988 and the USSR's final breakup. Metropolitan Detroit is now home to some 96,000 Jewish Americans. Of this number about 75 percent live in southern Oakland County, many within walking distance of their synagogues.

Symbols of this Jewish woman's faith adorn her table—the menorah, the challah, and the candles lit at sundown to mark the Sabbath. Photo by Judy Kerwin. Courtesy Detroit Historical Museum.

Two of the largest groups to settle in Detroit were the Italians and the Greeks. The first Greek families began arriving in the late 1880s and settled on Monroe Street between Beaubien and St. Antoine. Later the settlement moved onto Macomb Street, where the first Greek coffeehouse opened. Although many Greek immigrants came from agricultural backgrounds, few became farmers in this country. Many of those who settled in Detroit sought jobs as railroad and auto factory workers. Many other Greeks were merchants and lived near their stores, and in many cases above their shops. The church has been especially significant in the life of Detroit's Greek community. By 1909, when no more than 250 Greeks had settled in the city, a campaign was begun to raise money to purchase space for a church. Within a year, sufficient funds were available to rent the second floor of a hall on Broadway Street, and the Annunciation Greek Orthodox Church was founded. Today people of Greek descent will be found throughout the Detroit tri-county region, but it is still Greektown, centered on Monroe

As ethnic communities moved to the suburbs, they opened new churches. Here parishioners gather for the blessing of a Greek church in Dearborn Heights. Photo by Lance Muresan. Courtesy Detroit Historical Museum.

Street with its bustling restaurants, coffeehouses, bakeries, and markets, that the Greek community calls home.

Italians first began arriving in Detroit in large numbers in the 1880s (the first families had arrived here as early as the 1850s). They settled on the near east side north of Fort Street and south of Gratiot in the neighborhood of Mullett, St. Antoine, and Orleans Streets. These first families came from northern Italy, but they were soon joined by people from other parts of their homeland. In 1883 a group of Sicilian immigrants arrived in Detroit from Cleveland, where they were fruit merchants; they soon opened similar businesses. Detroit was unique in that the Italians who settled here had come from all parts of Italy. Most other large U.S. cities had Italian colonies, but these were made up only of Italians from one or two regions of the country. As would be expected, many Italian set-

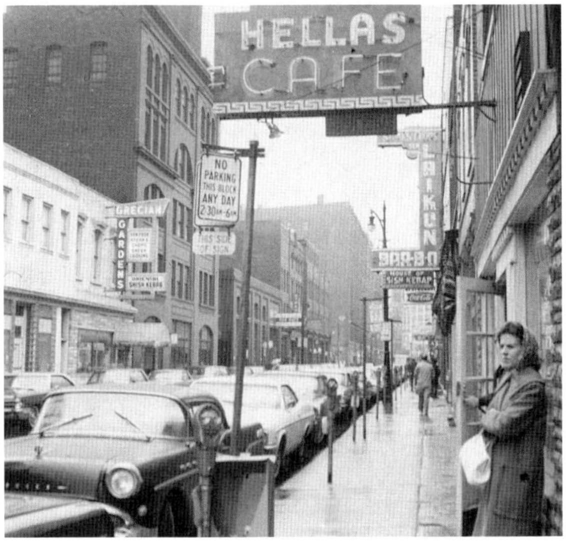

On the left side of Monroe in Greektown is the Grecian Gardens. The Hellas Café and the Laikon Café are on the right. Grocery stores, coffeehouses, and restaurants line this Greek cultural center, anchored by St. Mary's Catholic Church and Assumption Greek Orthodox Church on the next block. Courtesy Walter P. Reuther Library, Wayne State University, Detroit.

tlers in Detroit found employment in the city's factories, but many others established their own shops and markets. In 1930 the Italo-American Commercial Guide listed more than 120 retail groceries owned by Italians. Other Italians who came to Detroit were skilled artisans, particularly in tile work and decorative plaster, and their work graced many of the city's early mansions and office buildings. Today the Italian community is scattered throughout the tri-county area, but it is represented most heavily on Detroit's east side—in St. Clair Shores and Eastpointe as well as in other Macomb County suburbs.

The city's Polish citizens began to move from Detroit's lower east side into Hamtramck about 1910. As the Dodge plant grew, so grew Hamtramck's Polish population, and Polish street names began to appear there in the early 1920s. It is interesting to note that settling with the Poles in Hamtramck were Russians, Austrians, Lithuanians, and Czechoslovakians, all of whose homelands are contiguous with Poland in Europe. The Ukrainians were another important group to settle in the Hamtramck area. Like people of so many other nationalities, they first came to Detroit to work in the automobile factories. The second large influx of Ukrainians followed World War II, many coming to Detroit by way of Canada. These people were among the thousands caught homeless in displaced-person camps throughout Europe. They were political refugees who looked to America as a safe harbor. Today more than 200,000 Ukrainian Americans populate greater Detroit, most living in the suburbs on the east side. The hubs of Ukrainian-related activities, however, are in Hamtramck and Warren, which is home to the Ukrainian Cultural Center and St. Josephat Ukrainian Catholic Church.

The pressures for Americanization of the new arrivals began earlier in Detroit than in the United States generally. The initial stimulus was the high unemployment rate during the winter of 1914–15, when an estimated eighty thousand men were unemployed and homeless in Detroit. Of these, it was discovered that more than 60 percent did not speak English. As a result, English language instruction was undertaken in night schools conducted by the Detroit Board of Education. Then in 1919, as the number of immigrants continued to grow, a group of concerned citizens opened a "cottage" in downtown Detroit to serve as a center for newcomers to the city. The workers, primarily employees of the YMCA, gave assistance to the

Diners walk "Under the Eagle" into this tiny restaurant on Joseph Campau renowned for its excellent home-style Polish cooking. Photo by Larry Abegarian. Courtesy Detroit Historical Museum.

thousands of new residents who needed instruction in the language and in the rudiments of living in "the new world." From this beginning in a small brick building at the corner of Adams and Witherell Streets grew the International Institute. Today, located in its own building on East Kirby in the city's cultural center, the International Institute continues to serve Detroit's foreign-born residents with advice and help with immigration and naturalization matters, individual and family counseling, English language classes, interpreters, and translation of documents.

Several of the larger companies in the city had also begun classes in English language instruction. One of these, Ford Motor Company, went a step further than simply imparting a new language to foreigners. At the beginning of the twentieth century it was generally accepted that America was the great melting pot into which diverse immigrant groups entered. Their foreign cultures, languages, customs, and values would melt and the resultant broth would be "American"—a product of a new and uniform consistency devoid of the character of any of the individual ethnic ingredients. The Ford Motor Company carried this theory to an extreme. The graduation ceremony at its school included a large replica of a steaming pot on a stage. Into this pot would walk the graduates in their immigrant clothing. While the English instructors stirred the pot, graduates would emerge in American suits waving American flags.

Although the melting pot theory was a strong force in American life, a large number of the new immigrants continued their old-world customs. Fortunately, many of these customs survived and are still practiced today. Hungarians still celebrate "Locsolodas" (Easter Monday) and "Disznotor" (a ceremonial feast following the butchering of a pig). Many Polish families still practice the Christmas customs of breaking and sharing the Christmas wafer among relatives, placing

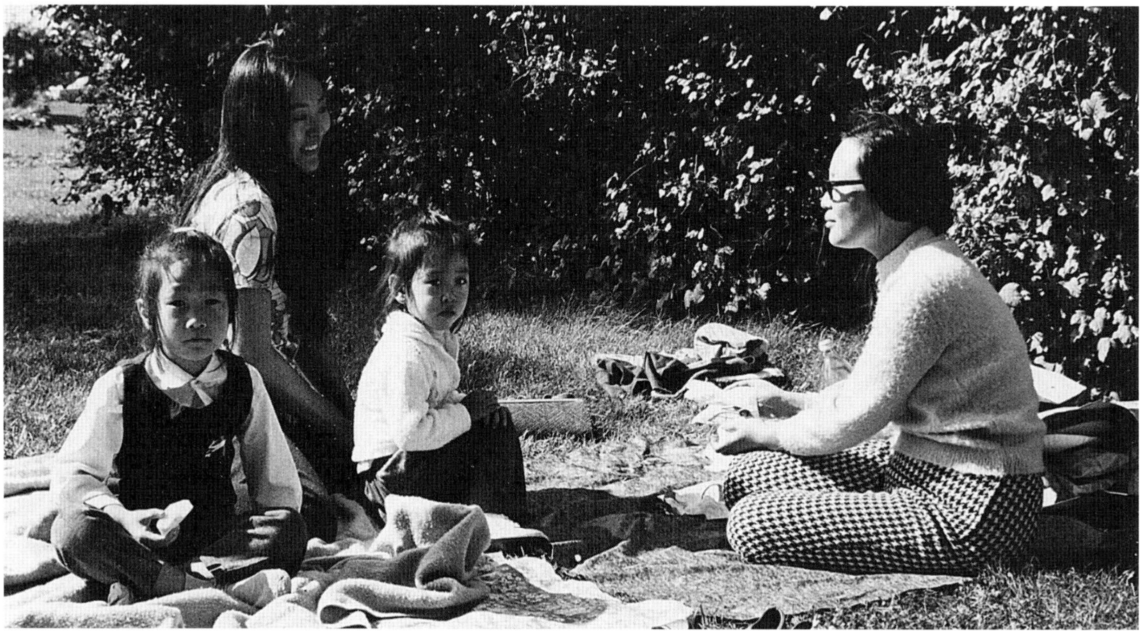

Korean family picnicking on Belle Isle, 1973. Photo by Paula Anderson. Courtesy Detroit Historical Museum.

Headquarters of the Detroit Chinese Merchants Association on Third Avenue and Porter Street decorated for the thirty-fifth annual convention in 1939. *Detroit News* photo. Courtesy Walter P. Reuther Library, Wayne State University, Detroit.

hay underneath the tablecloth, serving twelve varieties of dishes for Christmas Eve supper, and going around from house to house with "Christ's Crib" and caroling. The Ukrainians brought their holiday customs of "Sviat Veckur" (the holy supper), the "Korovai" (wedding bread), and the gaily colored "Pysanky" (specially decorated Easter eggs). The Greeks have shared with Detroiters their music and their dancing, the Lebanese and Syrians their fine food, and the Irish contributed St. Patrick's Day, when every Detroiter is an Irishman for a day.

Special festivals also continue to be celebrated in Detroit, such as the Hungarian Fall Festival of the Grape, the Mexican Feast of Our Lady of Guadaloupe, the Polish Strawberry Festival, the Chinese Moon Festival, the Japanese Cherry Blossom Festival held on Belle Isle, and the Scottish Highland Games, which have been held in Detroit every year since 1850 and are the oldest festival of their kind in North America.

In the late 1880s another ethnic group began to call Detroit home—the Latinos. Many came to Detroit primarily as workers for the railroads, as well as the sugar beet and meatpacking industries. It has been estimated that by 1920 some 15,000 Latinos lived in Detroit—mainly in the old Irish neighborhood of Corktown. Unfortunately, during the 1930s Detroit's Latino population lost significant numbers and endured considerable hostility as they were perceived as competitors for the few jobs that were available. In fact, during the Depression a "Mexican Bureau" was formed in Detroit to encourage Mexican Americans to return to Mexico. During the 1940s and 1950s the Latino community began to grow once again, and today there are an estimated 90,000 to 100,000 Latinos in metropolitan Detroit.

Mexican dancers perform with a live band at a holiday gathering. *Detroit News* photo. Courtesy Walter P. Reuther Library, Wayne State University, Detroit.

View of Mexican Village on Bagley at Eighteenth Street. Courtesy Walter P. Reuther Library, Wayne State University, Detroit.

Most live in the city's southwest neighborhoods of Corktown, Hubbard-Richard, West Vernor, Michigan Avenue, and Springwells, all in the parishes of Ste. Anne's, Holy Redeemer, and St. Gabriel. The Latino community, made up primarily of Mexican Americans, also includes people from Puerto Rico and Cuba and is today a thriving and economically stable neighborhood.

Another ethnic group that has grown in recent years is that of the Arabic-speaking peoples. The first Arabs came to Detroit as early as the 1890s from Lebanon and Syria. The largest influx, though, occurred in the last thirty years, with most coming as refugees fleeing the Middle East. In addition to the Lebanese and Syrians, the other major Arabic nationalities represented in the Detroit area are Jordanian, Palestinian, Iraqi-Chaldean, Egyptian, and Yemeni.

The opening of the Ford Motor Company plant in Highland Park played a pivotal role in the establishment of Detroit's first large Arab community. By the early 1900s, Highland Park had a number of Arab grocery stores, coffeehouses, and other businesses within walking distance of the plant. At this time, the community was mainly Christian in faith, but many Muslim immigrants also began to arrive. In fact, the first mosque in America was built in Highland Park in 1919.

Another significant event that affected the growth of Detroit's Arab community was the opening of Ford's giant Rouge plant. By the 1940s the Rouge had become the largest industrial complex in the world, employing

Lebanese market, 1974. Photo by Vicki Conover. Courtesy Detroit Historical Museum.

more than 90,000 workers. A large number of Muslims from Lebanon and other areas of the Arab world began to settle in Dearborn's south end next to the Rouge plant. During the following years, war and economic disaster in the Middle East resulted in a huge influx of people from the Arab world, and by the mid-1970s nearly 100,000 people of Middle Eastern descent lived in the Detroit area.

Like most other immigrant groups, Detroit's Arab community settled in enclaves reflecting the common bonds of nationality and religious persuasion. This ethnic community concept has persisted, and successive generations have migrated out into the expanding metropolitan area. Today Lebanese and Syrian Christians and Muslims represent over 55 percent of metropolitan Detroit's Arab American community. Lebanese and Syrian Christians established roots on Detroit's east side and eventually expanded in a northeast path in the Grosse Pointes, St. Clair Shores, Eastpointe, Roseville, and other Macomb County suburbs. Lebanese and Syrian Muslim residential patterns have concentrated in the Dearborn area and the western suburbs. Today, in fact, southeast Dearborn is 90 percent Arab American.

Palestinians and Jordanians make up over 20 percent of metropolitan Detroit's Arab community. These groups have settled along the east-west corridors established by the Lebanese and Syrian communities. The number of people emigrating from Yemen has escalated during the last twenty-five years, with settlement in both Dearborn and Hamtramck. Today, Yemeni American students represent over 70 percent of the enrollment in Hamtramck's public schools.

The Iraqi-Chaldeans are a unique cultural minority of Detroit's Middle Eastern community.

Arab family relaxing on their porch in Dearborn, 1995. Photo by Millard Berry. Courtesy the photographer.

These people first began to arrive here just before World War I and settled in the Seven Mile Road–Woodward Avenue area. With its row of small shops and restaurants, bilingual signs and names, the area earned the well-deserved designation as Detroit's "Little Baghdad."

The growth of the region's Arab American community continues. Now numbering more than 250,000 people, it continues to reflect the religions and ethnic diversity of the Arab world.

Thus it is that over the last seventy-five years, hundreds of thousands of immigrants from all over the globe have come to Detroit and made the city their new home. This influx is not a thing of the past, though. In 1997, for example, more than ten thousand legal immigrants settled in Detroit. Today the region can proudly boast of more than one hundred ethnic and nationality groups. Yet, while they represent a variety of languages, customs, and traditions, Detroit's ethnic communities have worked hard to create a feeling of respect and harmony. Detroit is indeed fortunate, for its multi-ethnicity has resulted in a better life not only for the peoples of these various cultures, but for all the region's residents.

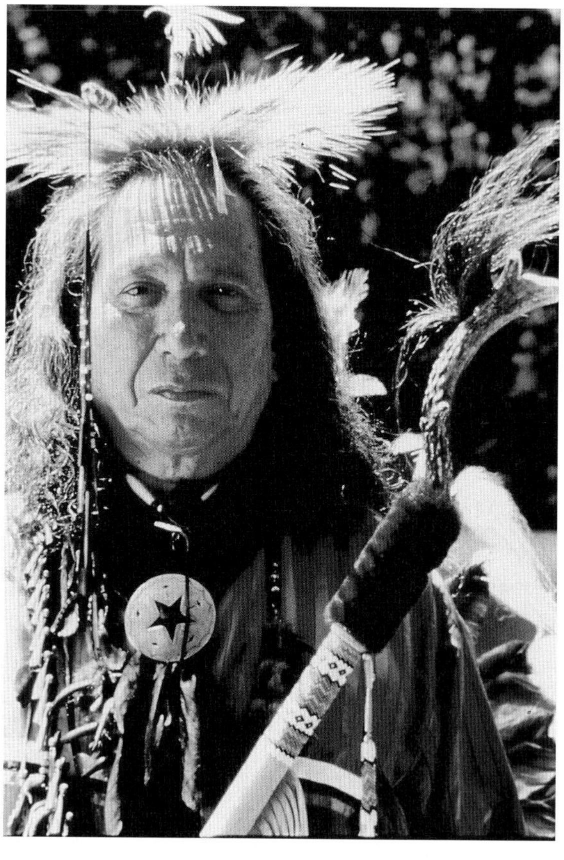

George Martin, Ojibwe/Eastern Shawnee Native American, is an elder, Midewin, and beadwork artist. Native Americans from many tribes, including descendants of the original People of the Three Fires, live in Metropolitan Detroit today. Photo by S. Kay Young. Courtesy the photographer.

Eighteen

Motown

To many, the name Detroit is synonymous with the automobile. Although the horseless carriage was not invented here, the city is recognized worldwide as the Motor Capital. To others, however, Detroit means something far different from the sound of assembly lines, stamping plants, and finely tuned engines. To many the name Detroit brings forth an image produced by a far different sound—it is the sound of music, the sound of Motown.

In 1959, a young African American, Berry Gordy, Jr., borrowed $800 from his parents and began a music recording company in a small house on West Grand Boulevard. Originally called Tamla Records, the company began as one of a number of small rhythm and blues record companies that sprang up in Detroit during the 1950s, partly in response to a demand for such music by black-oriented radio stations.

For his performers, writers, and producers, Gordy turned to Detroit's black community, the same environment in which the music itself had its roots. The company's first national release was "Money (That's What I Want)," recorded by Barrett Strong in August 1959. Shortly thereafter, Gordy, choosing a

Berry Gordy presents Motown's first gold record to William "Smokey" Robinson and the Miracles in 1961. Courtesy Motown Records Archives.

name which he felt reflected the Motor City, coined the word "Motown" and incorporated his company as the Motown Record Corporation on April 14, 1960. Motown's first major success was a song called "Shop Around" by William "Smokey" Robinson and the Miracles. Released late in 1960, the record quickly became a smash hit, selling more than a million copies by February 1961. It was to be Motown's first gold record.

The company went on to develop such artists as Stevie Wonder, a blind boy born in Saginaw and raised in Detroit who at age twelve recorded "Fingertips" and went on to win numerous Grammy Awards as a producer, writer, and performer. There was also Marvin Gaye, the Temptations, the Marvelettes, the Four Tops, Martha and the Vandellas, the Jackson 5, and many others. Their songs included such hits as "I Second That Emotion," "How Sweet It Is," "My Girl," "Up Tight (Everything's All Right)," and "I Heard It Through the Grapevine."

But it was really three young Detroit schoolgirls that brought success to Motown. They were Diana Ross, Mary Wilson, and

Hitsville U.S.A. is where it all began, the first home of Motown Record Corporation on West Grand Boulevard. *From left:* Edward Holland, Diana Ross, Mary Wilson, Lamont Dozier, Brian Holland, and Florence Ballard. Courtesy Motown Records Archives.

Florence Ballard, better known as the Supremes. The most successful singing group of the 1960s, they had more number one hits in a row than any other group in the history of popular music. Their songs, all of which were written by composers Brian Holland, Lamont Dozier, and Eddie Holland, included the hits "Where Did Our Love Go?" "Baby Love," and "Stop in the Name of Love."

In 1968, Gordy's company, which had now grown from a family-oriented business to an international enterprise, moved its business operations to a building on the northwest corner of Woodward and the Fisher Freeway. Recording continued to be done in Studio A in the original building, "Hitsville," on West Grand Boulevard. Here the recording artists were busy twenty-four hours a day, seven days a week. By 1971 Motown had over one hundred writers. One of the most prolific of these was "Smokey" Robinson, whom the Beatles called "the poet laureate of the pop world." By the end of its first decade, Motown was the largest manufacturer of 45 rpm singles in the world.

In 1972, Gordy expanded his operations and moved his headquarters to Los Angeles. There the company continued to grow at such a rate that by 1975, Motown Industries, with annual sales in excess of $40 million, was the largest black-owned corporation in the world. In California, Gordy expanded his operations from records, to tapes, to television, and finally to movies. The company produced *Lady Sings the Blues* (which received five Academy Award nominations), then *Mahogany,* and, in 1978, *The Wiz,* all starring Diana Ross. Finally, in 1988, Gordy sold Motown for $61 million to Boston Ventures.

Although the company has gone from Detroit, the sound survives and the memories of Motown have been preserved at "Hitsville USA," the original home of the company on West Grand Boulevard. Here visitors can tour Studio A with microphones ready for use and sheet music still on the stand. As one music historian wrote, "Motown combines elements of blues, gospel, swing, and pop with a thumping backbeat for a new dance music that was instantly recognizable." It is a special sound, born on the streets of Detroit, still listened to and enjoyed the world over by all who know the Motown sound.

The Supremes were the most successful singing group of the 1960s. This 1968 photograph was later used on one of their albums. *From left:* Diana Ross, Mary Wilson, and Florence Ballard. Photo by Tony Spina. Courtesy Walter P. Reuther Library, Wayne State University, Detroit.

Long before Motown, Detroit and Detroiters had an interest in music and the business of music. In 1854 a Detroiter named A. Couse wrote and published a song titled "The Detroit Schottische." It was not long before Couse's little tune became one of the nation's most popular songs. Thus began Detroit's music publishing business, a business that for the next seventy-five years was to flourish and grow, ranking Detroit second only to New York City in the publishing of music.

In the forty years that followed "The Detroit Schottische," Detroit's published music was largely for the local market. But with the 1890s, ragtime and Detroit rose to the top of the musical scene. Such tunes as "At a Georgia Camp Meeting" and "Dark

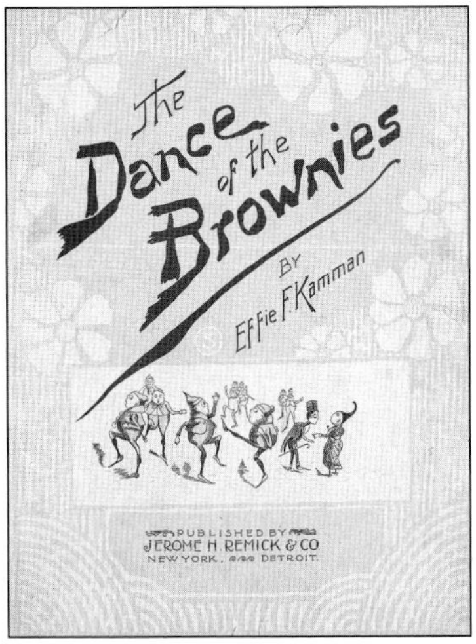

During the last half of the nineteenth century and the early years of the twentieth, Detroit was a leader in the music-publishing business, second only to New York City. Hits included "The Dance of the Brownies," "The Detroit Schottisch," and "The Cake Walk Winner." Courtesy Music and Performing Arts, Detroit Public Library.

Town Strutters Ball" began pouring from the presses of Whitney-Warner, Belcher and Davis, and other Detroit publishers. One of these tunes, "The Dance of the Brownies," was bought by Jerome H. Remick for ten dollars, and his investment set him on the way to becoming one of the largest music publishers in the world. From 1905 until he retired from the business in 1928, Remick's firm published more than sixty thousand songs.

While Detroit was busy publishing popular music, one of its citizens was becoming a leader in the field of black music. Her name was Emma Azalia Hackley. Born in 1867 and reared and educated in Detroit, this concert singer, choral director, and humanitarian devoted herself to the musical education of black people. Azalia Hackley traveled throughout this country and abroad raising funds for scholarships and working to revive interest in genuine black music. She died in Detroit in 1922, and in 1943 her private papers and memorabilia were presented to the Detroit Public Library by the Detroit Musicians' Association, the local chapter of

E. Azalia Hackley became a leading authority and promoter of black music in the early part of the twentieth century. Courtesy E. Azalia Hackley Collection, Detroit Public Library.

the National Association of Negro Musicians. Today the E. Azalia Hackley Memorial Collection, housed at the Main Library, is one of the nation's most valuable collections of research materials documenting the achievements of African Americans in the performing arts.

On the evening of November 19, 1914, Detroit's newly restructured symphony orchestra gave its first concert at the Detroit Opera House on Campus Martius. The conductor that evening was Weston Gales. On December 19, 1887, the Opera House was also the site of the first performance of a for-subscription concert season of a symphony orchestra in Detroit. The leading figure in the development of the new orchestra was Ossip Gabrilowitsch, who became conductor in 1918 and was one of the leading pianists of his day. In 1919 the symphony moved from temporary quarters into the beautiful new Orchestra Hall on Woodward Avenue at Parsons. Constructed in just five months at a cost of $590,000, Orchestra Hall is acoustically one of the finest auditoriums ever to be built in this country. For the next twenty years the concert hall was home to the symphony, but in 1939—at the end of the Depression, and three years after Gabrilowitsch's death—the symphony was to leave Orchestra Hall and move to more economical quarters.

In 1941, Orchestra Hall was reopened as the Paradise Theater and became "home" for many famous black performers in jazz, blues, and vaudeville. Among the performers who played the Paradise were Duke Ellington, Dizzy Gillespie, Billie Holiday, the Mills Brothers, Lionel Hampton, and Dinah Washington. But in 1951, economies forced the hall to close once again. Thereafter it was used occasionally as a concert hall, a recording studio, and even a church.

Detroit's famous Orchestra Hall at the time of its opening in 1919. Courtesy Burton Historical Collection, Detroit Public Library.

The leading figure in the early development of the Detroit Symphony Orchestra was Ossip Gabrilowitsch, who became conductor in 1918. Courtesy Burton Historical Collection, Detroit Public Library.

After leaving Orchestra Hall, the symphony gave its performances in the Music Hall, formerly the Wilson Theater, on Madison Avenue, or in the Masonic Temple auditorium. Then, in 1956, the Ford Motor Company and its dealers presented the city with the Henry and Edsel Ford Auditorium as a memorial to the two automotive leaders. The second structure to be erected in the civic center near what had been the foot of Bates Street, Ford Auditorium became the home of the symphony for the next twenty-two years. Once the orchestra left Ford Auditorium the building was occasionally used as a concert and lecture hall, but since 1990 it has stood vacant, its future use uncertain.

Following years of slow decay, Orchestra Hall was scheduled to be torn down in 1970, but a last-minute crusade by orchestra musicians and friends saved it from the wrecking ball. The next year the building was added to the National Register of Historic Places and a campaign was begun to restore this once beautiful concert hall. Finally, on September 15, 1989, after a nineteen-year, $6.8 million restoration, the Detroit Symphony Orchestra returned to its original home—Orchestra Hall.

Along with a world-class symphony orchestra, Detroiters have also long enjoyed their opera. In 1875 C. J. Whitney built an opera house on Fort Street where today's federal court building now stands. When the city's new post office was erected there in 1897, Whitney constructed a new house on the east side of Griswold just north of Michigan. Called the Garrick, it ran as a first-class theater until it closed in 1926.

Almost as well known was the Lyceum located on the east side of Randolph between Monroe and Lafayette. It began life as White's Grand Theater in 1880. White's was burned out in 1886 by the fire that destroyed the D. M. Ferry Seed Company, but it was immediately rebuilt as the Lyceum. After World War I the name was changed to the New Detroit Opera House, and it continued

During the 1920s Detroit became an important contributor to the development of big band jazz. Here, Floyd Hickman's Orchestra plays at the Palais de Dance on Jefferson. Other popular spots included the Arcadia, the Pier, and of course the famous Graystone Ballroom on Woodward at Canfield. There on Mondays ("colored only–night") three thousand people danced to McKinney's Cotton Pickers. Courtesy E. Azalia Hackley Collection, Detroit Public Library.

in operation until 1928, when its doors were closed for the last time.

Without question, however, the best-known of the old theaters was the famous Detroit Opera House on Campus Martius just east of Woodward Avenue. Built in 1868, it was opened in a glow of gaslight and was acclaimed by the *Free Press* as a "luxurious temple of art." The interior of the Opera House was lavishly decorated by Detroit artist Robert Hopkin. One of the building's most cherished features was the mainstage curtain, painted by Hopkin, with an idyllic scene that bore the following lines:

> *So fleet the works of men, back to their earth again, Ancient and holy things fade like a dream.*

The Opera House was designed with space for shops on the ground floor of the building, and it was there on April 2, 1881, that Joseph L. Hudson opened his first clothing store. Remodeled in 1887, the Opera House was completely destroyed by fire in 1897 but was immediately rebuilt. The Detroit Opera House was a grand theater, and it was there that the great performers of the late 1800s and early 1900s appeared, including the first performance of the Detroit Symphony Orchestra in 1914. It was a sad day in 1937 when the old Opera House was remodeled into a department store. The building was torn down in 1963.

In the same year the old Opera House was torn down, the Overture to Opera was established as an education/outreach arm of the

Detroit's most famous old theater was the Detroit Opera House on Campus Martius, just east of Woodward. All the great performers of the late 1800s and early 1900s appeared in this grand theater. Courtesy Manning Brothers Historic Photographic Collection, Detroit.

Detroit Grand Opera Association. In 1971 the organization presented its first mainstage season at the Music Hall on Madison Avenue. With the 1973–74 season, the company officially changed its name to the Michigan Opera Theatre with a mandate to serve the entire state. It is under this name that the company would later prosper and take a leading role in the rebirth of Detroit's theater district. That story will be told later.

There was little interest in art in early Detroit, but during the first half of the nineteenth century the city was home to several prominent painters. James O. Lewis, who came to Detroit in 1824, was noted for his portraits. John Mix Stanley won recognition for his landscapes and portraits. Thomas M. Burnham is best remembered for his portrayal of crowds and street scenes. Robert S. Duncanson, a black artist from Ohio whose training was financed by anti-slavery societies, had a studio in Detroit during the 1840s and lived in the city permanently after the Civil War. Alvah Bradish, in addition to being a fine portrait artist, frequently gave lectures in art appreciation. During the latter years of the nineteenth century, Detroit produced a number of other notable artists, including Robert Hopkin, Gari Melchers, Julius Rolshoven, Lewis T. Ives and his son Percy Ives, and Joseph W. Gies.

Although Detroit had no established art museum at this time, two very successful art exhibitions were held in the city in 1852 and 1853, and several smaller exhibits were held in later years. It was in 1883, however, that the first major art exhibition was held in Detroit. To organize this event, an Art Loan Association was formed.

To house the exhibition, a new skylighted brick exhibit hall was built on the north side of Larned between Randolph and Bates Streets. The exhibition, which contained over forty-eight hundred items, included works ranging from paintings and sculpture by American and European artists to what was frankly termed "bric-a-brac" in the exhibition catalogue. The exhibition, however, was a huge success, and for ten weeks, from September through November, 134,925 people paid twenty-five cents to visit the exhibit hall. Following the exhibition, the Art Loan

The impressive new Detroit Institute of Arts shortly after its opening in 1927. Courtesy Detroit Institute of Arts.

Association was disbanded and its assets were turned over to a newly formed museum association. In 1885, under the guidance of the members of the museum association, the Detroit Museum of Art was incorporated, and in 1888 it opened a new building at the southwest corner of East Jefferson and Hastings. In 1919 the Detroit Museum of Art gave the Jefferson Avenue building and its art collection to the city, and the private museum corporation became the Founders Society. The city's new museum was renamed the Detroit Institute of Arts, and the old museum's educational facility was spun off as Cass Technical High School. The new city charter of 1919 established an Arts Commission that was directed to build a new museum. The commission hired Paul Cret to design the building, and on October 6, 1927, a magnificent new museum opened on Woodward Avenue. It was substantially enlarged in the 1960s with the addition of two wings.

One of the museum's most notable holdings is a series of four murals by the noted Mexican artist Diego M. Rivera. When they were completed in the 1930s, the murals created a bitter controversy. Powerful in their depiction of Detroit's industrial life, the paintings led some to accuse Rivera of injecting Communist ideology into his portrayal. There was even talk of whitewashing the murals. Fortunately, they remained intact and may be viewed to this day.

Several other organizations also made important contributions to the history of art

Detroit Industry, north wall, 1932–33, Diego M. Rivera. This view of the north wall of the court at the Detroit Institute of Arts shows one of the four frescoes by Rivera. The north wall depicts the automobile industry, along with the medical, pharmaceutical, and chemical industries. Photograph copyright 1991 Detroit Institute of Arts, Gift of Edsel B. Ford.

and the Arts and Crafts movement in the Detroit area. Pewabic Pottery, founded in 1903 by Mary Chase Perry Stratton and Horace J. Caulkins, earned a national reputation for its tile work, unique vessels, and iridescent glazes. Today the Pottery, housed in an historic 1907 Tudor Revival building, is located out East Jefferson across from Waterworks Park. Also in 1907, the Arts and Crafts Society (today the Center for Creative Studies) was founded and was soon established as an art school of major importance. Its campus on East Kirby Avenue is located in the city's cultural center adjacent to the Detroit Institute of Arts. The Scarab Club had its beginnings in Detroit's artist colony in 1910. The clubhouse, built in 1928, is located at the northeast corner of John R. and Farnsworth in the cultural center. The club was organized, and still functions, for the artistic encouragement "of every facet of creative interest." In 1932, the famous Cranbrook Academy of Art was founded in suburban Bloomfield Hills. The Cranbrook complex, consisting of the art school, a church, a science museum, and a private school, was established by *Detroit News* publisher George G. Booth and his wife, Ellen Scripps Booth.

Mary Chase Perry Stratton laying Pewabic tiles. Courtesy Pewabic Pottery.

Like art, the theater had little success in early Detroit. This was due in large part to the antagonistic attitude toward the theater on the part of most of the city's Protestant churches. However, as early as 1816, American army officers stationed at the fort staged theatrical productions in the government warehouse at the foot of Wayne Street. In the 1830s a barn near the Steamboat Hotel was used as a theater, and the City Hall council chambers were occasionally used during the 1840s. It may be that the old City Hall rostrum was the first stage to be used by traveling or road companies.

The city's first real theater was finally opened in 1834 on the second floor of the Smart block where the City-County Building now stands. That same year a building at the corner of Gratiot and Library, originally intended to be a Methodist church, was converted into a theater. In 1849 the Metropolitan Theater on Jefferson between Randolph and Brush was built. A short time later two more playhouses, the Varieties and the Courique, appeared on the same block. For many years thereafter that part of town was known as Detroit's theater district.

Best known of the city's old theaters was of course the Detroit Opera House on Campus Martius, whose story has already been told. There was also the Lyceum, White's, and the Garrick. Later other popular legitimate theaters (that is, those using professional actors) were opened, including the Washington on

An artist in one of the studios at Detroit's famed Scarab Club. Courtesy Scarab Club.

Washington Boulevard near Clifford; the Orpheum, built in 1914 on Lafayette at Shelby and later renamed the Shubert-Lafayette; and the Cass, opened in 1926 on Lafayette near Washington. Eventually the Washington and the Shubert-Lafayette were torn down, and in 1965 the Cass was converted into a motion picture house. With these theaters' curtains lowered for the last time, downtown Detroit was left without a regular theater. In fact, by the 1960s the Fisher was the city's only professional legitimate theater. Remodeled in 1961 from a movie palace in the Fisher Building, the Fisher Theater was an immediate success and at the time boasted the largest full-season subscription audience in the country.

Along with professional legitimate theater, Detroit has had its share of community theaters. The most important of these was the Bonstelle Players, formed by Miss Jesse Bonstelle in 1910. After 1924 the group had its own theater, the Bonstelle Playhouse, in the reconverted Temple Beth El on Woodward Avenue. Miss Bonstelle was known as the "maker of stars," and among the great figures she encouraged were Katharine Cornell, Ann Harding, Frank Morgan, Melvyn Douglas, and William Powell. In 1928 the Bonstelle Players were reorganized as the Detroit Civic Theater. Four years later, however, Miss Bonstelle died, and the theater closed its doors the following year. Thereafter the facility was used as a movie house and for vaudeville until it was taken over in 1951 by Wayne State University as its undergraduate theater.

Today, community theater thrives in the Detroit area through Wayne State University's Hilberry (the only graduate repertory theater in the country), Bonstelle Theater, Youtheater, Detroit Repertory Theatre on Woodrow Wilson Street, Detroit Theatre for the Dramatic Arts, Plowshares Theatre Company, Detroit Puppet Theatre, the Theatre Company on the campus of the University of Detroit Mercy, Jewish Ensemble Theater in

West Bloomfield, Oakland University's Meadow Brook Theatre, Second City Detroit on Woodward at Montcalm, and Planet Art Theatre on Caniff in Hamtramck. In addition, there are more than one hundred other community theater groups in the Detroit area, making this one of the largest community theater centers in the United States.

Along with legitimate theater, Detroit had several fine vaudeville houses. The best-known was the Temple, which opened in 1901 on Monroe just around the corner from Campus Martius. Practically all the great vaudeville artists appeared there. The Temple had a regular clientele and in many respects was the city's most popular theater, but the movies dealt it a death blow. It closed in 1935 and was torn down a short time later. Burlesque too was popular in Detroit and had its well-known houses. One famous one was the Avenue, located on lower Woodward in the block now covered by the City-County Building. The Gayety on Monroe was also a favorite, as was the Cadillac on Michigan at Washington.

In 1896 a group of newspapermen and a few leading citizens were invited to the Detroit Opera House to witness the first demonstration in Detroit of a novelty called the eidoloscope, which was nothing more than a crude motion picture. It consisted of seven reels depicting a bullfight in Mexico, and those who saw it did not think very highly of it. A short time later a better show was staged (or screened) at the Wonderland, located on the east side of Woodward at Jefferson. That was *The Great Train Robbery,* generally acknowledged to have been the first American-made movie. It was well attended, and this time the public was impressed. A new form of entertainment had come to Detroit, and it would not be long before the motion picture put vaudeville out of business and darkened most of the legitimate theaters.

Detroit had several fine vaudeville houses. One of the most popular was the Miles Theatre on the east side of Griswold between State and Grand River, seen here in 1920. Courtesy Manning Brothers Historic Photographic Collection.

The first Detroit theater devoted exclusively to showing motion pictures was opened in 1905 at Monroe and Farmer Streets. Named the Casino Theater, it had been a variety house. The Casino was such a success that within a few years other new movie theaters were opened downtown. At first they were centered on Monroe between Campus Martius and Farmer Street, but before long stores were being converted into movie houses, not only downtown, but in the residential neighborhoods as well. The first of the neighborhood theaters was the Garden on Woodward between Selden and Alexandrine. Soon motion pictures became such a success that by the 1920s the city boasted more than 160 movie theaters.

Burlesque was popular in Detroit. Here is the Avenue in 1917, on the east side of Woodward just north of Jefferson. Courtesy Manning Brothers Historic Photographic Collection.

Without question, though, the most famous of Detroit's movie theaters were the grand movie palaces built downtown. These "great temples of amusement" were the product of the period of prosperity that preceded the Great Depression. Built on the outer perimeter of Grand Circus Park, these huge, opulent structures featured gilded carvings, ornate statuary, crystal chandeliers, and grand staircases. The first were the Madison and Adams Theaters, both of which opened in 1917. They were followed by the Capitol (1922) on Broadway and the State (1925) on Woodward. Then came the Michigan (1926) and the United Artist (1928), both on Bagley Avenue. Many of these beautiful buildings were designed by Detroit architect C. Howard Crane. By the end of his career Crane had completed some 250 theater buildings in the United States and Canada. His crowning achievement, however, was Detroit's Fox Theater (1928). Seating over five thousand people, it surpassed all the other movie palaces in the city in size. Then, no sooner was the Fox opened than Detroit moviegoers were treated to an equally grand palace, the Fisher. Opened in the fall of 1928 in the beautiful Fisher Building on West Grand Boulevard, the Fisher was the last of the great movie palaces to be built in Detroit. Eventually television, and then the large suburban movie theater complexes, brought an end to these grand downtown theaters. By the 1980s all had closed their doors.

Along with art, music, and the theater, Detroiters have long had an interest in reading and in books. The city's first library was a private organization known as a subscription

One of Detroit's "great temples of amusement" was the Michigan Theater, built in 1926. This view dates from 1929. Courtesy Manning Brothers Historic Photographic Collection.

library. Incorporated in 1817, the City Library Association sold shares of stock to raise funds, and only shareholders could borrow books. The association had rooms in the old University of Michigan Building on Bates Street.

It was not until after the Civil War, however, that Detroiters had their own free public library. In 1865 the board of education established the Detroit Public Library with a reading room at the rear of the city high school in the Old Capitol. In 1877 the library moved into its own building erected in Centre Park on Gratiot between Library and Farmer Streets. The site is today the location of the Downtown Branch library, built in 1932. The present Main Library, on Woodward between Putnam and Kirby Streets, opened in 1921. The architect for the new library was Cass Gilbert, who had also been the architect for the Scott Fountain on Belle Isle. Gilbert's design for the library was Italian Renaissance. Set back from Woodward Avenue with an approach of terraces, the white marble facade was a model of carefully studied proportion and detail. As one noted architectural historian wrote, the building "set a new standard of magnificence for Detroit." The library was substantially enlarged when its wings were opened in

The opulent interior of the beautiful Fisher Theater. Opened in 1928, the Fisher was the last of the great movie houses to be built in Detroit. Courtesy Manning Brothers Historic Photographic Collection.

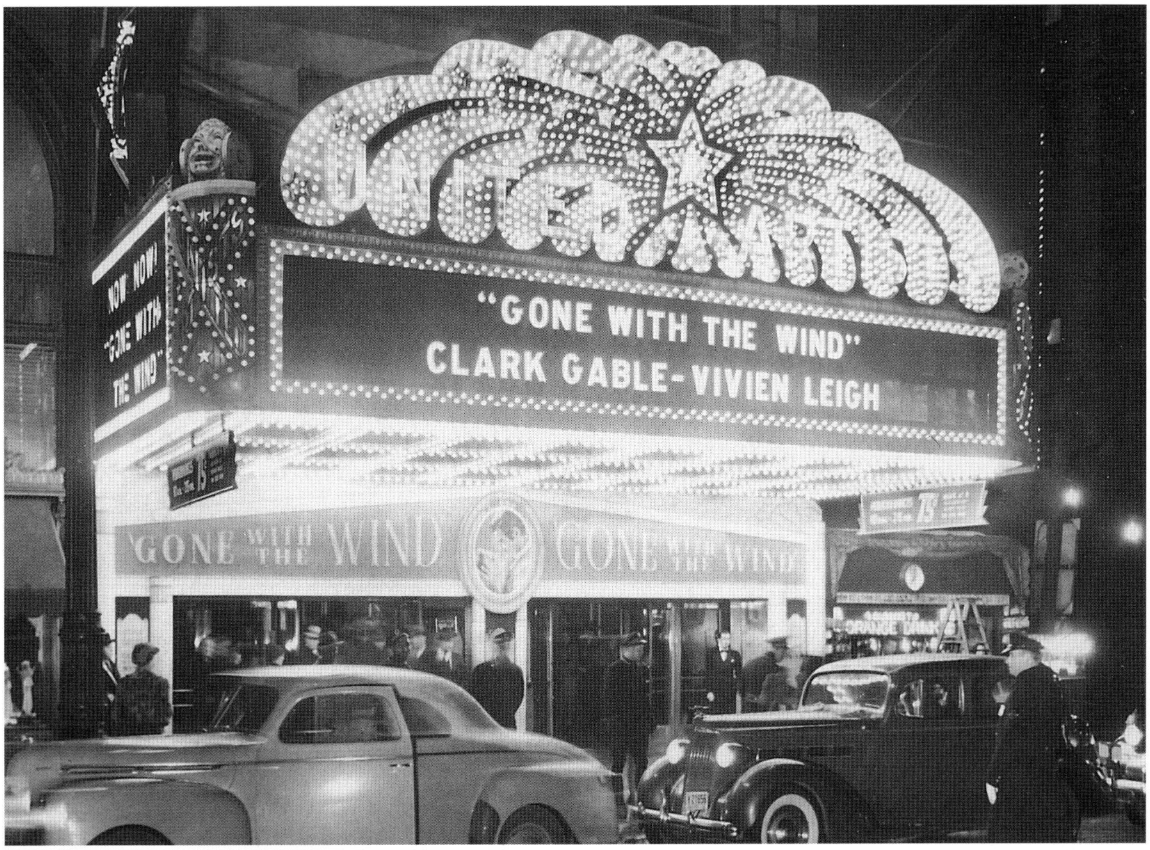

Gone with the Wind was playing at the United Artist Theater when this photograph was taken in 1940. Courtesy Manning Brothers Historic Photographic Collection.

1963, and today the Detroit Public Library is one of the nation's finest. With holdings of more than two million volumes, it has extensive reference and research collections in the fields of technology and science, music, cartography, and literature. It also houses the nationally known Burton Historical Collection and the National Automotive History Collection.

The life expectancy of a newspaper in Detroit during the last half of the nineteenth century was frequently short, and changes in ownership were numerous. Up to 1885, for example, 253 newspapers had been started in Detroit. By 1900 there were four major papers being published in the city. The *Free Press* and the *Tribune* were the morning dailies, while

The Cass Avenue entrance of Detroit's world-famous Main Library, built in the 1920s, and wings, which opened in 1963. Courtesy Detroit Public Library.

the *Evening Journal* and the *News* were the leading afternoon papers.

The News had been founded in 1873 by the colorful James E. Scripps, who over the years took control of several other papers, including the *Advertisor,* the *Tribune,* and the *Journal.* In 1960 the News purchased William Randolph Hearst's *Detroit Times,* leaving only the *News* and the *Free Press* as the city's major daily newspapers.

In 1987 the *News* and the *Free Press* announced plans to merge their business operations under the terms of a joint operating agreement. Following considerable controversy, the agreement was approved in the fall of 1989 and the two papers were joined under a newly formed Detroit Newspaper Agency. This action eventually led to a long and often bitter employee strike that was not settled until 1997. Finally, on July 26, 1998, the *Free Press* moved out of its old building on West Lafayette and into new offices down the street in the *Detroit News* Building. There today the two papers, while operating out of the same building, remain fierce competitors, each retaining its own identity.

Detroit's largest black-owned newspaper (and the oldest black newspaper continuously published in the state), the *Michigan Chronicle,* was established in 1936 by Louis E. Martin. Under editor Longworth M. Quinn, Sr., and later publisher Samuel Logan, the paper became an active voice in the community and today has a circulation of over forty-seven thousand. Other important ethnic papers published in the Detroit area today include the German *Nordamerikanische Wochen-Post* (founded in Detroit in 1854); the *Arab American Journal;* the *Hispanic El Central;* the *Chaldean Detroit Times;* the Belgian *Gazette Van Detroit* (published here since 1914); the *Italian Tribune;* the *Jewish News;* and the *Swait Polski* (Polish World).

In addition to publishing a leading newspaper, the *Detroit News* was also a pioneer in the field of electronic communications. On the evening of August 20, 1920, a radio station owned by the News broadcast the first regular radio program in the United States. Condenser dials were adjusted, generator brushes were cleaned, and strains of "Annie Laurie" and "Roses of Picardy" went out over the airwaves. Originally known as 8MK, the station was later named WBL, and finally, in 1922, WWJ. That year it initiated broadcasts of University of Michigan extension courses and Sunday services from St. Paul's Episcopal Cathedral. The first Tiger baseball game was broadcast by WWJ in 1927 with Ty Tyson at the microphone.

On May 4, 1922, another early station, WCX, later WJR, signed on. Today it broadcasts from studios in the "Golden Towers" of the Fisher Building. WXYZ, founded on October 10, 1925, as WGHP, was bought by George W. Trendle in 1929. He changed its name, moved its studios to the Maccabees Building (now the School Center Building), and in three years sent forth the cry of "Hi,

This staged picture was shot a few days after the August 20, 1920, inauguration of the *Detroit News's* makeshift studio where WWJ aired for the first time. Courtesy *Detroit News* Archives.

Ho, Silver" to join the immortals of radio. *The Lone Ranger, The Green Hornet,* and *Sgt. Preston of the Yukon* thundered out of the Maccabees Building across the country and made Detroit rank with New York, Chicago, and Hollywood as a radio center.

When it went on the air on November 7, 1956, WCHB AM 1200 in Detroit became the nation's third black-owned radio station. The call letters were the initials of the station's founders, Hamtramck dentists Wendell Cox and Haley Bell, who were the first minority members to build a station from the ground up. Today the WCHB stations, including WGPR FM and WQBH AM, are still owned by African Americans.

In the fall of 1946, the *Detroit News*'s WWJ-TV produced the city's first television broadcast at Convention Hall. On March 4, 1947, the station introduced the first commercial television program in Detroit from its studios on West Lafayette at Second. When the *Detroit News* sold WWJ-TV to the *Washington Post,* the new owners renamed the station WDIV-TV. In return for WWJ-TV, the *News* assumed control of the *Post*-owned WTOP-TV in Washington, D.C.

Detroit's first TV broadcast, WWJ-TV at Convention Hall on Woodward, November 22, 1946. Courtesy *Detroit News* Archives.

As Detroit grew from a busy nineteenth-century commercial town to a giant twentieth-century industrial city, its citizens' need for institutions of higher learning grew as well. Expanding business and industry called for workers with greater technical and professional skills. In addition, stay-at-home students needed new educational facilities at a lower cost than was possible from the established outstate colleges and universities.

Wayne State, the city's largest university, is an outgrowth of this need. It developed from the merger of several separate colleges maintained originally by the Detroit Board of Education. Although the university did not come into official existence until 1933, some of its colleges had been in operation for many years. The medical college was established in 1868 as the privately owned Detroit Medical College, and it is from the founding of this, its oldest college, that the university dates its origin. The college of education was founded by the city in 1881 as the Detroit Normal School. The liberal arts college is the outgrowth of post-graduate high school training offered at the old Detroit Central High School (now Wayne's "Old Main") beginning in 1915. Wayne University, as it was first named, remained under board of education control until 1956, when it came under state control and support and received its present name of Wayne State University.

Detroit's other major university, the University of Detroit Mercy, dates from 1877, when it was founded as the Detroit College by priests of the Jesuit order. It was first housed in a two-story residence on East Jefferson Avenue near downtown, and new colleges such as law, engineering, business administration, and dentistry were added over the years. As a result, the school was reorganized in 1911 and renamed the University of Detroit. The school continued to grow at such a rate that in 1922 a forty-two-acre site was obtained for a new campus at West Six Mile and Livernois. In 1927 this became the school's main campus. It was later named the McNichols campus (and Six Mile Road became McNichols Road) in honor of Father John McNichols, the university's president from 1921 to 1932. In 1941 the University of Detroit's neighbor, Mercy College of Detroit, was founded by the Religious Sisters of Mercy, and in 1990 the two schools consolidated to form the University of Detroit Mercy. Today the school is the largest independent Catholic university in Michigan.

Another important educational institution originally established to fill the need for technical skills and know-how is Lawrence Technological University. Originally founded in 1931 as the Lawrence Institute of Technology, the school opened in a building that had formerly been part of the Ford Motor Company's Highland Park plant. Supported largely by local industry, Lawrence Tech moved to a new campus at Ten Mile Road and Northwestern Highway in suburban Southfield in 1955. There, with a greatly expanded curriculum, the university has prospered, and since 1981 its campus has more than doubled in size.

The Detroit area's other major university, Oakland University, was founded in 1957 when Alfred G. and Matilda Dodge Wilson donated their fifteen-hundred-acre estate in

Wayne State University's "Old Main" at Cass and Warren opened in 1896 as Detroit's Central High School. Courtesy Wayne State University.

University of Detroit Mercy's McNichols campus. The university was founded in 1877 as the Detroit College. Courtesy University of Detroit Mercy.

suburban Rochester to Michigan State University to begin a new college in Oakland County. Originally named Michigan State University–Oakland, it became Oakland University in 1963 and then in 1970 was granted autonomy by the state legislature. From its beginning the university has flourished by providing its students with a broad liberal arts education. Today Oakland's cultural activities attract thousands of visitors to the campus each year to enjoy events offered through the university's Meadow Brook Theatre, Meadow Brook Art Gallery, and Meadow Brook Hall, and in the summer at the nearby Meadow Brook Music Festival.

Along with these four universities, Detroit is home to a number of other fine educational institutions, most notably the Merrill-Palmer Institute, Marygrove College, and the Center for Creative Studies–College of Art and Design.

During the early 1950s, when Detroit was developing its civic center on the riverfront, an important new addition was being made to the city's cultural center located adjacent to the campus of Wayne State University. On July 24, 1951, the new Detroit Historical Museum was opened at Woodward and Kirby across the street from the public library. In 1968 the museum was substantially enlarged with the opening of the Kresge Wing. The City Historical Department now comprises the main museum in the cultural center, the fine Dossin Great Lakes Museum on Belle Isle, and the military museum at Fort Wayne. Sadly, Fort Wayne has been closed to the public for the past several years and its future is uncertain. Fortunately, though, the National

Museum of the Tuskegee Airmen and the Great Lakes Indian Museum, both housed on the grounds of Fort Wayne, are open and available for public tours.

Today the cultural center has grown to include not only the Historical Museum, the Detroit Public Library, and the Institute of Arts, but also the Children's Museum, Your Heritage House, the Scarab Club, the Merrill-Palmer Institute, the International Institute, the Center for Creative Studies, the Detroit Science Center, and the impressive new Charles H. Wright Museum of African American History.

Along with the institutions of the cultural center, Detroiters are fortunate in having in nearby Dearborn one of the finest museum complexes in the world, Greenfield Village and Henry Ford Museum. Collectively known as the Edison Institute and founded in 1929 by Henry Ford, they show the sweeping changes that transformed America from a rural, agrarian society to a highly industrialized nation. At Greenfield Village, visitors are able to tour nearly one hundred historic buildings that have been brought here and placed in a village setting of nineteenth-century America. The adjacent Henry Ford Museum contains historic collections representing nearly all areas of human enterprise, including outstanding displays of decorative arts, transportation, communications, lighting, industry, agriculture, and domestic life. One of the most impressive exhibits is "The Automobile in American Life." Here all manner of motorcars, from the original Ford to the first production Mustang, are displayed amidst automotive memorabilia. The exhibit documents not only the evolution of the automobile and its industry, but also its cultural impact and how the American landscape changed with the roadside businesses and entertainment that emerged.

On July 24, 1951, Detroit's 250th birthday, the city dedicated the Detroit Historical Museum, at the corner of Woodward and Kirby. Courtesy Detroit Historical Museum.

NINETEEN

Tough Times

FOLLOWING THE RIOT OF 1967, Detroiters, both black and white, began to look at ways to rebuild their city. Out of the disaster on Twelfth Street a variety of steps were taken, such as the formation of New Detroit, to begin the rebuilding process. Without question, though, the most dramatic step in this process came in the fall of 1971 when Henry Ford II announced his plan for a $350 million riverfront development complex.

The area selected for the development was immediately to the east of the civic center, bounded by the Ford Auditorium, Jefferson Avenue, St. Antoine Street, and the river. To design his project, Ford called upon famed Atlanta architect John C. Portman, who was known for his many urban hotel designs, including the Peachtree Center in Atlanta. The plans that Portman prepared were impressive indeed. The first phase of the project was to consist of a seventy-three-story, fourteen-hundred-room luxury hotel and four thirty-nine-story octagonal office buildings surrounding the hotel. It was projected that

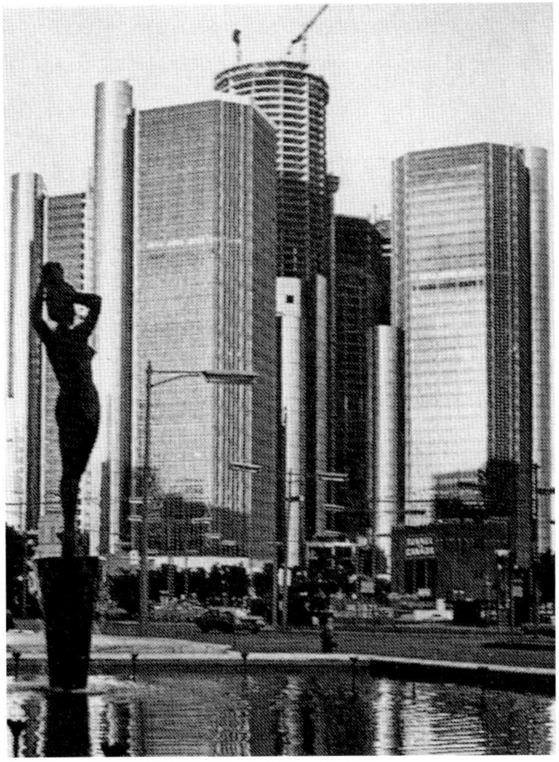

The Plaza Hotel rises above the completed office towers, July 13, 1976. Great things were expected of the Renaissance Center, but the promise in its name would be more than twenty years in coming. Photo by Harry Wolf. Courtesy Dossin Great Lakes Museum, Detroit.

when completed, the five buildings would employ more than twenty thousand people. The hotel was to be the tallest building in Michigan and, at the time of its construction, the tallest hotel in the world. The project was to be called the Renaissance Center.

On May 27, 1973, ground was broken and the project was begun. But in October, just as the heavy equipment was being moved into the area, an important historical site was discovered and a team of archaeologists was called to investigate. Working around the contractors and workers, the archaeologists began sifting out bits and pieces of nineteenth-century Detroit from the mud. It was found that the Renaissance Center was located on one of the oldest sections of Detroit. The hotel itself was going up directly on the 1820 site of the Brush farmhouse and the eastern stockade wall of the old city. By the time the digging was finished, the archaeologists had uncovered more than twenty thousand artifacts representing a complete cross section of life in Detroit between 1820 and 1850. The artifacts salvaged from the site included dishes, glassware, bottles, pewter forks and spoons, scissors, spools of thread, pieces of clothing, children's toys, and even a fragment of an April 3, 1833, edition of the *Detroit Advertiser.* As the items were uncovered they were taken to the Detroit Historical Museum for preservation and cataloging. In May 1974 the archaeological dig was completed and the bulldozers began their work in earnest.

On March 15, 1977, less than four years after groundbreaking, the hotel, named the Detroit Plaza, was opened. The first two office towers opened in 1976, the third in late spring 1977, and the fourth in the fall of 1977. This completed the first phase of the project. Later, two twenty-one-story office buildings were added.

It was hoped by all that this project would be the catalyst for changing the image of downtown Detroit. And indeed, some progress along Jefferson Avenue did occur. In 1979 the riverfront Hart Plaza (named for U.S. Senator Philip A. Hart) was completed near the intersection of Jefferson and Woodward. This plaza included an open-air amphitheater, space for festivals, an ice skating rink, and Isamu Noguchi's Dodge Fountain. It was followed by the twenty-thousand-seat Joe Louis Arena built just west of Cobo Hall. Then the twin-towered twenty-nine-story luxury Riverfront West apartment complex was completed along Jefferson just to the west of Joe Louis Arena. But, sadly, while these projects were indeed impressive, the downtown renaissance promised by the complex's name would take more than twenty years to be realized.

Along with a major change in the city's skyline, there was also a major change in the office of mayor. In the summer of 1969, Mayor Cavanagh (he had been reelected in 1965) announced that he would run for the U.S. Senate. That fall Wayne County Sheriff Roman S. Gribbs defeated County Auditor Richard H. Austin, an African American, by the smallest margin in the city's mayoral election history. In 1973, Gribbs chose not to seek another term, and that November Michigan Senator Coleman A. Young was elected the first black mayor of Detroit, defeating former city police commissioner John F. Nichols. At this time, blacks made up about half of the city's population. Young won support from more than 90 percent of black voters and about 10 percent of white voters.

Born in Tuscaloosa, Alabama, in 1918, Young moved to Detroit with his family when he was five. Here he graduated from Eastern High School with honors, and during World War II he served in the army air corps as a member of the famed Tuskegee Airmen. During the late 1940s and early 1950s, Young was active in the city's labor movement and later became active in the Democratic Party.

In 1960 he won election as a delegate to Michigan's Constitutional Convention. From 1964 to 1973 he served in the Michigan Senate, and in 1968 he became the first black member of the Democratic National Committee.

On January 1, 1974, Coleman A. Young took office as mayor of Detroit, and for the next twenty years he was to serve as the city's chief executive. He was elected mayor five consecutive times, thus becoming the city's longest-serving mayor. Those twenty years were to be one of the most turbulent periods in the city's long history.

When Young took office in January 1974, he was faced with leading a very troubled city. It was a time of rising crime, white flight, economic recession, and forced school busing. One of Young's first tasks, the result of an oft-repeated campaign promise, was to disband

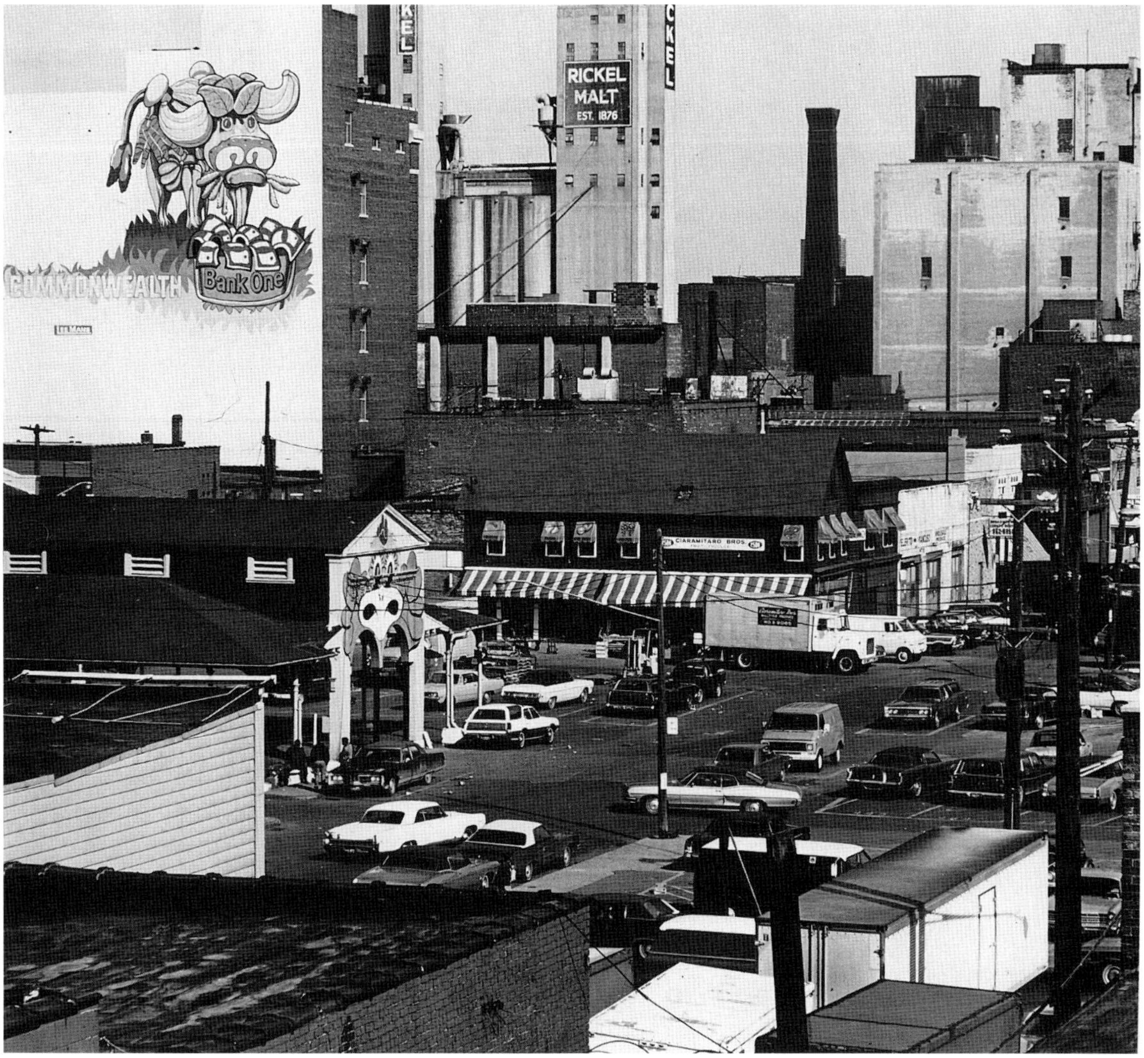

Long a favorite of urban and suburban Detroiters, this is the city's main produce terminal, more commonly known as Eastern Market. Here fresh food of all kinds—meats, fruits, vegetables—can be purchased by the bag full or the truckload. Photo by G. Edwynn Hank. Courtesy Detroit Historical Museum.

the police department's controversial STRESS (Stop the Robberies Enjoy Safe Streets) unit. Established in 1971 during the administration of Mayor Gribbs, the unit had been formed in an attempt to help control the city's escalating street crime. The unit, however, created more problems than it solved, particularly within the black community. After several black youths were killed by STRESS officers, a public rally was held to call for the unit's suspension. Later there were reports of other shootings, and when reports surfaced of a number of African Americans dying while in the custody of STRESS officers, the already severely strained relationship between the police and the black community deteriorated further. Thus Mayor Young, immediately after taking office, carried through on his campaign promise and swiftly brought an end to the STRESS unit.

Unfortunately, the disbanding of STRESS, the hiring of seven hundred new police officers, the desegregation of the city's predominantly white police force, and the appointment by Mayor Young in 1976 of William L. Hart, the city's first black police chief, failed to stem the tide of a rising crime rate. It was this fear of crime, both real and

Detroiters gather at an anti-STRESS rally in Kennedy Square on Woodward Avenue, September 23, 1971. Courtesy Walter P. Reuther Library, Wayne State University, Detroit.

perceived, that in large part contributed to a continued exodus to the suburbs by Detroit's white residents. Although this exodus had actually began in the 1950s, it increased dramatically following the riot of 1967 and Young's election in 1973. As a result, by 1980 the white middle class had largely abandoned the city of Detroit. Between 1970 and 1980 alone more than 310,000 white residents fled for the suburbs. The city's population dropped from 1,511,482 in 1970 to 1,203,339 in 1980, while the suburban population rose from 2,688,449 to 3,549,425 during this same period. Yet the percentage of blacks living in the city during this period rose from 43.7 percent to 63.1 percent. Thus, by 1980, Detroit had one of the highest black populations of any northern U.S. city.

When Detroit lost its white residents, it also lost a significant portion of its economic base. According to one noted geographer, when white Detroiters left for the suburbs "they took the majority of the important service, professional, and leadership activities of the Detroit Metropolitan system with them." By 1980 more than 20 percent of Detroit's largely black population lived below the nation's poverty line.

To be sure, the devastation of inner-city Detroit was not caused by white flight alone. Beginning in 1973, the nation as a whole began a slide into a severe economic recession. By the early 1980s, industrial capital had largely fled the urban North for low-wage and non-union areas of the country, and of the world. Every major industrial city in the North suffered in the recession of the 1970s and the deindustrialization of the 1980s. But once again, as had happened in the Great Depression of the 1930s, few cities suffered

The beautiful old Michigan Theater, one of Detroit's grand movie palaces, now serves as a parking garage. Copyright Camilo Jose Vergara.

In 1913, Detroit's grand Michigan Central Railroad Station was built at Michigan and Vernor. Once a major transportation center, the building was abandoned by Amtrak in 1988 and is now derelict. This view of the station's entrance is a painful symbol of Detroit's demise and is characteristic of the state of many of the city's historic buildings. Copyright Camilo Jose Vergara.

to the extent that Detroit did. And once again, the automobile industry was central to Detroit's economic problems.

During the 1960s, American Motors had considerable success with its emphasis on the production of the small-size car, or compact. At this time as well, the German manufacturer Volkswagen began exporting its compact Beetle into the United States. By 1959, Beetle sales reached 668,000 and U.S. companies turned to producing their own compact models. But the popularity of the Beetle continued to grow, and by 1968 Volkswagen sales passed the one million mark. The Japanese also entered the U.S. market at this time with their lines of small cars. The first was Nissan (Datsun) in 1965, followed by Toyota in 1966, Mazda in 1972, and Honda in 1974.

Adding to the challenge of the compact imports, Detroit's auto manufacturers were faced with new federal regulations as well. In 1966 President Johnson had signed the National Traffic and Motor Vehicle Safety Act, which regulated the safety performance of vehicles sold within the United States. This was followed by the Clean Air Act of 1970, which regulated tailpipe emissions, and the Energy Policy and Conservation Act of 1980, which mandated a series of gradual increases in fuel economy.

But it was not the sale of compact cars or federal legislation that hit Detroit the hardest. In October 1973 the automobile industry was rocked by the embargo of oil from the Middle East. Over the next year U.S. oil prices

Once a stately home in one of the city's finest residential neighborhoods, the Ransom Gillis house (built in 1876) on the northeast corner of John R. and Alfred Streets is today a symbol of the decay of Detroit's inner city. Copyright Camilo Jose Vergara.

jumped 350 percent. At the pump, car owners saw gasoline prices leap from 42 cents to $1.30 a gallon. Americans were faced with long lines at the pump and in many cases with signs of "No Gas Today." As a result of this oil shortage, the United States was faced with an energy crisis and a major economic recession.

As gasoline prices went up and supplies went down, Americans stopped buying full-sized cars and U.S. auto sales fell to their lowest level in twenty-five years. American Motors was the only U.S. car producer with sales increases—90 percent of their cars were compacts. The Japanese automakers benefited from the energy crisis, their sales rising to a market share of 10 percent in 1978 and 35.6 percent by 1989. In 1974, Congress tried to ease the oil crisis by reducing gasoline consumption when it passed legislation dropping the national speed limit to 55 mph. But the recession continued, and by 1975 U.S.

One white and three African American men share a porch on Trombly near Dubois, May 1981. Photo by Bruce Harkness. Courtesy Walter P. Reuther Library, Wayne State University, Detroit.

Downtown Detroit's most common skyline view is north across the river from Windsor. Looking south shows a different Detroit. Empty lots and the Fisher Freeway replace the sparkling waters of the river. Copyright Camilo Jose Vergara.

unemployment hit 8.5 percent. In Detroit, plants closed and the city's population dropped. As the recession worsened, GM laid off 38,000 workers indefinitely and placed another 48,000 on short-term leave. During the 1970s the city lost an estimated 208,000 jobs, one-third of its total employment. By 1975 Detroit's population had fallen to about 1,335,000, a 28 percent decrease since 1950. It was now also estimated that blacks made up 54 percent of Detroit's residents.

As the U.S. auto industry turned to building small cars, GM embarked on a plan to redimension its entire auto lineup for better fuel economy. Weight and exterior size were reduced while interior room and comfort were retained. The first "downsized" cars were GM's 1977 full-size autos, about a foot shorter and seven hundred pounds lighter than their predecessors. They proved to be an immediate success.

At Ford, along with changes in the types of cars being built, there was also an important change in the leadership of the company. On October 1, 1979, Henry Ford II retired from the position of chief executive officer, handing over that responsibility to Philip Caldwell. Caldwell also succeeded Ford as chairman of the board on March 13, 1980. Mr. Ford retired as an officer and employee of the company on October 1, 1982, but he continued to serve on the company's board of directors and as chairman of the finance committee until his death on September 29, 1987.

As important as these changes were at Ford and General Motors, none had the impact of the changes that came to Chrysler. As American consumer demand soared for compact, fuel-efficient cars, Chrysler began importing and distributing small passenger cars and trucks built by its Japanese partner, Mitsubishi Motors. Chrysler set sales records in 1972 and 1973, but the gasoline shortage, political uncertainty, high interest rates,

Henry Ford II stepped down as the company's chairman in 1980 but continued to serve on its board of directors until his death in 1987. Photo by Tony Spina. Courtesy Walter P. Reuther Library, Wayne State University, Detroit.

severe inflation, and weakening consumer confidence drove Chrysler into a financial crisis. In the midst of this crisis, John J. Riccardo became Chrysler chairman on October 1, 1975. Responding to the growing economic troubles, Riccardo hired Lee A. Iacocca as Chrysler president on November 2, 1978. Ten months later Riccardo resigned, and Iacocca was elected chairman on September 20, 1979.

Lee Iacocca came to Chrysler following a thirty-two-year career with Ford Motor Company. He had risen to the position of president at Ford, but after a falling out with Henry Ford II he moved to Chrysler. Iacocca applied his experience at Ford to meet the challenge of rejuvenating Chrysler's sagging operations. Chrysler reduced costs, restructured its management, and recruited new executives to deal with its serious financial problems. Despite these measures, however, the outlook for Chrysler became even more serious when a second recession hit in 1979. As a final move to survive, Chrysler turned to the federal government and sought assistance in the form of loan guarantees. Thus on

January 7, 1980, President Jimmy Carter signed the Chrysler Corporation Loan Guarantee Act, which provided Chrysler with $1.5 billion in federal loan guarantees.

Concessions from its UAW workers, white-collar employees, suppliers, creditors, and lenders kept Chrysler operating despite record losses of $1.7 billion in 1980. The corporation also cut inventories by $1 billion in its drastic efforts to manage its finances.

The second recession, in 1979, hit Detroit and Michigan particularly hard. Both interest rates and inflation rates rose to a staggering 18 percent, Japanese auto production out-paced that of the United States, and Michigan's unemployment rate was the highest in the nation. In 1981 Mayor Young was faced with a tough financial battle, the worst of which was a budget crisis that forced Detroit voters to approve an income tax hike and city officials to sell $125 million in emergency bonds. Mayor Young not only had to persuade city voters to go along with his plan to save the city from bankruptcy, but he also had to convince the state legislature and twist the arms of municipal workers to accept a two-year wage freeze. Black unemployment in the city stood at 25 percent and remained a particular problem for the mayor. But Detroit was not alone. By 1982 America was in its deepest recession since the Great Depression, and one in ten Americans were out of work.

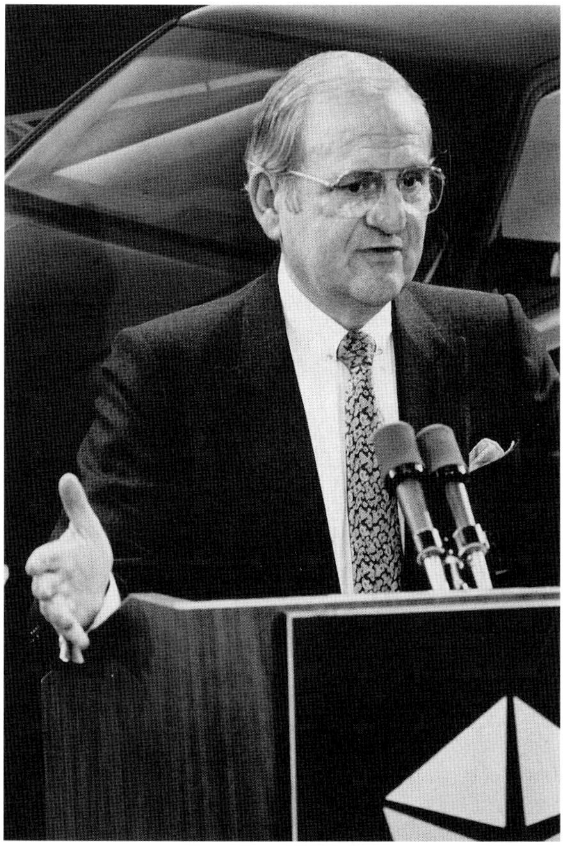

Elected chairman in 1979, Lee Iacocca met the challenge of rejuvenating Chrysler's sagging operations. He oversaw the repayment of the corporation's federal loan, the introduction of the minivan, and the dedication of the company's new Technology Center. Courtesy National Automotive History Collection, Detroit Public Library.

In 1981 Chrysler again reported record losses, but a new line of cars was introduced in October 1980—these were the Dodge Aries and the Plymouth Reliant. Code-named the "K-Cars," these vehicles were an immediate success. Then, in 1982 Chrysler reintroduced the convertible and the corporation finally began to turn the economic corner. The momentum continued, and for the first time since 1973 the company was profitable for four consecutive quarters. In August 1983, Chrysler paid off the federal loan guarantees seven years early, at a profit of $350 million to the federal government.

In November 1983, Chrysler introduced a whole new concept in automotive design—the minivan. With the production of the Dodge Caravan and the Plymouth Voyager, Chrysler created a new market segment and thus changed the way American families traveled. Minivans became Chrysler's best-selling vehicle, and the company was well on its way back to economic health.

By 1984 the recession was loosening its grip on Michigan's economy. The state's unemployment rate dropped to 7.2 percent, and along with Chrysler, important changes were occurring at General Motors. In 1980 demolition began of the old Dodge Main and Hupp factories in Detroit's Milwaukee Junction Industrial District, near the I-75/I-94 interchange. Here GM was planning to build a new automobile factory—the $750 million Poletown plant. The following year, amidst considerable local opposition and on occasion bitter controversy, the city condemned a seventy-seven-acre area and tore down a whole neighborhood and the Immaculate Conception Church for the new plant. A good percentage of the homeowners were happy to find a buyer for their modest frame homes, but others, including many elderly original owners and their defiant parish priest, were heartsick to see their old neighborhood and parish destroyed with the cooperation of labor unions and the Catholic archdiocese. Contrary to the impression left by national media, the new plant did not destroy the entire Poletown neighborhood, the site of Detroit's original Polish community, but only its northern third. Half of the displaced residents were Polish; many of the rest were African Americans.

Officially named the Cadillac Detroit/Hamtramck Assembly Center, this highly roboticized plant, which opened in 1984, was designed to make Cadillac Sevilles, Buick Rivieras, and Oldsmobile Toronados. The Poletown plant was the first major new automobile factory built in Detroit since 1928, when Chrysler's Plymouth Lynch Road assembly plant went up. Also in 1984, GM added Saturn to its vehicle divisions, thus gaining a sixth automobile brand. The Saturn headquarters were located in suburban Troy while the cars were built in a highly innovative plant at Spring Hill, Tennessee, thirty miles south of Nashville.

During the last half of the 1980s a number of other important changes came to Detroit's auto industry. In 1986 Chrysler began work on

Demolition of the old Dodge Main factory began in 1980 to make way for the new GM Poletown plant. Photo taken by Santa Falui. Courtesy Detroit Historical Museum.

Formerly St. Nicholas Byzantine Greek Catholic Church, the Temple of Faith Missionary Baptist Church on E. Grand Boulevard is demolished to make way for the Poletown plant. Photo by Bruce Harkness. Courtesy Walter P. Reuther Library, Wayne State University, Detroit.

a $1.2 billion project to update and rebuild its Jefferson Avenue Assembly plant and also began construction of its new Technology Center in suburban Auburn Hills. The following year Chrysler made its biggest acquisition when it purchased American Motors Corporation on August 5, 1987. The smallest of the "Big Four," AMC had moved its headquarters to suburban Southfield in 1976. The $800 million acquisition of AMC by Chrysler included the world-famous Jeep, three automotive assembly plants, and sixteen hundred dealerships.

In October 1991 Chairman Lee Iacocca dedicated the new Chrysler Technology Center. The new complex, covering 3.5 million square feet, would also be the site of the company's new world headquarters as the automaker completed plans to move out of its Highland Park offices. Then, during the following year, Chrysler dedicated its new Jefferson North Assembly plant. Located out East Jefferson Avenue, the plant was built to manufacture the Jeep Grand Cherokee sport-utility vehicle.

Detroit's economic problems of the late 1970s and early 1980s were not only due to the automobile industry and the loss of manufacturing jobs, however. If anything, commercial disinvestment in Detroit was even more catastrophic to the city than was any industrial abandonment. Certainly it was more visible to the eye. All one had to do was drive downtown, around the empty Kern block, then by the demolished remains of Crowley's Department Store, and past Hudson's shuttered downtown emporium—the three grand ladies of downtown Detroit's once thriving commercial district. Kern's Department Store, built in 1929, and the other buildings on its block were torn down in 1966 to make way for a shopping complex that was never built. Crowley's Department Store, built in 1907, was demolished in 1978 for nothing in particular.

The J. L. Hudson Company had long been Detroit's dominant retail power. In the 1940s, Hudson's twenty-five-story, two-million-square-foot store on Woodward at Gratiot generated three times the sales of its nearest Detroit competitor. But by 1950 Detroit's population was growing mostly on the fringes of the city. In 1951 Hudson's decided to build the Northland shopping center where the new Lodge Expressway intersected Eight Mile Road, as well as the Eastland shopping center in Harper Woods near Grosse Pointe and the planned Ford Expressway. Completed in 1953, Northland was the nation's first regional shopping center with a "hub design"—an anchor department store at the center of a cluster of smaller stores. Northland was an immediate success, and for fifteen out of the next sixteen years it was number one in sales among the country's shopping centers.

Hudson's downtown sales peaked at $154 million in 1953, about the same time the city of Detroit reached its high-water population mark. By 1959 Hudson's sales had fallen to $117 million, a 24 percent decline in six years, but by then Hudson's transfer of capital from downtown to Northland and Eastland was paying off handsomely. Combined sales at the Northland and Eastland shopping centers came to $103 million, more than offsetting the decline in sales at the downtown store.

In 1969 the J. L. Hudson Company merged with the Dayton Corporation of Minneapolis. Hudson's initiated the merger because it was growing slowly and needed capital. So the J. L. Hudson Company became the Hudson Division of the Dayton-Hudson Corporation. Then, in 1978, Dayton-Hudson sold Northland, Eastland, Westland, Southland, and five other shopping centers to the Equitable Life Assurance Company. The Hudson department stores were now owned by a firm in Minneapolis, and the shopping centers by a New York insurance company.

In January 1983 the Dayton-Hudson Corporation closed its downtown Detroit department store—thus bringing to an end 72 years at the corner of Woodward and Gratiot and 102 years in downtown Detroit. The company cited declining sales and increased operating costs as the reasons for the closing. Then, in March 1984, the Minnesota corporation announced that its last remaining central-city operation, the Hudson Division headquarters, would be combined with the Dayton Corporation headquarters in Minneapolis, and the rest of Hudson's corporate staff would leave the city.

Mayor Young charged the Dayton-Hudson Corporation with "pulling up stakes and moving out" of a city that had helped it grow into one of the nation's largest department store chains. But in reality, Hudson's was merely making its contribution to a more general trend. In 1958, ten of the Detroit region's twenty major shopping areas were located within the city. By 1977 that number had dropped to one, and with the closing of Hudson's in 1983 the city of Detroit—with a population of 1.2 million people—was no longer home to even one major regional shopping center.

Along with a rising crime rate, the loss of its white middle class to the suburbs, the loss of thousands of jobs within its automotive and manufacturing industries, and the closing of its last major department store, Detroit was faced with yet another major crisis during the 1970s and 1980s—the court-ordered desegregation of its school system, which resulted in the forced busing of thousands of its public school children.

As early as the 1960s, African American parents in Detroit were expressing their concern over the inadequate and segregated public schools in the city's black neighborhoods. As a result, in 1964 a liberal pro-integration majority was elected to the city's school board. In the following year the new board altered school boundaries to promote racial integration, increased the number of black teachers and administrators, and pressured publishers to produce textbooks that provided a more accurate picture of the races. Parents' dissatisfaction continued, however, and in 1967 blacks boycotted the Detroit Public Schools to protest racism in the city's educational system. Then, in 1969, in response to growing pressure within Detroit's African American community, the state legislature passed legislation (PA 244) that required the decentralization of the city's school system by providing for the election of regional school boards. In the Detroit Board of Education's view, while integration remained their primary goal, this new decentralization, or "increased community involvement," would help bridge the gap between themselves and the city's black residents.

Sadly, in 1970 a new plan by the Detroit Board of Education for the desegregation of the school system spurred a bitter school board recall election. This in turn led to a series of events that culminated in a court-ordered plan for the desegregation of the public school systems of the entire metropolitan region. The recall came about because of a modest proposal to desegregate the city's high schools. On April 7, 1970, the Detroit Board of Education voluntarily adopted a plan to effect a more balanced distribution of black and white students in twelve of the city's twenty-one high schools. This so-called April 7 Plan was to take effect over a three-year period. The plan was designed to reduce segregation in a school system that was then 63.6 percent black.

The introduction of this plan resulted in such a public outcry that a campaign was begun to recall those board members who had backed it. The state legislature, responding to powerful public pressure, passed legislation that was signed by the governor as PA 48 on July 7, 1970, which in effect nullified the plan. The following month the board members who had supported the plan were recalled, the governor appointed four new board members, and the April 7 Plan was rescinded.

As a result of this action the NAACP filed a suit challenging the constitutionality of PA 48 and asked for restoration of the April 7 Plan. The complaint alleged that the Detroit school system was segregated on the basis of race as the result of the actions and policies of the Detroit Board of Education and of the state of Michigan.

On April 6, 1971, the NAACP suit went to trial in U.S. District Court before Judge Stephen J. Roth. After extensive hearings, Judge Roth ruled, on September 21, 1971, that Detroit schools were indeed segregated and that they had been deliberately segregated over a long period of time. To remedy this situation a number of plans were proposed. Judge Roth ruled, however, that the solutions that involved only Detroit were inadequate since desegregation within the school district could not result in a "racial balance" that represented the "racial composition" of the Detroit metropolitan area. The only acceptable solution, he stated, would be one that included the suburbs.

Thus, in June 1972, Roth settled on a plan for the busing of students between Detroit and fifty-three suburban school districts across the tri-county area. The plan involved about 780,000 children. At the time of this ruling Detroit schools were 65 percent black, the suburban schools less than 10 percent black.

Suburban reaction to this "cross-district" desegregation plan was immediate: deep-seated and widespread opposition. The ruling was appealed to the Sixth Circuit Court of Appeals in Cincinnati, which in December 1972 affirmed Roth's ruling of segregation in

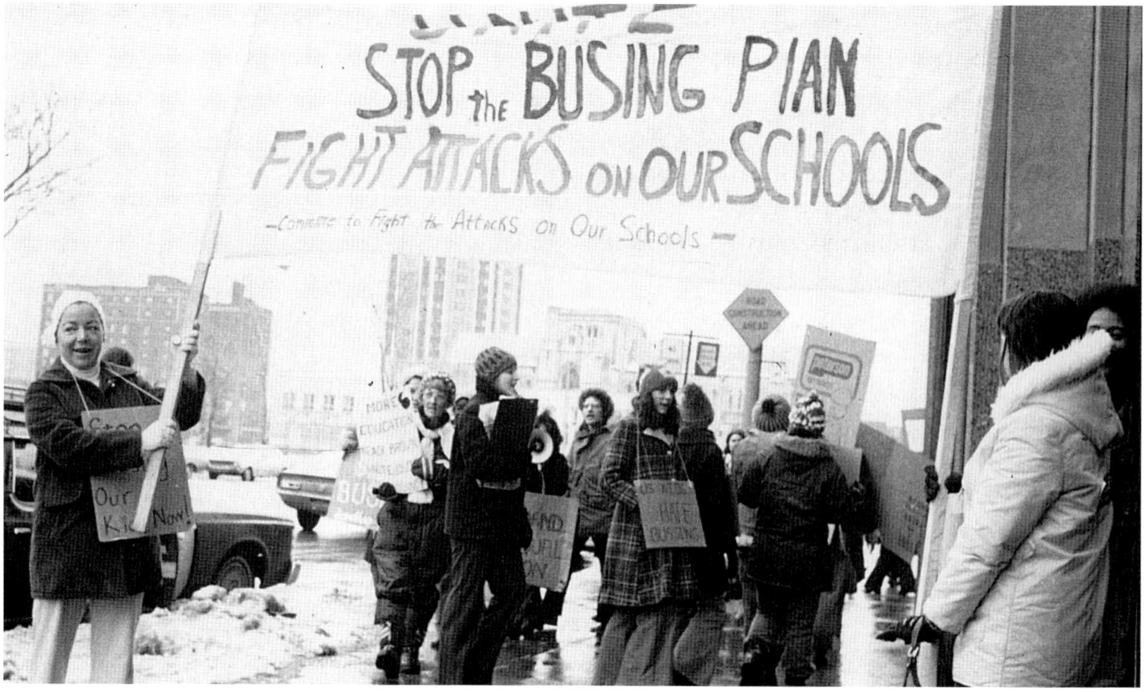

Parents picket the School Center Building on Woodward at Putnam, January 26, 1976, the day court-ordered busing of Detroit's public school students was to begin. Courtesy Walter P. Reuther Library, Wayne State University, Detroit.

Detroit's schools as well as his conclusion that the desegregation remedy must not be confined to only the city of Detroit.

The state of Michigan and the suburban school districts then took the case to the U.S. Supreme Court. When the Supreme Court heard the case, known as *Milliken vs. Bradley,* it overturned the multi-district solution and ruled that the solution must be found within Detroit's city limits. On July 25, 1974, in a five to four ruling, the Court held that because only Detroit had been found guilty of segregation, the remedy must be confined to the city, and that the Detroit Board of Education must desegregate its schools. The Supreme Court then remanded *Milliken vs. Bradley* back to the district court to fashion a new remedy that would affect only Detroit's schools.

In April 1975, U.S. District Court Judge Robert DeMascio began hearings on plans for desegregation. The case had been assigned to Judge DeMascio because of the death of Judge Roth, which had occurred just before the Supreme Court handed down its decision. DeMascio issued a series of court orders on various aspects of the proposed remedy, which included ordering the school board to institute comprehensive remedial education, testing, training, counseling, and guidance programs; create a new code of ethics for student conduct; and establish community participation through the appointment of a fifty-five-member monitoring commission. DeMascio also directed the state of Michigan to pay half the costs of implementing these programs.

Finally, on November 4, 1975, Judge DeMascio ruled that the Detroit city school system must begin integration by January 26, 1976. On that date the reassignment of some twenty-eight thousand students began, about twenty-two thousand of these being bused. On that first day of busing, school attendance was off by over one-third as many parents kept their children at home fearing violence. The busing proceeded peacefully, however, and the next day attendance was near normal.

In June 1977 the U.S. Supreme Court unanimously upheld the educational components of Judge DeMascio's order over the objections of the state of Michigan concerning its obligation to pay a large share of these costs. The following year Judge DeMascio declined to expand busing in view of the declining proportion of white students within the district, now only 15 percent of the total school population.

Busing in Detroit continued for another ten years. Finally, in 1988, U.S. District Court Judge Avern Cohn ruled that the busing of Detroit's schoolchildren for purposes of integration should end as there were no longer any pockets of segregation within the schools, and since "we have achieved all that we can." With this ruling, busing in the city of Detroit came to an end and the suit resulting in *Milliken vs. Bradley* was finally brought to a close.

Many believed that due to the results of *Milliken vs. Bradley,* there was more urban school financial aid for equipment and supplies than might otherwise have been available, and that the decision helped to create Head Start–type programs. Many others, however, believed that the decision did nothing more than create a greater racial schism between the city and the suburban school districts, increase white flight to the suburbs, and cause an even greater rift between the residents of the city and their neighbors.

Fortunately, not all that was happening in Detroit at this time dealt with economic

Children on their way to Detroit's Carrie School, January 26, 1976, the day the city's court-ordered school integration plan began. Courtesy Walter P. Reuther Library, Wayne State University, Detroit.

Pope John Paul II visited Detroit in 1987. Here the pope and Archbishop Edmund C. Szoka pray in the chapel of the Cathedral of the Blessed Sacrament, where they paused before going into the cathedral. Photo by Tony Spina. Courtesy Walter P. Reuther Library, Wayne State University, Detroit.

decay, suburban flight, and lost jobs. In September 1985, for example, the Detroit Medical Center was officially formed. Bounded by Woodward, the Chrysler Freeway, Warren, and Mack, the medical center dates from the mid-1950s. Originally it included Harper, Grace, Women's (now Hutzel), and Children's Hospitals. They were later joined by the Rehabilitation Institute, and these institutions joined together to coordinate services with Wayne State University's Medical School. The medical center's founding members have long been part of Detroit's history. Harper Hospital opened on October 12, 1864, to care for Civil War wounded. The Detroit College of Medicine, now Wayne State University's Medical School, was founded May 18, 1868. Detroit General Hospital, now Detroit Receiving Hospital, became an active member and built its new hospital on the medical center's campus in 1980. Over the next several years the center was expanded to provide joint strategic planning, budgeting, financing, and other responsibilities. Then, in 1985, the old Medical Center Development Corporation was restructured as a holding company and became the Detroit Medical Center. In 1986 Huron Valley Hospital (now Huron Valley–Sinai Hospital) became an affiliated member of the medical center. Grace Hospital consolidated its services with neighboring Mt. Carmel Mercy Hospital and moved into larger, more modern facilities in northwest Detroit in 1991. Then, in 1997, the Detroit Medical Center experienced further expansion with the addition of Sinai Hospital of Greater Detroit. Most recently, in 1999, the center consolidated the services of Sinai Hospital and Grace Hospital to form Sinai-Grace Hospital. Today the Detroit Medical Center is the largest health care provider in southeastern Michigan, operating seven hospitals, two nursing centers, and more than one hundred outpatient facilities. It maintains an affiliation with the Barbara Ann Karmanos Cancer Institute and serves as the teaching and clinical research site for Wayne State University, now the nation's fourth-largest medical school.

As its medical center was growing, Detroit witnessed the completion of yet another major development during the late 1980s. Located several blocks south of the medical center on Woodward Avenue, this project, however, was one of renovation and restoration. On November 19, 1988, the largest surviving "motion picture palace" of the 1920s and the second-largest theater in the nation, the Fox Theater, was reopened. After nearly a yearlong restoration, this grand movie house was completely renovated, with more than 80 percent of its original interior finish being preserved. The Fox Theater and its adjoining office building had been purchased in July 1987 by Little Caesars and Detroit Red Wings owners Michael and Marion Ilitch from businessman Chuck Forbes, of whom much more will be heard later. The multimillion-dollar renovation project restored not only the Fox, but also the surrounding office building that eventually would house the world headquarters of Little Caesars Enterprises (moved to downtown Detroit by the Ilitch's from suburban Farmington Hills in November 1990).

The Fox, built by motion picture pioneer William Fox, originally opened on September 21, 1928. With seating for nearly five thousand, the interior of the theater was embellished in gold leaf, hand-stenciled walls, throne chairs, intricately cast brass ornamentation, and exquisite plaster finishes that simulated marble. All this was restored to its original opulence. In late 1989, the Fox was awarded status of a National Historic Landmark, and in 1991 the Michigan Historical Commission named the building to the State Register of Historic Sites.

Work continued on the Fox following its reopening, and over the next four years the

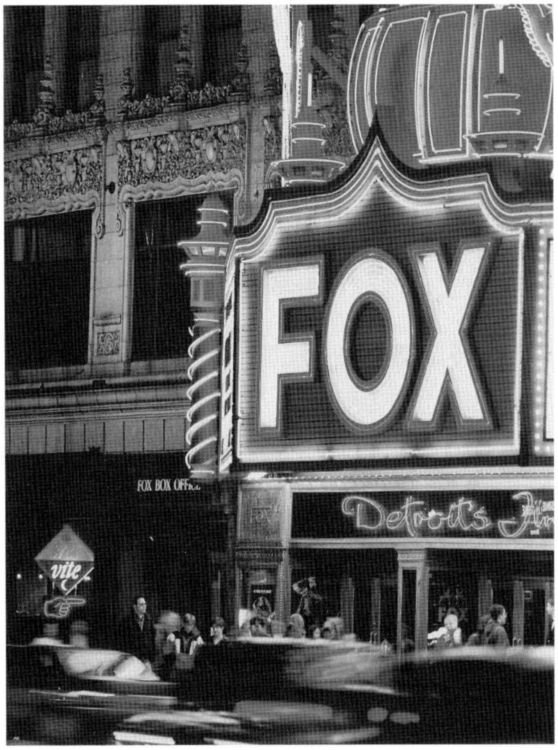

A multimillion-dollar restoration project culminated in the gala reopening of the Fox Theater on November 19, 1988. Courtesy the Fox Theater.

After nearly a year-long restoration, the Fox Theater was completely renovated; more than 80 percent of its original interior finish was preserved. Courtesy the Fox Theater.

total investment in the restoration and redevelopment of the Fox Center (as the theater and adjoining buildings came to be known) reached $50 million. Today the Fox has become the center of the city's revived theater district as it attracts record crowds back to downtown Detroit for a mix of concerts, annual variety and Broadway shows, restored classic films, and other family entertainment.

In November 1989, Coleman Young was elected to his fifth consecutive term as mayor of Detroit. It would also be his last term. As Young began his final four years in office, the city was still plagued with a declining population (in 1990 just over a million at 1,027,974, a drop of nearly 15 percent since 1980), widespread poverty (one-third of Detroiters lived below the federal government–determined poverty level), an extremely high unemployment rate (between 1974 and 1991 the rate in Detroit rose from about 9 percent to more than 20 percent, and the number of jobs had fallen by about one-third), glaring deficiencies in the public school system, block after block of burned-out or boarded-up houses, and a still substantial crime rate (the most prominent crimes involving the sale and use of drugs).

Although beset by myriad problems, Mayor Young had accomplished much of which he could be proud: the GM Poletown plant; the Chrysler Jefferson Avenue plant; Joe Louis Arena; the Riverside West apartment complex; the expansion of Cobo Center; the new parks on the river at the foot of Chene Street and St. Aubin Street; the People Mover; the restoration of the Fox Theater; the expansion of City Airport; the Millender Center; the development of Victoria Park and the renovation of Virginia Park subdivisions; Detroit Receiving Hospital; and the New Center One retail and office center.

While much had indeed been accomplished during his twenty years as mayor, Young was criticized by many as being anti-business, antagonistic toward the suburbs, and caring little about neighborhood development versus downtown development and big-ticket projects. Yet many of his supporters viewed him as a fighter who brought Detroit through tough, changing times; when many businesses and residents were fleeing to the suburbs, he brought key projects into town that kept the city afloat. But age and poor health were catching up with the mayor, and in the summer of 1993 he announced that he would not seek a sixth term.

With Young's withdrawal from the upcoming mayoral race, former Michigan Supreme Court Justice Dennis W. Archer became the front-runner in the field of twenty-two declared candidates. Archer campaigned promoting his "vision of what Detroit can be." He pledged to make Detroit a "well-run, well-

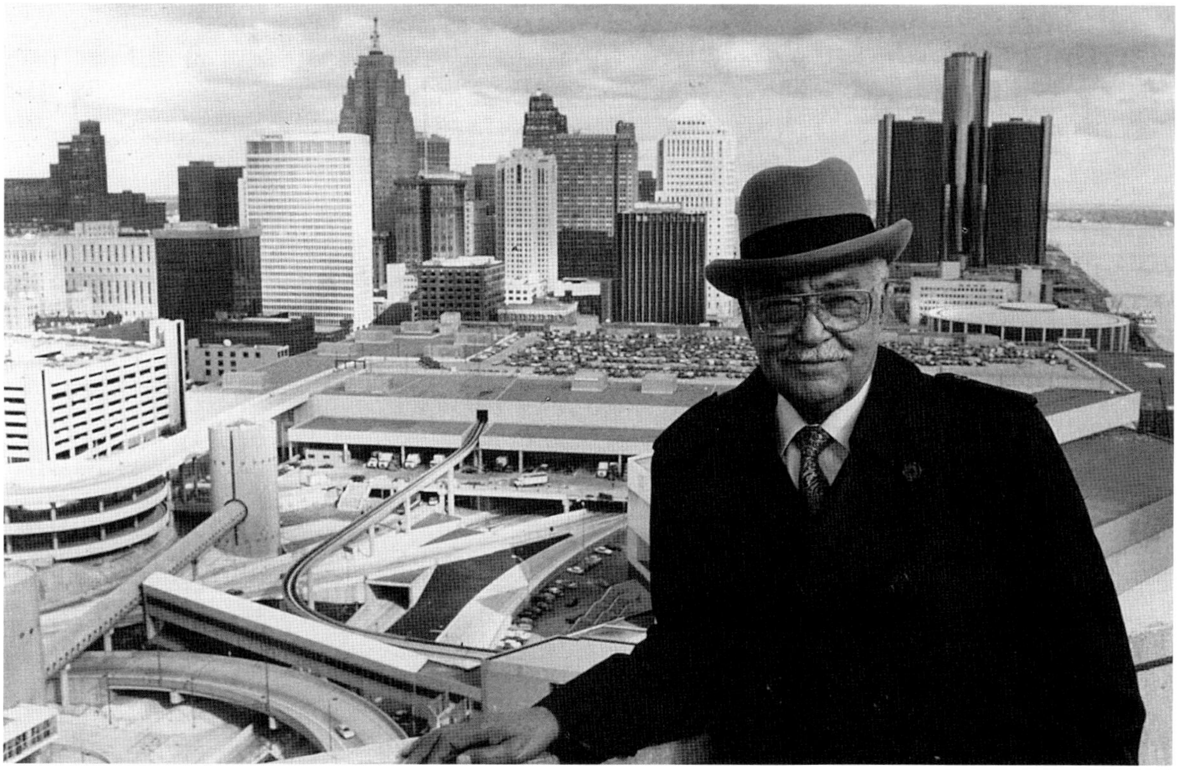

From the roof of the Riverfront West apartments, the city of Detroit spreads out like a panorama behind its mayor, Coleman A. Young. To the left is a stretch of the People Mover track; to the right is Joe Louis Arena. Photo by Tony Spina. Courtesy Walter P. Reuther Library, Wayne State University, Detroit.

managed city" that, in becoming a safer, more habitable place for its citizens, would attract business and create jobs. Winning the September primary with 53 percent of the vote, Archer had faced Sharon McPhail, who had come in second with 26 percent. As the general election approached, Archer received the endorsement of, among many others, three dozen labor unions and many business leaders. McPhail was endorsed by Mayor Young and backed by some of Young's most powerful supporters, among them the Detroit branch of the NAACP and various black church groups. Archer overcame these obstacles, however, and on election day, November 2, 1993, he won handily, capturing 57 percent of the vote.

On January 1, 1994, Dennis W. Archer was sworn in as Detroit's new mayor. In impressive

In 1987, after years of delays and cost overruns, Detroit's controversial People Mover began operations. Built at a cost of more than $200 million, the 2.9-mile system has been plagued with poor ridership, constant service problems, and rising costs. Courtesy *Detroit News* Archives.

ceremonies at the newly renovated Fox Theater, Archer called for "a new era of self-reliance." As he began his term he pledged to carry out his campaign promises, stating, "We will pick up our garbage on time, our police officers will be in the neighborhoods, and we will have a master plan." Archer also sent a message of conciliation to suburbanites, offering an end to the racial demagoguery of the Young era and an approach based on regional cooperation.

Detroit had a new mayor and a new outlook—the city was on the threshold of a new beginning.

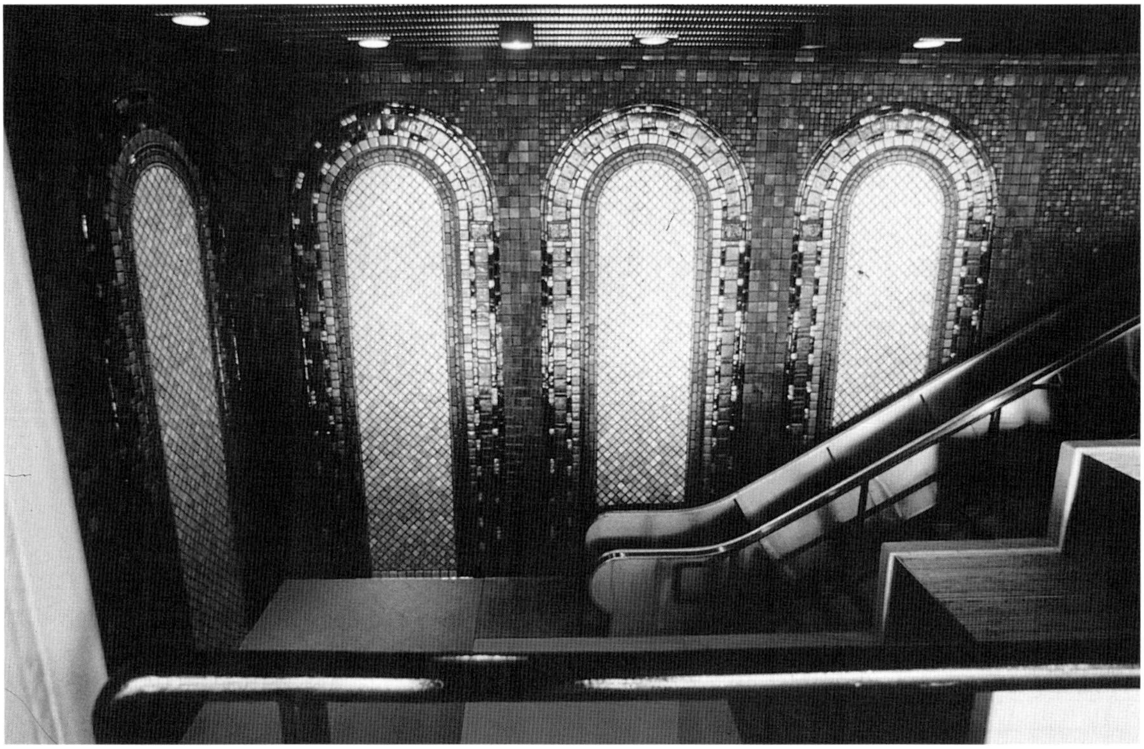

Although the system itself has been a disappointment, the artwork commissioned for the People Mover's thirteen stations is impressive. At the Cadillac Square Station, a profoundly rich green hue emanates from the luminous arches surrounded by the Pewabic tiles that were originally fired for the Stroh Brewery in 1955. Courtesy Pewabic Pottery.

Epilogue
A New Beginning

After the election of Dennis Archer in the fall of 1993, the city of Detroit entered an era of extended economic prosperity and development. This growth followed an economic boom felt throughout the state of Michigan and across the nation.

During the 1990s, the U.S. economy underwent a fundamental change. Fueled by a boom in technology and a powerful combination of low inflation, favorable interest rates, productivity gains, and increased flexibility, the nation's economy proceeded on an unparalleled growth track. Led once again by the automotive industry, Michigan's economy surged ahead as well with low inflation and high employment. By 1997, for example, the state's unemployment rate had fallen to 3.9 percent, almost a full point lower than the national level.

While the 1970s and 1980s had been, for the most part, a period of economic decline and even recession for the city of Detroit, the 1990s were to be a period of unprecedented growth and prosperity. The renaissance promised by Henry Ford II's great riverfront development of the early 1970s had finally begun.

For Detroit this era of prosperity really began in 1991 with real estate developer Chuck Forbes, the Gem Theatre, and the development of the city's new theater district. Detroit probably had more grand, historic theaters and concert halls than any other major U.S. city—partly because downtown collapsed so quickly in the 1960s and stayed down so long. In other cities, historic stages fell to the wrecking ball to make way for new development. In Detroit, however, the curtain came down, the doors were padlocked—and there the theaters sat, the seats rotting, the plaster friezes crumbling. Forbes was one of the first to realize what a popular draw the restored old theaters could be.

In the early 1980s Forbes purchased the Gem Theatre, which had been closed since 1978. Forbes also owned the Fox and State Theaters, selling the Fox to the Ilitch family in 1987. The Gem, built in 1927 adjacent to the Century Theater on East Colombia off Woodward Avenue just a block from the Fox

Theater, had served a variety of purposes. In 1990 Forbes began restoration of this quaint 450-seat Spanish Revival–style theater. Layers of black paint were stripped from proscenium panels, and the carpet design was re-created from a small section of the original carpeting found in the basement of the theater. The Gem reopened on New Year's Eve 1991 with the musical revue "The All Night Strut!" The newly restored Gem and its first production were an immediate success, and the rebirth of Detroit's theater district was under way.

Along with the Gem, the Fox, and the State Theaters, the renovations and restorations continued with the new Second City, the Music Hall, the Detroit Opera House, and Orchestra Place. Located next to the Fox Theater, the 350-seat Second City opened in 1993. Based on the Chicago and Toronto troupe theme, the Second City featured classic sketch comedy. The Music Hall reopened its doors on Madison Avenue across from the Detroit Athletic Club when its six-year, $6.5 million restoration was completed. Now a venue for musical shows and plays, the theater originally opened in 1928 as the Wilson. Built by Matilda Dodge Wilson, the theater was renamed the Music Hall in 1945 when it became the home of the Detroit Symphony Orchestra. Today many Detroiters will remember the Music Hall as the site of Lowell Thomas's "Cinerama." Phase one of the $80 million Orchestra Place, located on Woodward next to Orchestra Hall, was completed in 1998. This phase consisted of office space for Detroit Medical Center and Detroit Symphony Orchestra employees, an eight-hundred-space parking deck, and an upscale restaurant. Future plans for Orchestra Place include the Detroit High School for the Performing Arts, the Jacob Bernard Pincus

Phase one of the impressive new Orchestra Place, located on Woodward Avenue next to Orchestra Hall, was completed in 1998. © Glen Calvin Moon.

More than 450,000 people annually hear the Detroit Symphony Orchestra at historic Orchestra Hall and in concerts around the world. Led by Neeme Järvi, a music director who is also one of the world's most recorded conductors, the Detroit Symphony Orchestra has a larger radio audience than any other American orchestra. Courtesy Detroit Symphony Orchestra.

Music Education Center, and an expansion of Orchestra Hall.

As important as these projects proved to be, however, the most spectacular theater restoration was to be the Detroit Opera House. This restoration project was a long time in coming. It began back in 1988 when the Michigan Opera Theatre (MOT) first put money down on the nearly ruined Grand Circus Theater. Located on the corner of Broadway and Madison just off Grand Circus Park, the theater was originally known at its 1922 opening as the Capitol. Under the leadership of general director David DiChiera, the MOT began acquiring property immediately adjacent to the theater to make room for the 75,000-square-foot stage, backstage, and rehearsal space that was to be built entirely from scratch. The major project, however, was the daunting task of restoring the old theater's interior, which had been gutted by water damage when its pipes froze after its 1985 abandonment. Especially critical was the reconstruction of the hall's plaster walls, ceilings, and proscenium arch, about 70 percent of which had been destroyed, and which called upon nearly forgotten plastering arts to reconstruct in its original detail. Finally, all

Once the old Capital Theater had been purchased for the new opera house, restoration of the old theater interior began. Courtesy Michigan Opera Theatre.

was in readiness, and on April 22, 1996, the beautifully renovated theater was opened. Detroit once again had a magnificent Opera House. In February 2000 the Detroit Opera House announced a $10 million restoration of its western facade on Broadway that will include a two-hundred-seat performance theater, media studios, costume center, research library, museum shop, and café.

Also benefiting from the strong economy and the renewed interest in Detroit were several institutions in the city's cultural center. The Detroit Institute of Arts (DIA), for example, launched a five-year, $320 million fund-raising campaign that would include about $200 million in endowments. The DIA was able to expand hours, open previously closed

On April 22, 1996, the beautifully renovated theater was opened and Detroit once again had a magnificent opera house. Photo by Mark Mancinelli. Courtesy Michigan Opera Theatre.

galleries, renovate the building, and bring in major new exhibitions. The Detroit Historical Museum was also to raise its donations and thus become less dependent on state and city money. In 1992, 85 percent of its $4.7 million budget came from government funds; by 1997, only 57 percent of its $4.8 million budget was made up of public money. In the fall of 2000 the museum also announced the receipt of grant funds to make major enhancements and improvements to the exterior of its main building at Kirby and Woodward. Another major building program was also begun at this time by the Center for Creative Studies, and the Detroit Science Center announced plans to increase its exhibit space more than ten times with a $30 million building expansion.

Without question, though, the major addition to the cultural center came in 1997 with the opening of the impressive new Charles H. Wright Museum of African American History. Originally started as the International Afro-American Museum in three row houses on West Grand Boulevard at Warren in 1965 by Dr. Charles H. Wright, a Detroit obstetrician/gynecologist, in 1985 the museum moved into a $3.5 million, 28,000-square-foot facility located on Frederick Douglass Drive between John R. and Brush in the cultural center. Then, in 1993, ground was broken for the third building—a 120,000-square-foot state-of-the-art facility built at a cost of $38.4 million. With its opening on April 12, 1997, the museum became the world's largest institution dedicated to the African American experience. Located on Warren at Brush, next to the Detroit Science Center, the museum features four exhibition areas, a one-hundred-foot architecturally acclaimed glass-domed rotunda with a terrazzo tile mosaic titled "Genealogy," a research library,

The two main entrances are among the most impressive aspects of the Charles H. Wright Museum of African American History. The magnificent aluminum- and gold-plated, ten-foot-high stainless steel masks hang over the brass doors. Courtesy Charles H. Wright Museum of African American History and Felecia Hunt Taylor, photographer.

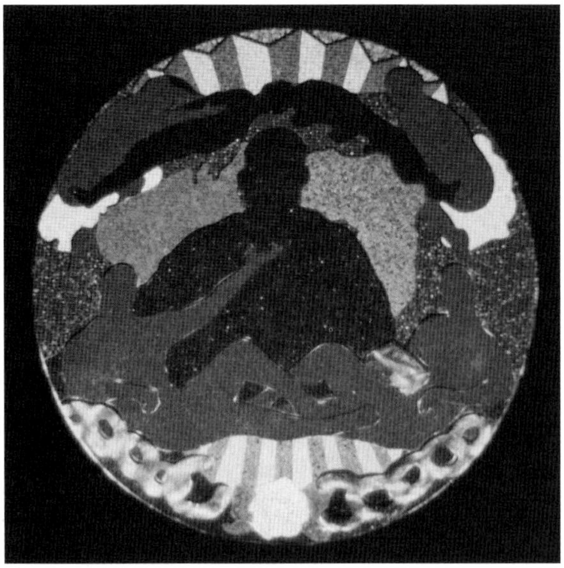

The rotunda's impressive terrazzo floor, designed by artist Hubert Massey and titled "Genealogy," features historic figures who symbolize the struggles of African Americans in this country. Courtesy Charles H. Wright Museum of African American History and Felecia Hunt Taylor, photographer.

a theater, and a museum store. Within a short time, the museum became one of the city's major attractions and a leading cultural institution.

Down the street from the cultural center, at the Detroit Medical Center, changes were also under way. At the Karmanos Cancer Institute's Hudson-Weber Cancer Research Center, a $22 million, six-story tower was built atop the institute. Out West Grand Boulevard at the Lodge Freeway, the Henry Ford II Pavilion—a $75 million, four-story structure—was added to the west side of the Henry Ford Hospital complex in 1998 in what administrators called the hospital's "commitment to the city of Detroit." Originally founded in 1911 as the privately owned Detroit General Hospital, the institution ran into financial problems and was taken over by Henry Ford in 1915. The present main building was opened in 1917, and the hospital continues to this day as one of the region's leading health care facilities.

As these institutions were expanding, growth was also occurring downtown. In 1992 the Atheneum Suite Hotel and Conference Center opened in Greektown. The Harmonie Park district prospered as well with lofts, several fine restaurants, an art gallery, a state-of-the-art recording studio, office space, and a $6 million renovation of the Harmonie Club, a former German social hall dating to 1895.

At the corner of Fort and Cass the venerable Detroit Club was facing the real possibility of closing in 1996 due to falling membership. Founded in 1882, the club was the city's oldest, and the clubhouse, built in 1892, was a longtime center of the city's business and social life. When the old board of directors announced the closing, a group of younger members took control and brought new life to the club. Today the clubhouse is being handsomely restored room by room, and the Detroit Club is now an important part of the revival of the city's central business district.

Up Woodward Avenue another area was being developed—the Necklace District. The area is defined, and thus so named, by the pattern of radial streets and triangular blocks that represent the strands of a necklace, with Grand Circus Park as the clasp and Campus Martius as the pendant. The Necklace District contains some of the most significant surviving remnants of Judge Woodward's original street plan of 1807. Here developers have begun the rehabilitation of a number of historic buildings. Capitalizing on the area's unique setting, the developers have created a loft district with living space on the buildings' upper floors, and commercial sites, retail shops, restaurants, and entertainment spots at street level. Thus the developers have provided, in this new district, a central location to bring people back to live and shop downtown.

On opening day, April 11, 2000, Tiger fans streamed through the main entrance of their new baseball stadium, Comerica Park. Photo by Deborah R. Kingery. Courtesy the photographer.

On September 27, 1999, an era came to an end when the last baseball game was played at Tiger Stadium. After 103 years, professional baseball was leaving the corner of Michigan and Trumbull. While many Detroiters were saddened that the old ballpark would be gone, they were excited that on opening day, April 11, 2000, their Tigers were playing on a new field—Comerica Park. Built on the block bounded by Adams, Witherell, Montcalm, and Brush, the new ballpark was another key element in the revival of the city. Constructed at a cost of over $360 million ($245 million from the Ilitch family and $115 million from public funds) and with seating for 40,000, the new stadium was more than just a baseball field. It was designed with families in mind. Included in the new ballpark were a host of attractions: the world's largest scoreboard towering above

The new ballpark features stainless-steel statues of six Tiger greats. Included is the sculpture of power-hitting outfielder and 1968 World Series star Willie Horton. Photo by Deborah R. Kingery. Courtesy the photographer.

the leftfield backdrop, huge water fountains beyond center field, a carousel, and even a Ferris wheel. Marked by these high-tech features and a sense of airiness along its pathways and concourses, the new stadium soon became a favorite with the fans.

Plans for the new baseball stadium had been formally announced in 1996, but before construction could begin a decision had to be made concerning three historic buildings. Standing on the site, and in the way of the new stadium, were the Gem Theatre, the adjacent Century Club, and the 1936 art deco Elwood Bar and Grill. The buildings were owned by developer Chuck Forbes, and just six years after restoring the Gem he was faced with the choice of either seeing the buildings destroyed or moving them. Forbes decided to move them, and in mid-October 1997 two bulldozers and four excavators with two thousand feet of cable literally pulled the Gem Theatre/Century Club building from its old home on Columbia at Witherell to its new home at Madison and Brush. Weighing more than five million pounds, the building was moved five city blocks and into the *Guinness Book of World Records* as the heaviest building ever relocated on tires. After eighteen months of moving and reconstruction, and after laborious restoration of the Century building, the Gem Theatre reopened on September 9, 1998. The Century building,

In order to save the historic Gem Theatre and Century Club, developer Chuck Forbes had the two buildings moved five city blocks and into the *Guinness Book of World Records*. Courtesy Forbes Management.

In 2000, after twenty-five years in suburban Pontiac, the Detroit Lions announced their move back to downtown Detroit. Their new stadium—Ford Field—will be completed by the 2002 football season. Courtesy Detroit Lions.

constructed in 1903 as a women's club and closed for more than forty years, reopened as the two-hundred-seat Century Theatre on April 14, 1999, and the Century Club Restaurant on May 16, 1999. Later the Elwood was also moved and relocated next to the Gem and the Century. Thus a major new development was completed and a part of Detroit's historic past was preserved.

Sadly, while the Gem, Century, and Elwood were moved and restored, a fourth building on the stadium site was left behind and destroyed. The old YWCA building, designed by Albert Kahn, was torn down; fortunately, however, many of its unique architectural items were saved by Forbes and incorporated into the new Gem/Century building. These items included three fireplaces, a balustrade, chandeliers, leaded glass doors, woodwork, stained glass, Pewabic tile, and over one hundred pieces of original furniture.

On November 16, 1999, following the reopening of the Gem and the Century, and as the Tigers were completing construction of their new ballpark, another groundbreaking took place for another sports stadium—Ford Field. And so it was that twenty-five years after leaving the city for the suburbs, Detroit Lions owner William Clay Ford was moving his football team back to downtown Detroit. The domed stadium would be built at a cost of over $300 million, and its principal architectural feature would be its dramatic view of Detroit's skyline. The new stadium will be joined to two refurbished Hudson's warehouses (which will include luxury football suites, office space, shops, and restaurants) and will have an entrance with a glass wall several stories high facing Brush Street just across from Comerica Park. With its completion expected in time for the 2002 football season, another important part of the renewal of downtown Detroit is under way.

On July 29, 1999, after years of often bitter debate and controversy, the first of Detroit's three temporary casinos, the MGM Grand, opened to the public. Five months later the second casino, the MotorCity, opened. The third casino, located in Greektown, was scheduled to open shortly after the other two but remained temporarily closed due to financial difficulties and state regulatory problems. It finally opened on November 10, 2000.

Gaming casinos owned and operated by Native American tribes had long been in operation in outstate Michigan, and casinos had also been up and running for several years across the river in Windsor. In Detroit, however, casinos were approved by voters only after a long struggle. It had taken supporters seven elections dating back to 1976 to win voter approval. Proponents of casino gaming (originally supported by Mayor Coleman Young) argued that casinos would bring tax income, jobs, and visitors to Detroit and thus help the city overcome its severe economic problems. Opponents, led principally by local church leaders, argued that gaming casinos would bring higher crime and substantial increases in family discord and violence, that the jobs generated would be only low-paying service positions, and that the financial rewards promised by supporters were greatly exaggerated.

Finally, however, in 1996 state voters approved casino gaming for Detroit by a margin of 51 to 49 percent. With the needed state law in place, Mayor Archer selected three syndicates to open their casinos in temporary quarters: the MGM Grand on the Lodge Freeway service drive between Howard, Michigan, and Third Streets in a building formerly occupied by the Internal Revenue Service; the MotorCity in the old Wonder Bread Bakery Building on Grand River and the Lodge Freeway between Trumbull, Spruce, and Elm Streets; and the third casino in a converted warehouse in Greektown.

During the two casinos' first full year of operation their revenues far exceeded expectations, and in that respect they were most successful. Spinoff revenues for area hotels, shops, and restaurants, however, proved to be disappointing. The long-range impact of casinos on the city's economy, however, is uncertain, as is the location for the permanent casinos. Their proposed location is out Jefferson Avenue on fifty-seven acres of property along the riverfront east of the Renaissance Center. However, there is considerable opposition to using valuable riverfront property for the casinos, and the final choice for location has not yet been determined.

The economic success that Detroit and Michigan enjoyed during the 1990s was derived largely from the growth of the automobile industry—both the Big Three and the industry's parts suppliers. Production reached record levels and the industry experienced seven straight years of unprecedented growth, with North American vehicle production reaching 17,615,611 units in 1999. Along with production records, downsizing within the industry caused profits to reach record levels as well. Yet during the later half of the 1990s each of the Big Three produced important news in addition to record production and record profits.

On Wednesday, December 22, 1999, one of Detroit's most famous signs—the red glowing letters atop the General Motors Building on West Grand Boulevard—went dark. With a flip of a switch, GM turned off the letters that had proclaimed its industrial power for more than forty years. Thirty minutes after

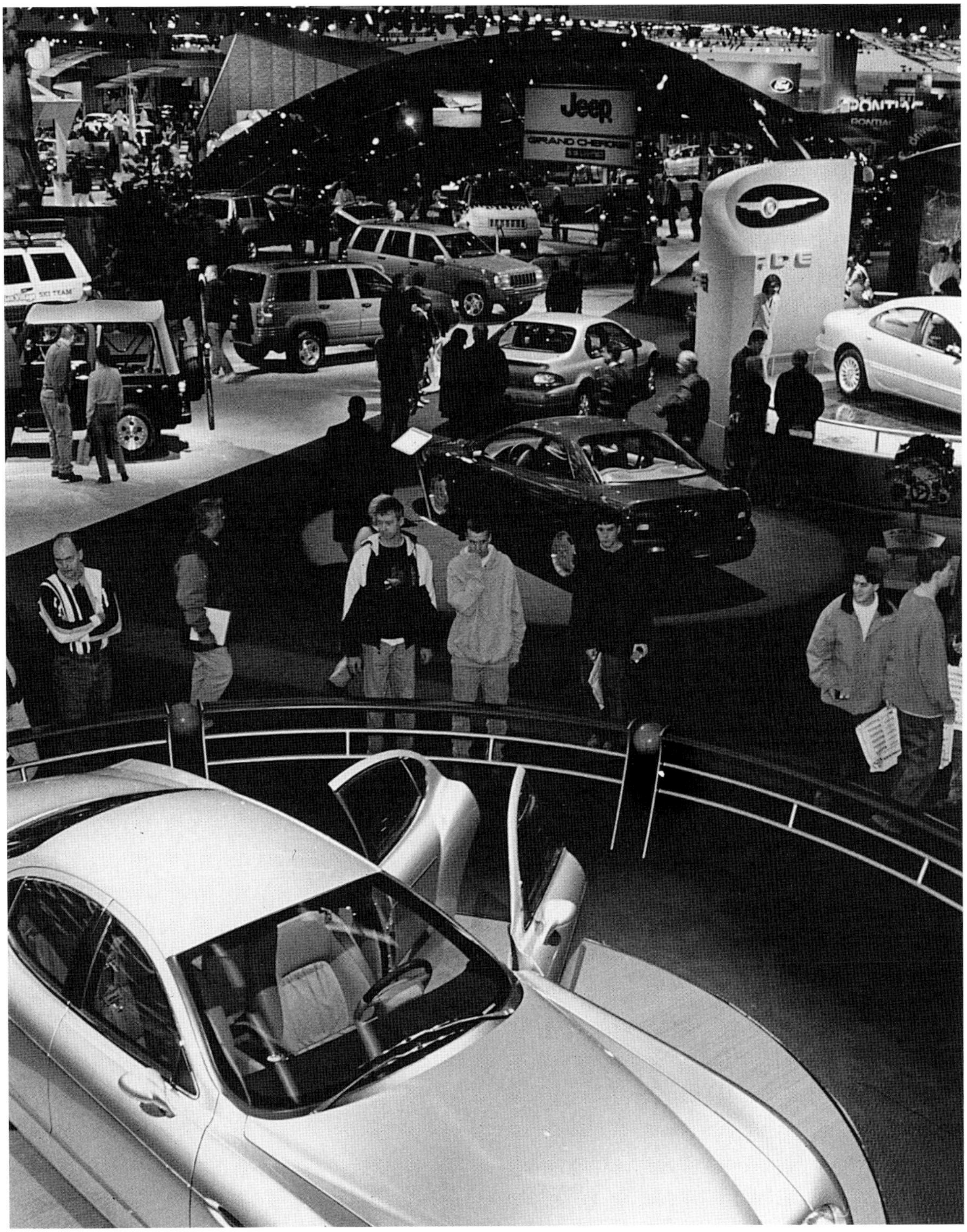

One of Detroit's premier events is the North American International Auto Show. Although auto shows have been held in the city since the earliest days of the industry, this international show ranks as one of the five most important auto shows in the world. This view is of the 1998 show. Photo by Tom Sherry. Courtesy National Automotive History Collection, Detroit Public Library.

the old sign was turned off, GM turned on a temporary sign over the Jefferson Avenue entrance of its new global headquarters—the Renaissance Center. The automaker had purchased the Ren Cen office, hotel, and retail complex for $73 million in 1996. Fortunately, however, the darkening of the old sign did not mean the end of the General Motors Building. Following GM's move to the Ren Cen, it was announced that the state of Michigan had signed a twenty-year lease to occupy the New Center building and that state employees would be using the building's entire 1.1 million square feet of office space.

At the time it purchased the Ren Cen, GM announced that it would also be spending $750 million to renovate the complex. Since its opening in 1977, the Renaissance Center had suffered from a fortress-like appearance and a maze-like interior. This was a situation that GM vowed to fix. In addition, GM announced plans to remove the big, forbidding berms on Jefferson and create a new, pedestrian-friendly entrance. Then, in June 1999, GM announced that it would not only be renovating the Ren Cen, but also transforming twenty-five acres of surface parking lots just east of the complex into a bustling district of riverfront shops, lofts, offices, condominiums, and restaurants. This new development was to be called River East and would be part of the new Detroit River promenade reaching from Cobo Center to the Renaissance Center. This promenade would eventually become part of a grand pedestrian walkway that will stretch from the Ambassador Bridge to Belle Isle's MacArthur Bridge.

As General Motors was moving ahead with the development of its new world headquarters, the Ford Motor Company was making plans for its future as well. On September 11, 1998, it was announced that a member of the Ford family would once again, after an absence of eighteen years, sit at the head of the Ford Motor Company. And so, on January 1, 1999, William Clay Ford, Jr., became chairman of the world's second-largest automaker. Young Ford was appointed to his new position after having held a series of progressively responsible positions following his joining the company in 1979. With this new appointment Ford was given the responsibility of leading the board of directors in its support of the management running the business. The company's day-to-day operations were to be handled by Jacques Nasser, who was named president and chief executive officer.

Ford's promotion to chairman gave shareholders assurances that their interests were aligned with the man at the top—the Ford family itself controlled 40 percent of the company's voting stock. The promotion of Nasser to president gave the company one of the industry's most respected executives. This power-sharing arrangement—potentially disastrous if roles were not clearly defined—offered the company a leadership team unique in American industry: a chairman whose fortunes and those of his family were tied to the company bearing his name, and a chief executive with a proven track record.

Henry Ford II, the uncle of William Clay Ford, Jr., had been the last chairman from the family. He had stepped down in 1980. Henry had become president in 1945 when the family took control of the company from his aging grandfather. Old Henry Ford's son Edsel had served as president from 1919 until his death in 1942. The news of the appointment of William Clay Ford, Jr., was met with approval throughout the automobile industry, and thus a new era began at the Ford Motor Company.

As General Motors and Ford were making plans for the future, so was the Chrysler Corporation. On May 7, 1998, Detroiters awoke to the stunning news of a $36 billion merger between Chrysler, the maker of Jeeps and minivans, and Daimler-Benz, the German maker of Mercedes-Benz luxury cars. In joining with Daimler-Benz, Chrysler gained security heading into a period of great uncertainty for the auto industry. Pressures to expand globally while cutting expenses, the move by Asian automakers to escape their region's economy, too much automaking capacity seeking too few buyers, and big investments to design environmentally friendly cars for the next century all threatened to severely stretch Chrysler's resources. On the other hand, Chrysler offered Daimler-Benz instant expertise in a booming North American market that Mercedes had begun to enter seriously only in 1997. With a solid manufacturing and sales presence in the United States, Daimler acquired a foothold that would have taken it several years and billions of dollars to develop independently.

Separately, Chrysler and Mercedes were important mainly in their home markets. Together they became the worlds fifth-largest automaker in cars built and number three in sales. That made the new Daimler-Chrysler Corporation a world force, joining the General Motors Corporation, Ford Motor Company, Toyota Motor Company, and Volkswagen AG.

The seeds for the Daimler-Chrysler deal were sown in 1995, when Chrysler fought off a takeover bid by its biggest shareholder, billionaire Kirk Kerkorian, and its retired chairman, Lee Iacocca. Their startling grab for the smallest of the Big Three sparked secret talks between Chrysler and Daimler. Although these talks broke down, they set the stage for the final talks between Daimler Chairman Juergen Schrempp and Chrysler Chairman Robert Eaton. The union of Chrysler and Daimler, with joint headquarters in Auburn Hills, Michigan, and Stuttgart, Germany, was to be a merger of equals, but Schrempp and Daimler soon emerged as the unquestioned leader when Eaton abdicated power by agreeing to retire within three years of the merger.

Detroit has always had a great deal of pride in calling itself the Motor City and in being home to the Big Three. Now it is to be home to the Big Two and a portion of a new transatlantic entity.

While Detroit prospered and grew during the 1990s, Detroiters were to witness the loss of parts of the city's long history. On Tuesday, February 9, 1999, Stroh Brewery Company, the nation's fourth-largest brewer and one of Detroit's oldest firms, announced that it was getting out of the beer business and sellings its brands to Pabst and Miller. Founded in

On October 29, 1998, demolition experts turned a switch and in a matter of moments the old J. L. Hudson Building on Woodward Avenue imploded into a pile of shattered brick, concrete, and twisted steel. Photo by Tom Sherry. Courtesy the photographer.

1850 by German immigrant Bernhard Stroh, the company had long been one of Detroit's icons, but a shrinking market share and a sizable debt made the sale of the beer business inevitable. The Stroh Company was to remain headquartered in Detroit, however, concentrating on its real estate business and its longtime support of civic and cultural activities by the Stroh family.

The closing of Stroh's brought to an end 149 years in Detroit and a vestige of the passing century as it joined such bygone landmarks as Tiger Stadium, Vernor's, Sanders, Parke-Davis, Olympia Stadium, and the Bob-Lo boats. Without question, though, the city's most notable loss was the grand old lady of Woodward Avenue—the J. L. Hudson Building. On October 24, 1998, demolition experts turned a switch, 2,728 pounds of explosives were ignited, and in a matter of moments the great building, so fondly remembered by generations of Detroiters, imploded into a pile of shattered brick, concrete, and twisted steel.

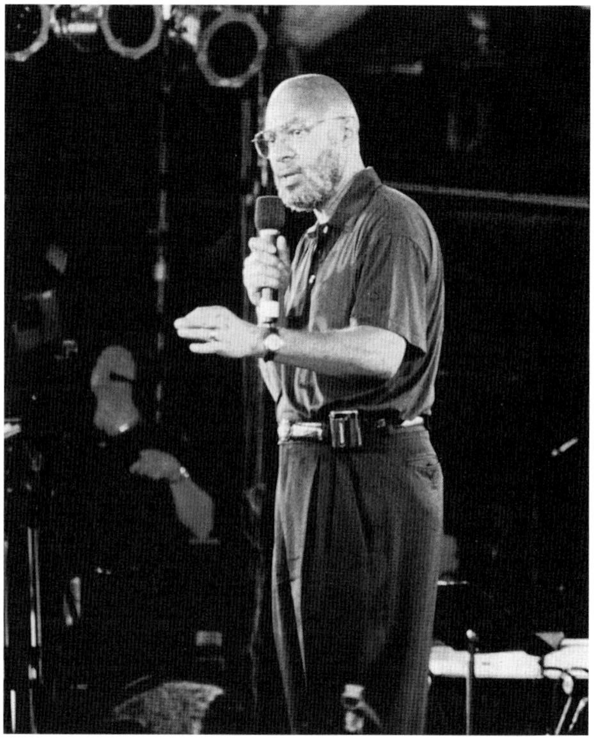
Mayor Dennis Archer extends the city's welcome to the crowd at the 2000 Ford Detroit International Jazz Festival. Courtesy Jazz Festival.

The loss of this downtown landmark was overshadowed, however, by the exciting news of what was to be built in its place. On November 24, 1999, officials from the city and from Compuware Corporation (located in suburban Farmington Hills) unveiled plans for the construction of the company's new $800 million world headquarters at the northeast corner of Woodward and Monroe. Fronting on Campus Martius, the sixteen-story building will be a state-of-the-art office tower designed for the computer age. Thus, after fifty years, during which it made more sense to move out, a high-tech, world-class corporation is now moving from the suburbs back to downtown Detroit.

In addition to its headquarters building, Compuware also announced plans to build a $400 million office building for its automotive and health care businesses just east of the Renaissance Center. In all, it is estimated that these new Compuware projects will bring more than ten thousand jobs back to the city.

At Campus Martius, the new Compuware headquarters will be joined by a multibillion-dollar development that is expected to encompass nine blocks and include a mix of mid-rise office towers, stores, restaurants, and a hotel. The first building in the district will be an underground parking structure to be constructed on the basement ruins of the old J. L. Hudson Building. Above the structure will be an office building.

The location of this new development has a significant place in the history of Detroit. Named by Judge Woodward and included in his 1807 plan for the city, Campus Martius—"Field of Mars"—originally comprised four large areas at this intersection and included

Since 1979 Hart Plaza has been center stage for the world-renowned Ford Detroit International Jazz Festival. Held annually for four days over the Labor Day weekend, the festival brings together the region's finest jazz musicians. Courtesy Jazz Festival.

The first Detroit Electronic Music Festival, the largest in the world, was held in Hart Plaza in May 2000. Detroit is considered the birthplace of Techno music. Courtesy Pop Culture Media.

part of what is now Kennedy Square. Campus Martius was once the corner on which the city's life turned. It was the site of the elegant Detroit Opera House and later of the Kern and Crowley's department stores. For the Detroit and Pontiac Railway and the city's electric streetcars, Campus Martius was the end of the line. When Detroiters decided to build a monument to honor those who had served their country in the Civil War, they built it across from Campus Martius.

In the 1890s, Campus Martius was a lush green space with wide walks, fountains, and beautiful flower beds. Here, Michigan Civil War regiments mustered, holiday parades were conducted, and presidents addressed huge crowds. A wholesale food market occupied the adjacent Cadillac Square, and Detroiters built a stately city hall directly across the street. And so today, Campus Martius, one of the city's most historic sites, is to be the center of the city's new development—the center of the city's new beginning.

As Detroiters prepare to celebrate the three hundredth anniversary of the founding of their city, exciting times do appear to be ahead—the renaissance promised by Henry Ford II's great riverfront complex has indeed begun. The city is still faced, however, as are most of America's urban centers, with serious problems: neighborhood decay, inadequate mass transit, crime, a shrinking tax base, racial tension, air and water pollution, a faltering school system, and the financing of

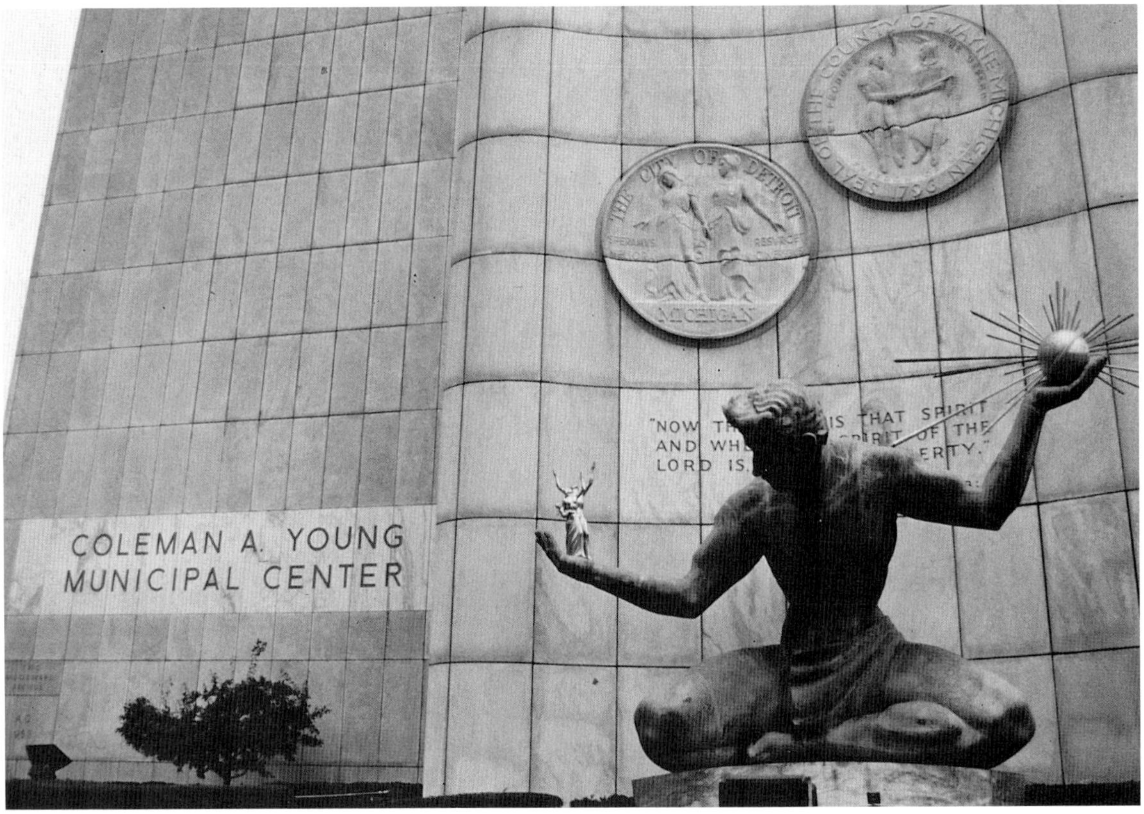

On November 29, 1997, Coleman A. Young, Detroit's first black mayor and its longest-serving chief executive, died after a long illness. In his honor, the City-County Building was renamed the Coleman A. Young Municipal Center. Photo by Deborah R. Kingery. Courtesy the photographer.

municipal services. But these are problems that can and will be solved. For, as we have seen, over its long history, Detroit and Detroiters have solved problems far greater.

Today Detroit is entering a new century and a new era. The 1990s proved to be a decade of substantial growth and prosperity for the city. It would appear though, that even more exciting times are ahead. What is to come, we of course do not know. What Detroit is to be, what will be its triumphs and its disappointments, must remain a matter of conjecture. History stops at this moment—the next second lies in the future.

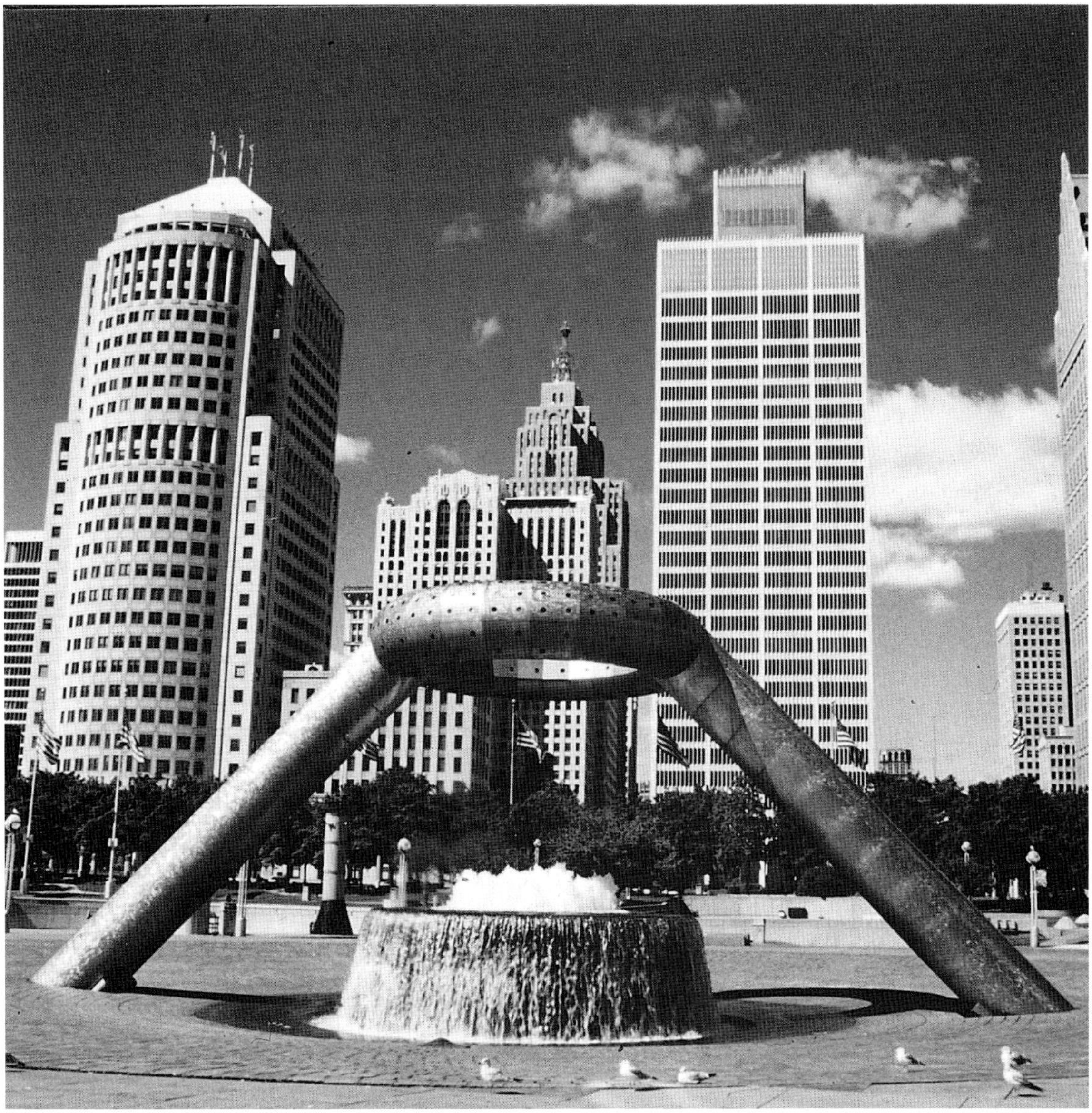

A view of Hart Plaza and Detroit's new skyline on the eve of the city's 300th anniversary. Photo by Deborah R. Kingery. Courtesy the photographer.

One of the region's most popular events is the annual fireworks display held on the Detroit River for the International Freedom Festival. Cosponsored by the cities of Windsor and Detroit, the event honors July 4th, Independence Day in the United States, and July 1st, Dominion Day, in Canada. Photo by Robert L. Stewart. Courtesy the photographer.

Suggestions for Further Reading

Abraham, Nabeel, and Andrew Shryock, eds. *Arab Detroit: From Margin to Mainstream.* Detroit: Wayne State University Press, 2000.

Anderson, William M. *The Detroit Tigers: A Pictorial Celebration of the Greatest Players and Moments in Tigers' History.* Detroit: Wayne State University Press, 1999.

Bak, Richard. *The Corner: A Century of Memories at Michigan and Trumbull.* Chicago: Triumph, 1999.

———. *Detroit, 1900–1930.* Charleston, S.C.: Arcadia, 1999.

———. *Detroit: A Postcard Album.* Charleston, S.C.: Arcadia, 1998.

———. *A Place for the Summer: A Narrative History of Tiger Stadium.* Detroit: Wayne State University Press, 1998.

———. *Turkey Stearns and the Detroit Stars: The Negro Leagues in Detroit, 1919–1933.* Detroit: Wayne State University Press, 1994.

Bald, F. Clever. *Detroit's First American Decade, 1796 to 1805.* Ann Arbor: University of Michigan Press, 1948.

———. *Michigan in Four Centuries.* New York: Harper, 1961.

Barcus, Frank. *All Around Detroit.* Detroit: Frank Barcus Art Studio, 1939.

Blum, Peter H. *Brewed in Detroit: Breweries and Beers since 1830.* Detroit: Wayne State University Press, 1999.

Brown, Henry D. et al, eds. *Cadillac and the Founding of Detroit: Commemorating the Two Hundred and Seventy-Fifth Anniversary of the Founding of the City of Detroit, by Antoine Laumet de Lamothe Cadillac on July 24, 1701.* Detroit: Wayne State University Press, 1976.

Bukowczyk, John H. et al., eds. *Detroit Images: Photographs of the Renaissance City.* Detroit: Wayne State University Press, 1989.

Burton, Clarence Monroe. *History of Wayne County and the City of Detroit, Michigan.* 5 vols. Chicago: S. J. Clarke, 1930.

Capeci, Dominic J. *Race Relations in Wartime Detroit: The Sojourner Truth Housing Controversy of 1942.* Philadelphia: Temple University Press, 1984.

Catlin, George B. *The Story of Detroit.* Detroit: Evening News Association, 1926.

Chafets, Ze'ev. *Devil's Night and Other True Tales of Detroit.* New York: Random House, 1990.

Conot, Robert E. *American Odyssey.* New York: Morrow, 1974.

Cotsonika, Nicholas J. *Century of Champions.* Detroit: Detroit Free Press: 1999.

Darden, Joe T., ed. *Detroit, Race and Uneven Development.* Philadelphia: Temple University Press, 1987.

The Detroit Almanac: Three Hundred Years of Life in the Motor City. Edited by Peter Gavrilovich and Bill McGraw. Detroit: Detroit Free Press, 2000.

Detroit Black Writers' Guild. *Paradise Valley Days: A Photo Album Poetry Book.* Detroit: Detroit Black Writers' Guild, 1998.

Detroit Institute of Arts. *American Paintings in the Detroit Institute of Arts.* New York: Hudson Hills, 1991.

Detroit Public Library. *Detroit in Its World Setting: A 250-year Chronology, 1701–1951.* Edited by Rae Elizabeth Rips. Detroit: Detroit Public Library, 1953.

Dunbar, Willis Frederick. *Michigan: A History of the Wolverine State.* Grand Rapids: W. B. Eerdmans, 1995.

Eckert, Kathryn Bishop. *Buildings of Michigan.* New York: Oxford University Press, 1992.

Farmer, Silas. *The History of Detroit and Michigan: Or, the Metropolis Illustrated; A Chronological Cyclopaedia of the Past and Present, Including a Full Record of Territorial Days in Michigan, and the Annals of Wayne County.* Detroit: S. Farmer, 1884.

Ferry, W. Hawkins. *The Buildings of Detroit: A History.* Detroit: Wayne State University Press, 1980.

Fine, Sidney. *Violence in the Model City: The Cavanagh Administration, Race Relations, and the Detroit Riot of 1967.* Ann Arbor: University of Michigan Press, 1989.

Ford Motor Co. *Global Journeys in Metro Detroit: A Multicultural Guide to the Motor City.* Detroit: New Detroit, 1999.

Galbraith, Stuart. *Motor City Marquees: A Comprehensive, Illustrated Reference to Motion Picture Theaters in the Detroit Area, 1906–1992.* Jefferson, N.C.: McFarland, 1994.

Gibson, Arthur Hopkin. *Artists of Early Michigan: A Biographical Dictionary of Artists Native to or Active in Michigan, 1701–1900.* Detroit: Wayne State University Press, 1975.

Glazer, Sidney. *Detroit: A Study in Urban Development.* New York: Bookman Associates, 1965.

Green, Jerry. *The Detroit Pistons: Capturing a Remarkable Era.* Detroit: Detroit News, 1991.

Hennepin, Louis. *A New Discovery of a Vast Country in America.* New York: Kraus Reprint, 1972.

Henrickson, Wilma Wood, ed. *Detroit Perspectives: Crossroads and Turning Points.* Detroit: Wayne State University Press, 1990.

Holli, Melvin G. *Detroit.* New York: New Viewpoints, 1976.

———. *Reform in Detroit: Hazen S. Pingree and Urban Politics.* New York: Oxford University Press, 1969.

Horan, James David. *North American Indian Portraits: 120 Full-Color Plates from the McKenney-Hall Portrait Gallery of American Indians.* New York: Crown, 1975.

Hyde, Charles K. *Detroit: An Industrial History Guide.* Detroit: Detroit Historical Society, n.d.

Katzman, David M. *Before the Ghetto: Black Detroit in the Nineteenth Century.* Urbana: University of Illinois Press, 1973.

Kornhauser, Arthur. *Detroit as the People See It: A Survey of Attitudes in an Industrial City.* Detroit: Wayne University Press, 1952.

Kubiak, William J. *Great Lakes Indians: A Pictorial Guide.* New York: Bonanza, 1970.

Mason, Philip P. *The Ambassador Bridge: A Monument to Progress.* Detroit: Wayne State University Press, 1987.

———. *Detroit, Fort Lernoult, and the American Revolution.* Detroit: Wayne State University Press, 1964.

———. *Rumrunning and the Roaring Twenties: Prohibition on the Michigan-Ontario Waterway.* Detroit: Wayne State University Press, 1995.

McFarlane, Brian. *The Red Wings.* Toronto: Stoddart, 1998.

Moon, Elaine Latzman. *Untold Tales, Unsung Heroes: An Oral History of Detroit's African American Community, 1918–1967.* Detroit: Wayne State University Press, 1994.

Morgan, Carl. *Birth of a City.* Windsor, Ont.: Border, 1991.

Motor Vehicle Manufacturers Association of the United States. *Automobiles of America: Milestones, Pioneers, Roll Call, Highlights.* Detroit: Wayne State University Press, 1974.

Murray, Mike, ed. *Lions Pride: Sixty Years of Detroit Lions Football.* Dallas: Taylor, 1993.

Nawrocki, Dennis Alan. *Art in Detroit Public Places.* Detroit: Wayne State University Press, 1999.

Parkins, Almon Ernest. *The Historical Geography of Detroit.* Lansing: Michigan Historical Commission, 1918.

Peckham, Howard Henry. *Pontiac and the Indian Uprising.* Detroit: Wayne State University Press, 1994.

Pflug, Warner. *The UAW in Pictures.* Detroit: Wayne State University Press, 1971.

Poremba, David Lee. *Detroit, 1860–1899.* Charleston, S.C.: Arcadia, 1998.

———. *Detroit, 1930–1969.* Charleston, S.C.: Arcadia, 1999.

———. *Detroit, City of Champions.* Charleston, S.C.: Arcadia, 1998.

Quaife, Milo Milton. *This Is Detroit, 1701–1951: Two Hundred and Fifty Years in Pictures.* Detroit: Wayne University Press, 1951.

Rich, Wilbur C. *Coleman Young and Detroit Politics: From Social Activist to Power Broker.* Detroit: Wayne State University Press, 1989.

Schoolcraft, Henry Rowe. *Historical and Statistical Information Respecting the History, Condition, and Prospects of the Indian Tribes of the United States: Collected and Prepared under the Direction of the Bureau of Indian Affairs per Act of Congress of March 3rd, 1847.* Philadelphia: Lippincott, Grambo, 1851–57.

Sinclair, Robert, and Bryan Thompson. *Metropolitan Detroit: An Anatomy of Social Change.* Cambridge, Mass.: Ballinger, 1977.

Smith, Suzanne E. *Dancing in the Street: Motown and the Cultural Politics of Detroit.* Cambridge, Mass.: Harvard University Press, 1999.

Spina, Tony. *Tony Spina, Chief Photographer.* Detroit: Detroit Free Press, 1988.

Stanton, Samuel Ward. *Great Lakes Steam Vessels.* Meriden, Conn.: Meriden Gravure, 1962.

Sugrue, Thomas J. *The Origins of the Urban Crisis: Race and Inequality in Postwar Detroit.* Princeton: Princeton University Press, 1996.

Tanner, Helen Hornbeck et al., eds. *Atlas of Great Lakes Indian History.* Norman: University of Oklahoma Press, 1987.

Thomas, Richard Walter. *Life for Us Is What We Make It: Building Black Community in Detroit, 1915–1945.* Bloomington: Indiana University Press, 1992.

Vergara, Camilo J. *American Ruins.* New York: Monacelli, 1999.

The WestSiders. *Remembering Detroit's Old Westside, 1920–1950: A Pictorial History of the WestSiders.* Detroit: WestSiders, 1997.

Wilson, Sunnie. *Toast of the Town: The Life and Times of Sunnie Wilson.* Detroit: Wayne State University Press, 1998.

Wolf, Eleanor Paperno. *Trial and Error: The Detroit School Segregation Case.* Detroit: Wayne State University Press, 1981.

Woodford, Arthur M. *Detroit, American Urban Renaissance: A Pictorial and Entertaining Commentary on the Growth and Development of Detroit, Michigan.* Tulsa, Okla.: Continental Heritage, 1979.

———. *Detroit and Its Banks: The Story of Detroit Bank and Trust.* Detroit: Wayne State University Press, 1974.

Woodford, Frank B. *Father Abraham's Children: Michigan Episodes in the Civil War.* Detroit: Wayne State University Press, 1999.

———. *Gabriel Richard: Frontier Ambassador.* Detroit: Wayne State University Press, 1958.

———. *Lewis Cass, the Last Jeffersonian.* New Brunswick, N.J.: Rutgers University Press, 1950.

———. *Mr. Jefferson's Disciple: A Life of Justice Woodward.* East Lansing: Michigan State University, 1953.

Woodford, Frank B, and Arthur M. Woodford. *All Our Yesterdays: A Brief History of Detroit.* Detroit: Wayne State University Press, 1969.

INDEX

Great Lakes Books Series

Freshwater Fury: Yarns and Reminiscences of the Greatest Storm in Inland Navigation, by Frank Barcus, 1986 (reprint)

Call It North Country: The Story of Upper Michigan, by John Bartlow Martin, 1986 (reprint)

The Land of the Crooked Tree, by U. P. Hedrick, 1986 (reprint)

Michigan Place Names, by Walter Romig, 1986 (reprint)

Luke Karamazov, by Conrad Hilberry, 1987

The Late, Great Lakes: An Environmental History, by William Ashworth, 1987 (reprint)

Great Pages of Michigan History from the Detroit Free Press, 1987

Waiting for the Morning Train: An American Boyhood, by Bruce Catton, 1987 (reprint)

Michigan Voices: Our State's History in the Words of the People Who Lived It, compiled and edited by Joe Grimm, 1987

Danny and the Boys, Being Some Legends of Hungry Hollow, by Robert Traver, 1987 (reprint)

Hanging On, or How to Get through a Depression and Enjoy Life, by Edmund G. Love, 1987 (reprint)

The Situation in Flushing, by Edmund G. Love, 1987 (reprint)

A Small Bequest, by Edmund G. Love, 1987 (reprint)

The Saginaw Paul Bunyan, by James Stevens, 1987 (reprint)

The Ambassador Bridge: A Monument to Progress, by Philip P. Mason, 1988

Let the Drum Beat: A History of the Detroit Light Guard, by Stanley D. Solvick, 1988

An Afternoon in Waterloo Park, by Gerald Dumas, 1988 (reprint)

Contemporary Michigan Poetry: Poems from the Third Coast, edited by Michael Delp, Conrad Hilberry and Herbert Scott, 1988

Over the Graves of Horses, by Michael Delp, 1988

Wolf in Sheep's Clothing: The Search for a Child Killer, by Tommy McIntyre, 1988

Copper-Toed Boots, by Marguerite de Angeli, 1989 (reprint)

Detroit Images: Photographs of the Renaissance City, edited by John J. Bukowczyk and Douglas Aikenhead, with Peter Slavcheff, 1989

Hangdog Reef: Poems Sailing the Great Lakes, by Stephen Tudor, 1989

Detroit: City of Race and Class Violence, revised edition, by B. J. Widick, 1989

Deep Woods Frontier: A History of Logging in Northern Michigan, by Theodore J. Karamanski, 1989

Orvie, The Dictator of Dearborn, by David L. Good, 1989

Seasons of Grace: A History of the Catholic Archdiocese of Detroit, by Leslie Woodcock Tentler, 1990

The Pottery of John Foster: Form and Meaning, by Gordon and Elizabeth Orear, 1990

The Diary of Bishop Frederic Baraga: First Bishop of Marquette, Michigan, edited by Regis M. Walling and Rev. N. Daniel Rupp, 1990

Walnut Pickles and Watermelon Cake: A Century of Michigan Cooking, by Larry B. Massie and Priscilla Massie, 1990

The Making of Michigan, 1820–1860: A Pioneer Anthology, edited by Justin L. Kestenbaum, 1990

America's Favorite Homes: A Guide to Popular Early Twentieth-Century Homes, by Robert Schweitzer and Michael W. R. Davis, 1990

Beyond the Model T: The Other Ventures of Henry Ford, by Ford R. Bryan, 1990

Life after the Line, by Josie Kearns, 1990

Michigan Lumbertowns: Lumbermen and Laborers in Saginaw, Bay City, and Muskegon, 1870–1905, by Jeremy W. Kilar, 1990

Detroit Kids Catalog: The Hometown Tourist, by Ellyce Field, 1990

Waiting for the News, by Leo Litwak, 1990 (reprint)

Detroit Perspectives, edited by Wilma Wood Henrickson, 1991

Life on the Great Lakes: A Wheelsman's Story, by Fred W. Dutton, edited by William Donohue Ellis, 1991

Copper Country Journal: The Diary of Schoolmaster Henry Hobart, 1863–1864, by Henry Hobart, edited by Philip P. Mason, 1991

John Jacob Astor: Business and Finance in the Early Republic, by John Denis Haeger, 1991

Survival and Regeneration: Detroit's American Indian Community, by Edmund J. Danziger, Jr., 1991

Steamboats and Sailors of the Great Lakes, by Mark L. Thompson, 1991

Cobb Would Have Caught It: The Golden Age of Baseball in Detroit, by Richard Bak, 1991

Michigan in Literature, by Clarence Andrews, 1992

Under the Influence of Water: Poems, Essays, and Stories, by Michael Delp, 1992

The Country Kitchen, by Della T. Lutes, 1992 (reprint)

The Making of a Mining District: Keweenaw Native Copper 1500–1870, by David J. Krause, 1992

Kids Catalog of Michigan Adventures, by Ellyce Field, 1993

Henry's Lieutenants, by Ford R. Bryan, 1993

Historic Highway Bridges of Michigan, by Charles K. Hyde, 1993

Lake Erie and Lake St. Clair Handbook, by Stanley J. Bolsenga and Charles E. Herndendorf, 1993

Queen of the Lakes, by Mark Thompson, 1994

Iron Fleet: The Great Lakes in World War II, by George J. Joachim, 1994

Turkey Stearnes and the Detroit Stars: The Negro Leagues in Detroit, 1919–1933, by Richard Bak, 1994

Pontiac and the Indian Uprising, by Howard H. Peckham, 1994 (reprint)

Charting the Inland Seas: A History of the U.S. Lake Survey, by Arthur M. Woodford, 1994 (reprint)

Ojibwa Narratives of Charles and Charlotte Kawbawgam and Jacques LePique, 1893–1895. Recorded with Notes by Homer H. Kidder, edited by Arthur P. Bourgeois, 1994, co-published with the Marquette County Historical Society

Strangers and Sojourners: A History of Michigan's Keweenaw Peninsula, by Arthur W. Thurner, 1994

Win Some, Lose Some: G. Mennen Williams and the New Democrats, by Helen Washburn Berthelot, 1995

Sarkis, by Gordon and Elizabeth Orear, 1995

The Northern Lights: Lighthouses of the Upper Great Lakes, by Charles K. Hyde, 1995 (reprint)

Kids Catalog of Michigan Adventures, second edition, by Ellyce Field, 1995

Rumrunning and the Roaring Twenties: Prohibition on the Michigan-Ontario Waterway, by Philip P. Mason, 1995

In the Wilderness with the Red Indians, by E. R. Baierlein, translated by Anita Z. Boldt, edited by Harold W. Moll, 1996

Elmwood Endures: History of a Detroit Cemetery, by Michael Franck, 1996

Master of Precision: Henry M. Leland, by Mrs. Wilfred C. Leland with Minnie Dubbs Millbrook, 1996 (reprint)

Haul-Out: New and Selected Poems, by Stephen Tudor, 1996

Kids Catalog of Michigan Adventures, third edition, by Ellyce Field, 1997

Beyond the Model T: The Other Ventures of Henry Ford, revised edition, by Ford R. Bryan, 1997

Young Henry Ford: A Picture History of the First Forty Years, by Sidney Olson, 1997 (reprint)

The Coast of Nowhere: Meditations on Rivers, Lakes and Streams, by Michael Delp, 1997

From Saginaw Valley to Tin Pan Alley: Saginaw's Contribution to American Popular Music, 1890–1955, by R. Grant Smith, 1998

The Long Winter Ends, by Newton G. Thomas, 1998 (reprint)

Bridging the River of Hatred: The Pioneering Efforts of Detroit Police Commissioner George Edwards, by Mary M. Stolberg, 1998

Toast of the Town: The Life and Times of Sunnie Wilson, by Sunnie Wilson with John Cohassey, 1998

These Men Have Seen Hard Service: The First Michigan Sharpshooters in the Civil War, by Raymond J. Herek, 1998

A Place for Summer: One Hundred Years at Michigan and Trumbull, by Richard Bak, 1998

Early Midwestern Travel Narratives: An Annotated Bibliography, 1634–1850, by Robert R. Hubach, 1998 (reprint)

All-American Anarchist: Joseph A. Labadie and the Labor Movement, by Carlotta R. Anderson, 1998

Michigan in the Novel, 1816–1996: An Annotated Bibliography, by Robert Beasecker, 1998

"Time by Moments Steals Away": The 1848 Journal of Ruth Douglass, by Robert L. Root, Jr., 1998

The Detroit Tigers: A Pictorial Celebration of the Greatest Players and Moments in Tigers' History, updated edition, by William M. Anderson, 1999

Father Abraham's Children: Michigan Episodes in the Civil War, by Frank B. Woodford, 1999 (reprint)

Letter from Washington, 1863–1865, by Lois Bryan Adams, edited and with an introduction by Evelyn Leasher, 1999

Wonderful Power: The Story of Ancient Copper Working in the Lake Superior Basin, by Susan R. Martin, 1999

A Sailor's Logbook: A Season aboard Great Lakes Freighters, by Mark L. Thompson, 1999

Huron: The Seasons of a Great Lake, by Napier Shelton, 1999

Tin Stackers: The History of the Pittsburgh Steamship Company, by Al Miller, 1999

Art in Detroit Public Places, revised edition, text by Dennis Nawrocki, photographs by David Clements, 1999

Brewed in Detroit: Breweries and Beers Since 1830, by Peter H. Blum, 1999

Detroit Kids Catalog: A Family Guide for the 21st Century, by Ellyce Field, 2000

"Expanding the Frontiers of Civil Rights": Michigan, 1948–1968, by Sidney Fine, 2000

Graveyard of the Lakes, by Mark L. Thompson, 2000

Enterprising Images: The Goodridge Brothers, African American Photographers, 1847–1922, by John Vincent Jezierski, 2000

New Poems from the Third Coast: Contemporary Michigan Poetry, edited by Michael Delp, Conrad Hilberry, and Josie Kearns, 2000

Arab Detroit: From Margin to Mainstream, edited by Nabeel Abraham and Andrew Shryock, 2000

The Sandstone Architecture of the Lake Superior Region, by Kathryn Bishop Eckert, 2000

Looking Beyond Race: The Life of Otis Milton Smith, by Otis Milton Smith and Mary M. Stolberg, 2000

Mail by the Pail, by Colin Bergel, illustrated by Mark Koenig, 2000

Great Lakes Journey: A New Look at America's Freshwater Coast, by William Ashworth, 2000

A Life in the Balance: The Memoirs of Stanley J. Winkelman, by Stanley J. Winkelman, 2000

Schooner Passage: Sailing Ships and the Lake Michigan Frontier, by Theodore J. Karamanski, 2000

The Outdoor Museum: The Magic of Michigan's Marshall M. Fredericks, by Marcy Heller Fisher, illustrated by Christine Collins Woomer, 2001

Detroit In Its World Setting: A Three Hundred Year Chronology, 1701–2001, edited by David Lee Poremba, 2001

Frontier Metropolis: Picturing Early Detroit, 1701–1838, by Brian Leigh Dunnigan, 2001

Michigan Remembered. Photographs from the Farm Security Administration and Office of War Information, 1936–1943, edited by Constance B. Schultz, with Introductory Essays by Constance B. Schultz and William H. Mulligan, Jr., 2001

This Is Detroit, 1701-2001, by Arthur M. Woodford, 2001